Before Babel:
A History of Basque Literatures

Joseba Gabilondo

BαRβαποaK

Design: Joseba Gabilondo.
Photographs: Wikimedia commons.

ISBN: 978-1530868322
Library of Congress Cataloging Data: PH5281 .G33 2014

Barbaroak, LLC. www.barbaroak.com

Only Basques preserve, to our days, their vulgar and barbarian language, which does not show any elegance, and is very different from the rest of languages and the most ancient of Spain, […] it is said that the whole Spain made use of the Basque language before the Romans entered these provinces and, with their arms, spread their language. It is also said that, because these Basque people were vulgar, ferocious, and wild […] and the mountains they inhabited were inaccessible, they never fell completely under the yoke of the foreign empire, or they shook it swiftly.

Juan de Mariana, *General History of Spain*, (1601).

What are we waiting for while congregated in the forum?
The barbarians are expected to arrive today.
Why is there such lack of action in the senate?
Why are the senators sitting still and do not legislate?
Because the barbarians will arrive today.
…
Why are the streets and public squares becoming empty?
And everybody is going home with skeptical thoughts?
Because night has fallen and the barbarians did not arrive.
Some people came from the border
And reported that the barbarians do not exist anymore.
Now what are we going to do without barbarians?
These people were after all a kind of solution.

Constantine P. Cavafy. "Waiting for the Barbarians." (1904;
translation by Konstantinos Karpozilos).

To Carlos Blanco Aguinaga

Generosity, intellectual breath, and political commitment never came together in such an inspiring way.

Introduction

"The past is never dead. It's not even past"

William Faulkner, *Requiem for a Nun* (Act.1, sec. 3)

1. Writing Difference

To this day, there is not a history of Basque literature written originally in English with a global audience in mind. There are two translations (Igartua and Zabaltza; Olaziregi *Basque Literary*) but the two best remain untranslated (Aldekoa, *Historia*; Urkizu *Historia*). Although there is an immediate need for such a history, this book is not another traditional history of Basque literature; rather, it intends to be a cultural history written against the nationalist grain that has informed Basque literary history to this day. So far, Basque literature has been considered that which is solely written in Basque language or *euskara*. Conversely, literatures written by Basques in state languages such as Spanish, French, or English, have been relegated to their respective state canons: Spanish, French or North-American literature. This tendency to equate language and state in the name of a putative cultural and historical unity, the nation, is prevalent not only in the Basque Country but in Europe and the world at large. Surprisingly enough, it shows how dominant nationalist ideology continues to be in literary studies since its initial elaboration by the Schlegel brothers at the beginning of the 19th century in Germany.

The following is a postnational history of Basque literature(s): it encompasses all the literatures written by the Basques in all their languages, while also showing the violence, conflicts, and differences that these literatures create, represent, and reflect. Here, thus, "postnational" means a position critical of nationalism and, therefore, a way of historicizing that comes after nationalism and nationalist history.

Yet, the reference to "national" in "post-national" intends to emphasize the fact that nationalism neither has disappeared nor has been superseded—it remains the ghost of all literary and cultural histories. As Benedict Anderson claimed in 1983, "the 'end of the era of nationalism,' so long prophesied, is not remotely in sight. Indeed, nation-ness is the most universally legitimate value in the political life of our time" (12); his claim still holds true these days.

To my knowledge, no postnational history of literature exists in Europe—and, in this sense, this project presents innovative ideas that might

3

affect or change most literatures in Europe. The concepts of "literatures of the Americas" (Jordan, Brotherson, Pérez Firmat), "Latin American literature" (Rama, González Echevarría and Pupo-Walker; Valdés and Kadir), African literatures (Olaniyan and Quayson; George), "Indian literature" (Chauduri, Gupta), or "literatures in the Iberian Peninsula" (Cabo Aseguinolaza, Tarrío and Domínguez) come closest to a postnational understanding of literature in the western and southern hemispheres. Yet, even in most of these cases, minority literatures written in other languages than Spanish, Portuguese, French, and English are still marginalized or omitted *tout court* under the umbrella theory of postcolonialism, which gives preference to imperialist languages with terms such as Francophone, Anglophone, Lusophone, etc. As Gayatri Spivak has noted, "[I]n the field of literature, we need to move from Anglophony, Lusophony, Teutophony, Francophony, et cetera. We must take the languages of the Southern Hemisphere as active cultural media rather than as objects of cultural study by the sanctioned ignorance of the metropolitan migrant" (*Death of a Discipline* 9). Yet, even her work has contributed to the *imperium* of English. Obviously, Basque literature is, in the northern hemisphere, part of what Spivak only locates in the southern —although Basque has been written in countries such as Argentina since the 19th century (Aramburu and Eskerro).

The main goal of writing a postnational literary history is to walk away from the narrative and teleology of a single nationalist subject, which, very much in a Hegelian fashion, celebrates the formation, development, critical moments, and final maturation or self-realization of such a national subject within its state. This postnational history aims at underscoring that Basque culture and literature have been marked by diglossia, internal conflict, external repression, and stereotyping through discourses such as Orientalism, Occidentalism, and primitivism. Therefore, to approach Basque literature as solely written in a single language betrays, in its nationalist zeal, the complex, heterogeneous, and divided history of Basque culture. The goal of this postnational history, thus, is to be *historical* by stepping outside the prefixed box of a putative Basque nation that gains historical consciousness and becomes a full historical subject by writing itself into its national language.

Conversely, the other goal of this history is to question the even more hegemonic ideology that pervades both literary history and state nationalism. Such ideology posits that every subject is national and, therefore, s/he writes on behalf of and for the interest of the nation-state. Basque difference shatters this ideology in the Spanish, French, and (North)

4

American states. Most first-world literary histories follow this state-nationalist tendency, with the institutional and economic support of the State. Yet, this is not a specifically Basque, Spanish, French, or (North) American problem; it is a nationalist problem *tout court*. In this respect the other important effect of a Basque postnational history is to reterritorialize Basque literatures and authors who have been considered so far Spanish, French, (North) American, etc. In short, a postnational history cuts into state-nationalist canons and makes them secondary and dependent on minority literatures such as the Basque. Let us take perhaps the two most fetishized and discussed Basque authors of the 20th century who wrote in Spanish, Unamuno and Martín Santos. In this new postnational history, they become, first and foremost, Basque, and only secondarily Spanish, so that the Spanish canon becomes dependent on and secondary to the Basque.

Although Basques might not read much literature, especially in times of globalization,[1] Basque literature—or literatures—is more than a literary corpus, a reading practice, a cultural ideology, or even a private pleasure. Basque literature is at the core of Basque politics and history, for Basque difference has been formed around certain texts, read by few but discussed by most. A history of Basque literatures is more about writing a difference, one that is not ethnic, properly speaking, neither simply cultural nor political. It is not even a singular difference: there are many Basque differences. Hence, I use here Basque literature/s and difference/s interchangeably in singular and plural.

At least since the late Middle Ages, Basque language has been evoked and referenced in other languages to articulate a geopolitical difference in so many ways that Basque difference has to be rethought retrospectively from our new global situation. In our postmillennial present, the nation-state is in crisis, the state is being reorganized and reinforced according to neoliberal ideologies (including neonationalism), and biopolitical differences such as gender, sexuality, and race are emerging independently of the modern nation-state on a global scale. It is here that Basque differences must be located and historicized.

Basque difference has always been traumatic to the surrounding states (especially Spain) and, more generally, to Europe and the Americas. Therefore, it allows to understand not only the formation of the Basque

---

[1] Ironically enough, Spanish Basques rank among the most avid readers in Spain and Europe, especially of newspapers (Pérez de Pablos). Among minority languages, the use of twitter in Basque is one of the highest in the world (indigenoustweets.com)

Country, but also the imperialist history of states such as Spain and France. Basque differences are at the core of the colonial and nationalist formation of Europe and the Americas, in which Basques played the role of the "oldest Europeans," "the true European natives," "the first Oriental (=Spanish) people whom the romantic, northern-European traveler encounters on his/her way south," "the last remnants of Atlantis," or "the true imperialist Spaniards." Even when it came to theorizing such a fundamental concept as democracy, in the case of Rousseau, Basque difference was summoned quite conveniently (*Instrucción*). John Adams in his *A Defense of the Constitution of the United States* also mentioned the Basques, people of "Celtic extraction" (310), as an example of republicanism and anti-colonialism. In short, Basque difference has been mobilized to legitimize very different political agendas.

Similarly, in the Basque Country, Basque language and culture were invoked and historicized, willingly or unwillingly, as the political and cultural heart of the nation in the 20th century (Krutwig). Literature was the textual representation of Basque national identity: an identity that would go all the way back to the Renaissance and, sometimes, further back to an oral culture that supposedly originated in the Neolithic (Oteiza). However, this literary practice and interpretation has reached a standstill, a crisis, in the Basque Country, Spain, France, and the diaspora. Because of globalization, the Basques are entering a new phase that is reminiscent of the Renaissance when differences were not yet understood nationally.

Therefore, we have to revisit Basque literature, not as the chronicle of a hypothetical "Basque nation," but rather as the historical witness of a Basque difference that, these days, appears historical but does not have a consensus as to how to interpret it, since it no longer is nationalist. As I will explain in the following, I call this historical Basque discourse of differences *materia vasconica*. The new postnational development of *materia vasconica* requires that we rethink Basque differences anew, altogether, in its historicity from the eruption of globalization. Perhaps the goal is to conclude that there no longer is such a thing as Basque history or Basque difference—or Spanish, French, and American histories. Perhaps the goal is to conclude that other geo-biopolitical formations are defining our desires and politics. Yet, a new global and postnational exploration is necessary in order to determine what a new, negative or positive, history of things Basque would be. Thus, a new postnational and global history of Basque literatures is crucial to situate the Basques, as either Basque or otherwise, historically and globally. At the same time, a postnational approach must offer also a Basque reading of globalization and the neoliberal states that constitute the Basque Country in Europe and the Americas. Perhaps the conclusion can be the opposite: states such as Spain or France are doomed because of differences such as the Basque. In short, it is important to attempt what in Hegelian discourse is considered the dialectical universalization of the particular (the difference).

2. The Basque Country

Although these days there are a number of introductions to the Basque Country and its culture (Kurlansky, Woodworth, Caro Baroja, Watson, Zallo), no book can presume a familiarity with the subject on the part of the English reader. Thus, as in the case of most minority languages or cultures, one must submit to the unavoidable introduction and re-presentation of the Basque "identity and difference"—and endless repeating presentation that, instead of freeing the Basques from the shackles of otherness, always ends up perpetuating their bondage to exoticism.

The Basques live in Europe on both sides of the Atlantic Pyrenees. They reside in two states, Spain and France, and in three political entities: the Autonomous Basque Community (ABC), the Chartered Community of Navarre, in Spain, and the administrative region of Aquitaine-Limousin-Poitou-Charentes, Department of the Atlantic Pyrenees, in France. The Spanish side is considered the South of the Basque Country and the French side is called the North. The historical provinces that constitute the Basque Country are seven. Three are located in the North: Lapurdi (Labourd), Nafarroa Beherea (Lower Navarre), and Zuberoa (Soule). Four are located in the South: Nafarroa (Navarre), Gipuzkoa (Guipuzcoa), Bizkaia (Biscay) and Araba (Alava). The last three provinces constitute the ABC. Navarre and Lower Navarre were part of the same kingdom till 1512 when Ferdinand of Aragon invaded it and annexed the high territories, in what is now Spain, reducing the kingdom to its lower territories in the North, hence the name Lower Navarre. The annexed territories of the kingdom became known as Navarre proper. The traditional adjectives for those seven provinces are lapurtar/Labourdan, baxenafar/Lower-Navarran, zuberotar/Souletin, nafar/Navarran, gipuzkoar/Guipuzcoan, bizkaitar/Biscayan, and arabar/Alavan.

1 France
2 Spain

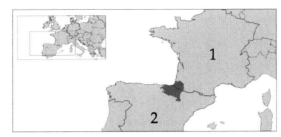

Autonomous Basque C.
1 Bizkaia
2 Gipuzkoa
3 Araba

Chartered C.of Navarre
4 Nafarroa

Dpt. Atlantic Pyrenees
5 Lapurdi
6 Nafarroa Beherea
7 Zuberoa

(Source of images:
Wikimedia Commons)

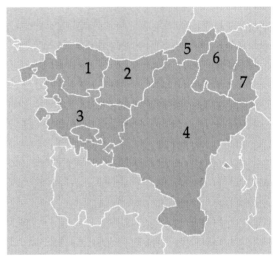

As of 2014, the total of Basque inhabitants in the seven provinces amounts to over 3 million. According to the most recent census figures, there are 280.046 (2006) in the Department of the Atlantic Pyrenees, 644,566 (2012) in Navarre, and 2,166,184 (2014) in the Autonomous Basque Community. The population is slightly less than that of Uruguay (3,404,189) and slightly more than that of Lithuania (2,923,360) or Albania (2,895,947; all 2014 figures).

Basque speakers are no longer monolingual; they also speak either Spanish or French (in addition to varying degrees of English and Gascon). They amount approximately to 850.000 and the majority live in the South. Only 80.000 speakers remain in the North.

The total area of the Basque Country is 20,947 km². The Basque territory is approximately half the size of Switzerland (41,285 km²), the same approximate extension of the New York metropolitan area (17,405 km²) and twice that of Puerto Rico (9,104 km²) or Jamaica (10,991 km²). In comparison, Catalonia is 32,114 km², Galicia 29,574 km², and Andalusia 87,268 km².

The Basque diaspora is hard to quantify but its numbers could be estimated between 1 and 2 million. They reside mainly in the Americas and Europe, although there are diasporic communities in other continents and countries such as China or Australia (Totoricaguena). There are about 200 Basque institutions and/or centers around the world (euskosare.org).

Except for the furthermost southern area, which borders with the Ebro river, and thus is a fertile land for agriculture (wine, wheat, etc.), the rest of the Basque Country is rather mountainous and ill equipped for agriculture. Thus, the Basque economy has historically relied on industrialization (from shipbuilding and iron mining to specialized manufacturing), trade (from wool and cocoa to iron ore), and fishing (from whales and cod to sardines). Yet, except for an elite class, which was also very successful in its dealings with the Castilian/Spanish crown (more so than its French counterpart), the Basque Country has always been a poor area. In the Middle Ages the Basques were described as barbarians and thieves, most famously by Aymeric Picaud (Gerson). During the modern era, peasant revolts (*matxinadak*), especially during the 17th and 18th centuries, and wars, in the 19th and 20th centuries, marked its history, which also led to massive migration waves starting in the 19th century. As late as the end of the 19th century, before the beginning of industrialization in Biscay, the Basque Country was one of the poorest areas in both Spain and France.

The North, although constituted originally by three different political entities (Labourd, Lower Navarre, and Soule), which during the late Middle Ages were under the control of the English crown, ultimately were absorbed by the French state. The development of the Navarran kingdom, which began as the County of Pamplona in the 9th century, defined the South. As Navarre became a kingdom in the 10th century, it expanded west and southward, alongside the Astur-Leonese kingdom. In the 11th century, the kingdom was splintered and the Castilian fragment, originally a county, became a dominant kingdom that absorbed the Astur-Leonese kingdom and, after joining Aragon, the kingdom of Navarre itself. The three provinces of the South (Biscay, Guipuzcoa and Alava)[2], joined originally the Navarran kingdom but, after several interest conflicts, were absorbed by Castile after the 13th century, while retaining their founding charters or *fueros*.

---

[2] Technically, Alava and Biscay were not provinces but more complex political entities that contained "merindades" and "señoríos."

9

The North endured the French revolution (1789) and both World Wars (1914-1919, 1941-1945), whereas the South was involved in a series of civil wars of dynastic succession (1833 through 1876) called Carlist wars (*karlistadak*). Although the Spanish state remained neutral in both world wars, in 1931 became a republic, which lasted 5 years. In 1936, a fascist coup d'état led to another civil war (1936-1939). The coup, in turn, gave rise to both a dictatorship that lasted 36 years (1939-1975) and an armed struggle led by the Basque terrorist organization ETA (1959-2011), which contributed to the demise of the dictatorship. Despite the fact that Spain became a post-dictatorial, liberal democracy in 1975, ETA lingered as the last chapter of a long-drawn civil war; in 2011 the terrorist group finally declared a permanent cease-fire.

Yet, through all these ordeals, the South experienced a steady increase in industrial production (mining and manufacturing) in the late 19th century and throughout the 20th. As a result, the ABC became in 2012 the community with the highest per-capita income and the lowest unemployment rates in the Spanish state; Navarre followed closely (Pozuleo-Monfort). The northern Basque Country, because of French policies directed to preserve the area as a tourist site, did not grow at the same pace as its southern counterpart. Since the borders between the Spanish and French states were dismantled in 1995, the South began to invest more in the North in ways that, sometimes, bordered on internal economic imperialism. The global economic crisis (2008-) and the ensuing European political crisis define the entire continental Basque Country today.

3. Origins of the Basques: On *Materia Vasconica*

The Basque language has been the reason or pretext for most political and identitarian quarrels among the Basques and their neighboring states. *Euskara* or Basque has always been connected with the discourses of historical origins and, consequently, with the legitimation of the Spanish and French states—and even more generally with the origins and legitimation of Europe. Since, in the following chapters, this book will cover Basque history and literature from the Middle Ages to the 21st century, it is worthwhile dwelling here on the prehistoric genesis of the Basques and their language. This prehistory says very little about the Basques and much about the Western obsession with origins and the difficulty of fixing them. This ever-present obsession generates a discourse of "mysterious" origins, which always compel the West to deploy a large apparatus of scientific discourses to solve them. In short, Europe's origins, and thus Basque prehistory, are always originated in the present as a past mystery.

Before approaching the "mysterious" origins of the Basques, it is important to contextualize and historicize the very same debate about origins. With very few exceptions, the local elites never embraced Basque language as a cultural language in the modern era. More generally, the upper classes never attempted to develop cultural institutions and infrastructures in the Basque Country beyond priesthood seminars (the two exceptions being the University of Oñati in the 16th century, and the School of Bergara in the 18th century). Yet, the language of peasants, fishermen, and laymen, that is, the subaltern language of the Basques, became the basis of political and identitarian disputes as early as the 13th century with Rodrigo Jimenez de Rada, the chief architect of Castilian imperialist historiography. These disputes expanded in the 16th century and became a new form of discursive politics for and against the (subaltern) Basque Country. From the French and Spanish Inquisition to the Basque landholding nobility of the 16th and 17th centuries, from European anthropologists to tourist developers of the 19th, everybody deployed Basque language as a political (albeit not cultural) tool of legitimation, condemnation, repression, and exoticization. At the same time, Basque subaltern classes, which were oppressed and exploited precisely for being monolingual Basques, developed a counter-hegemonic subaltern culture. This culture became political mainly in the form of mutinies and wars; in everyday life, they developed forms of resistance that are now considered "infrapolitics" (Scott).

This ever-growing way of "doing politics with a subaltern language" constitutes the foundation of what can be called *materia vasconica* and represents the object of study of this book.[3] In the Basque Country "Literature" proper (with capital L) cannot be distinguished from the rest of lettered and non-lettered practices (i.e. literature with lower-case, as in popular literature with no "quality," as well as "oral culture") and, in my opinion, this has been the major political mistake of previous literary histories. A 'written tradition in Basque" does not exist, properly speaking, and does not make historical sense, unless it is explained as part of a larger lettered and non-lettered (hegemonic and subaltern) political and cultural history—something that the colonial field in Latin American

---

[3] Mitxelena ("Contra Lekobide" 292) and Juaristi (*La memoria* 212) have already used "materia de Vasconia" and "materia de Cantabria," respectively, but in a more restrictive sense.

studies has clearly established, at least since Angel Rama's *The Lettered City*. In short, to pretend to study "literature of the 16th century written in Basque" and to attempt to find different "genres," is simply a form of further oppression, as it ultimately pretends to treat Basque literature as a "major literature." This approach denies Basque literature's most historical characteristic: the fact that it is based on a minority, subaltern language deployed by hegemonic classes who write in other languages (Spanish, French, Latin...) to produce a political discourse of origins.

More recently, there has been at least one attempt to give an account of the different languages and literatures used by Basque writers: Enrique Ayerbe's *Basque Literature* (2002). However, the book is organized by authors; they are presented divided by language and territory, side by side, as additional traditions that, at most, have different geographies within the Basque Country. The underlying ideology of this non-conflictive presentation of Basque literatures is (neo)liberal, as it implies an un-explained coexistence and harmony among authors and languages. It is rather the opposite: *Basque literature is the history of two literatures*, a subaltern "literature" in Basque, and a hegemonic "Literature" in hegemonic state languages. Basque literature is the history of a conflict and repression mainly enforced through diglossia to which other biopolitical differences are subsumed, as in the case of gender: starting in the 16th century Basque language is feminized and identified with witchcraft, and vice versa.

Thus, establishing the "origins" of the Basques and their language is not simply a scientific exercise on some prehistoric data, but a political endeavor loaded with centuries of discussion, debate, and oppression. This historical discourse has come to shape the Basques and cannot be separated from them; it is the very same matter of which they are made. The debate and the origin become inseparable: they become what I call *materia vasconica*. This "Basque matter" is what truly defines the Basques, more so than the origins themselves, which, as we will see, escape sound scientific inquiry even today —and thus remain "mysterious."

The scientific facts about the Basque language and its connection to early Basque inhabitants leave no room for any clear hegemonic narrative, nationalist or anti-nationalist (Spanish, French, Basque or otherwise). Let us mention some widely accepted facts. The Basque language is a pre-Indo-European language; it is an isolate or island language with no other relatives (except perhaps Aquitanian, a dead language who might have been an older form of Basque). It is the only language that predates the Indo-European invasion, which, during the Iron Age (1500-500 BC), laid the linguistic foundation for the rest of European languages (with the exception of Finno-Ugric languages such as Finish, Sam, Estonian, and Hungarian as well as other dead languages such as Etruscan or Iberian; Trask, *A History of Basque* 11). The fact that Spanish imperialism, more so that the French, never managed to eradicate the Basque language entirely, as it was its intention, is due to many historical reasons, which cannot be simplified or reduced to a single cause. The poverty of the Basque land, its sea-borne economy, the decline of Spanish imperialism since the 17th century (and the French after the 18th), the hold of the Catholic church on the Basque language as a mode of mass indoctrination, the exotization of the language starting in the 19th century, and the rise of Basque nationalism in the 20th, constitute some of these reasons. Yet, compared to other minority languages of a similar isolated nature, Basque language remains an exceptional case only because it is situated in Europe and not in the Global South—where it would become just "another" minority, indigenous language among thousands.

Although there are remains in the Basque Country that date back to the lower Paleolithic (150.000 BP), and the direct ancestor of the present wo/man, the Cro-Magnon (*Homo sapiens*), settled in the Basque Country in the Upper Paleolithic (35.000 BP), there is no direct way of establishing a connection between these early settlements and contemporary Basques—let alone the Basque language (MacClancy). Nevertheless, traditional Basque anthropology, heralded by Joxe Migel Barandiaran, and "scientific" contemporary genetic anthropology, developed by scholars such as L. Luca Cavalli-Sforza from Stanford University, continue to perpetuate the myths first elaborated in the formation of *materia vasconica* in the 13th century. Bertranpetit and Cavalli-Sforza in their study from 1991 conclude:

> […] the major difference in the Iberian Peninsula is that between people originally of Basque and non-Basque descent. The recession in time of the boundaries of the Basque-speaking area seems correlated with the progressive genetic dilution of the Basque genotype in modern populations, as we move away from the centre of the Basque area. Clearly, there must have been a close relationship in *the progressive loss of the Basque language and increasing genetic admixture with neighbours. Most probably, Basques represent descendants of Paleolithic and/or Mesolithic populations* and non-Basques later arrivals, beginning with the Neolithic. (51, my emphasis)

Although Bertranpetit and Cavalli-Sforza have not scientific basis to establish the "Paleolithic origin" of the Basque language, they mix it with genetic analysis to recreate the founding myth of *materia vasconica*.

Later, Cavalli-Sforza, in one of his most important works, *Genes, Peoples, and Languages*, further concludes:

> During the last Paleolithic period the Basque region extended over almost the entire area where ancient cave paintings have been found. There are some cues that Basque descends from *a language spoken 35,000 to 40,000 years ago,* during the first occupation of France by modern humans, who most probably came from the southwest, but possibly from the east as well. The artists of these caves would have spoken a language of the first, preagricultural Europeans, from which modern Basque is derived. (121, my emphasis)

Once again, there is no scientific basis to establish the Paleolithic antiquity of the Basque language or to connect it with the inhabitants of the Basque Country of that period.

More recently in 2006, Stephen Oppenheimer, from Oxford University, claimed, in his *The Origins of the British*, that the early British people, from the western British Isles, descend from "the Basques" (the Mesolithic population on the northern western coast of the Iberian Peninsula) who migrated to Britain during the last ice age (10.000 BP). Although the language of the following quote is highly technical, the conclusion is not:

> One observation shines bright from the genetics. The bulk of informative male gene markers among the so-called Atlantic Celts are derived from down in south-west Europe, best represented by people of the Basque Country. What is more, they share this Atlantic coastal link with certain dated expansions of mtDNA gene groups, representing each of the main, archaeologically dated, putative colonization events of the western British Isles. One might expect the original Mesolithic hunter-gatherer colonists of the Atlantic coast, over 10,000 years ago, to have derived from the Ice Age refuges of the western Mediterranean: Spain, south-west France and the Basque Country. And that was indeed the case: shared genetic elements, both in the British Isles and Iberia, did include such Mesolithic mtDNA founding gene lines *originating in the Basque region.* (5, my emphasis)

According to Oppenheimer, the Eastern British Isles, instead, were populated later, in the Neolithic from tribes coming from northwestern Europe (6000 BP). Yet, this scientist, pulled by the gravitational power of *materia vasconica*, clearly slips into unscientific speculation when he imagines that the original populations of Britain "spoke Basque" or a language similar to Basque. There is no scientific proof of this:

> Clearly, the deep time perspective and the size of ancient male and female recolonizations of north-west Europe rather blunts simplistic claims, based on similarity of genetic markers, that the ancestral insular-Celtic languages must have come from Spain, or that English results from a replacement of Celts by Anglo-Saxons based solely on the extraordinary genetic similarity between people of the respective regions. This is partly because of the huge time gap since those recolonization events after the Ice Age, which means that whatever languages those early hunters and gatherers may have spoken it was unlikely to have been Celtic or Germanic. In fact, sub-structural linguistic evidence within both these modern branches of Indo-European suggests *the oldest language of the British Isles may have been more like Basque.* (151, my emphasis)

Therefore the discourse of *materia vasconica* continues to be well and alive, not only among Basques, but among many scientific communities around the world.

The list of scholars not considered scientific enough to be taken seriously constitutes an army too long to list here; their claims range from Atlantis (d'Abartiague) to a pan-European or pan-Mediterranean common language-family of which Basque would be the last remnant (Vennemann; Arnaiz-Villena and Alonso, respectively).

The first time in which the Basque language can be connected to a community is during the Roman occupation. There are few hundred inscriptions in the northern Basque Country, which are approximately 2000 years old and point to a language that is very close to Basque and was spoken by a group called Aquitanians. Whether this is old Basque or a different language related to Basque, remains an open discussion. Most recently in 2008, and following Luis Michelena, Larry Trask concluded "Aquitanian represents an ancestral form of Basque" (*Etymological Dictionary* 6). There are only three Basque inscriptions from the Roman era in the southern Basque Country, all of which are situated in eastern Navarre. The Navarran area was inhabited by a tribe called *Vascones* (from which the word *Basque* derives). Yet, the western area of the Basque Country, or what we now consider the Autonomous Basque Community, which contains today the largest community of Basque speakers, was inhabited during the Roman occupation by other tribes (Varduli, Verones, Caristii, Autrigones). There is no record of what language they spoke, and the only recorded names are not Basque but Indo-European and probably Celtic (Trask, *Etymological Dictionary* 7).

The above scenario has already opened room for much debate among linguists and philologists. Defending the view of a minority of linguists, Trask concludes:

> Since the western part of the modern Basque Country retains a number of toponyms which are non-Basque, probably Indo-European and very likely Celtic, we may wonder whether Basque was already spoken in its historical region at this time, or whether it spread westward only after the collapse of Roman power in the west. (*Etymological Dictionary* 7).

Therefore, there is a possibility, defended by a minority of linguists, that the actual majority of Basque speakers, which live in the area presently recognized as the ABC, do not speak Basque as their original "prehistoric" language, but rather as a result of an eastern invasion of Vascones from today's Navarre, who would have imposed their language. As early as the Middle Ages, this idea was transformed by Castilian imperialism into a new name for the Basque language: *vascue**nce*** (parallel construction to *roma**nce***), which means "language of those made Basque, or the language of those linguistically conquered by the Basques." Trask concludes, "we now see Basque as a language of Gaul [Aquitania, the North] which has spread south and west" (*The History* 38).

Yet, a majority of linguists, following the lead of Luis Michelena (*Languages and Protolanguages, On the Past of the Basque Language*), defend that these areas might have been bilingual and therefore Basque was originally spoken alongside other Indo-European languages. Similarly, Joseba Lakarra ("Gogoetak") and Joaquín Gorrochategui ("Vasco Antiguo") are against a late basquization of the western Basque Country (as late as the fall of the Roman Empire). After discussing the expansion of Basque to Eastern Soria (a Spanish area located south-west of the Basque Country) during the Roman era, Gorrochategui concludes:

> All these data go against, in my opinion, of a late introduction of the Basque language in the Basque Country [ABC], let us say, during the Visigoth or Franc era… If we contemplate all the Pyrenean territory and its extended flat lands on both sides of its mountain range through the valleys of the Ebro

[Spain] and Garona [France], we can see that, from a long-duration perspective, there have been advances and retreats by the Basque language from its Pyrenaic nuclei to the lower lands in an accordion-like movement. (551)[4]

Finally, Joan Coromines (*Estudis*) has shown through toponymy that Basque extended all the way to western Catalonia, to the valley of Arán, on a territory that stretches approximately 250 kilometers outside the contemporary Basque Country.

Therefore, even the most scientific debate about language, geography, and origins continues to form part of *materia vasconica*. The tension between the possibility of being able to ascertain "the origin of Western Europe," on the one hand, and the realization of not being able to explain fully a heterogeneous body of (pre)historic data and objects, on the other, makes the Basque Country the perfect object for many Western political fantasies and anxieties about Europe's origins. Spanish, French, and Basque nationalist discourses have built their discourses of inception around, on top, and against *materia vasconica*, which has the potential of unsettling any discourse of political legitimation that bases its political privileges and/or rights on its origin.

The title of this book is meant to capture the (pre)historical and political structure of *materia vasconica* and Basque literature, as it is always condemned to live simultaneously in the present and in the past (in the Paleolithic, so to speak) in a Moebius-band like structure that connects both times by bending history. In this sense, Basque literature always comes *before* the European modern division of languages, that is, before Babel: the Biblical myth that the Renaissance mobilized to explain the modern proliferation of state and national languages after the demise of Latin, as well as the "discovery" of other languages in the New World and the Orient. Yet, Basque literature's contemporary situation is always defined by its situation *in front of, facing, being before* our contemporary, global Babel, as a language that, to this day, has been denied its political status as national or state language. This double sense of "before," in time and space, defines the Basque Country. In this sense, the title of this book is also a reply to

---

4 "Todos estos datos van en contra, en mi opinión, de una introducción tardía del vascuence en el País Vasco, digamos en época visigoda o franca... Si contemplamos todo el territorio pirenaico y sus extensas zonas llanas a uno y otro lado de la cadena hasta los valles del Ebro y el Garona, vemos que en una perspectiva de larga duración ha habido avances y retrocesos de la lengua éuscara desde sus núcleos pirenaicos a las tierras bajas como en una especie de movimiento en acordeón."

one of the most influential contemporary reflections on language, translation, and literature: George Steiner's *After Babel*. Steiner, in the introduction
to the second edition of his book, had to reconsider some of his original
theses:

> At the time when [my book] *After Babel* was in progress, the increasing domi-
> nation of an Anglo-American Esperanto across the planet looked to be obvi-
> ous and possibly irreversible [...] None the less, the picture now strikes me as
> somewhat less clear than it was. Fierce ethnic and regional atavisms are resur-
> gent. Determinant of, determined by tribal, regional, and national passions for
> identity, languages are proving more resistant to rationalization, and the bene-
> fits of homogeneity and technical formalization, than one might have expected.
> (xvii)

The civilizational Steiner, from his privileged imperial North-American
positon, would place Basque and *materia vasconica* among the forms of "re-
surgent fierce ethnic and regional atavisms" driven by "tribal, regional, and
national passions for identity." As Iban Zaldua noted (*That Language*), Steiner
gave an interview to the Spanish journal *El País*, and literally reinforced the
stereotype of "atavistic and passionate" Basques:

> When the IRA conflict was coming to an end, I published an article stating
> that it would happen the same with ETA. But no, ETA continues killing…
> This *mysterious language* is *very strange, very powerful*. That is why perhaps it is so
> difficult for some of those people to accept the exterior world. (Cruz, my
> emphasis)[5]

Yet, Steiner is not aware that, after taking a post-Babelian civilizational
position, he is contributing to the discourse of *materia vasconica* by repeating
and perpetuating some of its most foundational myths. In short, Steiner,
and other writers in the same position (Juaristi *Vestiges of Babel*), are the true
atavistic and passionate critics who are contributing to "fierce ethnic and
regional atavism and resurgence," hence confirming the pre-Babelic structure of Basque literature, identity, and politics. Benjamin's dictum that behind every civilization there is a history of barbarism and destruction is
confirmed by Steiner.

---

[5] "Cuando el asunto del IRA estaba llegando a su fin, publiqué un artículo conside-
rando que con ETA pasaría lo mismo. Y no, ETA sigue matando.... Ese idioma tan mis-
terioso es muy raro, muy poderoso. Quizá por eso a alguna de esa gente le resulta tan
imposible aceptar el mundo exterior."

To the (especially) non-native Anglo-American reader, a pre-Babelic ancestry of 35,000 years seems an unthinkable or fundamentalist reality. Yet many Basques believe, with the legitimation of Anglo-American anthropology and linguistics, that indeed they are the direct descendants of those "Paleolithic Basques." For them, the constitution of the Spanish and French states about six centuries ago appears a small historical bump soon to disappear in the relentless Basque march towards a future self-government. The persistence of *materia vasconica* makes clear that the above pre-Babelian or Paleolithic position cannot be pushed aside as a non-scientific myth, for it comes back with the unbound force of the uncanny (even among enlightened and civilized critics such as Steiner). In short, the Basques cannot adopt a post-Babelic position. Yet, simultaneously, this myth has to be viewed as a historical construction that has been developed for the last eight centuries. Gayatri Spivak uses the term "strategic essentialism" in the context of deconstruction, but it can also be used here in order to explain the politics of pre-Babelian Basques: "Since one cannot not be an essentialist, why not look at the ways in which one is an essentialist, carve out a representative essentialist position, and then do politics, according to the old rules, whilst remembering the dangers in this?" (*The Postcolonial Critic* 45).[6] Basques cannot simply deny a (pre)history that takes them/us back 35.000 years to a position that always risks becoming a non-historical essence; they/we must adopt it strategically, fully aware that it is the result of a historical discourse called *materia vasconica* that originates in the Middle Ages as Castile (Spain) and France begin to expand as empires.

Ultimately, *materia vasconica* is a shared European political fantasy of origins. Basques are the subject-to-know-Europe's-origin. If psychoanalytical post-Marxism is to be believed, political fantasy is the element that structures our social being; the field of European/Western politics would collapse without this type of fantasies, not the other way around (Zizek).

---

[6] "I would read it, then as *a strategic use of positivist essentialism* in a scrupulously visible political interest. This would put them [subaltern historians] in line with the Marx who locates fetishization, the ideological determination of the 'concrete', and spins the narrative of the development of the money-form; with the Nietzsche who offers us genealogy in place of historiography, and the Derrida of "affirmative deconstruction'. This would allow them to use the critical force of anti-humanism, in other words, even as they share its constitutive paradox: that the essentializing moment, the object of their criticism, is irreducible" (Spivak, "Subaltern Studies" 13-4).

4. On the Open Structure of the Book

Although in the first chapter I will elaborate the theoretical and historical reasons for my postnational approach, some readers might want to scape this chapter, which deals with epistemological and critical issues, rather than Basque literature proper. For those readers, I will just advance that, at this point there is no author, or even team of specialists, who can write a coherent and comprehensive postnational history of Basque literatures.

Today, there is not enough information and discussion to complete a comprehensive postnational history. This book is only a first step towards such a history; its completion made me realize that further research, writing, and translation is required. Here, I simply advance several ideas and hypotheses that I would like to bring forward, so that readers can discuss, criticize, and implement them, and, thus, turn this book into a part of a larger collective effort. The reader is encouraged to contact me and provide comments, suggestions, and criticisms (joseba@joseba.net). The reader will also be able to see further developments and translations at the publisher's website: www.barbaroak.com.

Since this book's goal is to promote a more extensive postnational discussion of Basque literatures, I will eventually present it, not only as a historical monograph, but also as a pedagogical text with guides and questions. I do not think that a theoretical and historical presentation should require of a monograph, such as this, to forgo a pedagogical dimension. Therefore, this book is meant to grow as both research project and pedagogical model. Minority literatures such as the Basques cannot afford to dismiss any of their potential readers or venues of dissemination.

This history is first and foremost an open, ongoing, in-process work. Furthermore, although foretelling the future is a fools' errand, my intent is to continue to upgrade the book every year, incorporating more ideas, authors, texts, and analysis. Furthermore, this history does not contain almost any secondary critical literature on the works and history analyzed. The purpose of this history was just to open a new historical approach and inquiry in order to show the basis of what a future, more elaborate version could look like. As the book progresses, the secondary critical literature will also be incorporated. Yet, for the reader who seeks only the historical overview of a minority literature, this introductory history will remain valid in the near future. This is also a way of avoiding one of the main problems of this type of histories: their rapid obsolescence.

Since no publisher would put up with a yearly revision of the same book, I have resorted to a company that supports open publications, Barbaroak. The reader will not only find the upgrades of the work but also a way to contribute to its expansion with comments on each page—rather than a long chain of never-ending disconnected comments at the end. Technology has advanced in very interesting ways. The reader only needs to ask permission to add comments or questions by writing to the author: joseba@joseba.net. Then s/he can proceed to add their comments or questions on each page on barbaroak.com/beforebabelcomments.pdf.

Although the book can be purchased on paper form through the main online retailers for the minimum price of its production, the digital version in pdf format will remain free. Presently, publishers are charging exorbitant prices for academic books and yet the profits do not reach the authors—except in the case of few bestsellers. The book is also meant as an experiment in publishing and providing new ways to evaluate the content of a book: the comments received, the number of downloads, the reviews of the publication as well as the number of references and quotations will constitute the basis of its evaluation.

For the purpose of reading fluidity, and in order to avoid unnecessary linguistic diversification, the titles of works cited as historical reference are always given in English, even if they have not been translated to that language. Only when a work is analyzed, quoted, and referenced in detail does its title appear in the original language with its English translation next to it, regardless of whether it has been translated or not. Unless noted otherwise, the translations of texts not available in English are all mine. In these cases, the original text is given in a footnote, rather than in the text following the translation—even though the general practice is to give the original after the translation in the same text in square brackets. I find this practice very cumbersome, unpractical, and more importantly, alienating.[7] Since the goal of this book is to reach a wide audience that might not necessarily have ready access to public libraries, I have given priority to online sources for the texts studied and referenced, even if sometimes those sources do not meet the highest academic standards of thoroughness and exactitude. Most notably, I have always referenced most Basque classical books to the great initiative of Armiarma online: *klasikoen gordailua* (the classic archive): http://klasikoak.armiarma.eus.

---

[7] There is a website to find out works written in Basque that have been translated to other languages: http://www.ehu.es/ehg/eli/

Finally, it is important to emphasize that this type of book cannot be completed without the help of a very varied and competent group of friends and colleagues. They all know the different ways in which they have contributed to this book: Iñaki Aldekoa, Isabel Alvarez-Sancho, Iker Arranz, Elixabet Ansa, Ur Apalategi, Eduardo Apodaka, Ibai Atutxa, Mikel Ayerbe, Josu Bijuesca, Miguel Cabañas, Jon Casenave, José Colmeiro, Elena Delgado, Cesar Domínguez, Ibon Egaña, Karmele Etxabe, Gillermo Etxeberria, Imanol Galfarsoro, Teresa Garulo, Ricardo Gomez, Mikel Hernandez Abaitua, Kirsty Hooper, Felix Ibargutxi, Kenneth Kid, Jon Kortazar, Jo Labanyi, Xabier Landabidea, Santi Leoné, Jonah Magar, Luis Madureira, Jeremy MacClancy, Xabier Mendiguren Elizegi, Helena Miguelez, Laura Mintegi, Cristina Moreiras, Douglas Noverr, Olasegun Obasanjo, Juanjo Olasagarre, Iratxe Retolaza, Ramon Saizarbitoria, Oier San Martin, Patri Urkizu, Mark Ugalde, Mitxelko Uranga, Blanca Urgel, Juan Luis Zabala, Iban Zaldua, and Mary Jo Zeter.

1. Literary Theory and History

1. Postnationalism

The German philosopher Jürgen Habermas has developed the concept of "postnationalism" following the original proposal of Karl Dietrich Bracher. According to Habermas, there is a historical teleology from dynastic, prenationalist societies to nationalist and, finally, multicultural postnationalist states in a unified Europe. Reflecting on the history of the nation-state and the future of a unified Europe, Habermas reevaluates the collective identity of the nation and concludes:

> If this form of collective identity was due to a highly abstractive leap from the local and dynastic to national and then to democratic consciousness, why shouldn't this learning process be able to continue? … These experiences of successful forms of social integration have shaped the normative self-understanding of European modernity into an egalitarian universalism that can ease the transition to postnational democracy's demanding context of mutual recognition for all of us—we, the sons, daughters, and grandchildren of a barbaric nationalism. (102-03)

By ignoring the history of European imperialism and colonialism, Habermas concludes that this evolution is internal to Europe and naturally generates postnational, multicultural societies. He just adds a normative character to this internal logic: these societies have to recognize collective rights. As he states, "[M]ulticultural societies require a 'politics of recognition' because the identity of each individual citizen is woven together with collective identities, and must be stabilized in a network of mutual recognition" (74). Habermas means to solve the politics of recognition within the framework of the (neoliberal, neoimperialist) European state, wherein each individual is primarily a citizen—once again ignoring the postcolonial history of (illegal) immigration in Europe. John Rawls has also made popular a similar (neo) liberal theory in North America after the publication of his foundational *A Theory of Justice* in 1971.

Yet, Habermas when referring specifically to the Basque and Irish cases, dismisses them as a nationalist problem of the past, which do not require a "politics of recognition:" "Here I am not referring primarily to nationalist conflicts such as those in the Basque regions of Spain, or in Northern Ireland. Nothing of the seriousness and gravity of these conflicts is lost if one sees them as the delayed consequences of a history of nation-building that has generated historical fault lines" (72). In short, even when the problem of terrorism comes to an end, for Habermas the

25

cases such as the Irish or the Basque do not fall within the problem of multicultural recognition, but rather represent an anachronistic throwback to the era of national conflicts. Habermas establishes a general theory of postnationalism in Europe, but dismisses the cases that do not fit his theory, thus, negating the principle of recognition upon which his theory is built in the first place. In this respect, Habermas' theory is neither multicultural nor postnational. It aims to reorganize the existing European states along diversity lines that conform to the needs and goals of neoliberal democracy and capitalism in Europe.

In the following, the Basque case will be rethought in postnational terms so that the corresponding politics of recognition and multiculturalism are historically addressed. Such a history requires challenging Habermas's understanding of the European state as the ultimate horizon of postnationalism. His approach still remains nationalist (neonationalist), since he still upholds retrospectively the European state and its historical national identity, based on the history of its majority groups as the only institutional *locus* of recognition.[8]

This neonationalist ideology is precisely what prompts Habermas to dismiss the Basque case: he cannot historicize the French and Spanish states and their heterogeneous nationalist cultures; they are beyond postnationalism and multiculturalism. The neonationalist nature of Habermas' thought also explains the reason why his political theories have become one of the most important ideological foundations of the neoliberal, European State—including Spain, where Habermas has received ample recognition among the left and right (Aizpeolea). Here, thus, I will present the Basque case, not as the anachronistic exception to Habermas' neonationalism, but rather as the rule and model of a future postnational Europe and, more generally, of a multicultural, globalized world.

Although I have discussed elsewhere in a more elaborate way my political theorization of postnationalism ("Posnacionalismo"), here I will just state that a historical theory of postnationalism has to affirm simultaneously two seemingly contradictory facts. On the one hand, nationalism continues to be an important form of political ideology for neoliberal states, at least in Europe and in the Americas. On the other, nationalism no longer is the hegemonic ideology that structures the neoliberal state in globalization. Nationalism, rather, works as an ideology of contention

---

[8] Hence the complementary idea of "constitutional patriotism" to implement his neonationalist proposal as state ideology

or reaction vis-à-vis global phenomena such as immigration, multinational capitalism, and new social and ethnic formations intensified by globalization (feminism, queer activism, green movements, etc.). In this sense, this reactive form of nationalism represents its new realignment and organization along neoliberal lines and, therefore, it will be identified here as *neonationalism*. Arjun Appadurai has argued that the nation-state has reached a crisis and "state and nation are at each other's throats, and the hyphen that links them is now less an icon of conjuncture than an index of disjuncture" (39). However, my contention is that neoliberal nationalism or neonationalism is out of sync with the State in globalization and, yet, it is mobilized against the latter. The ideological dissonance between nation and state does not announce the crisis of nationalism or its replacement by non-nationalist forms of state ideology such as "constitutional patriotism:" the latter constitutes the hegemonic doctrine of neonationalism.

The consolidation of Basque culture in Spain (and, to a lesser extent, in France and the Americas), along other minority cultures such as Catalan, Galician, etc. only points to this new postnational condition in which nationalism does not disappear. Rather, different forms of nationalism continue to multiply while none of them can legitimize the State (not even Spanish state nationalism or, its latest neoliberal incarnation, "constitutional patriotism"). This decoupage or slippage between nationalism and State must be articulated through a sound multicultural theory of postnationalism that also questions the political nature of the State. Otherwise, different forms of fundamentalism will continue to gain strength, fueled by clashes between different forms of nationalism—ethnic, religious, and otherwise. Will Kymlicka is one of the first theorists to emphasize the postnational nature of contemporary multiculturalism (33-37). However, and as I will explain in the following, most multicultural theories in the first world do not challenge the political nature of the State, while most proponents of postnationalism do not fully embrace multiculturalism---as in the case of Habermas and the Basque Country. In this respect, I do not embrace traditional multiculturalism, but *radical difference*, in a way that challenges multiculturalism. However, I will use the word "multiculturalism" strategically in few contexts.

Here, thus, I would like to affirm that the Basque Country and its literatures, in their Atlantic spread, constitute one of the most interesting locations, cultures, and literatures from which to begin to think postnationalism in conjunction with cultural difference, while avoiding any form of fundamentalism or neonationalism.

Multiculturalism, as political reality, is an ideology that was officially sanctioned for the first time in Canada and Australia in the 1970s and expanded as an unofficial ideology to the USA and the UK in the 1980s and 90s, as a result of the civil rights struggles of the 60s and 70s. In the case of Canada, Australia, and the USA, multiculturalism was articulated as a response to states that were populated by immigrant groups which, in the past, marginalized or exterminated indigenous populations and enslaved others. Furthermore, multiculturalism emerged as a reaction to earlier ideologies of immigrant heterogeneity such as the US credo of the "melting pot." In the case of the UK, multiculturalism responded to the increasing presence of postcolonial migrants and, thus, it is a postcolonial phenomenon. In academia, multiculturalism became a central debate in the 1990s in the humanities (Goldberg) and political sciences (Kymlicka, Parekh, Young; Taylor and Gutman) and evolved into an institutionalized discourse in the 2000s (Laden and Owen; Shohat and Stam).

German chancellor Angela Merkel claimed in 2010 that multiculturalism had "utterly failed" in Germany, thus emblematically closing the door to multiculturalism in Europe and probably in the USA in the 21st century (Weaver). This only shows that multiculturalism as an official ideology had been already absorbed by both the state and the market (Galfarsoro *Multicultural*). Yet, even after the "failure of multiculturalism," biopolitical difference (racial, gender, sexual, ethnic…) continues to be a historical problem and challenge that awaits an answer. Radical difference, beyond multiculturalism, continues to defy the (post)nation-state and globalization.

In southern and central European states such as France and Spain, the idea of multiculturalism, historically speaking, is new and, from a geopolitical point of view, foreign. At the height of their respective modernities, the Spanish and French states propounded theories of assimilation and homogenization. From the 15th through the 17th centuries, Spain enforced religious conversion as a way to assimilate and control diverse populations (Moriscos, Jews, Basques,[9] etc.). France, since the end of the 18th century, implemented Jacobin republicanism as a way to assimilate heterogeneous populations and cultures: any difference, ethnic, racial, or cultural, was turned into a non-political reality that lied outside the

---

[9] With the help of local authorities, the inquisiton conducted massive witchcraft trails in the 16th and 17th centuries in the Basque Country as a way to exert control over populations that remained, until that point, not fully assimilated in the newly formed Spanish state.

French state—as in the case of different French languages that were marginalized as "patois." Yet, even in the case of France, the most successful case of republican nationalism, assimilation takes place late in history: the majority of French citizens did not speak French at the turn of the 19th century (Weber).

By the end of the 20th century, both France and Spain experienced the failure of their respective nationalist projects, when earlier non-fully assimilated historical realities, mainly ethnic and/or postcolonial, refused to go away. In the case of Spain, and starting in the late 19th century, several groups organized themselves as nationalist communities in areas such as the Basque Country, Catalonia, and Galicia. By the late 20th century these realities were recognized, although in conflictive ways (which also produced forms of terrorism), by the Spanish state while, at the same time, the last Spanish colonies gained independence from the metropolis (Equatorial Guinea, Western Sahara). Similarly, and in the case of France, the failure to account for its postimperialist history opened the gates for many postcolonial groups that were marginalized by the nationalist ideology of Jacobin republicanism. These groups defined themselves in many different ways, including violent and fundamentalist ones, against and in favor of the French state. As Immanuel Wallerstein concludes, "France is a multicultural country par excellence still living the Jacobin dream of uniformity." France's resistance to sign the European Charter for Regional or Minority Languages (ECRML), which would require to change the second article of the French constitution ("the language of the Republic is French") is another example of this republican nationalism, which has been widely criticized (Nature).

In both Americas, the hegemonic discourses of "mestizaje" and "the melting pot," respectively, were hegemonic in the 20th century but are undergoing a crisis in the 21st as a result of challenges by indigenous and migrant people who do not subscribe to those assimilationist theories. These challenges also require to rethink the Basque diaspora and to contribute to the debate from a Basque position.

Therefore, in the case of the Basque Country and the states that define its reality, a new theory of historical difference or "multiculturalism"—a locally situated and historically based multiculturalism—is necessary. Furthermore, this differential theory must be defined vis-a-vis state-nationalism, through postnational theory, in order to articulate a historical discourse that redefines retrospectively state nationalism as an ideology in crisis while also challenging its new neonationalist-neoliberal articulation in globalization. In conjunction with postnationalism, "multiculturalism" must theorize state (neo) nationalism as an ideology bound to create further tensions and crises, due to the violence that it generates when rejecting other forms of postnational and postcolonial culture, which then also tend to respond in violent and fundamentalist forms. The continuation of ETA in Spain until 2011 or the riots in the suburbs of Paris in 2005 constitute the most radical manifestations of this violence (Wallerstein). Thus, and unlike in the case of North-American and British multiculturalism, which experiences a crisis of their nationalist-multiculturalist project in globalization, Spanish or French "multiculturalism" has to be articulated as a global redefinition and reexamination of an already differential history, which goes back at least to the Middle Ages and is eminently imperialist and colonial. In short, such differential theory or "multiculturalism" must be simultaneously postnational and postcolonial.

In the case of Spain, the Middle Ages and its culture of tolerance, mostly in Muslim states (caliphate and *taifas*), represents an important reference, which, to this day, has not been fully explained in political and theoretical terms; it is simply evoked through the non-politicized idea of tolerance (Castro, Menocal). Furthermore, in the case of Spain (but also of France), the reexamination of a differential history has to be exerted in connection with Latin America. At least since the processes of colonial independence of the 19th century, *mestizaje* or creolization, in its varied formulations and variants, has also become a state ideology of homogenization in Latin America. Nevertheless, *mestizaje* does not negate a multicultural diversity; it assimilates this diversity through mixing, while depoliticizing the concept of mixture (in *mestizaje* "everybody becomes a mixed, national subject" at least since Martí). Newer forms of mixing proposed in the 20th century, such as transculturation (Ortiz, Rama) or hybridization (García Canclini), simply reformulate the same ideology of *mestizaje* in more cultural terms, now adapted to the new revolutionary history of many nations (Rama's transculturation) or to the new effects of globalization (García Canclini's hybridity).

2. History

Basque history and, more specifically, Basque literary history offers a privileged position to rethink both literature and history, precisely because things Basque do not have an easy fit in any modern category: language, state, nation, modernity, class, heteronormativity, gender, and race. Actually, it would not be too difficult to prove that there is no such thing as "Basque literature" if national, modern European standards were applied. Yet, this lack of an easy fit in modernity gives Basque literary history a vantage point in order to observe the smooth, hegemonic sutures between language and institution, nation and state, class and race, etc. Therefore, Basque history offers a strategic location from which to think the historical disjunctions that state hegemony renders so natural, so ahistorical, i.e., so non-ideological. Thus, to the question of whether Basque literary history should be national, European, Atlantic, Global, and/or Multicultural, the answer is excessively positive: all of the above. This excessive, affirmative answer aims at underscoring the fact that no category fits easily and, therefore, every category contributes to explaining the uneasy fit, the disjointedness of the categories upon which Basque literary history can be predicated.

If the Marxist tenet is always to historicize, and even Nietzsche proposed that the remedy to too much historicism was indeed to historicize historicism (103), then perhaps we ought to approach the problem of literary history in a historical way, so that it sheds light on the new global Babel that constitutes (contemporary) literary history in Spain and France as well as in Europe and the Americas—the historical backdrop for Basque literary history.

One of the earliest philosophers to connect culture and nation, and, thus, to precipitate romanticism in Europe is Johann Gottfried Herder. Until recently, those who have not read his work critically (Kristeva) have stereotyped him as the philosopher of the most fundamentalist and essentialist form of nationalism (ethnic nationalism, which then is opposed to civic nationalism; J. Azurmendi). Moreover, his work has been reduced to a few ultra-nationalist appropriations perpetrated much later. Yet, it is important to remember that Herder's initial innovation, at the end of the 18th century, was precisely to emphasize the irreducibility of particular history, rather than the ahistorical "essence of the nation." When his work is read critically, one can determine that Herder brandishes the historicity of the particular, of the singular (rather than that of the immutable nation), against the despotic enlightened state, of which European colonialism represents its final and most exploitative embodiment. In this respect, he is the predecessor and inspiration of thinkers of the singular and particular such as Nietzsche, Deleuze, and Guattari—as well as of their philosophizing style. At a time in which Emmanuel Kant published his *Anthropology from the Pragmatic Point of View* (1798), where race hierarchies were defended philosophically, and his colleague Johann Friedrich

Blumenbach, founder of German physical anthropology, proposed the well-known 5-race classification in the 1795 edition of his *On the Natural Variety of Mankind* (1775) for the first time, Herder clearly stated his anti-imperialist approach to European colonialism and nationalism in his *Letters for the Advancement of Humanity*:

> What, finally, is to be said of the culture that has been brought by *Spaniards, Portuguese, Englishmen,* and *Dutchmen* to the East and West Indies, to Africa among negroes, into the peaceful islands of the southern world? Do not all these lands, more or less, cry for revenge? ... The diversity of languages, ethics, inclinations, and ways of life was destined to become a bar against the presumptuous *linking together* of the peoples, a dam against foreign inundations—for the steward of the world was concerned that for the security of the whole each people and race preserved *its* impress, *its* character; peoples should live *beside* each other, not mixed up with and on top of each other oppressing each other. (381-83)

Historically speaking, thus, the birth of the credo of particularity —and later the nationalist understanding of literary traditions rooted in the particularity of each language and people—is a reaction against the totalizing ideological effects of the imperialist enlightened state: the despotic state. Although I would agree with Benedict Anderson that the "birth" of nationalism has to be located in the (Latin) American colonial wars of independence in the 19th century, the theorization of nationalist culture is carried out in Germany. Herder still understands the imperialist underpinnings of the European enlightened state and, thus, his reaction towards particularism is not nationalist, as it has been argued, but rather anti-imperialist.

It is only in the 19th century, after the Napoleonic wars turned anti-enlightened criticism into a nationalist, reactive ideology, that Frederick and Wilhelm Schlegel nationalized Herder's anti-imperialist understanding of particularity and singularity. In their work, the Schlegel brothers narrowed national literature to the field of European imperialism: Spain, Italy, France, England, and Germany. As a result, the two brothers incorporated the "new" literary traditions outside Europe, which they described as an orientalist extension and reflection of European nationalism and imperialism, to their literary histories, i.e. to the first modern literary histories. In short, the original anti-imperialist thrust present in Herder's philosophy was incorporated and neutralized by the Schlegel brothers into a nationalist ideology that consequently became European and imperialist in design. This shift has to do with the aftermath of the Napoleonic wars and, more specifically, with the repositioning of the Jena Circle (the Schlegel brothers and Novalis) in German culture after Goethe.

In the first lecture of his 1815 *Lectures on the History of Literature Ancient and Modern*, Frederick Schlegel, the founder of modern philology and literary history, proclaims his nationalist credo. Given the centrality of this idea for our critical historiography, it is worth quoting at length:

> We shall best discover the dignity and the importance of the arts and sciences represented in a spoken and a written form, if we trace their intimate connection with the moral worth and the destiny of nations in the long chapter of the world's history. *The real character of literature, as the summary of a nation's intellectual capacity and progress*, is then exhibited in its fullest extent.
>
> One of the most important advantages to a nation, in regard to its further development and especially its intellectual condition, is seen to be judging by historical and relative evidence, the possession of a store of national traditions; these as they become more and more faint in the long vista of ages, it is the especial business of poetry to commemorate with imperishable splendor. Such traditions, the most glorious heirloom of a country, are indeed a possession which deeds of past ages, embodied in matchless strains of poetry, kindles the noblest feelings of a people and fires their bosoms with a glorious ardour... (8, my emphasis)

Frederick Schlegel clearly naturalizes the relationship between teleological, national history and literature, when he states his object of study: "the development and spirit of literature among the principal nations of ancient as well as of modern times... its influence on practical life, on the destiny of nations, and on the progress of ages" (1). Furthermore, Schlegel defines literature as the repository of "national genius" (3). Finally, and since Schlegel is focused on studying the spirit of European nations in their literatures, he turns other non-European literatures into orientalist complements of the European nation: "as my primary object is to present a picture of *European* culture, and especially to point to the influence of literature on life, it will be more convenient to adduce Oriental modes of thought and systems of philosophy in such a form as shall serve to illustrate its effects on the habits of the European mind" (11, my emphasis). This is the founding text, with Wilhelm Schlegel's *Lectures on Dramatic Art and Literature* (1808), of what we now consider *literary history*, which is ultimately national and, because of its tendency to naturalize the literary field (spirit, genius…), also nationalist.

Therefore, the contemporary global resurgence of multi-nationalism-lingualism and, more generally, of radical difference, is not symmetrically opposed to the nationalist credo of a monocultural literary tradition and history (the Schlegels), since, in its origins, the latter was also anti-imperialist and particularist (Herder). Rather, multiculturalism constitutes a de-naturalization of nationalism, since the former further emphasizes particularity at a point in which the advances of the neoliberal state and its apparatuses threaten to totalize and homogenize diversity through a (neo)nationalist ideology that, ironically enough, was originally developed to emphasize historical diversity and particularity. Furthermore, globalization's effects on state hegemony and sovereignty allow us to view— through the cracks of this moment of crisis—the fact that nationality is simply a form of diversity-particularism favored by the modern State and its hegemonic class, the bourgeoisie. Moreover, nationalism must be now retrospectively contemplated as yet one more form of diversity among others, even though it still presents itself as the hegemonic form of diversity (and hence the only acceptable form of particularism, or in Lacanian terms, the *quilting point* of diversity).

Moreover, and although this would require a separate study, it could be posited that nationalism is the phantasmatic structure that shapes and haunts any other multicultural reality against its own particularism. If Carl Schmidt concluded that "[A]ll significant concepts of the modern theory of the state are secularized theological concepts" (36), one could conclude that many multicultural theories are shaped by de-nationalized concepts of the nation, hence the "identity-politics" shape that multiculturalism has taken in many instances—even though most multicultural realities have no direct relationship with the nation. Only an anamnesis of the particularist history of nationalism and multiculturalism would allow a theory of difference to rethink this haunting exerted by nationalism. Nationalism is in crisis and, yet, it is already attempting to reformulate and uphold its hegemony through neoliberalism—hence the need to emphasize the historical persistence of nationalism rather than its disappearance, as Habermas has attempted to do. The latter option only promotes the continuation of uncritical, unchallenged nationalism. Perhaps it would be fitting to call *neonationalism* to the new refashioning of nationalism under the hegemony of neoliberalism and to separate it from classical nationalism or nationalism proper.

Many schools and trends of literary history have sprung since the seminal work of the Schlegel brothers at the beginning of the 19th century. Some authors, such as David Perkins, claim the impossibility of literary history from a positivist-liberal point of view. Yet, such ahistorical claims seem untenable in the light of their epistemological naiveté. The necessity of a multiculturalist history that challenges (neo)nationalism makes any claim on the impossibility of historiography suspect of neoliberalism. In 1992, Perkins, in one of the most canonical theorizations of literary history, denounced multiculturalist histories as projections into the past:

> The movements for liberation of women, blacks, and gays produce literary histories for the same motives, essentially, that inspired the national and regional literary histories of the nineteenth century. These groups turn to the past in search of identity, tradition, and self-understanding. Their histories do not usually stress discontinuity but the opposite. They find their own situation reflected in the past and partly explained by it. (10)

However, after dismissing any form of literary history, Perkins concludes with a very vague and liberal invocation to "learning," "growing up," and "feeling otherness:" "Thus, to learn to read with the perspective of literary history is like growing up. We encounter a wider, more diverse world of books, expressing mentalities that challenge us by their difference... A function of literary history is, then, to set the literature of the past at a distance, to make its otherness felt" (184-85). His other suggestion concerns the "usefulness" of literary history: "to produce useful fictions about the past... [literary history] projects the present into the past and should do so; it makes the past reflect our concerns and support our intentions" (182). In short, he ends up embracing that which he has denounced earlier.

The Anglo-American school of literary criticism known as "new historicism," heralded by Stephen Greenblatt, is perhaps the last school to develop a new and differentiated theory of literary history. Similarly to Perkins, Greenblatt follows Foucault and claims that the ultimate goal of his literary history of the English Renaissance is "to analyze the collective dynamic circulation of pleasures, anxieties, and interests" (*Shakespearean* 12). Greenblatt echoes the Elizabethan critic George Puttenhams's idea that language has the ability to cause "a stir of the mind" and underlies the fact that, in the Renaissance, such effect was named "*energia*." Therefore, Greenblatt sets to study "the social energy initially encoded in those works" as way to interpret the "'life' that literary works seem to possess long after both the death of the author and of the culture for which the author wrote" (6). Ultimately, for Greenblatt, the study of the circulation of social energy is a way "to speak with the dead" and, thus, to make literary history (1). He concludes that his own history has led him to realize that "[I]f I wanted to hear one, I had to hear the many voices of the dead. And if I wanted to hear the voice of the other, I had to hear my own voice" (20).

The problem of Greenblatt's proposal, and of new historicism in general, is two-fold. On the one hand, since literature always positioned at the center of other institutions and discourses, with which it is compared in order to isolate the "circulation of social energy," literature always ends up being the institution that problematizes other institutions; yet, because of its teleological centrality in the new historicist discourse, literature becomes ahistorical and non-institutional. In short, any discourse or institution can be compared to literature and since the latter always becomes the most complex or subversive institution of all, at the end, we have a very mechanical and predictable circuit, in which literature's centrality cannot be challenged when studying the circulation of social energy. As a result, the canonicity of Shakespearean literature and, more generally, the centrality of the British Empire remain unquestioned in Greenblatt's new historicism. Consequently, we are back to a more sophisticated refashioning of the literary ideology advanced by the Schlegel brothers: the traditional spirit of the nation is refashioned into the social energy of the European imperial state.

On the other hand, since Greenblatt studies the circulation of social energy as a way to speak with the dead, he organizes his discourse so that the circulation of energy takes a single direction, from the past to the present. Therefore, the present is the time that is not dead: it is ontologically separated from the dead past. For Greenblatt the past and the dead are a supplement of his present desire to speak; there is a clear ontological difference and hierarchy between past and present. In short, the past is a supplement of the present, and history becomes a supplement of a critical subject, Greenblatt, who is not dead.

If we follow Walter Benjamin's theses on history and Jacques Derrida's discourse on ghosts, we can see the ultimately liberal position that supports Greenblatt's history. Following Benjamin and Derrida, and departing from the Basque case, the opposite of Greenblatt's liberal stance seems more historical. It is not we (I) who speak with the dead, who want to speak with the dead; rather the opposite, it is the dead who speak with us. Moreover, in an even more radical formula, I would propose that the dead continue to speak *through* us. We are spoken *by* and *through* the dead. Thus, in this new formulation, the present is the time that is the supplement of an ongoing history, the so-called past. Consequently, Greenblatt's liberal ontology on the separation of past and present disappears. Or to put it in a succinct and ironical way, the only ones who are alive are the dead; we are the dead of the dead. Before I am accused of renouncing to any form of agency or subjectivity, I would rather proclaim that I am arguing for a more historical agency and subjectivity, one that is truly grounded in history rather than on the liberal and still Cartesian illusion of the Greenblattian "I."

To bring the above criticism to the Basque territory, let us say that any Basque literary history emphasizes the lack of a present subject. The liberal-Cartesian Greenblattian subject, wanting to speak with some dead who seem to be silent and thus need to be spoken *to* and *for*, does not exist. There is no present Basque subject who can speak with the dead; it is Basque history, in its many forms of oppression, diglossia, and violence, which continues to exist as a difference that cannot be claimed by any given present subject, least of all, a confident liberal-Cartesian subject á la Greenblatt. The Basque difference, in its historicity, is the present crack, break, or slippage from which the dead continue to speak to us, continue to speak *among* themselves *through* us.

In a more recent debate dating from 2002, a very important disagreement seemed to erupt between Greenblatt and Linda Hutcheon on the issue of literary history. However, as I will show, the disagreement only manages to refashion and ultimately re-legitimize the nineteenth-century, Schlegelian agenda. Let me quote Greenblatt at length, since he also summarizes Hutcheon's claims:

> Hutcheon... is... writing... about recent attempts from a wide range of positions within current identity politics—class, race, ethnicity, gender, sexuality, and a host of other categories with which people self-identify—to forge a usable past. "Interestingly" she observes, "the newer literary histories often adopt precisely the same developmental, teleological narrative model used earlier by nations".... This is a model that Hutcheon asks us to endorse, if not ringingly then at least with two cheers. I have invoked *The Cambridge History of Latin American Literature*... because I want to acknowledge the possible tactical efficacy of such artificial memories and fabricated histories. Still more, I want to acknowledge that the strategy is by no means necessarily reactionary,

that it may serve progressive ends. The acknowledgement is not without cost, for me at least, because when I hear words like racial memory or *volk*, my blood runs cold.... [Greenblatt invokes Yugoslavia] I respond to such stories with distaste and something like horror, but I can remind myself ... that in certain circumstances the construction, along traditional, nationalist or ethnic models, of a particular cultural narrative, the story of a group's struggle to take control of its destiny, to find its voice, to honor its forebears, to transmit its heritage, and even to access its racial memories may be an aesthetic achievement and even seem to some an ethical act. Yet, this reminder does not ultimately induce me to share Hutcheon's endorsement, cautious though it is, of the appropriation of these old models. This appropriation, however useful strategically, seems to me a serious mistake... ("Racial" 56-7)

Ironically enough, when he uses the word "empire" his blood does not run cold and he does not invoke colonialism and slavery. After elaborating a very careful and sophisticated list of caveats and warnings against any minority literary history, he concludes by demanding from these histories precisely that which he has never achieved himself for English literature:

From this perspective, the acceptance, even if it feels clever and tactically enabling, of the traditional model of literary history, with its concern (in Eliot's phrase) to purify the language of the tribe, robs the hitherto marginalized groups of their revolutionary potential: a potential that lies in the impurity of languages and ethnicities, in tangled lines of access and blockage, in the flesh-and-blood intensity of loss, assimilation, and invention, and in the daring intersection of multiple identities. The new literary histories that these groups are poised to write should do more than put them on the map; they should transform the act of mapmaking. (60-1)

In short, Hutcheon and Greenblatt, both hailing from majority traditions, from hegemonic literary histories, end up displacing the problem of literary history onto the field of the other, of the minority, thus, moving the ghost of "the racist, oppressive nation" into the field of minorities. In this way, they have opened, once again, the gates of empire and of postimperialist literatures such as English for the free circulation of *energia* and, more generally, of a guilt-free global social energy, so that even Shakespeare can now be globalized without guilt. In short, their discussion reassures us that the problem of the nation is a problem of the other, of minorities. As for Shakespeare, new historicism, Elizabethan literature, or even the postmodern novel, the problem of the nation has been overcome long ago according to these critics. As the above exchange reveals, the most reactionary ghosts of national literary history continue to haunt hegemonic histories, now disguised as the ghosts of the other, of the minority.

Since the discussion between Greenblatt, Hutcheon et al. on literary history in the early 2000s, no other serious proposal has been advanced to rethink literary history per se. Furthermore, it seems that there is a revival of semi-positivist, material histories that vindicate maps (Moretti) and digital approaches (Jockers) connected to the digital humanities.

Only the school of South Eastern Asian Subaltern Studies (Guha) and the shorter-lived Latin American Subaltern Studies Group (Rodriguez and Lopez) have open up a new way to approach, not literature per se, but history: the history of the subaltern classes, mainly of the colonial period (in India). However, this approach is central to a reconsideration of literary history for two reasons. On the one hand, subaltern studies centers precisely on what the cultural project of the nation leaves outside or "below:" subalternity, the oppressed classes without a political voice, without a written discourse. On the other, some of the research of the Subaltern Studies Group has changed as a result of its encounter with poststructuralism, especially in the area of literature, thus opening up a new field of studies called postcolonial literature. Although there has been much discussion about "the end of postcolonial studies," it is important to revisit this new development in order to understand where literary history must head in the 2010s.

Following Gramsci's theorization of subalternity, Guha defines subalternity in the preface of the first volume of essays of the group entitled *Subaltern Studies* as follows: "The word 'subaltern' in the title stands for the meaning as given in the *Concise Oxford Dictionary*, that is, 'of inferior rank', it will be used in these pages as a name for the general attribute of subordination in South Asian society whether this is expressed in terms of class, caste, age, gender and office or in any other way" ("Preface" vii). This apparently simple definition had important repercussions for writing history. Guha outlined the consequences of historicizing subalternity in the opening article of the first volume published by the group, which is entitled "On Some Aspects of the Historiography of Colonial India." Yet, he has elaborated them more thoroughly in his *Dominance without Hegemony*:

Subaltern Studies made its debut by questioning that assumption [of a nationalist unified history] and arguing that there was no such unified and singular domain of politics and the latter was, to the contrary, *structurally split between an elite and a subaltern part*, each of which was *autonomous* in its own way. Much of what we have to say has indeed concerned with documenting the existence of these two distinct but interacting parts as well as with arguing why such a structural split between them was historically necessary. (*Dominance* ix, my emphasis)

Guha's claim to the autonomy of the subaltern classes means a break with Western Marxism, which was teleological in its narration of history as an inevitable shift from feudalism to capitalist, industrial societies. As Guha understood well, his claim to the subaltern subject's autonomy and structural difference from the elite has an important non-teleological consequence: "[T]he co-existence of these two domains or streams [...] was the index of an important historical truth, that is, the *failure of the Indian bourgeoisie to speak for the nation*" ("On Some Aspects" 41). In short, Guha opens up a new way to analyze history, which breaks away with the hegemonic model, centered on the bourgeoisie and nationalism. Western Marxism imposed this historiographic model in Britain, France, and Germany. In this way, Guha inaugurates a new history for what, in this book, I call "minorities and/or differential subjects." Although lately, there have been some critiques of the subaltern historiographical method (Chibber), I believe it remains vital and central to a postnationalist history of Basque literatures.

Yet, the confluence of subaltern studies and minority politics in the USA opened the field for a more general and theoretical form of analysis and historiography, which was also endorsed by Edward Said—the other important figure of a way of historicizing against the European grain. Said prefaced a selected collection of articles of the Subaltern Studies Group in 1988 and one of the later collaborators of the group, Gayatri Spivak, wrote the introduction (Guha and Spivak). On the aftermath of this initial North American confluence, Homi Bhabha published his *On the Location of Culture* (1994), and, as a result, this new North American cluster of contributions became known as "postcolonial theory," which relied more on literary analysis and poststructuralist theories than on historiographical analysis; Spivak's own article "Can the Subaltern Speak" published in 1988 set the tone for postcolonial studies.

Postcolonial studies, although closer to literary analysis, did not yield a renewed debated on literary history per se. As Spivak acknowledged, it was a cluster of interventions and collaborations, rather than a well-articulated theory. The issues of subalternity and autonomy were thus transposed by postcolonial studies from an Indian colonial setting to the more general one of Western colonialism and globalization. This more generalized and less historical form of analysis yielded contradictory effects. In one of the early canonizations of postcolonial literary studies, Neil Lazarus concluded that

> [...] the version of subalternity that has proven most influential in post-colonial studies is that proposed by Gayatri Chakaravorty Spivak [...] This conceptualization seems to me to come close to fetishizing differ-ence under the rubric of incommensurability. The central problem with Spivak's theorization of subalternity is that in its relentless and one-sided focus on the gap of representation, representation as political ventrilo-quization, it contrives to displace or endlessly defer other questions [...] an *epistemological* question [...] and a *methodological* question, concerning the relation between theory and practice. (9-10)

As late as 2012, in a debate organized by the journal *New Literary History*, Robert Stam and Ella Shohat summarized well the list of critiques against postcolonial studies, although the two authors remained committed to the project.

> To name just a few of the critiques, they include censure for: (1) the eli-sion of class [...]; (2) a tendency to subjectivize political struggles by re-ducing them to intrapsychic tensions, [...] (3) an avoidance, noted by Marxists, of political economy in a globalized age where neoliberal eco-nomics drives many of the cultural shifts registered by the theory; (4) an obsessive antibinarism that ignores the intractable binarism of colonial-ism itself [...] (5) a haughty superciliousness (noted by Ann du Cille) to-ward fields such as "ethnic studies," which shared many axioms with postcolonial critique and helped open up institutional space for postcolo-nial studies, yet which were dismissed as essentialist; (6) a tendency to focus on faded European empires while ignoring the actually existing U.S. neoimperialism that surged into the vacuum left by the receding empires; (7) a Commonwealth-centrism which, while valid in its own terms, sometimes quietly assumes the British-Indian relation as paradig-matic, while neglecting vast regions such as Latin America, Africa, the Middle East, and the indigenous "fourth world" (including that within India itself); (8) a lack of historical precision (noted by historians such as Frederick Cooper), linked to a vertiginous rhetoric of slippage that al-lowed little concrete sense of time or place except when the theoretical helicopter "landed" on a random historical example; (9) the inordinate

privileging of themes of hybridity, diaspora, and elite cosmopolitanism, to the detriment of refugees and displaced persons and the racialized division of international labor; and (10) a failure to articulate postcolonial theory in relation to ecology and climate change. (371-72)

Although the critique of postcolonial theory exceeds this introduction to literary history, it is important to note that some of these criticisms are pertinent and therefore a return to subaltern studies, in a more historical and material way, is necessary. Hence, the following history will take as a departure point the above critique of postcolonial studies.[10]

The other way in which the consequences of postcolonial literary history can be measured is by analyzing two of the most important literary histories published in the last few years. In the history mentioned above by Lazarus, he sums up the results of postcolonial theory for literary history in the following way:

> To read, teach, or write about contemporary literature today is inevitably to feel the impact of this decentering [triggered by postcolonial studies…] Where "English" literature, for instance, meant, more or less unproblematically, writing produced by white Britons—or, at most, by them and Anglo-Americans—today not only is the case that English is demonstrably a world language […] it is also obvious that the cultivation, preservation, and enrichment of English (as a literary language) are today tasks undertaken as much by "non-Anglo" as by "Anglo" writers […]. (14)

As the above quote shows, "decentering" is the ultimate word that sums up a history of postcolonial literature, where the emphasis is on English (Anglophone) and other imperialist languages and, consequently, small and native languages are ignored. In short, postcolonial literary history looks too much as a celebration of the decentered legacy of European colonialism to the detriment of any other literary reality. Even one of the latest

---

[10] As Sumit Sarkar states, the new direction taken by postcolonial studies has also changed the later Subaltern Studies: "In South Asian historiography, however, the inflated reputation of late Subaltern Studies has encouraged a virtual folding back of all history into the single problematic of Western colonial cultural domination. This imposes a series of closures and silences, and threatens simultaneously to feed into shallow forms of retrogressive indigenism. […] A simple binary of Westernized surrender/ indigenist resistance will necessarily have major difficulties in finding space for sensitive studies of movements for women's rights, or of lower-caste protest: for quite often such initiatives did try to utilize aspects of colonial administration and ideas as resources" (316-7).

histories of literature, *A New Literary History of America* (2008), edited by Greil Marcus and Werner Sollors, offers only fragmentariness and heterogeneity as historiographical criteria.[11]

Therefore, and in order to avoid the burden of philology, the discipline that traditional literary histories have deployed in order to organize the raw historical material of the nation, and which is conspicuously embraced by newer developments such as New Historicism or postcolonial literary studies, this Basque literary history will not be divided according to centuries, "periods" and/or cultural movements, although these categories are used strategically within a larger historical framework. This history is organized according to more local, historical developments and, in this respect, is more concrete and situated. There are no separate Baroque and Neoclassical periods exported from universal European history and forced onto a primal Basque historical matter, for example. This book does not look for "romanticism," celebrating or regretting the Basque fit or lack thereof to a predetermined European historical grid of categories. At the same time, this very local history is explained within a context larger than that of the nation-state. In this way, the local recovers its full historical complexity. Thus, this history departs from the fact that Basque culture and literature are not circumscribed to a single state and, rather, the different negotiations that take place between Basques and the imperialist states that define them on both sides of the Atlantic are at the core of their history.

Therefore, this books describes and situates Basque culture in five moments or phases in which the negotiations between several imperialist states and the Basques are redefined and resituated both geopolitically and biopolitically across the subaltern/elite divide. In short, this history has a geo-bio-political logic of its own in which a violent, political fracture between the elite and the subaltern takes place across several imperial states. This violent fracture, rather than a national subject, is the main historical object of study of this book. The above mentioned five moments coincide with the imperialist and colonial expansion and decadence of the Spanish and French states and, more recently, with that of North American imperialism, which is also known as postmodernism and/or globalization. In this sense, this history is ultimately and eminently Atlantic, and follows the new Atlantic histories that have emerged

---

[11] I have discussed the theory of subaltern studies in the field of Iberian and Basque studies elsewhere ("Spanish Nationalist Excess").

in recent years (Gilroy, Bailyn). Moreover, this discourse does not attempt to fit Basque history into the history of European and North American imperialisms as a pre-existing object that fits neatly in a preorganized larger historical scheme or puzzle. Rather the opposite, this history seeks to explore the ways in which Basque differences and European-American imperialisms constitute each other, without being able to be reduce each other to a single political subject or hegemony; hence the ever-present divide between elites and subaltern classes inside Basque history.

That is why the word "difference" is inscribed on the title of each chapter and in the historical description of each chapter. Although, in a near future, a history of Basque literatures could be written through other guiding principles or criteria that denote indifference, rather than difference, today, the differential approach is the only way to think and historicize Basque literary history in its radical complexity. In short, (subaltern) difference is invoked historically and strategically to counter the general state of indifference or homogeneity that pervades most postimperialist, nationalist literary histories in Europe and the Americas.

Chapter 2 analyzes Basque literatures from the late Middle Ages to the Renaissance. It centers on the multiple cultures, ethnicities, races, and languages that coexisted in continuous quarrel and, sometimes, in peace and tolerance while political borders kept shifting and different political processes of unification took place. This period is one in which Basque is just one difference among others and, therefore, one could also speak of Basque indifference. The chapter studies the discourses and historical changes that transform all these differences, in their complex historical relationship, into the first discourses in which Basque subjects are articulated through the discourses of travel literature (Aymeric Picaud), historiography (Jimenez de Rada) and pactist literature (*fueros/foruak* or founding charters). The chapter emphasizes the ways in which imperialist discourses of Castilian identity and originality create, as effect, counterdiscourses of Basque identity and originality that, in turn, trigger further Castilian discourses: a double genre in which Basques such as Jimenez de Rada give rise to a genre and discursive activity I call "the tradition of invention," against Hobsbawn's theories, and which will persist through the Generation of 98 and the new Basque neonationalists of the turn of the second millennium (Savater, Juaristi, etc.). At the same time, this chapter also studies other discourses that are born out of the highly multicultural reality of the southern Basque Country, which, in turn, give rise to forms of cosmopolitism (Benjamin of Tudela) and fundamentalism

(Judah Halevi) in the Jewish community of Tudela. The chapter ends with a reevaluation of oral "literature:" ballads and women's improvisational poetry. The chapter studies the ways in which the nobility and the subaltern classes share this oral culture, thus, producing literary realities that cease to exist in the Renaissance: poetry written by the Basque nobility (Lazarraga), improvisational poetry by women (Milia Lastur), and epic ballads ("Bereterretxen khantoria"). The chapter traces the reasons why the nobility abandons the Basque language as a cultural medium and women begin to be prosecuted for participating in the public sphere as subjects of culture. Against most European historiography, this chapter does not narrate a history from a dark period to one of enlightenment and humanism, but rather the opposite: the Basque Renaissance is the beginning of a dark age.

Chapter 3 examines the history and relationship between the Atlantic expansion of Europe, especially the Spanish empire (1492), and the formation of Basque difference around medieval consuetudinary law (*foruak/fueros*), which is now written and upheld against the homogenizing and centralizing impulses of the French and Spanish empires. The chapter centers on the consequent Basque expansion in the Atlantic, economic and cultural, so that Basque difference is argued and legitimized through the mobilization of Basque language against the racial discourse of the Spanish empire; this will result on the formation of a specifically Basque elite that deploys Basque difference against subaltern subjects. This chapter concludes at the end of the Enlightenment when the crisis of the Spanish monarchy and the rise of French imperialism give rise to a differential Basque enlightened culture (The Royal Basque Society of Friends of the Country), which defines itself by attempting and failing to give an Atlantic answer to the new ruralization and impoverishment of the subaltern rural classes. The chapter concludes by analyzing the ways in which the monopolistic trade of the Basque enlightened elites with Caracas (Royal Guipuzcoan Society of Caracas) serves as a conduit for the dissemination of the enlightened discourse in Latin America and for the increase in revolts against these Basque elites. This Atlantic traffic makes possible the anti-colonial, independentist discourse, which, in turn, brings the demise of the economic and cultural trade of the Basque enlightenment, already under attack by the Inquisition and the Spanish monarchy as a result of the former's French and, more generally, European affiliations and sympathies.

More specifically, this chapter centers on the ways in which the ideology of Basque antiquity, already present in the Spanish historiography of Jimenez de Rada in the Middle Ages, is fully developed by the Basque nobility in the form of the discursive genre of the "apology" (defense) in order to create a Basque difference that permits to uphold medieval rights while also gaining new privileges in the Spanish monarchy and bureaucracy as other "different groups" such as Jewish converts and Moriscos lose their position. The chapter also studies the ways in which French and Spanish monarchies deploy the Inquisition in order to contain Basque difference and turn Basque language into that of witchcraft, thus curtailing lower classes from having access to political institutions that, until that moment, conducted business in Basque. The chapter also centers on the other important discursive genre of the Basque Baroque: the religious manual written in Basque. By studying the work of Loyola and Axular, this chapter traces the contradictions and unintended effects of the Basque religious discourse of the Baroque. Finally, by studying the discourse of two exceptional Basque individuals, Lope de Aguirre and Catalina de Erauso, the chapter highlights the "monstrous" contradictions that allowed a minority such as the Basque to mobilize their difference across the limits imposed by an imperial-colonial order.

Chapter 4, entitled "Colonial Difference and the Nation," emphasizes the fact that the Basque Country is caught in a European imperialist shift from Spanish and Portuguese dominance to French and British hegemony. In this transition, the Basque Country becomes an internal, imaginary colony to the new rising imperial powers: an internal pseudo-colonial other. This process of othering the Basque Country is organized according to the new emerging discourses of anthropology, biological racism, linguistics, tourism, and Orientalism. The othered Basque Country becomes the object of the discourses of European and Spanish origin and antiquity, which trigger an essentialist discourse that is used by both Europeans and Basques for different purposes and is at the base of the formation of Basque nationalism at the end of the 19th century. This discourse is highly racialized and gives rise to racist discourses towards both Basque natives and immigrants to the Basque Country. It is also the phase in which the second most important wave of Basque emigration to the Americas takes place. This is also the time in which any essentialist formation is equated with idealized femininity (motherland, matriarchalism, etc.) and masculinity begins to be represented as lacking or castrated. This finally is a phase of economic polarization and social unrest, which leads to several uprisings (*matxinadas*) and, ultimately, the Carlist Wars. The final decline of Spanish imperialism in 1898 is chosen as a symbolic date to mark the transition to a new historical moment.

Chapter 5, entitled "State Difference and Strategic Essentialism," centers on the nationalization of Basque culture and difference in the Spanish Basque Country, whereby history, culture, and difference become framed within the discourse of the nation-state and, thus, Basques take an active part in the formation of Spanish nationalism as well as in the project of a putative Basque nation-state in the 20th century (1898-2012). By reversing Hobsbawn's felicitous coinage, this is "the long Basque 20th-century." This phase coincides with the rise of the middle class as national subject, the beginning of women's active participation in the formation of the nation (both Basque and Spanish) and the eruption of a new racist discourse on the migration to and from the Basque Country. This is also the time when the state mobilizes the school as the main institution through which Basque language becomes finally marginalized and moved to a diglossic state in which it begins to be threatened with extinction and ultimate subalternity. This final development is even more pronounced in the French Basque Country and represents the almost full assimilation of Basques into the French republican project. This phase also coincides with the third largest wave of subaltern migration to the Americas and with the political exile of Basques from Spain to France.

Chapter 6, entitled "Global Difference and Multiculturalism," is an extension of the previous, as a way to examine the most recent history in a more detailed way. It centers on the eruption of North American imperialism or globalization, which takes hegemonic hold in the 1990s in the Basque Country. As a result, the nation-state stops being the hegemonic model of cultural formation. Neoliberalism and new forms of state nationalism (neonationalism), defined by their hostility towards any global phenomenon (economic and exilic migration from the Global South, Americanization, Europeization...), create a new scenario whereby, for the first time, different models of the Basque Country are discussed and promoted simultaneously on both sides of the Atlantic in democratic states: from independence, sovereignty, and self-determination to a democratic transition into infra-state political solutions such as autonomy (Spain) and departments (France). At this point, Basque difference begins to lose its essentialist articulation and gives rise to a heterogeneity of discourses, among which the neonationalists emerge, ironically enough, as fundamentalist. This coincides with a wide array of biopolitical movements, from feminism and ecology to radical culture, LBGT movements, yuppyism, neonazism, and fundamentalist neonationalism (Spanish, French...), which are both a result of the expansion

47

of globalization and contestatory formations against it. Here, Basque culture and difference are also thought of as both a biopolitical difference that has a place within the neoliberal state and a difference that is not directly connected to language; at the same time, Spanish and French states start to lose their legitimation on nationalism and develop new forms of neonationalism that linger on fundamentalism. More specifically, and as the French republican project experiences a crisis, the French Basque Country begins to open to new political alternatives, including Basque nationalism. At this point, no political option is clearly hegemonic or counter-hegemonic in the Basque Country. This period is also defined by the new polarization of social classes, so that the middle class begins to lose ground, economic subalternity reemerges, and new forms of global migration define the Basque social space.

3. Literature

A postnational-multicultural approach to literature also requires we rethink Spanish, French, and American cultures and literatures. The reflection on what constitutes minority cultures in Spain and France —the two states that comprise the main European Basque territory—and, more specifically minority literatures, has never yielded well-grounded and far-reaching results. Moreover, some promising starts have not developed into broader theories and discussions (JanMohamed and Loyd). To my knowledge, there has not been an attempt to consider culture and literature from a differential *and* postnational point of view with an emphasis on subaltern history.

It suffices to peruse few histories of Spanish and French literature to understand that the multicultural, ghostly specter of minority literatures is always repressed or, in more vulgar terms, "dismissed," and yet it comes back, so that most histories arrive to a very uncomfortable standstill: they cannot ignore the problem altogether, but they push it to the side nonetheless.[12] This logic affects not only national minorities but also

---

[12] Iris Zavala's history of peripheral women's literatures is very innovative in this respect, but fails to account for the tensions between central-Spanish and peripheral literary traditions, which, ultimately ends up upholding the nationalist paradigm.

The only European exception seems to be an anthology: David Damrosch's *The Longman Anthology of British Literature*, which includes Welsh, Gaelic, and Irish texts in English translation. To follow the debate that it ensued in regards to the only-English *Norton Anthology* by Abrams, see the "Roundtable" published by *Pedagogy* with contributions by Roger Sale, George Drake, Karen Saupe, and David Damrosch.

many different minorities: women, gays, exiles, etc. At the same time, some of the canonical authors whose work is very much influenced by their multicultural makeup—such as Unamuno, just to mention a canonical Basque writer—are treated as if they were "fully" Spanish in their "national identity" and, thus, any other non-Spanish difference, such as being Basque, becomes an accident in their biographies and writings—a "regional" accident in Unamuno's case.

In Spain, the issue of minority languages and their (lack of) relationship to the state language, Spanish, has been elaborated mainly from within the literary histories of those minority traditions. In the case of Galician, Basque, and Catalan literatures, there is a nationalist consensus (and, thus, local hegemonies) that the historical particular language of each area constitutes their respective literary tradition and history and, therefore, Spanish is not part of it. Most literary histories of Galician literature (Carballo Calero, Vilavedra, González-Millán, Tarrío Varela, Blanco Pérez, Fernández del Riego), Catalan literature (Riquer, Espadaler, Fuster, Terry, Roca-Pons, Bohigas, Vallverdu), and Basque literature (Villasante; Michelena *Historia*; Sarasola; Juaristi *Literatura*; Urkizu *Historia*; Aldekoa *Historia*) confirm this point by explicitly or implicitly affirming the linguistic exclusivity of each literature.[13] It is worth quoting at length the major history of Galician literature, authored by Ricardo Carballo Calero under the Franco dictatorship (1963), as one of the most explicit and conscious affirmations of this linguistic exclusivity:

> In this work, I conceive the history of Galician literature as an exposition of the accomplishments and the development of Galician language in the literary field. This is the easiest and most natural meaning that can be attributed to the expression "history of Galician literature." [...] No matter how Galician is considered *The Palace of Ulloa* [written in Spanish by Galician author E. Pardo Bazán's], it does not proceed to classify this work within Galician literature. I understand by Galician literature that which is written in Galician. [...] There is no reason to oppose the fact that an author might study the literary work of Galicians in all the languages they have cultivated. If s/he wants to entitle such a study "history of Galician literature", s/he should do it from far away. Words have already an acquired value of their own. In this book, the language serves to delimit the material of our study. We follow,

---

[13] The exception is Stewart King's *Writing Catalanidad*. I have written elsewhere more extendedly about the negative effects of this approach ('Spanish Nationalist Excess").

therefore, philological criteria, which we deem most scientific, for language is the foundation of literature. (11)[14]

More recently, in 1999, Dolores Vilavedra, referring to Carballo Calero, upheld the linguistic criteria, now reframed within the theory of the literary systems—as an autonomous and autochthonous system— rather than within those of philology, as in the times of Carballo Calero (15-21). Only Xoán González-Millán has come to historicize this option when he has defined the history of postdictatorship literature written in Galician as the historical "transition from literary nationalism to a national literature"[15] (*A Narrativa* 29; *Literatura* 12-13; *Silencio* 15). However, he has not questioned or explored the political implications of such a historization.[16]

Similarly, Spanish literary histories take the complementary action of defining Spanish literature as that constituted by literature written in Castilian by Spanish citizens (thus excluding Latin American and foreign writers residing and writing in Spain). In other words, contemporary Spanish literary criticism still writes under the pretense of considering works written in Castilian the natural and universal literature of the Spanish State. Francisco Rico's canonical collection of essays on contemporary Spanish literature written in Castilian is a good example of such pretense: *Historia y crítica de la **literatura española**. Los nuevos nombres: 1975-1990* (*History and criticism of **Spanish literature**. The New Names: 1975-1990*, my emphasis). The opening study written by the editor of the collection, Darío Villanueva, captures the contradiction between the title of the volume and the literary language studied. When referring to the conflict that takes place in the "peripheries" of Spain between local literatures (Basque, Catalan, and Galician) and Castilian, Villanueva affirms

---

[14] "Concibo nista obra a historia da literatura galega como a esposición das realizacións e do desenrolo da fala galega no orde literario. Íste é o senso máis doado e natural que cabe atribuir á espresión "historia da literatura galega".... Por moi galego que poda ser o mundo de *Los pazos de Ulloa*, tampouco compre crasificar ista obra dentro da literatura galega. Entendo por literatura galega a literatura en galego [...] Ren hai que opor ao fito de que un autor estude a obra literaria dos galegos en todos os diomas que teñan cultivado. Se quer titular ise estudo "historia da literatura galega", fágao embora. As verbas teñen decotío un valor convencioal. Mais niste libro é idioma o que nos serve para escolmar o material do noso estudo. Seguimos un criteio, pis, filolóxico, que nos parez o máis científico, xa que o idioma é o estormento da literatura."

[15] "paso do nacionalismo literario a unha literatura nacional"

[16] It is due to his untimely demise. He was always at the forefront of Galician literary history.

that it is "a conflict of languages which, entangled in politics, tends to provoke a dialectic between two cultures, the vernacular and the *ill-labeled "Castilian,"* about the supposition that there is no place for balance, and rather one will have to uproot the other" ("Los marcos" 15, my emphasis).[17] Villanueva's collection then goes on to exclusively studying literature written in Castilian as "Spanish." As a result, his study "uproots" the other Spanish literatures not written in Castilian from the volume, thus making true the scenario he condemns in the peripheries of the Spanish state in the first place.

Although the *Suplemento 9/1 (Suplement 1 to Vol. 9)* to Rico's original literary history represents a quantum leap, it still leans towards a nationalist-linguistic definition, after noting, but not solving, the problem. As Jordi Gracia notes on the introduction:

> The very same definition of contemporary Spanish literature is a thorny and controverted issue: the debate about what that sintagm designates nowadays is waking up in Spain but, most of all, outside Spain [...] However, this volume continues to respect the linguistic criterion over that of literary history, which should perhaps prevail over the more restricted philological one. (8-9)[18]

This nationalist consensus across the linguistic divide has held so far in a way that seems most contradictory, since none of these literary histories would defend nationalism as their main political tenet, although they all are nationalist. Their main political and epistemological assumption is that a language creates a tradition that coincides with the geopolitical limits of a state or an autonomous region (nationality) that might still become a state. The latest refashioning of this paradigm, by which each national language becomes a "literary system" (Even-Zohar), only gives sociological depth to a still fundamentally nationalist paradigm—hence its popularity among Spanish critics.

---

[17] "un conflicto de lenguas que, entreverado de política, tiende a provocar una dialéctica entre dos culturas, la vernácula y la mal llamada 'castellana', sobre el supuesto de que no cabe punto de equilibrio, sino que una deberá erradicar a la otra."

[18] "Cuestión espinosa y controvertible es la definición misma de la literatura española actual: el debate sobre lo que designa hoy ese sintagma está despertando en España, pero, sobre todo, fuera de España [....] Sin embargo, este volumen ha seguido respetando el criterio lingüístico frente al criterio de la historia literaria, que debería quizá prevalecer sobre el restringidamente filológico."

José Carlos Mainer edited the latest canonical literary history in 2010, entitled *The History of Spanish Literature*, which, in 9 volumes, continues to uphold the nationalist, philological criterion. Only the latest two volumes dedicated to the history of literary ideas and the location of literature, respectively, problematize the issue to some extent, but only as an after-thought that does not alter the historical criteria (nationalist, philological) of the previous volumes.

The final irony is that the addition of all these nationalist literary traditions creates a *nationalist excess* for which no literary history can account: if Spanish is the sole literary language of Spain, are Catalan or Basque literatures Spanish, and if so, how? If Basque is the sole, literary language of the Basque Country (in any of its geopolitical formulations) then is Spanish or French not a literary language of the Basque Country? Is Galicia a double literary-system and if so, how? In short, the exclusive and separatist structure of nationalist literary identities and histories in Spain creates an irreconcilable excess of nationalist identity that no literary history can encompass. Even the latest, and to this point, most engaging and challenging attempt, Brad Epps and Luis Fernández Cifuentes's collection, *Spain Beyond Spain*, does not question the Spanish state itself as subject of literary formation and, thus, does not interrogate the institution that legitimizes this excess as national reality—thus excluding, for example, the possibility of French Basque literature as Basque.

Yet, this irreconcilable excess points to the need to theorize literary history beyond nationalist tenets, according to a postnationalist theory, which would account for this excess in non-exclusive terms. Although at first, a simple liberal answer such as "all literary traditions are Spanish" would seem to solve the problem—as Jürgen Habermas has proposed more generally for Europe and its multicultural states—reality shows that such an answer is not viable; it only hides the geopolitical tensions and conflicts that underline the coexistence of these literary traditions whereby one continues to be hegemonic. The ultimate proof of the impossibility of this liberal proposal is indeed the fact that no such a history exists.

For starters, any history of this nature would have to historicize the political struggles, tensions, exclusions, and repressions that have taken place among those literary traditions. This history could be summarized by stating that Spanish literary history, if contemplated in its multinationalism, is *a history of literary diglossia*. The historically imperialist Spanish state, on the one hand, has successfully pushed several languages to the brink of extinction (Leones, Navarran, Aragonese, Arabic, Hebrew...)

but, on the other, has also failed to do so in the case of other languages (Galician, Catalan…), even at the height of a dictatorship (Franco) opposed to diversity. This is partly due to the (lack of) linguistic mobilizations undertaken by the respective peripheral bourgeoisies and middle-classes since the 19th century. As I stated elsewhere, literary diglossia makes it impossible to accept a liberal history of coexistence by which all literary traditions are Spanish, since the latter denies the historical existence and importance of literary diglossia and therefore becomes complicit in the state's cultural repression, exclusion, and subalternization ("Towards a Postnational History"). At the same time, and as I will develop in the following in detail, minority languages, when are finally embraced by the local bourgeoisies and/or middle-classes, also proceed to mimic state diglossia and repression so that internal (biopolitical) diversity is repressed and subalternity enforced.

The difficulty of this historiographical problem becomes even more pronounced if contemplated under the light of globalization, since the new migrational flows triggered by the latter have had a very clear effect in Spain. The presence of what seems "new" languages in Spain, such as Chinese or Arabic, must be rethought, especially in the light of the latter's medieval vitality and influence, alongside Hebrew—in a way that might help to rethink multiculturalism in the Middle Ages, since accounts such as Menocal's do not explain the political crux of "tolerance" beyond the accidental migration of an Omeya heir to Al-Andalus (5-13). In short, the celebration of the "birth of a modern Spain in the first Golden Age of Arabic-Jewish literature and culture in the 10-11th centuries" continues to be a traumatic and unthinkable moment for any "Spanish" literary history—and its connection with the present even more so.

In the French case, and as Denis Hollier, the editor of the most influential history of French literature in English clearly states, the reduction of French literature to national literature already was traumatic in the 19th century: "For the French, who, throughout the Enlightenment, considered their language to be the voice of the universal, this nationalization almost came to mean their own cultural death" (xxiii). Echoing a felicitous coinage by 19th-century French critic Charles-Augustin Saint-Beuve, Hollier notes that the French "chauvinisme transcendental," or dismissal of multiculturalism and difference, also permeates 20th-century culture and literature. Hollier cites the notorious case of Jean Paul Sartre:

This blindness to one's own nationalism survived the twentieth century. Ingrained against the most obvious goodwill, it would lead Sartre himself,

53

in the same year that he wrote his diatribe against 'La nationalization de la littérature'... to publish *Qu'est-ce que la littérature* (*What is Literature?*), a dazzling short history of French literature whose title seems to imply that for him there simply was no literature outside France" (xxiii).

Although French criticism has made important strides to incorporate literature written in French by citizens and subjects of other (postcolonial-diasporic) countries under the term of "Francophone" literature (Larousi and Miller), the literatures written by French citizens in France in languages other than French (Briton, Basque, Occitan, Corsican, Arabic, etc.) still remain silenced. Hollier's history does not make a single reference to Basque literature in its 1150 pages.[19] In this respect, the idea of Francophone literature, ultimately a postimperial discourse, must be supplemented and combined with a postnational conception of "French literatureS" (Basque, Occitan, Briton, etc.). France's refusal to ratify the European Charter for Regional or Minority Languages, as of 2016, is very telling of prevailing French nationalism.

As for France overseas, Edouard Glissant has most lucidly problematized the history of the concept of Francophone literature by stating that

> In the nineteenth century, after the Spanish language had expanded into South America and the Portuguese language into Brazil, the French and English languages successfully accompanied the widespread expansion of their own respective cultures around the world. [...] Our aim here is to advance the notion that, within the limited framework of one language— French—competing to discover the world and dominate it, literary production is partly determined by this discovery, which also transforms numerous aspects of it poetics: but that there persists, at least as far as French is concerned, a stubborn resistance to any attempt at clarifying the matter. (*Poetics of Relation* 23)

---

[19] Although overgeneralizations are always risky, it would be safe to say that postcolonial theory has mainly engaged literatures written in imperialist languages. References to minority literatures of the Asian subcontinent in Homi Bhabha's canonical postcolonial text, *The Location of Culture*, are almost absent (Hindi 154, 168; "Hindoustani" 146). As his introduction makes clear, references to a rainbow of what he considers the (post-colonial) third space are constituted by writers such as Gomez Peña, Salman Rushdie, Tony Morrison, Nadine Godimer, etc. i.e. authors writing in (post)imperialist languages. Yet, and to remain within the Asian subcontinent, and more specifically in India, the number of official national languages is 18. Similarly, Salman Rushdie's own evaluation of post-independence Indian literature, published in *The New Yorker* in 1997, ends up celebrating English as the most important Indian literary language and, thus, himself as its most central representative.

His analysis of French creole as a language already internally split by the trauma of slavery (*Caribbean Discourse*) makes his work urgent to theorize (Basque) literary history.

The problem of multi-nationalism-lingualism becomes further complicated by the fact that, once national diversity is accepted as a historical problem, other forms of biopolitical diversity (gender, sex, race, class, etc.) bring to the fore the issue of the nationalist paradigm's predominance and hegemony. In short, it is not self-evident and, thus, we must inquire why is nationalism, and nationalist literary language, the main parameter by which the history of literature is organized. Already in 1947, Simone Beauvoir had clearly stated this problem in more general terms, when analyzing the fact that women were divided by class and race (and one could add, nation):

> They [women] live dispersed among the males, attached through residence, housework, economic condition, and social standing to certain men —fathers or husbands— more firmly than they are to other women. If they belong to the bourgeoisie, they feel solidarity with men of that class, not with proletarian women; if they are white, their allegiance is to white men, not to Negro women. (xxv).

Beauvoir's claim that the geopolitical overrules the biopolitical, and in our case, the fact that the nation overrules gender, sex, race and class still remains a problem to be questioned.

Therefore, the acceptance of a nationalist diversity also requires theorizing and historicizing the very fact of nationalist hegemony, which, once it is questioned, appears in its political nakedness. In Louis Althusser's felicitous dictum (159-62), one could conclude that the nationalist ideology's "lack of history" already points to the fact that it is clearly political at its core and, thus, must be questioned.

4. Postnational Literary History

In order to finish this introduction, I would like to add few notes in order to explain my subalternist-postnational-differential approach, while justifying some of the specific choices I made in each chapter. These notes should be expanded and organized elsewhere in a more structured way. For the sake of economy, I will use the term "SPD history" for "subalternist-postnational-differential history." I will also use a single adjective, as in "subalternist history" or "postnational history" to refer to "SPD history" for the sake of variation.

A SPD history cannot be a policing history where identity, a single national identity, is sanctioned or rejected. Rather, a postnational history is meant as an approximation to an area, an object, a time, which draws its historical value from its lack of exact borders and unique identities. The goal of a subalternist history is precisely to blur these borders in order to challenge any nationalist understanding and policing of identity. Therefore, questions such as "Is Judah Halevi's literature Basque?"; "Why do you include Victor Hugo in a Basque literary history?"; "If Itxaro Borda is Basque, can she be French?"; "Are those two identities incompatible?"; "How to choose?" are not questions that this history is interested in answering; rather, it aims at questioning the political presuppositions that make such questions possible. Yet, this challenge to the philological and nationalist policing of literary identity does not imply a mindless dance, a neoliberal, postmodern market of identities, in which one can choose as if they were consumption commodities. Rather, a SPD history blurs the borders of any philologically policed, nationalist identitarian space in order to explore the historical problems that those borders rely on, in order to grasp their specific, particular history. In short, this history blurs borders precisely to question and historicize them. In this sense, a differential history is radically historical and aims at showing that any national history is ultimately a-historical. In last instance, a subalternist history implies a border theory (Anzaldúa; Mignolo, *Local Histories*).[20]

Similarly, a postnational history is not interested in explaining literature as a system (Even-Zohar), a very popular and prevalent approach among Basque critics. It is more interested in explaining where the system fails, i.e. the cracks and noises of any system. It aims at historicizing any system and ultimately questioning the very idea of a system.

A SPD history also questions the Cartesian idea of a national literature written by national subjects for other national subjects, in a perfect circuit of national-self recognition—what we could call the *literary cogito*: "I write and read, ergo I am the nation." Following Freud and Lacan, it is clear that the Other/other has a role in the imagination of the self. A

---

[20] Literary histories, as they stand, are not very well equipped to account for a history of reading. It would be essential also to theorize a postnational reader as a Basque reading subject who reads and listens, or cannot read and listen, in several languages. The access of lack thereof to different languages in the Basque Country also represents a very political history of social privilege and subalternity.

differential literary history pays special attention to the ways in which the Other constructs, deflects, and reflects the self, in order to create the imaginary moment of literary reading and recognition. Therefore, and especially in the case of the Basque Country, this postnational history resorts to writers, anthropologists, tourists, etc. of other origins (European, African, etc.) in order to analyze how the discourse of the Other is internalized, repressed, deflected, and transformed by Basque literature. Therefore, Hugo's orientalist discourse is as important as Iparragirre's anthems to the *foruak/fueros*, for example, when explaining the "essentialization" of Basque literature in the 19th century. There is no way to understand Mogel's ruralism and custom literary style (*costumbrismo*) without studying Humboldt's romantic research on the origins of the Basque language and Europe. Hugo and Humboldt are not simply a "contextualizing" or "introductory" reference to the "true, native" discourse. They are as historically active and central as any Basque author is to the formation of Basque literature.

Against a philological, nationalist history that privileges written over oral discourse and divides literature in centuries, movements, and genres, thus, marginalizing oral discourse to a supplemental status in the opening or closing chapters of literary history, a SPD history aims at re-historicizing the political borders that the texts, discourses, and codes (oral/written) themselves create along the subaltern/elite divide. For example, the issue is not whether we have "true" Basque literature during the 16th, 17th and 18th centuries, a period when religious manuals written in Basque are the main genre that defines the field of written Basque literature. The two important *literary* genres of these two centuries are the religious manual in Basque and the linguistic apology of the Basque language written in Spanish as complementary discourses that organize the literary and cultural fields of the Basque Country. While religious manuals in Basque become baroque technologies for the subjection of subaltern masses, linguistic apologies in Spanish legitimize the very same elites that encourage the production of religious manuals in Basque. At the same time, oral poetry is not simply a supplement with which to deal in a separate first or final chapter; it is one of the discourses that rural subaltern classes organize against the technologies of the self deployed by religious manuals. In short, the field of literature in the 16th, 17th and 18th centuries is not divided according to the classical genre structure of "poetry-theater-narrative-essay." If this ahistorical division is adopted, Basque literature is "missing narrative," and is clearly "deficient" in (written) theater and poetry. The historical genres that define Basque literature as a historical reality are the religious manual, the linguistic apology, and oral poetry. These three "genres" also have specific languages (Spanish, French, Basque, and Latin) and are deployed historically by different social classes for different political purposes.

A postnational-multicultural history cannot either historicize according to the traditional code of the "aesthetic discourse," whereby only texts produced and received with an aesthetic function are considered literature. In the Basque case, literature is defined as the discourse that organizes Basque subjects and classes around their geopolitical differences. Aesthetic pleasure is only one literary pleasure among others. Basque subjects, when imagining their differences, deploy a more general category of "literary pleasure or enjoyment" that exceeds the aesthetic. Here "imagination" refers to Anderson's concept of nation formation as well as to Lacan's concept of the imaginary, whereby the subject constitutes itself in relationship to a desire that ultimately can never be fulfilled as either identity or possession when directed to the Other.

An initial mapping of a postnational history requires choosing specific texts and authors as a way to guide that mapping. However, this choice of a very limited amount of texts and authors cannot be confused with the canonization process that takes place in major literatures and goes against the subalternist grain. Here, it is rather the lack of previous mappings, the precariousness of the task, its initial stages, which force a subalternist history to limit the corpus. Moreover, this specific Basque history is directed to English readers and yet there are not many translations of Basque texts in English. Therefore, a careful choice of texts, authors, and historical events becomes more meaningful than a long list of names, works, and historical developments, to which the reader might never have access. I know this is a balance that will never be satisfactory to all readers. Eventually some Basque readers and critics familiar with previous literary histories will chastise me for not being specific enough, for leaving too many things out. Readers who are not specialists in Basque literature will criticize me for being too specific, too local, even too parochial, and, thus, for missing the larger picture, the only one that matters to them. I can only argue as a defense that this is more of a sketch of what a future, elaborate postnational history of Basque literatures could and should be. I have also quoted and translated many texts in this history, as I am aware that most of them will not be available to the reader otherwise. In short, I also had to present a corpus of literature and history within the text; something other canonical literatures do not need to do as the referenced works are readily available in English or in English translation and oftentimes are well known by the reader. The very incipient automatic translation of texts in Basque started by Google in 2010 is still insufficient.

Although, in this initial stage, this book is not definitive, a more complete postnational-multicultural history should also point to historical relations with other neighboring minority literatures such as Occitan, Galician, etc. and, on a more theoretical level, with other minority literary histories and discourses. Ngugi Wa Thiong'o's *Decolonising the Mind* (already published in Spanish in the Basque Country) or the earlier mentioned Edouard Glissant's *Caribbean Discourse* are two cases in point.

Finally, I would like to add few notes on the mechanics of this text. In several chapters, I have adapted work I have previously published, cutting and mixing it with newer ideas and more pedagogical explanations. Given the level of mixing, it has been difficult to identify a clear, direct relation between previously published work and its new arrangement in this text. Therefore, I decided to list all the published work in the bibliography without attempting to explain throughout the text where I have borrowed and mixed from it. The new mixings and rewritings have altered the old texts to the point that the original copyrights are no longer an issue.

2. Middle Ages: The Age of Differences

1. Travelers and Outsiders (Picaud, Ibn Hayyan, Al-Makkari)

The Basque Middle Ages resemble in many aspects the history of contemporary globalization: many cultures, ethnicities, sexualities, races, and languages coexisted in continuous quarrel and, sometimes, even in peace and tolerance. Political borders kept shifting; unification processes were taking place with different levels of success by emperors, monarchs, and communities alike. Finally, cutting across most differences, a stark polarization between a warrior elite and a destitute rural class defined the social class structure, which now we know by the term popularized by Montesquieu: feudalism.

This period is also known as the Dark Ages because, in contrast, the age of the Roman Empire was thought of as an enlightened period. Yet, it is also dark, from our distant 21st century, because there is little documentation, especially in the peripheries, and, thus, this age can only be approached through the scant references and texts that have survived. Yet, the darkness of this period is a reminder that new documents and vestiges can be found, which can shed new light and overthrow every assumption made to that point. By the same token, the darkness of the age also allows for much retroactive falsification and apocryphal literature, a tradition that begins in the very same Middle Ages. As I will discuss in the following, this active alteration of records yields one of the most interesting Basque literary genres: the narratives of consensual historical pacts, which define the legal status of most Basque communities and legitimizes them as politically different.

Yet, the thin line between discovering new documents and creating apocryphal ones continues to our days. In 2006, archeologists claimed to have found Basque inscriptions in the Roman city of Veleia in Iruña-Oka, Alava, dating back to the 3rd-5th centuries, that is, to the beginning of the Middle Ages. Soon after, philologists rang the alarm of fabrication (Provincial Government of Alava). What would have amounted to the oldest inscriptions of a contemporary language and tradition in Spain simply seemed a fabrication. Yet, the possibility of finding other documents remains. Similarly, a manuscript containing poetry and pastoral narrative in Basque, written by the Alavan Joan Perez de Lazarraga[21] and dating back to the late 16th century, was found in 2004 (Gartzia), thus adding a fifth

---

[21] He is usually referenced as "Lazarraga" without "Perez de." In the following, I will follow this convention.

work to the only other four published in Basque in that century. Finally, we have only indirect references to interesting historical characters such as a Basque woman who lived in the Muslim court of Cordova and was well known for her poetic abilities. The Arab historian Ahmed Mohammed Al-Makkari (c. 1578 -1632), in his *The History of the Mohammedan Dynasties in Spain* (also known as *Analectes*), mentions a Basque woman in the court of Abd-ar-Rahman II (788-852), named Kalam, who was famous for her singing and recitation skills and, probably, for her ability to improvise poetry (*Analectes*, I 225; II 96).[22] Therefore, the Middle Ages continue to be the (dark) age that is most likely to shed new light in our history.

The multicultural, conflictive life of the Middle Ages cannot be reduced to a single historical narrative. Aymeric Picaud, in his *Codex Calixtinus*, recorded a description of the Pilgrimage Road to Santiago de Compostela, thus giving rise, in the 12th century, to what later will become another important genre in Basque literature: the touristic and anthropological account of the Basques. Tudela, a Navarran city founded by Muslims in 802 and conquered by Christians in 1119, is the origin of several Jewish writers and intellectuals who wrote poetry (Judah Halevi), travel narratives (Benjamin of Tudela) as well as religious exegeses (Abraham Ibn Ezra) in Hebrew and Arabic.[23] Rodrigo Jimenez de Rada, born in Gares, Navarre, in the 12th century, went on to write the first history of what he conceived as "Spain" (*Hispania*), thus giving rise to a "very Basque" genre that has lasted, via the Generation of 1898, to our days: the invention of Spain. Also in the kingdom of Navarre, and after the negative effects of the Champagne dynasty in the 13th century, an apocryphal introduction to the *General Fuero [charter, constitution] of Navarre*, gave rise to the "narrative of pactism." This narrative genre redefined the

---

[22] Julián Ribera quotes Al-Makkari stating, "Abdu'r-Rahman II was the monarch who most furthered the acclimatizing of Oriental Arab music in Spain. He had a special section of his palace set aside for the women singers, among whom three from the great school of Medina were outstanding. They were called the 'Medinans,' and their room in the palace was known as the Medinans' room. They were Fadal, Alam, and Kalam [....] The singer Kalam was not behind them in perfection of song, exquisite elegance, and fine courtesy. She was a Basque maiden who had been sent as a child to the Orient, particularly to Medina, where she became very learned, even to the point of knowing by heart many literary and historical works. She was eminent in various studies and a great reciter of Arab verses" (99-100).

[23] Doubts still persist as to whether Halevi and Ibn Ezra were born in Tudela or Toledo.

relations between kings, on the one hand, and territories and subjects, on the other, as a consensual pact. This historical genre eventually became the basis of most of the *fueros* written in the Basque Country in the late Middle Ages. Finally, we only preserve the vestiges of a rich oral improvisational culture in Basque, shared by both peasantry and nobility, in which women played a central role. The infinite intersections among these genres and traditions constitute Basque literature in those very global Middle Ages, of which the Basque Benjamin of Tudela gave us the first global map. He travelled east and mentioned China (in its present name) for the first time in medieval Europe, thus, foreshadowing the expansion of the Silk Road and the later travels of Marco Polo in what became a global western hemisphere spanning from Spain to China and from Scandinavia to the South Saharan regions.

In the 12th century, Aymeric Picaud, the presumed compiler of the *Codex Calixtinus* (*Calixtinian Code*), gave one of the earliest accounts of the Basques; he also cited several words in Basque. The *Codex* is a guide for the pilgrims of the Way of St. James, whose tomb was supposedly buried in Santiago de Compostela in North-Western Spain. The pilgrimage to St. James was the most traveled way in the Middle Ages, due to the fact that Jerusalem was caught up in the wars of the Crusades. Book V of the *Codex*, "Iter pro peregrinis ad Compostellam" ("A Guide for the Travelers to Compostela"), which many authors such as Américo Castro (154) and Nancy L. Frey (13) characterize as the first European tourist guide, contains some of the most famous remarks about the Basques. According to the *Codex*, Basques were hostile towards the pilgrims and, thus, their characterization is utterly negative:

> These are ferocious people, and the land in which they dwell is considered harsh, both in its forest and in its savage ways; the ferocity of their faces and their barbaric speech arouse great fear in the hearts of those who see them. Although by right they ought not to exact so great a toll except from merchants, they also get it unjustly from pilgrims and from all who pass. (Gerson 25)

After narrating the Navarrans' customs and citing several words in Basque, Picaud concludes with a severe condemnation of all Basques:

> This is a barbarous race unlike all other races in customs and in character, full of malice, swarthy in colour, evil of face, depraved, perverse,

perfidious, empty of faith and corrupt, libidinous, drunken, experienced in all violence, ferocious and wild, dishonest and reprobate, impious and harsh, cruel and contentious, unversed in anything good, well-trained in all vices and iniquities, like the Geats [of the Black Sea or Germanic] and Saracens in malice, in everything inimical to our French people. For a mere *nummus* [coin], a Navarrese or a Basque will kill, if he can, a Frenchman. (Gerson. 29)

Regardless of the accuracy or reasons for such a description, it is clear that the "French" point of view of the Basques was differential; the Basques are perceived as different from French or Galician and closer to an earlier orientalist identity: the Saracens. Furthermore, they already represent the ultimate form of European otherness: "[T]his is a barbarous race unlike all other races." This differential characterization is also confirmed by other Franc chroniclers of the 7th century, who refer to the Basques as "Wascones rebelles," i.e. as rebellious (Bazán 203).

Similarly, Arab historians such as Ibn Hayyan (987 – 1075) in the 11th century and Al-Makkari, still in the 16th, when referring to Musa's campaign in the north, write: "[A]fter this, Músa invaded the country of the Basques and made war against them, until they all came to him in flocks, as if they were *beasts of burden*. He then took the route of the country of the Franks" (Hayyan lxxvi, my emphasis). The negative, differential characterization continues as Hayyan does not even bother to register the Basques as worthy enemies; they are simply animals on the edge of "civilization." In this respect, Hayyan agrees with Picaud.

2. Jewish and Arabic Writing (Halevi and Benjamin of Tudela)

Judah Halevi (1070 or 1075-1141) and Benjamin of Tudela (1130-1173), both Jews born in the Navarran city of Tudela, wrote in a transitional moment and, to a large extent, their writings were a response to that historical juncture.

After the Muslim invasion of 711, the Visigoth chief of the lower area of Navarre, Casio, converted to Islam in 713 in order to preserve his position of power; his family became known as the Banu Qasi and were appointed representatives of the Omeyas in Navarre. Farther north, and after several power changes, the region of Pamplona went to the hands of Eneko Arista in 816, whom made a pact with the Banu Qasi against the Navarran factions that were in favor of an alliance with the Christian Carolingians of France. By the end of the 10th century, Arista's hold over the Pamplona area gave rise to the kingdom of Navarre. This new kingdom, in conjunction with the Asturian kingdom, attacked the Muslim kingdom of Zaragoza, which extended to the lower area of Navarre, including Tudela. In 1118, the Navarran-Aragonese king Alfonso I the Fighter conquered Zaragoza and, the following year, Tudela. To put this Navarran expansion towards the south and the east in context, it will suffice to add that Toledo was conquered by Alfonso VI of Castile in 1085. Only Cordoba, Seville, and Granada remained Muslim cities of culture and commerce through the 12th century.

Although Halevi had migrated to Al-Andalus by the 1090s, he saw, in his lifetime, Tudela change from a Muslim to a Christian city. Yet, Al Andalus was also in transition. In 1086, Almoravid troops crossed the strait of Gibraltar and entered Al-Andalus in order to battle the Castilian king Alfonso VI. They gave way to a new wave of fundamentalism, which ended the Andalusi era of tolerance and cosmopolitism and put the Jews once again in a dangerous position, to the point that many, including Halevi's mentor, Moses Ibn Ezra, crossed the border northward and relocated in the less developed and less cosmopolitan Christian territory. Moreover, the first crusade had already begun in Jerusalem in 1099 and, therefore, a return to Israel was not an option for most Jews.

Benjamin of Tudela was born about sixty years later than Halevi (1130), and yet, both saw the rise of Arabic fundamentalism. Unlike Halevi, Benjamin of Tudela lived long enough to witness the Almohad expulsion from Al-Andalus of Jews who did not convert, starting in 1149. Similarly, both writers grew up in a Basque city that was more cosmopolitan and urban than most other Christian cities in central and northern Navarre. In Tudela during the 11th and 12th centuries several languages were spoken: Basque, Romance (Navarran, Aragonese, and Castilian), Latin, Hebrew, and Arabic. In this respect, Tudela was probably more multicultural than many cities further south. This multicultural situation and the ever-changing political landscape of Navarre prepared both writers to leave their home city for larger cosmopolitan places: Constantinople, Baghdad, and Samarkand in Benjamin's case, Toledo, Granada, Cordoba and Cairo in Halevi's.

Yet it is almost perplexing to observe the diametrically opposite answers given by both authors to their historical juncture of transition: Benjamin of Tudela undertook a long voyage around the Mediterranean and, through the Silk Road, to Baghdad, Yemen, Persia and India. After three years (1169-71), he returned home to the city of Tudela. Halevi, instead, moved to Toledo and Granada and, eventually, left Al-Andalus for Palestine. Yet, he was welcomed in Egypt and ultimately died in Cairo without ever reaching his final destination. In short, Benjamin of Tudela returned home; Halevi did not return to either of his homes (Tudela, Palestine).

In the account of his travels, and after his long journey, Benjamin of Tudela concludes that the Jewish communities around the known world show the strength and continuity of a thriving culture. In order to arrive to this conclusion, he resorts to a very rare style at the time among Jewish writers: a non-religious, referential, factual account of what he encounters, from people to customs. Yet, the only people he does not describe are precisely his own, the Jews of Tudela—including himself. Halevi, on the other hand, resorts to poetry and essays (*The Kuzari* or *The Book of Khazars*) and writes in both Hebrew and Arabic to find a way out of the cultural and political situation of the Jewish communities around the known world. He propounds a return to a non-philosophical religion and to the only place where this religion can be lived without the classical Greek and Muslim influences, which, according to him, have distanced Judaism from its religious core: Jerusalem. Later, another important Jewish philosopher and scholar, Maimonides (1135-1204), after being forced to leave Spain by the Almohad invasion (1149), remained faithful to the idea of joining Greek philosophy (mainly Aristotle) and the Jewish faith. Convert Petrus Alfonsi's anti-Semitic writings were also written around the same time (*Dialog against the Jews*, 1110). Therefore, Halevi represents a unique option: a fundamentalist answer to an extreme situation forced by Muslims and Christians alike. Yet, the difference between Benjamin of Tudela and Halevi's response is almost radical.

Benjamin of Tudela departed from his home city in 1169, headed to Tarragona and, through southern France, arrived to Rome and Naples. He crossed over to Greece and then headed to Constantinople (Istanbul). He traveled south to Jerusalem and finally arrived to Baghdad (*The Itinerary* 99), where the Jewish population, 40.000 according to him, surpassed the entire population of southern Navarre. In his travel account, he refers to the Abbasid Caliph, and encounters the most important authorities of the Jewish exile:

> The chief rabbi, Samuel, the Head of the yeshiva Gaon Jacob [school], who in conjunction with the other Betlaninm judges all those that appear before him. And at the head of them all is Daniel, the son of Hisdai, who is styled, "our Lord, the head of the Captivity of all Israel."

He possesses a book of pedigrees going back as far as David, King of Israel. The Jews call him, "Our Lord, Head of the Captivity," and the Mohammedans call him, "Saidna ben Daoud," and he has been invested with authority over all the congregations of Israel at the hands of the Emir al Muminin, the Lord of Islam. (99-100).

In an interesting reference, which is not clearly determined in today geography but most likely refers to the capital of Yemen, Sanaa, Benjamin of Tudela claims to find a Jewish community of 300.000 people— twice the population of the entire kingdom of Navarre (107).

Therefore, as Benjamin of Tudela headed east, he remained in familiar territory: a land he knew from the Talmud. Even in the Persian city of Susa, he recognized the tomb of Daniel (108). In other words, as he moved further east, he still could resort to Jewish history as his guide, in his travels through places that were not strange or foreign but rather part of the canonical book of his community. Only when he traveled to India, where he nevertheless found Jewish communities in Ceylon, did he finally find himself outside the territory of the Talmud and of any Western discourse (122). He was also the first European traveler to mention China: "Thence to cross over to the land of Zin (China) is a voyage of forty days. Zin is in the uttermost East, and some say that there is the Sea of Nikpa (Ning-po?), where the star of Orion predominated and stormy winds prevail" (123). Giovanni da Pian del Carpine (1185-1252) and Marco Polo (1254 – 1324) traveled to China several decades later.

At the end of this long journey, Benjamin of Tudela returned home through Egypt and Sicily. He concludes the account of his travels with a reassuring view. He is fully aware of the exilic condition of the Jews around the world and, thus, is mindful of the eventual return to the Promised Land. Yet, he also stresses the livelihood and strength of the Jewish diaspora:

All Israel is dispersed in every land, and he who does not further the gathering of Israel will not meet with happiness nor live with Israel.... As for the towns which have been mentioned, they contain scholars and communities that love their brethren, and speak peace to those that are near and afar, and when a wayfarer comes they rejoice, and make a feast for him. (138-39).

In the last paragraph of his book, he refers to France and gives a positive outlook of the situation of Jews. After naming Paris, he concludes,

"[S]cholars are there, unequalled in the whole world, who study the Law day and night. They are charitable and hospitable to all travelers, and are as brothers and friends unto all their brethren, the Jews. My God, the Blessed One, have mercy upon us and upon them!" (140). His is a realistic assessment of the Jewish community around the known world; and as such, he does not express any fears or alarms over the future of the Jewish community.

Judah Halevi, who transformed traditional Hebrew into a contemporary secular language by infusing it with patterns of Arabic poetry, was known for his initial poems about friendship, love, benefactors, and homesickness (Zion). Among his friendship poems, homoeroticism defines many of them. As the poem "The Mirror" states:

> Into my eyes he lovingly looked,
> My arms about his neck were twined,
> And in the mirror of my eyes,
> What but his image did he find?
>
> Upon my dark-hued eyes he pressed
> His lips with breath of passion rare.
> The rogue! 'T was not my eyes he kissed;
> He kissed his picture mirrored there. (Ausubel 45)

One of his most famous poems, "My Heart is in the East," deals with his longing for Zion, thus elaborating the issue of exilic and diasporic sentiment:

> My heart is in the East, and I myself am on the western edge;
> How could I enjoy drink and food! How could I ever enjoy it?
> Alas, how do I fulfill my promise? My sacred vow? Since
> Zion is still in Roman bondage, and I in Arabic bonds.
> All goods of Spain are chaff to my eye, but
> The dust on which once stood the tabernacle is gold to my eye!
> (*Ninety-Two* 234)

Yet, starting in the 1130s, he abandoned the Andalusi ideal of friendship, patronage, and elitist cosmopolitism, whereby religious endeavors were combined with philosophical speculation in Arabic, following the Greeks. As a result, Halevi proposed a fundamentalist turn, a shift towards the fundaments of Judaism: non-philosophical religion grounded in the land of Israel. The year he finally abandoned Al-Andalus (1140), he published his influential *Book of the Khazars* in Arabic.

In his book, and taking the historical event of the conversion of the king of the Khazars to Judaism, Halevi constructs a dialogue between a rabbi and the king of the Khazars, Al Khazari, as a means to unravel his fundamentalist turn. After the king dismisses Christian and Muslim religions and chooses Judaism, a long discourse develops, in which Judaism is explained at length. The same discourse condemns rational Greek philosophy on behalf of religious communication and knowledge based on prayer and revelation—the only way to reach god for Halevi.

Towards the end of the book, Halevi, through his characters, explains the reasons why the actual return to Jerusalem is also necessary to complete fully the return to religion:

> The Rabbi: I only seek freedom from the service of those numerous people whose favour I do not care for, and shall never obtain, though I worked for it all my life. Even if I could obtain it, it would not profit me—I mean serving men and courting their favour. I would rather seek the service of the One whose favour is obtained with the smallest effort, yet it profits in this world and the next. This is the favour of God. His service spells freedom, and humility before Him is true honour. (294).

Furthermore, and unlike Benjamin of Tudela who waits because "the appointed time has not yet arrived nor been reached" (139), Halevi advances the idea that the time has come. After the Rabbi reminds the Al Khazari of the prayer "On account of our sins have we been driven out of our land," he concludes that the time has arrived, by quoting another prayer: "Thou shall arise and have mercy upon Zion, for the time to favour her, yea, the set time is come. For thy servants take pleasure in her stones and embrace the dust thereof" (295). The Rabbi, and Halevi with him, interprets this passage in the following way: "This means that Jerusalem can only be rebuilt when Israel yearns for it to such an extent that they embrace her stones and dust" (295). Therefore, Halevi takes an active approach to the return to the Promised Land and turns it into an actual task to be completed in his lifetime. The return to Zion shapes the rest of his life.

Although Halevi died in Cairo, celebrated by the Jewish community of Egypt, he had already abandoned Al-Andalus and his previous cosmopolitan and cultured life. Unlike Benjamin of Tudela, Halevi could only return home by going to Jerusalem.

Yet, *The Book of the Khazars* is written in Arabic and, ironically enough, mobilizes every category of Greek philosophy to criticize the latter. In short, the book is constructed as a logical, philosophical treatise in Arabic, which attempts to leap beyond that very same tradition.

In this respect, Halevi never left Al-Andalus and, more generally, the Basque city that, from its small yet multicultural social fabric, propelled him to the Andalusi cosmopolitism that shaped his intellectual horizon.

The responses that later Jewish authors and scholars gave to the Jewish diaspora in the modern era were shaped, to a great extent, by the two diametrically opposed responses that Judah Halevi and Benjamin of Tudela gave to their Basque-Jewish history in the 12th century.

3. Political Literature (Jimenez de Rada, Pactist Literature)

Rodrigo Jimenez de Rada (1170-1247), born in the Navarran town of Gares or Puente la Reina, was the son of a noble family, who grew up in the court of the Navarran king Sancho VI the Wise (1133?-1194) and eventually was sent to Paris and Bologna to pursue university studies that were not available in the Peninsula at that time. After befriending Alfonso VIII of Castile, this monarch appointed him chancellor, bishop of Osma, and eventually archbishop of Toledo (1209). Jimenez de Rada wrote two stories of the Goths in Latin (*History of the Huns, Vandals, Sueves, Alans and Silingi; History of the Ostrogoths*), a history of the Arabs (*History of the Arabs*), and most centrally the first Hispanic history till the year 1243, *De rebus Hispaniae* (*History of Things Hispanic*), which, unlike previous histories, encompassed all Christian Hispanic kingdoms and laid the foundation for all future Castilian historiography, including Alfonso X's *History of Spain* and *General History*. Antonio Tovar intimates that Jimenez de Rada's native language was Basque (17), as the use of this language was widespread in southern Navarre in the 13th century.

He is at the beginning of what will become another important literary genre in Basque literature: *The Invention of Spain*, a genre that reaches its most productive moment with the Generation of 98 (especially Unamuno and Maeztu) at the end of the 19th century and, more recently, at the turn of the 20th with Basque writers such as Fernando Savater and Jon Juaristi.

This genre, which relies basically on the author's dismissal and repression of his[24] own position as Basque, on the one hand, and on a compensational hypertrophy or idealization of the idea of Spain as either empire or nation, on the other, is a political fantasy based on the believe that the imperialist state is the subject to know and to have, i.e. the state regulates or is in charge of the entire symbolic order or society---in psychoanalysis one would say that it is the political fantasy of the state as possessor of the Phallus (Lacan). The relationship between both discursive moves (repression and hypertrophy) lies on the fact that these authors contemplate the Basque Country as a negative and threatening reality to the existence of "Spain" (Hispania, or greater Castile). They perceive that the fundaments upon which the idea of "Spain" is predicated upon reveal the Basque Country as an earlier or "purer" version of that very same "Spain." In short, they perceive the Basque Country as a more original Spain than Spain itself—more "Spanish" than Spain; therefore, they proceed to repress their own position and that of the Basque Country as traumatic or violent on behalf of the imperialist State: Castile and later Spain. The ultimate political fantasy is that this eliminates any political discord and establishes a state free of conflict outside history.

Sometimes this genre has the counter-effect of producing a discourse of Basque originality that veers on exceptionalism, fundamentalism, and essentialism. Ironically, enough, this other genre could be named *The Invention of the Basque Country*. Therefore, we should speak of a double genre, properly speaking, the Spanish and the Basque. Perhaps Jimenez de Rada is not the founder of this double genre but, nevertheless, he is the author of whom we have the earliest account. More generally, he establishes the core discursive structure and foundation of what I denominate *materia vasconica*.

In his book *History of Things Hispanic*, Jimenez de Rada shows a universalist-Christian and imperialist conception of the Iberian Peninsula, which he denominates *Hispania*. He approaches the Iberian Peninsula as a single entity and chooses the way he organizes the history of its kingdoms in order to create a universalist-Christian and imperialist historiography whose single subject is the Goths—a subject who is universal precisely because it does not originate in *Hispania*. Thus, nothing "Spanish," particularly or locally "Spanish," is left in his universal, Christian historiography of the Goths. When he narrates the historic significance of the

---

[24] So far, all authors have been men.

Arab invasion of the Peninsula in 711, he summarizes his understanding of "Spanish" history as universal in a very concise way:

> Oh the pain! Here ends the glory of the Gothic majesty in the year 711 AD; they who had subdued many kingdoms in many wars, the banners of their glory bowed down in a single war; they who had devastated Scithia, Pontus, Asia, Greece, Macedonia and Illiricus with various killings; and whose wives had dominated, by fighting, the borders of the East, they who, after defeating and capturing Ciro the great ruler of Babylon, Assyria, Media, Syria and Hicania, had drowned him in his own blood; they, in front of whom a vanquished Rome, ruler of provinces, knelt its knees and emperor Valens died in a fire; they to whom Attila king of the Huns recognized their victory in the Cathalanic wars, to whom the Alans ceded Pannonia after fleeing the field of war, from whom the Vandals fled in Gallia, and whose wars had frightened the entire world with threatening thunder, the recently started rebellion of Mohammed annihilated in a single war with unprecedented destruction, so that all may proclaim that there is no richness in the rich, no force in the strong, no wisdom in the wise, no sublime in the ruler's glory. (104-05)[25]

In short, Rada chooses the Goths as the people who give *Hispania* its universal, Christian destiny. He finally explains the "Goths' choice of the Iberian Peninsula, over any other land, as their final home by explaining that "they preferred her to all others, because among all the provinces in the world she excelled in its titles of fertility" (105).[26]

Finally, the newest invasion, the Arab, which is not dissimilar to the Goths' in so far as both people are foreigners to *Hispania*, is explained by

---

[25] "Pro dolor! Hic finitur gloria Gothice maiestatis era DCCLII [711 AD], et que pluribus bellis regna plurima incuruauit, uno bello uexilla sue glorie inclinauit; qui Scithiam, Pontum, Asiam, Greciam, Machedoniam et Illiricum uariis cedibus uastauerunt et eorum mulieres Orientalem plagam preliis subiecerunt et Cirum magnum dominum Babilonie, Assirie et Medie, Sirie et Hircanie uictum et captum in utre sanguinis extinxerunt, et cui uicta Roma prouinciarum domina flexit genu, cui imperator Valens cessit incendio, cui ille eximius Athila rex Hugnorum Cathalanico bello recognuit imperium, cui Alani fugitiuo prelio Pannoniam dimiserunt, cui Vandali cesserunt Gallias fugitiui, quorum bella minacibus tonitruis toti mundo a seculis intonarunt, Machometi nuper orta rebellio uno bello inaudito excidio consumauit, ut discant omnes ne diues in diuiciis, no potens in potentiis, ne fortis in fortitudine, ne sapiis in sapiencia, ne sublimis in gloria glorietur."

[26] "Ipsam omnibus pretulerunt, eo quod inter omnes mundi pouincias specialibus ubertatis titulis redundabat."

74

Jimenez de Rada as a punishment sent by God for the moral and religious decadence in which the Goths had sunk by the 7th century. As Jimenez de Rada historicizes the "Reconquista" of the Peninsula, he narrates the ways in which God rewards faithful, religious-minded monarchs with lands and riches. Although the Arab invasion is traumatic for Jimenez de Rada, it is simply part of God's larger plan and, therefore, it is not an insurmountable test for the universalization of Goth history in *Hispania*. In order to show the idiosyncrasy of Jimenez de Rada's historiography, it is enough to compare it to contemporary French historiography, which chooses Rome as model, thus, turning Charlemagne and his progeny as the inheritors of the Holy Roman Empire. Instead, Jimenez de Rada chooses a "Holy Gothic Empire" as the subject of his history.

Therefore, it is of outmost importance to analyze the ways in which Jimenez de Rada narrates the history of the only indigenous people in Spain who retain their non-Gothic identity: the Vascons and Navarrans, as he calls them alternatively, meaning his own ancestry and himself. In what becomes a rhetorical trope, he refers to his own people as "those rebellious and unruly savages" who always rise against surrounding monarchs; are always vanquished; and, yet, rise again in new revolts. This repeating discursive trope comes close "the return of the repressed" (Freud). The reference to the rebellious and savage Basques are numerous in Jimenez de Rada's history. When speaking of the Goth king Suinthila who, according to Jimenez de Rada, dominated all the people of Peninsula from sea to sea, he adds: "At the beginning of his reign, [Suinthila] curtailed the incursions of the Basques, who infested the province of Tarragona, whereby these mountain people, terrified of his arrival, suddenly aware of their duties, dropping their arms and putting their hands together as to pray, humbly lowered their necks in front of him" (66).[27] Later on, when chronicling the life of the Goth monarch Wamba, he adds:

> While all these things happened, the Basques, ignorants of peace, invaded and pillaged several places in the Pyrenees and Cantabria, as the facts and desires of these people prove even today, for they rob what is others' at will. When this became known to Wamba, he proceeded

---

[27] "In inicio regni incursus Vasconum coarthauit qui Terrachonensem prouinciam infestabant, ubi montiuagi populi aduentus eius terrore perculsi, confestim quasi debita iura noscentes, remissis telis et complosis ad precem manibus, supplices submitterent ei colla;"

with the full extent of the law against those wrongdoers and drove them off to the ends of Cantabria and the Pyrenees. (77)[28]

Later he chronicles the life of king Fruela I, son of Alfonso I. After narrating the former's incursion in Galicia to stop the Arab general Omar, Jimenez de Rada refers once again to the Basques and, this time, he differentiates between Navarrans and Vascons (Guipuzcoa, Alava, Biscay, and perhaps people from the northern Basque Country[29]): "He attacked the Navarrans, whom had also risen, and took as spouse Monina, of royal Navarran progeny, and with their help he subjugated the Vascons, whom were defiant of his rule" (122).[30]

Still later, during the monarchy of Ordoño I, the same reference appears once again: "The first year of his reign, he gathered an army against the rebellious, belligerent Vascons, and coerced by force, he subjugated their country under his rule" (134).[31] Only once appears a reference to a collaboration between Goth kings and Basques, during the rule of Alfonso III: "Here, wanting to dedicate his time to the wars of the Lord, he received the help of the Gauls from Gothia and the people from Navarre and Vasconia, and he attacked, with famine, fire, death, and incursions, the lands held by the Arabs" (137).[32]

Most tellingly, when accounting for the only territories left after the initial invasion of the Arabs in 711, he enumerates the "belligerent Vascons" separately, by their provinces, and situates them at the core of the Gothic resistance, the last territories left to Christian hope:

---

[28] "Dum hec agerentur, Vascones quietis ignari loca Pirenei et Cantabrie inuaserunt rapinas agentes, ut eius gentis etiam hodie facta et desideria atestantur, qui libenter rapiunt aliena. Quod cum ad Bambe noticiam peruenisset, contra iniuriosos de iure procedens a finibus Catabrie et Prienei confusos abegit."

[29] Reminder: the terms northern Basque Country and French Basque Country can be used interchangeably. Conversely, southern Basque Country and Spanish Basque Country can too.

[30] « Nauarros etiam rebellantes inuasit et sibi concilians uxorem ex eorum regali progenie, Monninam nomine, sibi duxit et cum eis Vascones sibi infestos sue subdidit ditioni. »

[31] « In primo anno regni sui aduersus Vascones rebellantes exercitum congregauit et coactos cedibus suo iuri eos et patriam subiugauit. »

[32] « Hic uolens bellis Domini tempora dedicare, assumtis Gallis Gothie et populis Vasconum et Nauarrorum, terras quas Arabes detinebant fame, flama, cedibus et incursionibus coartauit; »

The Saracens occupied the entire Hispania, as the strength of the Gothic people was already diminished and no other place offered resistance, except for small pockets that remained in the lands of the Asturs, Biscayans, Alavans, Guipuzcoans, Ruchonians [probably Navarrans, although it is usually mentioned to describe parts of Asturias and Santander], and Aragonese, which the Lord had preserved so that the light of the saints was not extinguished in the Hispanias in front of the Lord. (114)[33]

Here Basques become saint-like Goths: the last hope of a vanishing Christian, Gothic empire. In short, references to Basques are rhetorical; they are in general negative and dismissive, except when, in front of the Arab menace, the need arises to account for them as the original foundation of the Christian people who regained the Peninsula from the Muslims. *In short, they become foundational but excluded from Jimenez de Rada's account of the origins of Hispania.*

Yet, this constant invocation of the unruly Basques, finds another moment of impasse and repression in the history of the kingdom of Navarre, which Jimenez de Rada attempts in chapters XXI-XXVI of book V. After the death of Vermundo III of Leon in the 11th century, the Gothic lineage stops and the Navarran king Sancho III the Great marries Elvira, daughter of the Castilian count Sancho, thus giving rise to a new Navarran lineage: the future king of Castile, Fernando, is also the son of Sancho III the Great. At this point, Jimenez Rada could have started a new Basque-Navarran, rather than Gothic, lineage for his project of an imperial-universal, Christian *Hispania*. Yet, the moment Sancho III's son, Fernando I, secures his place as king of Castile and Leon, the Navarran kingdom disappears from Jimenez de Rada's chronicle and his Gothic rhetoric resumes (194), as if there had not been any interruption. He proclaims Fernando I "monarch of the farther *Hispania*" (189).[34] In short, Jimenez de Rada is not looking for an indigenous historiography; he chooses a foreign invasion, because of its universal potential, as the subject of his historiography; then, he counter-poses it to the other historical invasion that defines the Peninsula, the Arab. However, he discards the latter, which presents the same universalist potential as the Gothic, because it is not Christian.

---

[33] « Sarraceni enim totam Hispaniam occupauerant gentis Gothice fortitudine iam contrita nec alicubi resistente, excepetis paucis reliquiis que in montanis Asturiarum, Bicagie, Alaue, Guipuscue, Ruchonie eta Aragonie remanserunt, quos ideo Dominus reseruauit ne lucerna santorum in Hispaniis coram Domino extingueretur. »

[34] "monarchus Hispanie Vlterioris"

However, the repression of the Basques and the hypertrophy of the idea of "Spain" in Jimenez de Rada is most intense and, at the same time, clearest at the very origin. Before the arrival of the Goths, Jimenez de Rada narrates the mythic history of Noah and the Flood, after which his son Japheth populates the West and, more specifically, the latter's son Tubal founds *Hispania*.

Following the original account of Titus Flavius Josephus (37– c. 100 AD), who located the arrival of Japheth's son, Tubal, to Iberia (modern-day Georgia in the Caucasian mountains), Saint Jerome (c. 347-420) re-fashioned eastern Iberia (Georgia) into the western one: Spain and Portugal. Finally, Isidore of Seville (c. 560 – 636) canonized this mistake, thus, making Tubal the first inhabitant of the "Iberian" Peninsula or *Hispania*.

In his *History of Things Hispanic*, Jimenez de Rada repeats Isidore of Seville's account but also gives a precise location for Tubal's settlement in the Peninsula, the Pyrenees: "Having arrived to Hispania, they lived first on the peaks of the Pyrenees and then multiplied in many tribes [peoples]"(13).[35]

He continues by adding a linguistic dimension to Tubal's arrival to the Pyrenees. Jimenez de Rada clarifies the original languages of *Hispania*. he retells the conventional account that, after the incident of Babel, Japheth's sons divided themselves into different nations and languages. He then cites Latin as the first language adopted by some of Japheth's descendants. Afterwards, he narrates the rest of nations and languages, and, at the end of that list, the Basque language appears unifying Vascons and Navarrans:

> And they were divided in languages and nations, and they used the one now called Latin. Similarly, the other sons of Japheth who settled in different places of Europe had other languages: the Greeks one, the Blakes and Bulgarians another. [...] and also the Basques and Navarrans [had another language, *euskara*]. And the Cetubals expanded into several peoples, descended [from the Pyrenees] to the flatlands of Hesperia [Hispania] and built towns, villages and forts next to the river now

---

[35] « qui in Hispaniam uenientes et Pirenei iuga primitus habitantes in populos ex-creuerunt.»

called Hiberus [Ebro] and settled thereby, those who were called Cetubales, were named Celtiberes due to the corruption of the name of
the river Hibero. (13-14)[36]

Antonio Tovar hesitates when interpreting this passage: "It would
appear that one cannot deduct from these texts that the Archbishop
[Jimenez de Rada] was thinking that the Basque language was brought to
the Pyrenees by Tubal's people" (19).[37] Later on, however, Tovar refers
to El Tostado, and he adds "And perhaps the Archbishop Don Rodrigo
was thinking of *euskara*, the Basque language, but, in truth, he does not
say so" (22).[38] Yet, the discursive continuity is clear. After mentioning
Basque and Navarrans, with no transition, he refers to the descendants
of Tubal (Cetubals): "and also the Basques and Navarrans [had another
language, *euskara*]. And the Cetubals expanded into several peoples, descended [from the Pyrenees] to the flatlands of Hesperia." Why this logical but nor causal continuity in the discourse between the Basque speakers and Tubal?

Given the historiographic plan of Jimenez de Rada to link the Gothic
invasion of Spain with the Castilian expansion to the south, the Basques,
or a he puts it, Vascons and Navarrans, become an impediment or hin-
drance to his plan. Yet, the discourse of origins, forces him to state that
the early (Cetu)Tubalians settled in the Pyrenees and then descended to
the Ebro valley. Given the wider expansion of Basque in the early Middle
Ages, Jimenez de Rada knew from first hand that Basque was originally
spoken in the Pyrenees all the way to both sides of the Ebro (including
Aragon, Rioja, and Burgos). He does not make an explicit reference to
the Basque language as the original language of Hispania. However, the
structural logic of his discourse dictates that, indeed, this is the case, and,
as a result, he needs to repress this fact: he must state in the contiguity of

---

[36] «Diuisi sunt in linguas et nationes et linguam que unc Latina dicitur obseruarunt. Alii
etiam Iapher filii qui in Europe partibus resdereunt linguas alias habuerunt : Greci aliam,
Blaci et bulgari aliam [...] similiter Vascones et Nauarri. Cetubales itaque in populos dila-
tati ad plana Hesperie descendenunt et iuxta fluuium qui nunc Hiberus dicitur uillas et
pagos et oppida construxerunt, et inibi remanentes, qui prius Cetubeles, ab Hibero fluuio
corrupto uocabulo Celtiberes se uocarunt.»

[37] "Parece que no se puede deducir sobre estos textos que el arzobispo pensara que
el vascuence fue traído a los Pirineos por los tubalianos."

[38] "Y tal vez el arzobispo don Rodrigo pensara en el euskera, aunque la verdad es
que no lo dice."

the discourse (Basques > Tubal), but not assert it directly and causally (Basques =/ Tubal).

That is, there is a constant tension in Jimenez de Rada's historiography between the discourse of origins, whereby the Basques emerge as the founding subject of *Hispania*/Spain, and the discourse of imperialist, Christian universality, in which Basques are the subject that must be dismissed and repressed. In short, for Jimenez de Rada, his own origin and ancestry becomes the biggest obstacle to his historiographic project of creating an imperialist, universal Peninsula with Castile at its center. Thus, Jimenez de Rada gives birth to this tension between Basque Country and Spain, which by the time Martinez de Zaldivia, Garibay, and other Basque apologists reappropriate it in the Renaissance, turns into its opposite: a widespread belief in the Spanish originality of the Basques. Already Pere Antoni Beuter and Pedro Medina at the beginning of the 16th century wrote about this belief. In short, Jimenez de Rada gave rise not only to Spanish historiography (The Invention of Spain) but also, against his own designs, to the discourse of Basque originality (The Invention of the Basque Country). Hence the double nature of this genre: the invention of Spain and the Basque Country and their origins come together in a political and discursive form that requires to exclude the origins of the other in a temporal logic by which the Basques always precede Hispania, Castile, and Spain. This is the foundational political fantasy at the core of *materia vasconica* (and, although it is not our current concern, *materia hispanica*). This is also a subaltern history: the denial of Basque historicity is what inscribes it in the imperialist history of Castile and later Spain. Furthermore, the Basques as such Basque political subject are articulated for the first time in this text: not the kingdom of Navarre, not the Basque speaking people of an area, but the Basques as political subject endowed with a political agency and identity. Therefore Basques are "born" (articulated, subjectified, interpellated…as political subjects) for the first time in the 13th century in Castilian imperialist historiography. This is the birth of "Basque politics" and its subject.

Pactist Literature

The Middle Ages also give rise to a literary genre that will be central to Basque culture at least through the 19th century. Against Eric Hobsbawn proposal of "the invention of tradition," as the main cultural structure of the formation of nationalisms, the opposite structure emerges early on in the Basque Country, which one could denominate "the tradition of invention," whereby different political structures and classes legitimize themselves by resorting to a "tradition of invented traditions." The latter are sometimes invented by other people and other times are refashioned from earlier Basque traditions invented for other purposes, thus, creating a thick maze of inventions, which constitutes a tradition of its own with a well-defined history. Starting in the Middle Ages, this tradition of invention has a clear political goal: to curtail the expansion of monarchical power. In order to do so, this tradition refers to the foundation of the Basque Country and its communities. Yet, it is important to emphasize that, against Hobsbawn simplistic epistemology of "truth vs. invention," or "genuine tradition vs. invented tradition" (8), here we have a more complicated and challenging inventive process that always incorporates earlier materials from other traditions and turns them into a hybrid of history and invention: a mix of other people's inventions and their own or a combination of oral-subaltern and written traditions. It is this mixture that gives this literary genre, this tradition of invention, its effect of truth and reality, which operates politically not only among the Basques but also among the surrounding kingdoms.[39]

Most founding Basque political charters, commonly known as *foruak* or *fueros,* derive from consuetudinary law transmitted in oral form until the 13th and 14th centuries. Against the attempts by surrounding monarchs to impose the Roman law, *foruak* were written down and provided with a foundation or historical legitimation, which the old oral form did not previously need. Thus, the historical shift from oral to written form prompted the need to originate these narrative foundations, which, nevertheless, always resorted to older documents and oral narratives, thus generating a retroactive effect of documented, historical "truth."

Needless to say, the legitimation of the Roman law that surrounding monarchs attempted to impose over the older consuetudinary law had a legitimation of its own, based on the nascent discipline and discourse of historiography, which also narrated the foundations of their respective kingdoms. The Roman law and its foundational legitimation were carried

---

[39] Anderson makes a similar critique of Gellner, about the latter's denunciation of nationalism as invented: "Gellner is so anxious to show that nationalism masquerades under false pretenses that he assimilates 'invention' to 'fabrication' and 'falsity,' rather than to 'imagining' and 'creation'. In this way he implies that 'true' communities exist which can be advantageously juxtaposed to nations. In fact, all communities larger than primordial villages of face-to-face contact (and perhaps even these) are imagined" (15).

away by two different institutions: the legal institution (the monarch, law specialists, courts...) and the historiographic institution (historians, monumental architects, etc.). However, in the case of the Basque Country, both the law and its foundation-legitimation were built within a single document, the *forua*, and, thus, the foundation took a different literary shape and structure: the single mythic foundational narrative, the myth of the original pact, which preceded the charter in the same written document.

Castilian or French historiography elaborated complex and hybrid myths that ranged from Biblical foundations and Greek mythology to Roman and Gothic mythography. For example, and as seen in the earlier section, Jimenez de Rada wrote the first "national" history of the Iberian Peninsula, which included all its kingdoms, as a way to legitimize the centrality of the Castilian monarchy at the beginning of the 13th century, precisely at the same time that Fernando III of Castile elaborated the first unified legal code for his kingdom, which was implemented by his son, Alfonso X the Wise (Montreal Zia 30). Jimenez de Rada resorted to a very heterogeneous material: Noah, his grandson Tubal, Hercules, the amazons, Alaric's destruction of Rome, and then the Gothic myths of their arrival to the Peninsula. This more complex foundational narrative was repeated from Alfonso X's *History of Spain* to Mariana's *General History of Spain* in the late16th century and the epigonic historiography of end of the 18th century with few changes. Therefore, there is not a tradition of invention, just an institutionalization of invention.

We have two different discursive structures here: the Basque tradition of invention versus the Castilian (or French) institution of invention. The Basque tradition centers on a single foundational myth: the narrative of a foundational pact. Therefore, it is appropriate to denominate this literature "pactist foundational literature" or, for short, "pactist literature." Later in the 16th and 17th centuries, as Basque language becomes the center of legitimation, the foundational myth of pactist literature is mixed with the linguistic myth of Basque originality, thus, producing a final, third racial narrative about the universal nobility of the Basques.

Jesús Lalinde Abadía retraces the origin of Basque pactist literature to the legend of the creation of "the *fuero* of Sobrarbe," which later influenced the Navarran and Biscayan old *foruak/fueros* in the 14th century ("El pactismo" 132-36). Yet, Andrés Mañaricua points out that, at the root of most pactist narratives, there could be an older oral narrative about a pact with a foreign leader, a narrative that would be intertwined with the Arthurian cycle. It is this ability to mix and hybridize older (oral, Arthurian) and even seemingly foreign narratives (*fuero* of Sobrarbe) that defines Basque pactist literature.

As Iñaki Bazán states, in the 13th century, after the death of Sancho VII the Strong (1234), the French house of Champagne took over the Navarran monarchy starting with Teobaldo I, identified in the *fueros* as "of foreign nation and foreign language" (180). Following the more modern, centralist model established in France by King Phillip August, Teobaldo I also attempted to overhaul the different institutions of the kingdom. Yet, the Navarran church and nobility reacted against the new policies that curtailed their privileges and rights. Therefore, they struck a compromise and the monarchy was rearticulated as a pact between the king and the people of Navarre.

In the *Fuero General de Navarra* (*General Law of Navarre*) written in 1237, the initial paragraph states that this book is a remembrance of the *fueros* as they were drafted in the Peninsula when "the mountaineers gained land without king;" a reference to the *Reconquista* or movement of conquering Muslim lands (Ilarregui and Lapuerta 3). The introduction states clearly the origins of the *fuero* and the pact between the monarch and the people. The reference is to the invasion of the "moors" as the reason why "Spain was lost and how was raised the first Spanish king" (don Pelayo). According to the introduction, Baztan, Berrueza, Anso, Jaca, Erronkari, Saraitzu, Sobrarbe and Ainsa resisted the invasion and provided the first people who started the "reconquest" of "Moor lands." The introduction continues narrating that, three hundred men in horses mobilized but, since there were disagreements and envy among them, they sent a request to Rome, Lombardy, and France seeking advice. Following the received advice, they selected a king who would lead them. Consequently, they wrote down and swore their "establishments" and "*fueros*," "as best as they could, as men who gained the lands of the moors." The introduction ends by informing that they elected Pelagius as king (Ilarregui and Lapuerta 5).

Following the introductory narrative of the *fueros*, Title I of Chapter I states the relationship between king and people. In Navarre, the king, instead of being crowned, was lifted on a shield to the hail of "royal!" The chapter is entitled: "How they have to crown [lift] the King of Spain and how he must swear:"

> It was first established by charter [*fuero*] in Spain to crown [lift] the King since immemorial time. Since no King who would be such would ever be bad to them; the council, as representatives of [under] the people,

83

crowned [lifted] him as King, and they gave him what they had and gained from the moors, provided he would first swear before they crowned [lifted] him over the cross and the Gospels that he would govern them right and he would always improve the *fueros* and not worsen them; he would divide the forces, and he would share the wealth of each land with the men of the land as it is convened with rich men, noble men, and village men; and he would not do so with foreigners of other lands. (Ilarregui and Lapuerta 7)[40]

In short, the king, before being crowned, was required to swear to respect the *fueros*, without curtailing them, and to share the wealth, a wealth that is gained for him by the men of the land—peasants are excluded.

Similarly, Biscay was instituted as a signori or lordship [señorío] in the 11th century within the kingdom of Pamplona, with Iñigo López or Eneko Lupiz. The founding charters or *foruak/fueros* of Biscay were transcribed from their earlier oral form in two partial documents in the 14th century (the legal codex of Juan Núñez de Lara of 1342 and that of Gonzalo Moro of 1394) and then redrafted in the *Old Fuero* of 1452. These *fueros* or *foruak* establish the requirement that the Lord swear them in Biscay. By 1452, the Lord was the Castilian king (Montreal Zia 35).

The Biscayan *foruak*, under title II, state again the pactist nature of the relationship between Lord and people, and therefore they state clearly the requirement from the Lord to swear and respect the *fueros* as well as the consequences of not swearing them:

He had to take the oath in the aforementioned church of Gernika and in certain other places to safeguard all the privileges and exemptions and liberties and fueros and usages and customs...

And the said Lord and King, as Lord of Bizkaia, could not take them away from them nor add to them nor give them any new [ones] unless he should do so in Bizkaia, beneath the Tree of Gernika in General Assembly and with the consent of the said Bizkaians....

---

[40] "Et fué primerament establido por Fuero en Espaynna del Rey alzar por siempre, porque ningun Rei que iamas seria non lis podies ser malo, pues conceyllo zo es pueblo lo alzavan, et le davan lo que eyllos avían et ganavan de los moros: primero que les iuras, antes que lo alzassen sobre la cruz et los santos evangelios, que les toviess á drecho, et les meioras siempre lures fueros, et no les apeyoras, et que les desfizies las fuerzas, et que parta el bien de cada tierra con los om bres de la tierra convenibles á richos hombres, á cabaylleros, á yfanzo nes, et á hombres bonos de las villas et non con extranios de otra tierra."

If he does not come, then the Bizkaians.... need not respond to the petition of the said Lord King, Lord of Bizkaia, nor to his treasurer or tax collector, nor should they receive or obey his letters until such time that he comes to swear and confirm the said exemptions and privileges and freedoms and laws and customs and lands and grants. (Montreal Zia 170-71)

In the Biscayan case, the foundational pact, was also kept in oral form, outside the written *foruak*, and later on developed as written narrative by early Biscayan historiographers in the 16th century. Lope García de Salazar (1399-1476), following an account of the Portuguese Count of Barcelos in the 14th century, gave a historiographic account of the foundational Biscayan pact pact in his *Adventures and Fortunes of Lope García de Salazar* (1471-1476). In this account, a mixture of oral tradition and Arthurian literature, the original Lord, becomes *Jaun Zuria* or White Lord, nephew of the king of Scotland, who does battle against the king of León who is attempting to subjugate the Biscayans. Since the Leones king does not deign to do battle against commoners, the Biscayans strike a pact with Juan Zuria and he leads them to victory in Arrigorriaga, which, in a false etymology, becomes the "place of rocks bathed in blood." Biscayan historians incorporated this narrative from the memoirs of García de Salazar to historiography in the 16th century, thus, giving a medieval dimension to an oral narrative that continued to found the *foruak* as pact in the 16th century.

In the case of Guipuzcoa, the *Decrees of the Brotherhood of Guipuzcoa*, which were originally drafted in 1375 and reshaped in its final form in 1463, point to a different situation, since the conquest of Guipuzcoa had taken place in 1200 and the Castilian king granted *fueros* to different villages in order to counteract the influence of the Guipuzcoan nobility. As a result, by the time the first consuetudinary law was written in 1375, Guipuzcoa had been annexed by Castile. Similarly, in Alava, the *Decrees of the Provincial Brotherhood* were drafted in 1463. Yet, starting in the 16th century, Guipuzcoan and Alavan historians such as Juan Martinez de Zaldivia (c. 1500-1578) resorted to the narrative of the founding pact in order to justify their respective charters. Unlike the case of the Navarran *fueros*, the Guipuzcoan and Biscayan counterparts did include the peasant classes. The movements to exclude the subaltern classes from these *foruak* started in the Renaissance.

In the case of Labourd and Soule, the French monarchy conquered them from the English in 1449 and, therefore, they were subject to a brand-new organization that was already incorporated to the centralist design of the crown: *Costumes of Bayonne and Labourd* in 1514 and *General Costumes* in Soule in 1520.

This tradition of invention that frames the expansionist policies of the French, Navarran, and Castilian kingdoms has been always narrated as a foundational act, and given that it relies on older oral and written traditions, still remains one of the main discourses of *materia vasconica*. It is important to note that if the Castilian imperialist historiography or "political literature" inaugurated by Jimenez de Rada is taking into consideration, pactist literature only further expands the Castilian imperialist narrative gap: the impossible logic of founding Castile by negating the Basque subject as original is enforced by pactist literature. They both lead to the negative affirmation of the Basque political subject. *In short, The Invention of Spain further strengthens The Invention of the Basques.* So far, the opposite has been defended by Basque and Spanish historiography and, therefore, it is paramount to underscore the new narrative and political logic that this postnational literary analysis unveils.

4. The Aristocracy, Ballads, and Improvisational Poetry (Milia Lastur, Lazarraga, Etxepare)

Perhaps the most central and, tragically, most disregarded literature of the Middle Ages, is constituted by a very rich tradition of ballads and improvisational poetry, of which only few fragments have been preserved. It was an oral tradition and was also cultivated by the nobility and the elite classes.[41] Perhaps, the widespread transmission of this oral tradition prevented this class from registering it on paper. Only a handful of the members of a very specific social group, the *letrados* or scribes (a large Basque group, proportionally speaking),[42] published some of those ballads and improvised verses: Esteban de Garibay and another group of mostly anonymous scribes who wrote a long chronicle of Biscay, known

---

[41] A detailed analysis of what segments of the aristocracy used Basque, Castilian, and other Romance languages remains to be done.

[42] Basque *letrados* in Spain constituted as much as 20% of the entire social group, according to certain estimates (Caro Baroja, *Los vascos y la historia* 75). In contrast, the Basques constituted 5% of the entire Spanish population. Even Sancho Panza makes a remark about the proliferation of Basque *letrados* in *El Quijote*. There was symbolic violence exerted against lettered Basque subjects for their attempt to enter the imperial burocracy. They were stereotyped for their corrupt or bad use of Castilian, which was attributed to the influence of their mother tongue, Basque (Bijuesca "Literatura eta mezenasgoa")

as the chronicle of Ibargüen-Cachopín. Given the tropes and topoi repeated in some of these ballads, as well as the formulaic structure of some of them, it is possible to conclude that it was a very lively and widespread genre. At the same, given the specific and historically situated nature of some of the events related by the ballads, it is also safe to assume that it was a highly improvisational genre.

Women also participated in improvising poetry and, furthermore, most historical evidence points to the fact that it was mostly performed by women. As we will see in the next chapter, this oral literature shows the existence of a linguistic unity between elite and peasant classes, which ceased in the Renaissance and, instead, gave rise to a "linguistic divide" by which literature in Basque became a subaltern practice while the elites embraced state languages such as Spanish and French for their cultural and political practices. Similar phenomena occurred with Catalan, Galician, and Occitan literatures, but unlike in those other traditions, Basque literature prior to "the linguistic divide" was defined by its oral transmission; it did not have a prestigious written tradition similar to the Galician *cantigas*.

Garibay also compiled a collection of proverbs, which exceeds mere tokenism and shows a concern for the content of oral literature—such attention to the oral form will not reemerge again until the 19th century. In the introduction to the collection, he already mentions the distinctive and rich acumen of *euskara* while also dismissing those who have only a superficial or referential knowledge of it. In short, he counts himself as knowledgeable in the language and, therefore, presents Basque as a language of culture, as his own cultural language:

> It [*euskara*] contains masculine and feminine verbs, like Hebrew, the first language of the world, and it is very different from Latin, Greek, and many others lacking this verbal distinction and many other marvelous concepts that are known to those who are knowledgeable of the language; with very few words, it is rich in moral sentences, as it is proven by its old proverbs, of which I transcribe few that come to mind in order to prove it. (Urquijo 2)[43]

---

[43] "Tiene verbos masculinos y femeninos, como la Hebrea, la primera del mundo, y es muy diferente de la latina y Griega, y otras muchas, carecientes desta distinción de berbos, sin otros marauillosos conceptos para los que la sauen con fundamento; debaxo de pocas palabras, es copiosa en sentencias morales, como lo manifiestan sus antiguos refranes, y dellos porné aquí algunos que me ocurren ahora para su comprouacion."

As a good example of these proverbs, it is worth quoting the following: "Guicon vearra, gogo us," which Garibay translates as "Hombre necesitado, pensamiento vazio" ("man in need, empty of thought" 10), but could also be translated as the opposite: "man in need, man full of thought (nothing but thought)."

Yet the most interesting and probably highest form or literary production in the Middle Ages is constituted by epic ballads. These ballads share the 6/7 and 8/10 syllable metric system, still present in contemporary, traditional improvised poetry; it is known as *zortziko txikia* and *zortziko handia* respectively. Yet, the ballads do not show a uniform line count, unlike its contemporary counterparts. We do not have enough documentation to ascertain which ones were the most popular metric forms. Michelena, echoing Lafon, points to the possibility that the metric system of the ballads comes from Latin hymns of the early Middle Ages (*Historia* 70). However, given their consistency across the Pyrenees, even an older origin could be posited.

Among the oldest ballads preserved, Garibay transcribes the opening stanza of "The Ballad of Beotibar," which refers to events that took place in 1340, when Guipuzcoans fought with Navarrans in Beotibar:

Mila vrte ygarota	After a thousand years
Vra vere videan.	The waters still follow their course.
Guipuzcoarroc sartu dira	The Guipuzcoans have entered
Gazteluco echean,	The house of Gaztelu
Nafarroquin batu dira	They have met the Navarrans
Beotibarren pelean	In the battle of Beotibar

(Michelena, *Textos* 66)

The non-causal or non-relational juxtaposition between the course of nature (After a thousand years / the waters...) and human events (The Guipuzcoans have entered...) is meant to signify, in mythic thinking, that human history is judged by its compliance to nature's laws. This rhetorical and mythical arrangement is a constant in many ballads and even in oral lyrical poetry. Moreover, this way of thinking mythically by juxtaposing nature and humans persists to our days in improvisational poetry.

Similarly, in the northern Basque Country, one of the few ballads that survived through the 20th century, and was made popular thanks to modern media, begins exactly with the same non-causal mythic juxtaposition

of natural and human elements. It is known as "Bereterretxeren khantoria" ("Ballad of Bereterretxe") and it was first published by JDJ Sallaberry
in 1879 (although it was collected by Agustin Chaho in 1844). According
to Jean Jaurgain, the ballad dates from 1434-49 and tells the story of the
murder of Bereterretxe by the mayor of Mauleon, Luis de Beaumont,
count of Lerin, as a result of the wars that took place between two family
clans: the Agramontese and the Beaumontese. It is worth quoting the
ballad at length in order to appreciate the way in which the action and
the temporal-spatial coordinates are narrated in a lively manner with a
great economy of recourses while stressing mythical juxtaposition.

Haltzak eztü bihotzik	The alder tree has no heart
Ez gaztamberak ezürrik	Nor does cottage cheese have bone
Enian uste erraiten ziela	I did not think that
Aitonen semek gezürrik	Noble men would tell lies
Andozeko ibarra,	The valley of Andoz
Ala ibar lüzia!	What a long valley!
Hiruretan ebaki zaitan	In three parts was cut
Armarik gabe bihotza.	My heart without weapons.
Berterretchek oheti	Berreterretxe from bed
Neakatuari estiki;	To the girl softly:
«Abil, eta so' ginezan	—Go and look
Ageri denez gizonik»	If there are any men in sight.
Neskatuak berhala,	The girl right the way
Ikhusi zian bezala,	As she saw it,
Hirur dozena bazabilzala	That there were three dozen
Leiho batetik bestera,	Going from window to window
Bereterretchek leihoti	Bereterretxe from the window
Jaon kuntiari goraintzi;	Salute to the Count.
Ehün behi bazereitzola	There were a hundred cows
Beren zezena ondoti.	Following their bull.
Jaon kuntiak berhala,	The Count right the way
Traidore batek bezala:	As a traitor:

«Berterretch, aigü borthala,	—Bereterretxe descend to the gate
Ützüliren hiz berhala.»	You will return shortly.
- «Ama, indazüt athorra,	—Mother, give me a shirt
Mentüraz sekülakua!	Perhaps one forever.
Bizi denak ohit ükhenen dü	Those who live will remember
Basko biharamena!	The morning after Easter-night.

(Sallaberry 212-14)

These ballads are structured with many rhetorical formulae and topoi, which serve as a mnemotechnic device and help audiences recognize and follow the narrative.

One of the few formulae that has survived shows the dramatism of these ballads: "The earth under my feet trembles, and so do my four limbs." The ballad relating the death of Martin Bañez, from the family clan of the Gamboas, at the hands of those of the Oñaz family clan, took place in 1464 and was transcribed by Garibay in the following way. The singer is the wife of Martin Bañez, Doña Sancha Ochoa de Oçaeta:

Oñetaco lurrau jabilt icara,	The earth under my feet trembles
Lau araguioc vere an verala,	And so do my four limbs.
Martin Bañes Ybarretan il dala.	Martin Bañes has died in Ibarreta.
Artuco dot escu batean guecia,	I will take the arrow in one hand
Bestean çuci yraxeguia,	The lit torch in the other.
Erreco dot Aramayo guztia.	I will burn down the entire Ara-
	maio. [the town of Aramaio]

(Michelena, *Textos* 90-91).

In the ballad of Peru of Abendaño, dating to events that took place in 1443, the same trope of earth and limbs shaking is used with the opposite function of denoting fear, rather than anger.

Yzarragati gora elcian joeala	As he was going over Izarraga
Jaun Peru Abendañococ esala:	Sir Peru of Abendaño said:
Oñetaco lurrau jauil<t> ycara,	The earth under my feet trembles
Gorpuceco lau araguioc berala.	And so do my four limbs.
Oi aldioneri albanegui empara,	If I could overcome this moment
Barriz enendorque Aramaioco	I would not come back against Ar-
contrara.	amaio

As the above-mentioned ballad of Martin Bañez makes clear, women were known to improvise ballads. Furthermore, the difference between ballads and improvised poetry is not clear from the documents that have survived. Garibay documents the tradition of women singing at funerals. Therefore, it is an established fact that women had an active participation in improvising poetry, funeral songs, and ballads. It is not clear if there was a gender divide as to the types of poetry or circumstances in which women could improvise poetry.[44]

Garibay transcribes the verses improvised by the sister of Milia Lastur in her funerals, as the widower, Pero Garcia de Oro, expresses his intention to marry Marina de Arrazola, a woman he has favored before the death of his wife. The first four lines sung by Milia's sister are as follows:

Cer ete da andra erdiaen çauria?	What is the present [wound][45] to the birthing woman?
Sagar errea, eta ardoa gorria.	Baked apples and red wine.
Alabaya, contrariomda Milia:	However, it is the contrary for Milia:
Azpian lur oça gañean arria.	Cold earth underneath and a tombstone on top.

In order to emphasize the dramatic nature of the situation and the repercussions that the widower's decision might have over the honor of the house of Lastur, Milia's sister resorts to mythic elements:

Iausi da cerurean arria,	A rock fell from the sky
Aurquitu dau Lastur-en torre barria,	It hit the new tower of Lastur
Edegui dio almeneari erdia.	It ripped half a battlement
Lastur-era bear doçu, Milia.	You must come to Lastur, Milia

(Michelena, *Textos* 75-76).

Pero Garcia de Oro's sister replies by stating that her brother has acted lawfully and with honor towards Milia Lastur. Therefore, the ex-

---

[44] There were laws (the *foruak* of Biscay) prohibiting women to improvise poetry in the 15h century (Larranaga Odriozola, "Del bertsolarismo silenciado" 65).

[45] "Çauria" literally means "wound." However, 'saria" means "present, gift, compensation." Most likely a misspelling or hypercorrection.

change between both sisters shows that women actively produced impro-visational poetry. This literature and culture represent a different world from the modern culture of the Renaissance, after which there are no news of women poets. Furthermore, and as the next chapter elaborates, the mythical thinking that is present in these ballads becomes one of the reasons for the Inquisition to persecute women in the 16th and 17th cen-turies.

These ballads, thus, show the end of a long, rich tradition, perhaps the most central literary production of the Middle Ages, in which women poets were also active participants. They also point to the beginning of what Walter Mignolo has very strategically named "The Darker Side of the Renaissance."

Lazarraga

In 2004, a manuscript containing poetry and pastoral narrative in Basque written by the Alavan Joan Perez Lazarraga (1548?-1605) was found in a second-had bookstore in Madrid (Gartzia), thus adding another work to the other four written or published in Basque in the 16th century: those of Leizarraga, Betolaza, Etxepare, and the anonymous collector of prov-erbs published in 1596 in Pamplona. Leizarraga is the author of a trans-lation of the Bible as well as other religious materials; Betolaza, similarly, published a Christian "doctrine;" only Etxepare wrote a book of poems.[46] Lazarraga's manuscript was written around 1567; philological investiga-tion has not been concluded yet and, therefore, many questions remain about the text and the possible author/s.

The manuscript was written during the rule of Philip II, at the height of Renaissance culture in the Habsburg Empire. Yet, Lazarraga's writing responds to a very medieval juncture: he is one of the last witnesses of a time in which the nobility still held on to Basque as language of (oral) culture. Lazarraga's exceptionalism is rather an index of an end, rather than the beginning, of a new historical period and culture. This epigonic characterization and historization could eventually be challenged, as we do not have a comprehensive understanding of the culture of that time. Rafael Micoleta, in his 1653 *Modo breve de aprender la lengua vizcaína (Brief*

---

[46] It is important to note that Leizarraga and Etxepare write in the Kingdom of Navarre, as the latter creates the only environment for the literary production in Basque. Similarly, Leizarraga mentions several members of the Navarran nobility as responsible supporters of his Basque work. In short, the nobility upholds Basque as literary language through the 16th century.

Method to Learn the Biscayan Language), is one of the few other references to what might have been a larger cultural trend to write in Basque. When exemplifying different ways or making verses in Basque, and after referring to popular genres, Micoleta also adds: "Some modern poets from the *Parnassus of the Bay of Biscay* have written *décimas*, lyres, and sonnets in Basque, with the same [stress] accents and rhymes that they have in Castilian, but it is not work of much distinction, as very few Basque readers understand this metric poetry, etc."(194).[47] It is unknown whether he refers to Etxepare's book published in 1545, or to other books and manuscripts, of which we have no information. It appears to be the latter case (Bijuesca "Praktika literarioaren"). Furthermore, even in the case of Lazarraga, it remains to be determined whether one or several authors were involved in the production of the manuscript.[48]

---

[47] "Tambien algunos modernos del *Parnaso Cantabrico* han escrito dezimas, lyras y sonetos en vasquenze, con los mismos accentos y consonantes que suelen tener en romance, pero es obrá de poco luçimiento, por los pocos que en vasquenze entienden este metro, etta."

[48] Oihenart in 1665 wrote in his *Basque Poetic Art*, about another two Basque poets Joan Etxegarai and Arnaut Logras. None of their writings has survived. Pedro Madariaga in his *Arte de escribir* (*Art of Writing*), originally published in 1565, also stated that "there are printed books in this language" (252). There are news of a Christian doctrine published by Antso Eltso in 1568 (Gómez López and Urgel 276) and another songbook or *cancionero* by Juan de Undiano in the late 16th century (Unzueta Echebarria). Patri Urkizu has published a list of theater plays performed at that time (Urkizu "Rolan" 660).

As Josu Bijuesca has shown ("Aránzazu y Sor Juana"), Lope de Vega and Sor Juana Inés de la Cruz incorporated and transcribed Basque poems in their work. These poems are of a cultured or learned nature; they are not popular. Therefore, in a first moment, and against what I have defended above, one could assume that, as late as the 17th century the Basque elite did not abandon the Basque language and had an active written tradition that reached Madrid (Lope de Vega; although he collected a Basque poem while traveling in Guipuzcoa) and Mexico (Sor Juana), in what can only be called *a modern, Atlantic, Basque written literary tradition*. However, in order to discuss this possibility or its lack thereof, we need to move to the realm of speculation. My speculative hypothesis is that such a possibility is "too good to be true." More texts would have survived if this written tradition had been so extended. A more realistic, yet, speculative hypothesis would have to account for the lack of surviving documents. Therefore, it is safer to conclude that already, at the end of the 16th century, the elite had abandoned Basque as the medium of a written literary tradition and only clung to an older oral tradition of aristocratic origin in the private sphere. In short, Basque aristocrats would still have sung some of these compositions in the private sphere and thus they would have orally transmitted them to writers such as Lope de Vega and Sor Juana Inés de la Cruz---or as in the case of Lazarraga, handwritten but not published.

Lazarraga wrote a short pastoral novel, *Silbero, Silbia, Doristeo and Sirena* and about 39 poems (*Eskuizkribua*). Furthermore, he is the author of the oldest reference to the term "Euskal Herria" (*Eusquel Erria*, 29). Although since the 19th century the pastoralization of the Basque Country is at the core of Basque literature and is developed by both the middle-class and the clergy, Lazarraga's pastoral novel cannot be historicized as a forerunner or reference for this 19th-century trend. His pastoral novel responds, as does the genre in general in Europe, to the nobility's tastes, which invents this new literary genre to legitimize an elite culture, after the chivalric novel reached its zenith with *Tirant lo Blanc* (1490) and *Amadis de Gaula* (1508) at the turn of the century. If Jacopo Sannazaro gave rise to the genre of the pastoral novel with his *Arcadia* (1504, translated to Spanish in 1549) and Jorge de Montemayor made the genre popular in Spain with *Diana* (1559), Lazarraga's pastoral novel, written in 1567, followed the new literary trends of the moment.

The novel is not complete. Yet it is a document that clearly points to the last moment in which a Basque nobility, still culturally connected to *euskara*, entertained the possibility of developing its mother tongue as a means of producing high or courtly culture. Although short, Lazarraga's novel delivers all the components of the pastoral novel: allegorical structure, classical location and names (most likely Italy), a retreat to nature (in this case to the countryside of Castile by the Ebro river), the transformation of courtly characters into shepherds, unrequited love interests as main plot device, mythic references (the god Mars, Cupid, a magician called Narvaez), and musical recitation of poetry. With the exception of Arnaud Oihenart in the 17th century, literature written in Basque would have to wait till the 18th century with Munibe and Barrutia to produce again non-religious texts. In the 16th and 17th centuries, the Inquisition and the Council of Trento dominated the subaltern Basque imaginary and the elite classes abandoned Basque language as a means of culture.

In Lazarraga's novel, the quarrel between the four lovers who are not corresponded by their respective love interests is a most delightful and rare witness to a historical situation that changes radically as the dark side of the Renaissance extends its control over the Basque Country. Only oral poetry, turned subaltern culture by then, will survive the religious onslaught of the late Renaissance and early Baroque; yet it will be compiled and transcribed in printed form starting in the mid-19th century with Agustin Chaho.

Lazarraga's poetry is also proof of this courtly culture he invents in his novel. Even when new vindications are mentioned by Lazarraga (the antiquity of the Basque language and the nobility of the Basques), they are framed in a courtly fashion in which love, beauty, and fame are invoked allegorically. Thus, in his poem "Great Fame Come to Me" (29-30), he opens and closes the poem with a manifesto for the "advantages" of the Basque people and the beauty of their women. The subtitle in Spanish reads: "Praise of the Basque ladies and gentlemen" ("Loa de las damas y galanes vascongados," 29). Yet, interestingly enough, this poem produces the first recorded reference to the Basque Country in opposition to the kingdom of Castile:

oi Gaztelako errege jauna	Oh lord king of Castile
erregiagaz ikasu	Learn with your royalty
zeure kortean dama ederrik	That in your court no beautiful lady
nola bapere ez dozun	You have left.
zegaiti Euskel Errian dira	For in the Basque Country
eder guztiok dotadu	All the beautiful ones have graced themselves.
ene berbaok jente noblea	My words, oh noble people,
ze daidizu pensadu	Do not think that
neure erria alabazerren	For the praise of my people
nik ditudala finjidu	I have feigned.
badanik bere jakin egizu	Instead, you should know
oita naxala fundadu	I have based myself
oi antxinako liburuetan	On books of antiquity
zeñetan ditut ezautu	Wherein I have learnt
Euskel Erriau oi nola eben	How this Basque Country
errege batek pobladu	Was populated by a king
jente noblez da lenguajeaz	With noble people and language
zenak eusten agindu	Who promised
zeruko jaunaren fede santua	The saint faith of the Heavenly Lord
oi legiela kunplidu	To uphold.
oi Salamonek eskribizen dau	Solomon writes,
jente noblea jakizu	Oh noble people do learn,
bere bizian oi ez ebela	That in his entire life
Jente obarik topadu	He did not find better people. (29-30)

Yet, in few instances, Lazarraga echoes oral poetry. In his poem "On Saint John's Eve" (31-4), there are echoes of the popular ballad "Ana Juanixe." Similarly, in his poem "The Open Ski is Full of Stars" (102-03), he resorts to a variant of one of the tropes most cited in medieval epic ballads: "ikara jabilt lau laurenok bildurez" (102, my four limbs tremble with fear). In his "Itai lelo i bai lelo" (107-08), he also repeats a variant of the popular "eta lelo hil bai lelo" (Lelo is dead). Perhaps his best poem is one dedicated to the allegorical figure of Love: "I Wanted to Go Against Her" (89). He does cite a certain Garcilaso in one of his poems, "I, This Graceless One, Went" (80-82), but the poem remains to be studied in detail in order to determine whether it is a reference to Garcilaso de la Vega.

With Lazarraga, the Middle Ages end in the Basque Country and the subalternization of the Basque language beings, as the nobility abandons it and makes room for what I have called "the linguistic divide" —a divide that has dire consequences, religious, economic, and cultural, for the rural and costal subaltern classes of the Basque Country. As Spanish and French imperialisms encroach on the Basque Country, the local nobility (*ahaide nagusiak*) is transformed and displaced by a new class of landowners (*jauntxoak*) who are subordinated to their respective imperialist states.

Etxepare

The first text printed and published in Basque, which has been preserved, is *Linguae Vasconum Primitiae* (*News of the Language of the Basques*; 1545) by Bernat Etxepare (c. 1480-?). It already contains an apology of Basque language written in Basque, as the title in Latin already points out. Yet, this book is as original as exceptional and marks the end of the Middle Ages and its carnivalesque culture, rather than the beginning of modern Basque literature.

Etxepare was a priest in the church of Eiheralarre, near Donibane Garazi in the kingdom of (Lower) Navarre. He wrote in the Lower-Navarran dialect. Unlike Joanes Leizarraga 25 years later, Etxepare did not attempt to create a unified linguistic model for his literature. The metric of his poetry is traditional, borrowed from oral poetry, and although the treatment of love and sexuality is medieval, his awareness of the novelty of publishing in Basque, of the new importance of local languages, places him at the end of the Middle Ages—which is confirmed by the religious content of the book (Aldekoa "Bernard Etxepare"). His work did not have much impact or was not known by most Basque authors; with very few exceptions, later writers do not mention him. It is worth quoting his apology of the Basque language, which, nevertheless, is not connected, as far as we know, to any defense of political rights and privileges. It is entitled "Sautrela" (Saltarella, a dance type):

Heuskara da kanpora, eta goazen oro danzara	Basque is out and let us all dance
O heuskara lauda ezak Garaziko herria	Basque praise the town of Garazi
Zeren hantik ukhen baituk behar duian thornuia	For you have received the rank you deserve there
Lehenago hi baitinzan lengoajetan azkena	For you were the last among languages
Orai aldiz izaneniz orotako lehena.	And now you will be the first among them
Heuskaldunak mundu orotan preziatu ziraden	Basques were valued in all places
Bana haien lengoajiaz bertze oro burlatzen	But they all mocked their language
Zeren ezein eskripturan erideiten ezpaitzen	For it was not found in any writings
Orai dute ikasiren nola gauza hona zen.	Now they will learn what a good thing it is
Heuskaldun den gizon orok alxa beza buruia	Everybody who is Basque raise your heads
Ezi huien lengoajia izanen da floria	For your language will be a flower
Prinze eta iaun handiek orok haren galdia	Princes and lords inquire about it
Skribatus halbalute ikhasteko desira.	If they can write it, they wish to learn it
Desir hura konplitu du Garaziko naturak	The nature of Garazi has fulfilled that desire
Eta haren adiskide orai bordelen denak	And its friend* who is now in Bordeaux
Lehen inprimizalia heuskararen hura da	He is the first publisher of Basque
Basko oro obligatu iagoitikoz hargana.	Thus obliging all Basques to it
Etai lelori bailelo leloa zarai leloa	[Untranslatable word play, sometimes translated as "Zara killed Lelo"]
Heuskara da kanpora eta goazen oro danzara. (70)	Basque is out and let us all dance! *The publisher *Françoys Morpain*

97

3. Imperial Difference and the Atlantic

1. The Renaissance: Language Apologies (M. Zaldivia, Garibay, Poza, Echave)

A history of the formation of modern Basque literature in the Renaissance requires, first and foremost, that the effects of the Catholic Church in the Basque Country be historicized. As Luis Michelena states, the movement of the Counterreformation marks modern Basque culture: "If an event in history had profound repercussions in the Basque Country, it is the Council of Trento, whose effects ended up conforming in a permanent way all aspects of life in the country. After the Council and as a consequence of it, the identification between Basque and Catholic, later made familiar, was materialized" (*Historia* 61).[49] Indeed, and as Michelena acknowledges, most of the religious production that dominates Basque literature till the 19th century derives from the Counterreformation's efforts to indoctrinate the masses in their own respective languages.

Yet, Michelena fails to note that there is a parallel movement to mobilize the Inquisition in order to extend the French and Spanish kings' power on both sides of the Basque Country. As a result of the activity of the Inquisition, which is oftentimes approached and summoned by local elites, culminates with the witch hunts of 1609-1610 in Labourd with Pierre Lancre and in Zugarramurdi (Navarre) with Juan Valle Alvarado respectively (Caro Baroja, *Las Brujas* 202-39). As a result, an identification begins to be made between (women) witches and Basque, their subaltern language.

The final combined effect of the Council of Trento and the Inquisition is more local and political. Starting in the 16th century, when the Inquisition makes its first appearances in Durango and in the upper valleys of Navarre (Aezkoa, Saraitzu and Erronkari), several legal resolutions are passed so that the attendance and participation in local and provincial legislative and judicial meetings (*batzarreak*) is restricted to those who speak and write in Castilian or French/Gascon. As a result, the elite classes abandon Basque as a cultural and political language, and, henceforth, *euskara* is relegated to the condition of subaltern language, which, then,

---

[49] "Si un hecho en la historia moderna ha tenido una profunda repercusión en Vasconia, este es el concilio de Trento, cuyos efectos llegaron a conformar de modo permanente casi todos los aspectos de la vida del país. Después de él y en su consecuencia va realizándose la identificación, luego familiar, de lo vasco con el catolicismo."

becomes the exclusive territory of the Catholic Church and its indoctrination of subaltern classes (villagers, rural peasants, and fishermen). In so far as witchcraft is identified mainly, if not exclusively, with women, Basque language becomes feminized and associated with the irrationality, excess, and threat that modernity adjudicates to women.

In this context, it is important to remember that European modernity began with the Reformation and the colonization of the Americas. The Reformation was a religious movement that allowed the North European princes to emancipate themselves from the jurisdiction of the Pope and, more specifically, in the political arena, from the subjection of the Habsburg empire ruled from Spain. In order to do so, the Reform claimed a political difference based on religion. Yet, this difference was consolidated by the *literary* deployment of *vernacular languages*, which begins with Luther's (1483-1546) translation of the Bible in German (1522).

In Spain, similarly, Basque *letrados* or scribes began to claim a political difference based on origin; they claimed that Basques were the oldest inhabitants of Spain.[50] Yet, this difference was articulated by the literary deployment of Basque language as irrefutable sign of antiquity—a language they had already abandoned as a cultural medium. The texts of these *letrados* are known as "apology" (defense and praise) and subsequently the *letrados* themselves became known as *apologists*.

Thus, Basque apologist literature must be aligned alongside the Reformation movement, as one more discourse attempting to claim a modernity that is defined by its resistance towards the expansion of Habsburg/Spanish imperialism and the hegemony of the Catholic church. As Benedict Anderson notes:

> Where Luther led, others quickly followed, opening the colossal religious propaganda war that raged across Europe for the next century. In this titanic 'battle for men's minds', Protestantism was always fundamentally on the offensive, precisely because it knew how to make use of the expanding vernacular print-market being created by capitalism, while the Counter-Reformation defended the citadel of Latin.... Inevitably, it was not merely the Church that was shaken to its core. The same earthquake produced Europe's first important non-dynastic, non-city states in the Dutch Republic and the Commonwealth of Puritans. (43-4)

---

[50] The concept of *letrado* must be further explained and develop in dialogue with Rama's *The Lettered City*.

Basque apologism can also be understood as the offensive deployment, on print, of a vernacular language against Spanish imperialism, which is Catholic. The apologists' claims enabled the Basques to preserve political rights that were established before the expansion of Castilian imperialism, although, then, those rights were legitimized as utterly modern and contemporary through language difference. If in the Middle Ages, the *foruak* or founding charters upheld those rights through a narrative of pactism, in the Renaissance, the *letrados* added a second narrative of originality and antiquity through the genre of linguistic apology. What in Jimenez de Rada led to the discourse of Spanish originality and universality, in the apologists, and following the former's lead, gave rise to the originality and universality of the Basques. It is the same genre, in its double, unstable articulation, which yields those two opposite political discourses on the origins of Spain and the Basque Country.

From the above rehistorization of apologism, we can now attempt a new approach to Basque literature as a very specific cultural and political discourse written in both Spanish and Basque. The reasons why apologism was conducted in Castilian (and Latin), whereas the other main discursive production of the Basque Country, religious manuals, was pursued in Basque, are not exclusive or contradictory: both literary practices respond to the same reality of the Counterreformation. Apologism was an attempt by the elites to position Basque culture in modernity, parallel to that of the Reformation, whereas religious literature in Basque responded to the opposite aim of containing and buffering modernity's influence among the low, illiterate classes; it was the genre deployed to control the subaltern classes.

In this way, any historically meaningful account of Basque literature must comprise both genres, the apologist discourse in Castilian and the religious manuals in Basque, as the two sides of the same cultural and historical coin. In turn, this specific double discursive production deployed around modernity explains why the Basque elite classes did not embrace Basque as a national language and, therefore, the latter remained a subaltern reality at least until the 19th century. Yet, it must be emphasized that most Basque dialects were written or published by the end of the 16th century: Biscayan, Navarran (low and high), Alavan, and Labourdan. Only Souletin and Guipuzcoan were published in the 17th century.

Furthermore, this new account centered on modernity and the Counterreformation explains why the enlightened culture fostered by Basques—beginning with the "Caballeritos de Azcoitia"—in the 18th century was not exceptional or unprecedented: it followed a very modern and Basque tradition inaugurated by apologism.

The Basque Discourse of Apology

In the aftermath of 1492, Basque authors such as Martínez de Zaldivia, Garibay, Poza, Oihenart, Echave, Henao, etc. (Tovar 26-47) wrote "apologies" or "defense discourses" about the rights and political legitimacy of the Basques and their language. These authors, known as apologists, mobilized the Biblical account of Babel in order to situate the unknown origins of Basque language within the Christian global orb and history, precisely at a moment when modernity, after the demise of Latin, was becoming a new Babel. The popularity that the Babelic account experienced in the Renaissance was due precisely to its ability to narrate the new Babel of modernity.

The idea of Basque as Babelic language was already suggested by non-Basque authors such as Italian Lucio Marineo Sículo (1460-1533; Tovar 26) and Spanish Pedro de Medina (1493-; Tovar 24) in the late Middle Ages. Tovar suggests that the origin of the idea is medieval, derives from the confluence of different and disconnected Biblical accounts such as Flavio Josephus, Saint Hieronymus of Seville, and Rodrigo Jimenez de Rada (Tovar 17-19). As my analysis of the latter's work shows, Jimenez de Rada could be considered one of the originators of this theory—yet in a negative way, by way of denial and repression, as his goal was to historicize the origins and development of a universal, Christian, Gothic Castile as the rightful heir to the entire Peninsula, *Hispania*. Thus, there is not enough evidence to determine the actual currency of the theory of a Babelic Basque in the Middle Ages. Furthermore, Tovar cites Alonso de Madrigal (c. 1400-1455) as already defending the Babelic origin of Castilian, by means of connecting it with the arrival of Tubal to Spain.

In the Basque case, the results of the new Babelic positioning are unprecedented: Basques and their language enter modernity (Juaristi *Vestigios*). Although each apologist varies in his account, most of them defend, in one way or another, that one of the descendants of the Babelic aftermath, Tubal, came to Spain and brought with him Basque language. During the same period, other Spanish authors attempted to situate Castilian in the new modern Babel that followed the fragmentation of Latin and the new cultivation of "vulgar" linguistic varieties as official state languages (Anderson 41-9).

The fact that Basque is defined as one of the languages that sprang from the fragmentation of the Biblical Babel gave modern legitimacy to *euskara* and, consequently, a new position for Basques in the new Babel of languages and nations brought about by European modernity. Consequently, Basque language became a tool of legitimation for Basques when entering modernity.

It is important to understand, first and foremost, the very contemporary and strategic sense of this positioning articulated by Basque apologists. When Antonio Nebrija published his Castilian grammar in 1492, he emphasized, as it is well known, the political importance of language in modernity by concluding that "language always is empire's companion " (99). Yet, fully aware of the new development and expansion of "vulgar" languages in the Babelic aftermath of the Renaissance, he admits to have written a Castilian grammar due to the fact that the latter "does not have a home of its own where to dwell" (107). At that point, Nebrija even refers to the Basques (Navarrans and Biscayans) when responding to an inquiry of Queen Isabella:

> When in Salamanca I presented her royal highness with a sample of this work. Your highness inquired as to its benefit. The reverend father Bishop of Avila took away the reply from me and answered on my behalf. After your majesty had put under her yoke barbarian people and nations of fleeting languages, and with their vanquishing, they needed to receive laws, which the conqueror gives to the vanquished with our language. Therefore, by means of my art, they would become knowledgeable of our language as we now learn the art of Latin grammar to learn Latin. For indeed it is certain that not only the enemies of our faith are in need of learning the Castilian language; but also the *Biscayans, Navarrans, French, Italians*, and all the rest who have dealings and conversations in Spain and are in need of our language. If they do not learn it from childhood through use, they will still learn it with my work. (109, my emphasis)[51]

---

[51] "cuando en Salamanca di la muestra de aquesta obra a vuestra real Majestad: y me preguntó que para qué podía aprovechar: el mui reverendo padre obispo de Ávila me arrebató la respuesta: y respondiendo por mí dixo. Que después que vuestra Alteza metiesse debaxo de su iugo muchos pueblos bárbaros y naciones de peregrinas lenguas: y con el vencimiento aquellos ternían necessidad de recebir las leies: quel vencedor pone al vencido y con ellas nuestra lengua: entonces por esta mi Arte podrían venir en el conocimiento della como agora nos otros deprendemos el Arte de la Gramática latina para deprender el latín. y cierto assí es que no sola mente los enemigos de nuestra fe que tienen

In other words, the discussions about the political legitimacy of languages were very much an open debate and struggle at the end of the 15th century. Jon Juaristi claims that in the case of Andrés de Poza (1530-1595), one of the foundational apologists, alongside Juan Martinez de Zaldivia, the former defends that Basque precedes even the language of paradise, Hebrew:

> From Poza's book, one can conclude that God chose to reveal its own nature to Tubal's lineage [the Basques], and that such revelation was superior to the first one of Eden, contained in Hebrew. When infusing this language in Adam, God made him participant in some of its mysteries, but the degree of that revelation was inferior to that of the Babelic revelation contained and expressed in Basque. This latter language would turn out to be a sort of proto-Gospel in which a Trinitarian theodicy was deployed. Basque—affirms tacitly Poza—is more perfect than Hebrew as language and theological philosophy. The religion from Babel was more accomplished and truer than that from Sinai, and the Basques, the truly chosen people. (*Vestigios* 86)[52]

According to Juaristi, Poza would be the most radical apologist. In Poza's case, Basque language becomes the possessor of Christianity's full revelation before any other language originating in the demise of Babel and, even, before the Edenic language itself. At the same time, Basque stands in front of modernity and its Babelic multilingual reality, as yet another modern language. Basque would be the most modern of all, given its outmost Christian or "cristiano viejo" status; since Basque precedes the arrival of Jews and Arabs to the Peninsula, the Basques are

---

ia necessidad de saber el lenguaje castellano: mas los vizcaínos. navarros. franceses. italianos. y todos los otros que tienen algún trato y conversación en España y necessidad de nuestra lengua: si no vienen desde niños a la deprender por uso: podrán la más aína saber por esta mi obra."

[52] "Del libro de Poza se desprende que Dios eligió revelar su propia naturaleza al linaje de Túbal, y que tal revelación fue superior a la primera o edénica, contenida en el hebreo. Al infundir esta lengua en Adán, Dios le hizo partícipe de algunos de sus misterios, pero el grado de tal revelación fue inferior al de la revelación babélica contenida y plasmada en el vasco. Esta última lengua vendría a ser una especie de protoevangelio en que se despliega una teodicea trinitaria. El vasco -afirma tácitamente Poza- es más perfecto que el hebreo como lengua filosófica y teológica. La religión de Babel es ya más cumplida y verdadera que la del Sinaí, y los vascos, el auténtico pueblo elegido."

exempted from the mixing that Spanish imperialism identifies as a sign of otherness. According to Juaristi, thanks to Poza, Basque language gives Basques their strongest legitimacy: Basque precedes modernity as well as the Edenic creation and thus Basques are the privileged subjects of God and, by extension, of the Hispanic modernity of the Renaissance.

Following Juaristi, but against his own conclusions, one could conclude that, according to Poza, Basque comes before the Christian West while constituting it. In this interpretation of Juaristi's reading of Poza, one could infer that the Basques stand as preceding and founding Europe (the West) as a result of their "beforeness." This position would not simply be historical or geographic but both, thanks to its unstable synecdochic logic, which would defy Western modernity. In short, when denouncing Poza, Juaristi provides, against his own political and critical objectives, the most suggestive and interesting reading of Poza. Basque could be considered the most modern and least modern of languages in the Renaissance. [53]

However, a closer examination of Poza's text runs against Juaristi's denunciation. When in chapters IV and VI of his book *De la antigua lengua: poblaciones y comarcas de las Españas (On the Old Language, People, and Lands of Spain*, 1587), Poza makes reference to Hebrew as the Edenic language, at no point does he claim for Basque a positionality anterior to that of Hebrew:

> Since humanity, in the times of the tower of Babylon, was already scattered throughout the world, it was also necessary for some time to pass, to suppress the original language, which as we have said, and everybody knows, it was the Hebrew. Because this general mother tongue of the world it was so settled, as there was no other, it is quite clear that the first arrivals, such they were those who spread from that tower of Nembroth, would name the islands and provinces to which they arrived, with the name that the [original] inhabitants and dwellers had given, just as now our Spaniards in the Indies, despite their language being Castilian, still name the provinces with their first names from the Indian language: Mexico, Peru, Chile, Cuzco, etc. (64-5) [54]

---

[53] In this sense, one could conclude that Poza is the first deconstructionist of logocentrism, as studied by Derrida, for Basque becomes the irreducible *différance* of the West.

[54] "Como el genero humano en aquellos tiempos de la torre de Babylonia, estuviesse ya muy derramado por el orbe, assi tambien fue menester algun transcurso de tiempo, para suprimir la lengua primera, que segun avemos dicho, y todos saben, fue la

In chapter VI, Poza clearly states that, even in the Basque Country, Basque language is a post-Babelic arrival, which might have oppressed and displaced the original inhabitants who spoke Hebrew: "As the Basques who came from Armenia and the fields of Sanaar multiplied, their language began to oppress Hebrew, till it suppressed completely its use and memory" (75).[55]

However, the Basques' apologies have a very important consequence for Basque language. If the Inquisition influenced and forced the nobility to abandon *euskara*, apologist literature itself provided another internal reason for that abandonment. Unlike the rest of modern languages that eventually served as basis for the construction of (imperialist) nation-states, Basque was located by apologist literature in front of modernity precisely in order to signify a position that was *exterior to modernity*. The reason is political: ultimately, Basque language's Babelic antiquity was mobilized to allow elite Basques to occupy a position of advantage and difference in the Spanish empire, which already had its own state language: Castilian. Unlike the rest of languages mobilized in modernity, which was geared towards the construction of a national and political interiority (national culture), Basque refered to a (modern) exteriority. The result was the lack of development for Basque. This language remained an object of writing but never became a literary language: the apologists' never wrote in Basque and the latter never became the basis for a potential national culture. To my knowledge, no other language fulfilled this function in the burgeoning modern Europe of the Renaissance. While the elite Basque subject and its discourse attained a locus in modernity, thus becoming modern, its language did not.

In order to understand the specific and historical way, out of the many possible ones, in which Basque entered modernity, it will suffice to

---

Hebrea, porque como essa lengua general y materna del mundo, estuviesse tan assentada, pues no avia otra ninguna, claro resulta que los advenedizos, quales fueron los que se derramaron de aquella torre de Nembroth, nombrarian las islas y provincias a que yvan, con el nombre que sus moradores y pobladores les avian impuesto, assi como ahora nuestros Españoles en las indias, sin embargo de su lengua Castellana, todavia nombran las provincias con sus nombres primeros de la lengua Indiana, Mexico, Peru, Chile, Cuzco, &c."

[55] "Con la multiplicacion de los Vascongados que vinieron de Armenia, y de los campos de Sanaar, fue su lengua poco a poco oprimiendo a la Hebrea, hasta quitarle de todo punto el uso y memoria suya."

remember the case of the Protestant queen of (Lower) Navarre,[56] Jeanne of Albret (1528-1572), mother of Henry IV, future king of France and daughter of Margarite of Navarre (1492-1549), author of the *Heptameron* (1559). Had (Lower) Navarre become Protestant under Albret's rule, the translation of the Bible into Basque, which was commissioned to Joanes Leizarraga by the Calvinist Synod of Pau, might have become the linguistic basis for a new state language next to Gascon---the actual official, administrative language. In this way, (Lower) Navarre might have followed a development similar to the one taken by the Protestant states of the bygone Sacred Roman Empire in the aftermath of Luther's translation of the Bible into German. However, the actual, specific development of Basque language, after the apologists' defense, followed the new economic and social structure of the Catholic, Castilian Basque Country. In this respect, and as Antonio Tovar notes, the French Basque apologist Arnauld Oihenart (54-8) was more preoccupied with establishing the Navarran origins of the Basques than their Biblical and post-Babelic origins. In other words, the Babelic theories were only of interest to the Castilian Basque elite.

As Juan Aranzadi already notes (288-317), the reorganization of a new rural nobility, emerging from the *banderizo* or family clan wars among the small nobility or *ahaide nagusiak* of the Middle Ages, did not require a national language, but needed, nevertheless, a cultural and political tool of differentiation in order to legitimize itself in the Spanish court. In this way, Basques emigrating from the rural Basque Country to the capital could join the new class of scribes in the imperial court; Basque proved the "old Christian" status of Basques and gave them automatically universal nobility and access to the imperial bureaucratic apparatus from which the Jews had been evicted. At the same time, the new class of nobles and *mayorazgos* (inheriting family members, landowners) remaining in the Basque Country could uphold their own economic privileges and interests in front of the Spanish crown. After the Inquisition trails of 1610, even this class abandoned Basque as its cultural language.

In other words, historically speaking, the apologists' particular legitimizing use of Basque language prevailed over its possible nationalist deployment geared towards the consolidation of nation-states, which was followed first by Protestant states and later on by Catholic empires such as the Spanish.

---

[56] The kingdom of Navarre on the French side of the Pyrenees that Castile-Aragon did not annex permanently.

Only an important issue remains to be studied in detail: if Basques, as modern subjects, were at the same time exterior to modernity as a result of the location of Basque language as "before," and if their *letrado* or scribe class occupied the vacant places left by the expulsion of Jews and Moriscos, to what extent did Basques become "phantasmatic internal Jews" to the Castilian empire? To what extent Basque anti-Semitism was not also a form of self-identification in the phantasmatic mirror of a Jewish exteriority now occupied by the Basques themselves? As Caro Baroja states, the Basque elite of the Renaissance "has become bourgeois by means of the [government] bureaucracy: a bourgeois who moves everywhere with ease… it will arrive a moment when the Basque predominance in government matters will appear abusive to some, so that they will argue that in so far as Basques are scribes, their relationship with the Jews becomes clear" (*Los vascos y la historia* 75).[57]

Genealogy of Apologists

Although Juan Martínez de Zaldivia (?-1575) wrote *Summa of Things Cantabric and Guipuzcoan* in 1564, the first important apologist is the official chronicler of the Spanish crown, Esteban de Garibay (1533-1599). The fourth book of Garibay's *Historical Compendium of the Chronicles and Universal History of all the Kings of Spain* (1571) contains most of his apologistic discourse.

Yet, Andrés Pozas's *On the Old Language, People, and Lands of Spain, in Which, Several Things of Cantabria are Discussed* (1587), constitutes, with Martinez de Zaldivia's, the first text upon which the apologist tradition was founded, in the sense that he wrote from a Basque position (commissioned by Basque institutions) rather than from that of a courtly scribe such as Garibay. Poza's text borrows most of its historical material from Garibay, but organizes it into the four different types of discursive elements that the rest of later apologists will follow: the reference to the Babelic incident in the Bible, the recourse to toponymic etymology as a way to prove the universality and originality of Basque language in Spain, the discussion of secondary or non-linguistic elements, such as attire, to confirm the toponymic etymology, and finally the narrative account of an early act of war against the Roman empire, by which the Basques

---

[57] "se ha hecho burgués por vía de la burocracia: un burgués que se mueve con soltura por todas partes… llegará un momento en que la predominancia vasca en cuestiones de gobierno parecerá abusiva a algunos, de suerte que afirmarán que en lo que los vascos tienen de 'escribas', se ve su relación con los judíos."

prove their original independence and nobility; this narrative is a variant of medieval pactist literature and becomes the generic basis of most 19th-century historical narrative, including the early work of Sabino Arana, the founder of Basque nationalism.

Baltasar de Echave (1558-1623) was the fourth canonical writer of the core-tradition of apologism. His *Discourses on the Antiquity of the Cantabrian Language* (1607) constituted a text that, although following Poza, marked the new direction of later apologists: linguistics. In his discourse, Echave resorts to baroque allegorical rhetorics and presents Basque language speaking directly as an old and venerable matriarch. The fact that he published his book in Mexico, that is, in the Basque diaspora, explains partly this more nostalgic and melancholic approach to apologist discourse. The fact that all apologists after Echave adopted his diasporic colonial point of view to write this genre is paramount; it confirms the Atlantic and anti-imperialist positioning of apologism. After Echave, most apologists resorted to the figure of Basque language as matriarch. At the same time, they subsumed the political thrust present in Martinez de Zaldivia and Poza under a more linguistic defense of Basque language and culture. Echave's linguistic turn came hand in hand with a tendency to expand the recourse to toponymic etymology so that any Castilian word could ultimately be explained as Basque. This etymological strategy culminated with Manuel Larramendi.

Arnaud Oihenart (1592-1667; *An Account of both Vasconias, the Iberian and the Aquitanian*, 1637) and Gabriel Henao (1612-1704; *Inquiries into the Antiquity of Cantabria*, 1689) constitute, with Echave, the other two important apologists of the 17th century. They are also the most original and different of the entire apologist tradition; however, they are not as influential as the rest. In Henao's work, which is also a biography of St. Ignatius of Loyola, the apology genre and the Counterreformation come together again. In this way, Henao seems to be the first one elaborating a mythological discourse on the origins of Cantabria and, at the same time, proposing the idea that Basques were Christians before the arrival of Christ.[58]

Finally, Manuel Larramendi (1690-1766) and his *On the Universality and Antiquity of Basque* (1728) represented a quantum leap in the linguistic turn

---

[58] Melchor de Oyanguren wrote the first grammar of Tagalog and a trilingual dictionary: Tagalog, Latin, and Basque. Unfortunately, this dictionary has been lost and the possible introduction to the dictionary, which could have contained very original thinking about the relationship between the three languages studied.

taken by Echave. Larramendi's later work constituted one of the earliest attempts to describe systematically the Basque language; it was eminently linguistic rather than strictly apologetic. In this sense, Larramendi consolidated apologism as a linguistic discourse that no longer addressed Basque language as a device to legitimize elite politics, but rather attempted to represent Basque language itself as its ultimate political object. After Larramendi, Basque language acquired an interiority for the first time (grammar, dictionary, etc.).[59] His work also coincided with the beginning of the crisis of the social order that *fueros* articulated.

Finally, and after the French revolution, Pablo P. Astarloa (1752-1806) and his *Apology of the Basque Language* (1803) became the last apologist systematization of the Basque language. Although still apologistic, Astarloa's work announces the arrival of modern linguistics and philology by the hand of the German scholar with whom he collaborated: Wilhelm von Humboldt. In this way, philology and linguistics superseded apology and, at the same time, benefited from the latter's rich acumen at the beginning of the 18th century.

2. Baroque and Subalternity: The Iron Century (Loyola, Axular, Oihenart, Erauso, Aguirre)

The Counterreformation and the consolidation of baroque culture were Spanish imperialism's two responses to Protestantism's Reformation movement as the latter sprang off the Renaissance and its humanist discourse. If Basque apologism represented a modern Atlantic movement within Basque culture and politics, articulated in response to the advances of Spanish imperialism, Basque religious literature became deeply and centrally involved in the anti-modern movement that Spanish and French imperialisms deployed on each side of the Pyrenees respectively. This anti-modernity was mainly expressed in Basque and yielded the first original literary production in that language: Axular's *Gero* (*Later*, 1643).

Axular's is a religious manual counseling its readers to fight indolence and the postponement of affairs for "later;" hence the title. 'Gero' means 'later' or 'future.' Ironically, enough, this first work became the foundation of modern standard Basque and, consequently its canonical reference. Axular is considered the Basque Cervantes, Shakespeare, or Sor Juana Inés de la Cruz. With him we can follow what Larramendi later

---

[59] In Galician, the first dictionaries and grammars originate in the 19th century (Carballo Calero, *Historia* 69).

calls the "iron age" of Basque literature and culture (Bijuesca "Euskara eta vascuence"), or what we could call the Iron Century, thus capturing the height of industrial and commercial development across the Basque Country, which was opposed to the colonial trade that defined French and, especially, Spanish imperialism. This colonialism could be symbolized by gold and, in this way, the term "Siglo de oro" or golden century takes its full colonial and cultural meaning.

Yet, the Basque Country also yielded the central religious character of the Counterreformation: Ignatius of Loyola (1491-1556). As José Antonio Maravall states, the order funded by Loyola to counteract the Reformation, the Company of Jesus, was "a pure expression of the baroque mentality" (77). Loyola's *Ejercicios espirituales* (*Spiritual Exercises;* 1530s), written outside the Basque Country in Spanish, became the other canonical work in the history of postnational Basque literature.

This was a historical moment full of turmoil in the Basque Country. In the 16th century, the kingdom of Navarre was assimilated by the Castilian-Aragonese crown (1512) and later on, the last independent part of the kingdom of Navarre, Lower Navarre, was incorporated to the kingdom of France after Henri IV (1620). Loyola participated in a war between Lower Navarre and Castile when the Navarran king, Henri d'Albret, attempted to retake the lost part of Navarre in 1521. As a result of the injuries sustained in the battle, Loyola abandoned his military career and embraced religious life.

In the 17th century, while the religious Protestant presence still persisted in France, on the one hand, and Spanish Jews and protestants crossed the border to find refuge in the province of Labourd, on the other, the French crown enforced its power in the Basque Country by sending the most famous and fanatic agent of the Inquisition, Pierre de Lancre (of Basque origin), to control and annihilate the proliferation of witches in the province of Labourd in 1609. According to Lancre, the increase in witchcraft was due mainly to "the demons that the missionaries had expelled from Asia" (Burns 169). Many of these missionaries were Basque, including Saint Francis of Xavier, companion of Loyola, who died in China.

When Axular presided over his parish of Sara in Labourd (1600-1644), he saw peasants, Protestants, Cagots, Gypsies, and even priest colleagues prosecuted and executed by Lancre. The traumatic effect of the witch-hunt was so profound in Axular, that he only makes one reference to the Protestant heresies in the introduction to his *Gero* and does not mention even a single time the word "witch" in his text.

Michel de Certeau captures well the historical context of Reformation and imperialism, against which religious writers such as Loyola and Axular composed their anti-modern, religious work:

> In the minds of the religious believers of the sixteenth and seventeenth centuries, a second state of affairs was inseparable from the foregoing situation—the humiliation of the Christian tradition. They were experiencing, in their shattered Christendom, another fundamental decline: that of the institutions of meaning.... In a symbolic gesture, Saint Ignatius of Loyola, Saint Teresa of Avila and many others wished to enter a "corrupt" order, not out of any taste for decadence, but because those disorganized places represented in their minds the state of contemporary Christianity.... More generally, their solidarity with the collective, historically based suffering—which was demanded by circumstances but also desired and sought after as a test of truth—indicates the place of mystic "agony," a "wound" inseparable from the social ill. (86)

De Certeau summarizes in a great metaphor the tension between the linguistic modernity of the Reformation (and Basque apologism), which brings back the myth of Babel as fragmentation, and the anti-modern and unifying thrust of the imperialist Counterreformation and its mystic writers: "Mysticism is the anti-Babel. It is the search for a common language, after language has been shattered. It is the invention of a 'language of the angels' because that of man has been disseminated" (88). Ironically enough, the language of the angels had to be brought to the people and, as a result, the Counterreformation ultimately fostered the dissemination of religion in the vernacular—in an act that mirrored the Reformation's Babelic ideology. Thus, the bishops of Calahorra and Pamplona issued "sinodales" to order the yearly writing of religious manuals in the Basque dialects of each region (Salaberri Muñoa 79). However, this new anti-Babel prompted by the Counterreformation was anti-modern for it ultimately did not celebrate linguistic difference; it only accommodated the "linguistic ignorance of the masses" towards the only true language of the angels. At this point, written Basque, and its standardized and classical writing, became the most important tool for the control and subjectivation of the subaltern classes.

Baroque

Maravall clearly states the centrality of Spanish imperialism in the Counterreformation's deployment of baroque culture, when he concludes that:

Spain, which contributed so effectively to the breakdown and removal of the Renaissance order, rapidly assimilated the incipient baroque forms of Italy, carried them to maturity, and diffused them into France, Flanders, Italy itself, and into the Protestant milieu of England and Germany. Counterreform, absolutism, and baroque went together, betokened by their Spanish base, and even the baroque art produced in Protestant countries was found to have a relation to the Hispanic influence—a thesis that others had already stated without playing down [...] the creative value of the Protestant baroque. (10)

Departing from this Hispanic centrality, Maravall defines baroque culture as the logic that articulates and organizes all the historical changes that consolidate the absolutist order in the 17th century: social upheavals, hierarchization of society, massification of the lower classes, brutal control exerted by the monarchies, etc. As Maravall concludes: "the crisis economy... the strengthening of seigniorial agrarian landholdings and the growing impoverishment of the masses foster a feeling of being threatened and of instability in one's personal and social life, a feeling that is held in control by the imposing forces of repression that underlie the dramatic gesticulation of the baroque human being..." (6). As a result, Maravall concludes that baroque culture is ultimately hierarchical, repressive, and massive. Baroque culture does not simply affect "the arts" but rather the entire cultural organization of European societies, which are ultimately controlled by increasingly absolutist monarchies. In Maravall's own words, "[T]he baroque monarchy made use of a large repertory of means [medios] to succeed in dominating the tension of adverse forces [...] It included aspects all the way from physical constraint, based on military force, which is the *ultima ratio* of political supremacy, to psychological expedients [resortes] that acted on consciousness and created within it a repressed psyche" (36).

More specifically religion, from manual to sermon, from prayer to religious drama, from sculpture to excessive architecture, became a very complex performative technology, by which the masses were addressed as spectators who were then incorporated in the religious spectacle, so that they found their "natural" place in a world that was hierarchically organized and controlled by God and its representative on earth, the absolutist monarch. [60] The massive incorporation of the spectator was implemented through a very detailed discursive and visual technology that aimed at provoking and controlling the masses' reactions and emotions (fear, crying, awe, etc.). As Maravall concludes "[D]istinct from the serenity sought by the Renaissance, the Baroque set out to stir and impress, directly and immediately, by effectively intervening in the motivation [resortes] of the passions... The efficacy in affecting, in awakening and moving the affections, was the great motive of the Baroque" (75). This baroque deployment of affective power can be seen in the works of Loyola and Axular. They are both technologies of the self: the self of individuals who, nevertheless, remain subaltern masses. [61]

Loyola and the Psychological Apparatus of Counterreformation

Loyola's writings are one of the most central and best exponents of baroque culture. As Yvonne del Valle claims: "Loyola can be seen as a personification of the Baroque, of a style, of the exercise of a will that 'constructs' the individual and at the same time designs an expansive plan of action which, rather than withdraw from the world, confronts it in order to incorporate, rearrange, and conquer it" (141). Following the baroque creed to organize and control the individual down to his or her innermost emotions and irrational excess, Loyola's *Spiritual Exercises* can be considered the blueprint of the baroque technology of subjectivation, of the baroque technology of the self. As del Valle states:

> The subject of Loyola's exercises would concentrate on directing... all of his senses, will and understanding towards a single goal: that of understanding himself solely within the teleological framework of his own relationship to the Christian tradition of salvation.... Loyola's program... equips the subject with a structure that contains a mechanism for self-conquest. (142)

---

[60] Baudrillard in his *Simulations* further elaborates the political logic of the Baroque: "This was the approach of the Jesuits who based their politics on the virtual disappearance of God and on the worldly and spectacular manipulation of consciences---the evanescence of God in the epiphany of power---the end of transcendence, which no longer serves as alibi for a strategy completely free of influences and signs. Behind the baroque of images hides the grey eminence of politics" (10).

[61] The Baroque requires revising the distinction between pastoral power (early modernity) and biopolitical power or biopower (18th century onwards) that Foucault presents in his *History of Sexuality*. The Baroque is a form of biopower.

116

The *Spiritual Exercises* constitute a *psychological apparatus* for the individuation of the baroque subject. This technology leaves no aspect of individual life unattended; even the non-spiritual is addressed. As del Valle stresses "the 'spirituality' of the exercises maintains a disconcerting respect for mundane activities" (142). The ultimate goal is precisely to create a very refined individual who, nevertheless, responds to the ideals of the Counterreformation. In this respect, Loyola attempts to create a form of individualism, which mirrors the one promulgated by Protestantism.

The *Spiritual Exercises* are directed not to the religious reader, but to the spiritual leader who later imposes the Jesuit psychological apparatus on his subjects. It is important to see that Loyola emphasizes the importance of paying attention not simply to the rational side of the "exercitant" (the addressee of the exercises) but also to his or her emotions (consolation, desolation, etc.): "When the director giving the Exercises becomes aware that the exercitant is not affected by any spiritual movements, such as consolations or desolations, and is not being stirred by various spirits, the director should question the exercitant closely about the exercises" (284). Later on, emotions are not simply controlled but also programmed, following the spectatorial "contemplation" of well-defined religious spectacles:

> The request must be adapted to the matter under consideration, so e.g. in contemplating the Resurrection one asks for joy with Christ joyful, but in contemplating the Passion one asks for grief, tears, and suffering with the suffering of Christ. Here I will ask for personal shame and confusion as I see how many have been damned on account of a single mortal sin. (295).

Finally, the "exercitant's" baroque vision and emotions elicited from him or her are expanded to the full body, so that "the eye of the imagination" extends to every sensory level: "The composition here is to see with the eyes of the imagination the length, breadth and depth of hell... To hear with one's ears the wailings, howls, cries, blasphemies against Christ Our Lord and against all the saints. To smell... To taste... To feel with the sense of touch..." (298-99). At that point, the mind and body of the "exercitant" are under the control of the spiritual leader and thus Loyola's baroque psychological apparatus succeeds in creating the perfect "religious individual" who can fully obey the orders of the Company (Loyola's religious order) in an individualized and perfectly controlled way. Loyola writes *the* manual to baroque subjectivation, the manual of the

117

baroque self, one in which, as Barthes concludes, even divinity is fully controlled (75).

Loyola wrote the first draft of his *Spiritual Exercises* in 1524. Twenty years later, he would write a *Spiritual Diary* for two years (1544-45). The most repeated and watched word in the diary entries is "tears." This word, or its correlate, "weeping," is repeated hundreds of times. In entries such as the one from Sunday February 24th, 1544, he notes:

> During the customary prayer, from the beginning to the end inclusive, I was helped by grace very far inside and gentle, full of devotion, warm and very sweet. While preparing the altar and vesting, the name of Jesus was shown me: I felt great love, confirmation and an increased resolve to follow Him: *I wept and sobbed.* Throughout mass, very great devotion and many *tears* so that quite often I lost the power of speech; all the devotion and feelings had Jesus as their object. (85, my emphasis)

Similar annotations, repeated hundreds of times throughout his diary, are a way to keep in check the religious excess and irrationality of his baroque subjectivity (devotion) while turning its bodily manifestations (tears) into the very signs that signify Loyola's control and self-mastery in his devotion. In short, those parts of his bodily existence that escape self-control are turned into the very signs that confirm self-mastery, self-control, and, thus, full, true surrender to religion and divinity—and its political institution on earth, the Church.

This discourse of was deployed by the Church as its main technology of the self in order to deploy Loyola's Company in a new mission to conquer not just the bodies of the Habsburg empire but also its minds and souls. This was a new phase in the control of the subaltern masses.

Axular and the Baroque Performance of the Vernacular

Although Axular is the canonical writer of Basque literature in Basque, there are no studies of his work in English. Pedro Dagerre Azpilikueta (1556-1644) is better known as Axular, after the farm in which he is born in 1556 in the Navarran town of Urdax. He studied at the University of Salamanca and was witness to the theological discussions that structured the baroque religious culture of the Spanish Habsburg empire. Later, he left the bishopric of Pamplona and joined the one in Bayonne relocating in 1600 to the Labourdan town of Sara. Axular dedicated his *Gero* (*Later*) to his vigorous bishop, Bertrand de Echauz, (alm-collector of Henry IV and Louis XIII, and friend of Richelieu) who was involved in fighting the

Protestant presence in Labourd. He was in part responsible for encouraging the production of religious literature in Basque. In Axular's words addressed to his bishop:

> When in those parts of Lower Navarre, as in many other places, the holy Catholic law [faith] was about to meager its figure, falter, and fall, everybody knows that your fatherly Lord, without taking note of his house, wealth, and life, went to Saint Palais, where the Navarran parliament was located at the time. And there, with great courage, with his noble Christian heart, began to shout, with unsheathed sword in hand, like a Matatias in his time, saying…. "Oh Christians, you all, whose being is [defined] by your Christian names, follow me and help me uphold and maintain the true law and faith." (7)[62]

Axular died in Sara in 1644, one year after the publication of his work, when the religious wars had finally subsided in Europe and, consequently, France remained Catholic. The political tension between the historical upheavals he witnessed and his own writings were at the center of the baroque culture that he helped consolidate in Basque.

Because of the prosperity that the province of Labourd was experiencing in the 17th century, triggered by its fishing and ship-building industries, a limited reading public emerged, one that nevertheless was more fluent in Basque (Salaberri Muñoa 55-7). As a result, several priests and cultured individuals congregated in the province of Labourd and collaborated in the production of different books in Basque: Materre, Etxeberri, Argaignarats, and Harizmendi. This group of writers has been known ever since as "The School of Sara," even though they did not pursue a programmatic agenda. Larramendi already noted in the next century that Axular's *Gero* was widely read on both sides of the Pyrenees (Salaberri Muñoa 78).

Axular was the first author among his colleagues who wrote an original work of religion in Basque. He details in the introduction the diffi-

---

[62] "Nafarroa behereko parte hetan, bertze anhitz lekhutan bezala, lege katolika saindua, iduriz flakatzera, kordokatzera eta erortzera zihoanean, badaki munduak nola zure aita Iauna, bere etxeaz, onez eta biziaz ere kontu guti eginik, ioan zen Donapalaiora, non baitzen orduan Nafarroako Parlamenta. Eta han ausartzia handi batekin, bere bihotz giristino noblearekin, hasi zen, ezpata biluzia eskuan harturik, oihuz, Matatias bat bere denboran bezala, erraiten zuela: […]. «Ea giristinoak, giristino izenarekin, izana duzuenak, bertze egiteko guztiak utzirik hurbil zakizkidate, iarraiki zakizkidate eta egiazko legearen eta fedearen mantenatzen eta sostengatzen, lagun zakizkidate»."

culties of endeavoring in such a work. However, the consistency and coherence of his writing set him apart from the rest of his fellow writers. If his language is compared with that of his predecessors, Leizarraga, Lazarra, or Etxepare, it is clear that his is not a cultist language; it is the language spoken in Sara at the time. In this respect, Axular clearly exemplifies the logic of baroque culture. It is a writing designed to address a wide reading public and to provide the latter with a psychological apparatus that serves to control and exert its inner self.

Furthermore and as Patxi Salaberri Muñoa states, works such as Axular's were also meant to be used in order to preach sermons and to read them out loud to an illiterate public (77-8). In this respect, Axular's language is massive and populist; it was meant *to be performed*. The repetition of words and the continuous punctuation are clear examples of Axular's attempt to reach a broad, literate and illiterate audience. The following example referring to Genesis makes clear that the purpose of Axular's profuse prose full of synonymous variations is to reach repeatedly a wide public that a single term might miss:

> When our Lord, next to all the other things in the world, created man, upon him, to his image and appearance, without sin and without the pollution of any sin, provided with all sorts of presents, gifts, and advantages, placed him where the earth had its best part and location, in the paradise of earth, in place full of pleasures. In addition, he ordered that man plow, cultivate, and take care of that paradise. (13, my emphasis)[63]

At the same time, Axular's work is fully embedded in the baroque religious rhetoric that follows Aristotle's *Poetics*. In this respect, the many references to the religious and philosophical authorities of the Middle Ages and Antiquity in the text point to the fact that the latter is designed to inscribe and articulate the oppressive hierarchy of baroque culture. This highly hierarchized text, while remaining popular, also marks the ignorance of the readership or audience. The hierarchical exclusion of the readership is also included and signified by and within the text. In this respect, Axular's text is not a Basque text written in Basque for a

---

[63] "Gure Iaungoikoak, munduko bertze gauza guztien ondoan, gizona bera, bere gainki, bere imajinara eta idurira, bat ere bekhaturik eta bekhaturen kutsurik ere gabe, anhitz donu, dohain, eta abantail suertez dotaturik, egin zuenean, ibeni zuen berehala, lurrak zuen parterik, eta aurkientzarik hoberenean, lurreko parabisuan, lekhu plazerez bethean. Eta manatu zuen lant zezala, labora zezala, eta begira ongi parabisu hura."

Basque readership, but rather a bilingual text, a text in translation, whose primal or original discourse continues to be in Latin, in the language of the religious elite, as if it were a palimpsest. In short, and recalling de Certeau's reference to Latin as the original language of angels, Axular's work remains written in the language of angels even though the text translates itself into the Basque vernacular as a way to emphasize an inner textual hierarchy between Latin, the language of angels, and Basque, the language of the masses. Just as in the case of apologist literature, here also Basque is simply a reference, a legitimizing tool whose final discourse and subject remains outside the Basque language and the subaltern class to which is addressed: the (religious) elite who reads in French/Castilian and Latin.

Furthermore, the main topic of the book, the perils and sins that derive from procrastination, is also thematized and explained in relationship with the baroque power of the absolutist monarch: "Aristotle says, that it is good, to eradicate and exile [people] from the land of laziness: and in order to ensure that the people do not rise against their monarch or other authorities, it is also good to build large projects, erect towers and castles, and employ people in them (Arist. lib. 5 Politic.cap. 11)." (15).[64]

Yet this very baroque excess, which attempts to control every aspect of the psyche of the subaltern classes, also yields contradictions and unplanned effects. Axular describes the dialectal diversity of the Basque Country and, consequently, interpellates Basque readers of all dialects as the ideal reader of his book, thus, creating the unintended effect of a baroque Basque community, in Anderson's sense, that defies the political divisions of kingdoms, which his baroque discourse aims at upholding or enforcing in the first place:

> I know that I cannot extend myself to all the different dialects of Basque. For it is spoken in many ways and in different manners in the Basque Country. In Upper Navarre, Lower Navarre, Soul, Labourd, Biscay, Guipuzcoa, Alava, and many other places. One says "to look" [*behatzea*] and others "to stare" [*so egitea*]. One says "to get angry" [*haserretzea*] and others "to enrage" [*samurtzea*].... Ultimately, each one in his own way, manner, and custom. Not all Basques have the same

---

[64] "Erraiten du Aristotelek, on dela, alferkeriaren herritik khentzeko, eta desterratzeko: eta herrien ere bere erregeren edo bertzeren kontra iaikitzetik begiratzeko, zenbait obra handiren hastea, zenbait dorreren edo gazteluren egitea, eta hetan iendearen enplegatzea (Arist. lib. 5 Politic.cap. 11)."

laws and customs, or the same Basque dialect, for they have different kingdoms. (11)[65]

In short, there is a political excess, an unintended political reality that emerges from this excess, which undermines the absolutist power legitimized by baroque literature: a unified Basque community of readers and listeners. And indeed this community represents a subaltern Basque class that shares a very heterogeneous but ultimately unifying language: *euskara*. This political excess is further emphasized by the masterful shift in personal pronouns that, although it is intended to interpellate and control the reader from different subjective angles, ends up producing the unintended excess of a Basque reading (listening) community in God that begins to resemble the communities of the Reformation. As a result of pronominal excess in the text, the "many" at the end of the paragraph below inadvertently excludes even the Basques. They have previously been interpolated by the pronouns "I," "you," and "we," and thus the Basques are not the "many" who will be either called or chosen to follow the Catholic Christ:

> Thus, *we* too find occasions, pretexts, delays, excuses and diversions, to commit sin, to spend time in lascivities and licentious desires. When anybody steers *you* away from good, and *you* are left behind, *you* answer to those who distract you in this way: please, now, at this present, *you* have to forgive *me*, I cannot do what you say. For a fantasy has entered my mind, and I have to fulfill that fantasy. And thus when it is said that many are called upon but few are chosen, it means Gentiles, Moors, Turks, Jews, Lutherans, and the rest of the world are called upon. (76, my emphasis)[66]

---

[65] "Badakit halaber ezin heda naitekeiela euskarako minzatze molde guztietara. Zeren anhitz moldez eta diferentki minzatzen baitira euskal herrian. Nafarroa garaian, Nafarroa beherean, Zuberoan, Laphurdin, Bizkaian, Gipuzkoan, Alaba-herrian, eta bertze anhitz lekhutan. Batak erraiten du *behatzea*, eta bertzeak *so egitea*. Batak *haserretzea* eta bertzeak *samurtzea*. [...] Finean bat bederak bere gisara, anzura eta moldera. Eztituzte euskaldun guztiek legeak eta azturak bat, eta ez euskarazko minzatzea ere, zeren erresumak baitituzte diferent."

[66] "hala edireiten ditugu bada *guk* ere okhasinoak, desenkusat, estakuruak, atxakiak eta itzurpideak, bekhatutan egoiteko, desirkundetan eta nahikundetan denboraren iragaiteko. *Nehork* ontasunera hersten zaituenean, eta gibela zaudenean, ihardesten dio*zu* hala hersten zaituenari. Othoi orai presenteon barkhatu behar derau*tazu*, ezin daidike*t* oraiño *zuk* diozuna. Zeren buruan sarthu baitzait fantasia bat, konplitu behar dut fantasia hura;

122

The combination between the popular language and the highly hier-archized rhetoric used by Axular defines *Gero*, next to Loyola's *Spiritual Exercises*, as the other great Basque exponent of the baroque psychologi-cal apparatus, which resorts to the vernacular and, by doing so, creates unintended political effects among subaltern classes, which remain to be studied.[67]

Oihenart: The End of Cult Basque Culture

Arnauld Oihenart (1592–1668) represents the first possibility of cult po-etry and, at the same time, the closure of such possibility. In the 16th century, Lazarraga embodied the renunciation of the local Basque-Span-ish nobility to the Basque language and its embrace of Castilian in the Renaissance. Lazarraga's or even Garibay's language was not cult or cul-tivated; it was simply popular *euskara* used by the nobility for its own purposes—hence the high rate of Castilian solecisms in their discourse.

When Oihenart turned 18 years old, Henry III of Navarre and IV of France (1553-1610), first ruler of both kingdoms, had recently died. In Oihenart's time, Basque and Bearnes (a dialect of Gascon) were spoken in the kingdom of (Lower) Navarre, even more so than French, the lan-guage of the Parisian court. Yet, Richelieu had just sanctioned the new French Academy and, thus, French language was beginning to make its inroads throughout the empire. Oihenart represents the last vestiges of a Navarran nobility that moved to Lower Navarre and, thus, did not nec-essarily depend on the languages imposed by the court of Paris or Ma-drid.

Of Souletin origin, Oihenart inherited his nobility-title through mar-riage to his second wife. As a new arrival to the court of Lower Navarre in Donapaleu, he wrote in Latin, Basque, and French. In 1625, he pub-lished in French his *Historical Declaration of the Unjust Usurpation and Reten-tion of Navarre by the Spaniards*. In 1638, he finished his major historical work in Latin: *An Account of the Two Vasconias, the Iberian and the Aquitanian* (reedited in 1656). Finally he published in Basque, although with a French title, his *Les Proverbes Basques, recueillis par le Sr. d'Oihenart; plus les poésies*

Eta hala erraiten denean anhitz *direla* deituak eta gutiak hautatuak, aditzen da Ientilak, Mairuak, Turkoak, Iuduak, Luterak, eta munduko bertze guztiak direla deituak."

[67] As a result, the 18th century became "the century of the religious manual," when Basque church books of this nature were published in most dialects and, in some cases, knew numerous editions.

basques du mesme auteur (*The Basque Proverbs, Gathered by Mr. Oihenart, And the Basque Poems of the Same Author*, 1657). In short, Oihenart represents the last vestiges of a local nobility that served the interests of a peripheral monarch, the king or queen of Lower Navarre, as this kingdom had begun to lose its political autonomy and the new French kings became rulers of both territories.

Similarly to Lazarraga, Oihenart also resorted to Basque language to write poetry. Yet, the baroque culture of the times demanded a linguistic refinement and organization that was unthinkable for Lazarraga. Among Oihenart's unpublished papers, a document entitled *L'art poétique basque* (*Basque Poetic Art*, 1665) was found that set the rules for the first time for a Basque metric system, departing from a comparison of Italian, French, Spanish, and Neo-Latin poetry. Oihenart cites the following poets in his *Poetic Art*: Plutarch, Sannazar, Petrarch, Ariosto, Buscelli, Juan de Mena, Montemayor, Cervantes, Lope de Vega, Desportes, Du Bartas, Saint Bernard, Jacobonus Tudertinus, Berterius, Howeden, Walter Map, Dominique Helion, Gariel, and Stapleton.

Moreover, although Oihenart does not cite the author, he quotes a poem in Biscayan dialect, which is clearly not popular and, thus, shows an awareness of cult poetry in the Basque territory, a tradition for which the only indirect reference is Oihenart's:

Atseyn andia da amore Eutea	It is great pleasure to possess love
Eta bere bada gustiz firmea	And if it is indeed most firm
Ecin essan Leydis ondo munduac	The world cannot tell well
Cein andiac diren are gustuac	How great its pleasures are.
Glorias beteric layo nindia	May I lie down full of glory
Icussias geuro Ceu, Ene Egusquia	As I see You, My Sun
(*L'art poétique* 205)	

Oihenart also cites Etxepare in order to condemn his unsophisticated populism. He also makes reference to two other Basque poets of whom we have no other information. Moreover, in his poetic self-awareness, which compels him to establish and revise the previous poetic canon in Basque, Oihenart cites Etxeberri of Ziburu precisely in order to clarify that the latter's poetry is religious but of low quality, since its purpose is not poetic but religious. Etxeberri, according to Oihenart, does not seek glory but faith: « And we will find that his verses are of the same measurement of fifteen syllables each and burdened by the vice and violence of quantity [...] it is a reason for charity rather than for any ambition or glory and has the zeal to benefit his fellow countrymen who must have a true religious man [to guide them with the reading]" (206).[68] Interestingly, Oihenart does not cite Axular, although his unpublished work remains to be studied. Thus, the origin of Oihenart's refinement and codification of Basque must be understood within the history of the Baroque—a culture that is both Basque *and* baroque in his case.

At a point in which the nobility reasserted its political and economic rights, while increasing the exploitation of the low classes, this elite class gave rise to a new culture that was both elitist and refined in order to denote its power. In each court (Paris, Donapaleu, Pau, and Madrid), poets began to cultivate a language that was complex, refined, excessive in its rhetorical or semantic structures, and ultimately spectacular in its deliverance. In Madrid and Toledo, culteranism and conceptism emerged as the two main forms of baroque poetry; in Italy, marinism represented a similar form of poetic refinement and excess. Finally in the French court of Paris, writers known as "the precious ones" (les précieux) arose as cultivators of a baroque literature known as "preciosism."

Oihenart's poetry represents precisely the same baroque and courtly culture in Lower Navarre. Furthermore, as he cites other poets and poems of which we have no further historical information, we must assume that his poetry was not an isolated attempt; it must have had a limited yet courtly readership or audience.[69]

Although Oihenart does not cite other contemporary baroque poets such as Quevedo, Góngora, or Vicent Voiture (he only references Cervantes and Lope de Vega), his poetry must be located within this baroque trend. He is the author of the first sonnet in Basque and, as the following poem shows, he seeks a level of complexity and refinement that distinguishes his poetry from any popular trend:

Zein ahal den egiati	Whom can be truthful
Zuk bezi ehork etziakizu,	No one, but you, knows.
Bain'engoiti Jainkoagati	But for God, please, as of today
Dakidan nik'er'egizu.	Make it so that I also do.
Ezi ordu dut jakinzu izan	For it is my time to be cognizant

---

[68] « Et nous trouuerons que ses uers sont de la mesme mesure de quinse syllabes chacun et tachez de pareil Uice de Uiolance de la quantite… un motif de charite que par aucune ambition, our Vainegloire, et quil auoit le zele de profiter a son prochain que doit avoir un veritable Ecclesiastique »

[69] As of now, there are no definitive historical or sociological studies on the issue of Oihenart's readership.

| Hil ala bizigei nizan. | If I am to die or remain alive. |
| (*Atsotitzak* 361-62) | |

Yet, as the court of Lower Navarre lost its power, this short historical moment in which a baroque, courtly, Basque literature surfaced, also disappeared with Oihenart.

The Monsters of Empire

Lope de Aguirre (1510-61) and Catalina de Erauso (1592-1650) represent Basque difference as Atlantic and colonial. They both engaged the Spanish monarch of their time and, in both cases, the monarch found a difference, a subject, who showed the limits of Spanish imperialism and its monarchy, a difference that it was shown by the object that symbolized their profession as soldiers, sword made out steel—hence the denomination of this Basque period as the Iron Century.[70]

Aguirre was the megalomaniac soldier who insulted Phillip II by letter, proclaimed his own kingdom in the Americas and, in this way, foreshadowed the future of a continent emancipating itself from the Spanish empire led by the elite creole classes of the 19th century. Erauso, the adventurous soldier coming back from the Indies, met personally Phillip IV in order to tell the story of her different life as a woman passing as man: she lived as a cantankerous soldier prone to fights, duels, and gambling in the Americas—she even killed her brother in a duel at night unaware of their kinship. Although the Spanish crown strictly enforced the control over the passage to the colonies, Erauso showed that even one of the most "evident" differences, gender, could hide from the empire in plain sight. Therefore, if any difference could evade imperial surveillance, Erauso became the embodiment of any difference that threatened the empire and its internal control of subjects. If women could defeat imperial control over the passage to the Indies, then, "Jews, Moors, and other heretics" could follow suit. In short, Erauso also foreshadowed the utopian possibilities of the colonies as the site where any non-accepted subject difference could prosper. She rendered the colonies the ultimate site of threat to the empire, as all its enemies could prosper there.

---

[70] Peter Bakker writes that the oldest pidgin language in North America created between Europeans and Indians originated with the exchanges between Basques and Native Americans in the 16th century in eastern Canada. Basque-American literature must be theorized as taking place between the subaltern trading pidgin of Basque fishers and the counter-imperialist discourses of Aguirre and Erauso.

Aguirre and Erauso are both "freaks" or, in the literal Latin sense of the word, monsters: subjects who de-*monstr*-ate, show, the limits of the Spanish monarchy. They "monstrate" empire's unthinkable, unimaginable side: one that is beyond the control of imperial body politics. Aguirre follows the imperial logic of sovereignty when proclaiming himself king; thus, he is eliminated. Erauso opens an unprecedented logic of gender bending and, nevertheless, she is allowed to survive, as the empire has no political logic of its own to deal with such transgression. Even her many murders are pardoned by the monarch. They are both monsters defiant of the power logic of the empire.

It is important to note that both are individuals, unique subjects, freakish unrepeatable monsters rather than representatives of a larger historical or biopolitical reality or class. Although they both foretell the future threats of the colonies, ultimately they contribute to enforcing the imperialist imagination of the colony as a land where the limits of the human and the political (the body politics) must be traced, enforced, and subjugated. Therefore, the imperial imagination can only represent this field as that of the monster: mythic animals, amazons, cannibals, and golden cities. Even El Dorado, after which Aguirre embarked in a large expedition, is a monstrous location where wealth loses its meaning and becomes a natural condition of the urban landscape: everything is paved in gold.

Thus, it is not a coincidence that both Basque subjects died in the Americas, after they interpellated the Spanish monarch: Aguirre was executed near Barquisimeto, Venezuela, and Erauso, after s/he received the permissions of the Spanish monarch and the Pope, returned to Mexico where s/he settled as a merchant and died twenty years later. As monsters, they belonged in the field of the colonial, the monstrous.

By the same token, and because of their unrepeatable monstrosity and uniqueness, both individuals became the two most celebrated subjects of Basque literature. They were both celebrated, revisited, and reinterpreted by Latin Americans and Europeans alike. They became myths in the real cognitive sense of the word; they became material with which the limits of the empire were represented, understood, and contested. To rephrase Lévi-Strauss, they were not the cooked and the raw, but rather the colonial soldier of empire and the monster beyond this very same empire. Thus, Simon Bolívar (1783-1830) celebrated Aguirre by proclaiming the latter's letter to the king the first revolutionary declaration of independence in Latin America.[71] Thomas De Quincey (1785-1859), in his ironic tone, celebrated Erauso as the end of the romance genre and, more generally, of any female fiction:

> The reader is to remember that this is no romance, or at least no fiction, that he is reading; and it is proper to remind the reader of real romances in Ariosto or our own Spenser that such martial ladies as the *Marfisa* or *Bradamant* of the first, and *Britomart* of the other, were really not the Improbabilities that modern society imagines. Many a stout man, as you will soon see, found that Kate, with a sabre in hand, and well mounted, was no romance at all, but far too serious a fact. (103)

Erauso

In Erauso's case, there was a network of family members, friends, and acquaintances that permited her travel throughout Latin America in Mexico, Peru, Chile, Argentina, and Colombia. This network was founded in their common bond as "vizcaynos." In her autobiography, published as *La historia de la monja alférez* (*The Lieutenant Nun*), she explains that when she left San Sebastian, she found her first employment with Juan de Idiaquez, king's secretary, and friend of her father (12). When she decided to embark for the Indies, she met the galleon owner Miguel de Echarreta, "from my home country" (13), and captain Esteban Eguiño, "my uncle, second cousin of my mother" (13).[72] In the vice-royalty of Peru, she found her first job with Juan de Urquiza from Trujillo. Later, Erauso managed to escape her first arrest in the following way:

> The sheriff took me personally to jail, as his deputies took care of the others, and he asked me who I was and where from, and as he heard that I was Basque, told me in Basque to loosen the belt from which he carried me when we walked by the main church and to take refuge there. (17)[73]

---

[71] "Peru de La Croix tells, in his "Diary of Bucaramanga," that in a certain occasion the Liberator Simón Bolívar refered the story of Lope de Aguirre and his death, choosing the passages and traits that were more interesting and heroic" (López 114).

[72] "natural de mi tierra;" "tío mío, primo hermano de mi madre."

[73] "Llevandome el propio Corregidor a la carcel, que los ministros se ocupaban de los otros, ibame preguntando quien era y de donde, y oido que Vizcaino, me dijo en vascuence que al pasar por la iglesa mayor le soltase la pretina, por donde me llevaba asido y me acogiese."

She met her brother Miguel de Erauso, whom did not know s/he was his sister. He assumed s/he was part of his family and helped her out in several situations, including one in which she was sentenced to death. The intimacy between both is even marked linguistically in the text. When she was arrested for a murder she committed as a result of gambling disputes, her brother secured her escape in a language her enemies did not understand: "My brother came then and told me to try to save my life" (21).[74]

Even when s/he was wrongly accused of another murder, and put to torture to confess, s/he was aware of the importance of her/his origin and status: "I denied to have any knowledge of that case; then [the sheriff] ordered me to strip naked and to place me on the rack. A delegate came and argued that I was Basque and, given my privileged status [nobility by birth], there was no legal ground to torture me" (29).[75] When she was arrested again for another murder and was about to be hung, in the last moment, she was saved by another "vizcaino:"

> As I was about to be hung, a postman from the city of La Plata came in running, dispatched by the secretary, and with orders from president, don Diego of Portugal, at the request of Martin de Mendiola, Basque, who knew about the predicament I was in, and handed a document to the sheriff, issued in front of a notary, which ordered the Court to stop the execution and to send the prisoner and the proceedings to the Royal Audience. (31-2)[76]

The references to the "vizcaino" or Basque network are endless in the text. Yet, when she returned to Spain, she traveled as far as Pamplona (46), but never returned to her home province and city, Guipuzcoa and San Sebastian. The only family members she met, after she became publically known to be a woman and received permission of the king and the Pope to live as a man, resided in Cadiz; they were soldiers located in that city.

---

[74] "Entro en esto mi hermano, y dijome en vascuence que procurase salvar la vida"

[75] "Yo negue totalmente saber del caso: luego paso a mandarme desnudar y pone en el potro: entro un procurado, alegando ser yo vizcayno y no haber lugar, por tanto, a darme tormento, por razon de privilegio"

[76] "Estando en esto entro corriendo un posta de la ciudad de la Plata, despachado por el secretario, por mandato del presidente, don Diego de Portugal, a instancia de Martin de Mendiola, Vizcaino, que supo el pleito en que yo estaba, y entrego en su mano al corregido un pliego, ante un escribano, en que le mandaba la Audencia suspender la ejecucion de justicia y remitir el preso y los autos a la Real Audiencia"

129

One can only conclude that she was also passing as Basque, not only as man. Her Basque origin was the other main difference that allowed her to travel and to survive in the Americas. In that respect, she is a monster, a freak, who shows the limits of the monarchy, not only because of her gender difference, but also because of her geopolitical difference—a Basque difference she also performs tactically, when needed, in order to continue her adventure. In this sense, and in her singularity, she shows the potential limits of the monarchy when faced with a Basque difference, which is performed in the colonial field as one that the Spanish empire cannot control and, rather, is challenged by.

3. Atlantic Enlightenment (Larramendi, Munibe, Lyrical Poetry, Etxeberri)

The Basque Enlightenment is a moment that must be thought anew, as most critical tools derived from the historiography of the European Enlightenment cannot be directly applied to the Basque Country. At first sight, it would appear that the origins of Basque nationalism could be traced back to the Enlightenment. One of the central intellectuals of this moment, Manuel Larramendi, in his *Sobre los fueros de Guipuzcoa (On the fueros of Guipuzcoa;* 1756-58), puts these words in the mouth of his alter ego, Puztaburu:

> What reason is there for the Basque nation, the early inhabitant of Spain… this privileged nation of most noble origin, not to be a separate nation, nation in its own, a nation exempted and independent from others? […] The project of The United Provinces of the Pyrenees is, without a doubt, wonderful and perfect. This republic will become famous with its aristocratic or democratic government, as it is more suitable, borrowing from the ancient republics all that made them renowned and famous in the world and from the modern ones everything that is convenient for its longevity and survival. (58-9)[77]

---

[77] "¿Qué razón hay para que la nación vascongada, la primitiva pobladora de España... esta nación privilegiada y del más noble origen, no sea nación aparte, nación de por sí, nación exenta e independiente de las demás?.... El proyecto de las Provincias unidas del Pirineo es sin duda magnífico y especioso. República que se hará famosa con su gobierno aristocrático o democrático, como mejor pareciere, tomando de las repúblicas antiguas todo lo que las hizo célebres y ruidosas en el mundo, y de las modernas todo lo que es conveniente para su duración y subsistencia."

Similarly, the founders of the enlightened *The Royal Basque Society of Friends of the Country*, which served as a model for the development of similar enlightened societies throughout Spain in the 18th century, contemplated in their inaugural essay of 1766 a "Pais Bascongado" (Real Sociedad 2, 31, 104) as well as the promotion of the Basque language ("Diccionario del Bascuence en castellano;" Real Sociedad 105-7) in their bylaws. Finally, and in the case of the French Basque Country, Dominique Joseph Garat, senator and "count of Empire" under Napoleon, suggested to the latter to establish an independent Basque Country as a buffer zone between Spain and France: an area to control any invasion from the south (Bazán 362). A putative, enlightened Basque nationalism would force historians to redraw the map of the 19th century, especially in Spain.

Yet, the period that extends from the end of the Thirty Year War and the treaty of Westphalia (1648)—when Spain lost its hegemony in Europe and the Atlantic—to the Napoleonic invasion of Spain and Europe (1808-14) cannot be defined in either nationalist or anti-nationalist terms. It is marked, not by nationalist unrest, but by the increasing economic decadence of the Spanish empire as well as of the Basque Country on both sides of the Pyrenees. Increasing unrest among peasants, taxations increases, and the consolidation of land ownership in the hands of an oligarchic elite, mostly formed by the nobility, define this history. The French Revolution (1789) is simply one of the forms in which social unrest was expressed throughout Europe and, with the North American revolution (1776), across the Atlantic.

In the Basque Country, the economic and political disintegration of the Spanish crown gave rise to political and economic tensions that were framed are dealt with, not within a nationalist framework, but rather within the politics generated by an Atlantic economy and culture. The Basque economy was eminently Atlantic until 1648: the fact that the Basque customhouses were not located on the coast but inland, on its southern border with Spain (Burgos, etc.), framed most taxation problems in an Atlantic context. Even in the French Basque Country, the Treaty of Utrecht of 1713, which ended the War of Spanish Succession, dealt a serious blow to the seaborne economy of Labourd, which lost fishing grounds in North America. Therefore, the Atlantic expansion that defined the Basque Country since 1492 came to an end with the Napoleonic invasion of 1808-14. This Atlantic expansion and later contraction defined the Basque Country and its difference since 1492.

As Emiliano Fernández de Pinedo explains in his summary of popular uprisings in Europe during the 1600s and 1700s, the popular rebellions that occured in the Basque Country against the rulings classes and the monarchy were not specifically Basque but European; their origins were not nationalist or anti-nationalist, but anti-absolutist. Furthermore, Fernández de Pinedo also recounts several attempts led by the Spanish nobility to seek independence for different regions of Spain, including areas lacking a previous political identity in the Castilian kingdom, such as Andalusia. Therefore, even independentist political uprisings and projects did not yield a nationalist formation in this period:

> The salt revolt in Biscay [1631-34] is one of many that shook up western Europe with the juncture changes. In the Iberian Peninsula, it was preceded by the sacaroses [sugar revolts] in Oporto (1628) and in Santarém (1629), the two of them of clear anti-tax bent. They were the first warnings of a profound unrest that would manifest in the Hispanic monarchy in the decade of the sixteen forties and which would reach its zenith with the rebellion of Catalonia and Portugal [1640], without forgetting the *independence* efforts in Aragon with the Duke of Ijar and in Andalusia with the Duke of Medinasidonia [...] The characteristics of the Biscayan uprising were similar to those that took place around the same time in France. The main cause, or at the least the most apparent, was the new taxes (75-6, my emphasis).[78]

Popular uprisings continued in the 18th century (1718, 1766) and became known as *matxinadak* (from the name of Saint Martin, patron of foundry workers). As the Spanish Basque Country's seaborne commerce-industry and inland customhouses proved, the Basque economy was eminently Atlantic. When the Spanish monarchy began to lose its Atlantic hegemony in the late 17th century, Spanish-Basque writers and ideologues sought to solve this economic decline in an Atlantic framework. After

---

[78] "El motín de la sal de Vizcaya [1631-34] es uno de los tantos que sacudieron al occidente europeo con el cambio de coyuntura. En la Península Ibérica había sido precedido por el de las sacarosas en Oporto (1628) y el de Santarém (1629), uno y otro de claro carácter antifiscal. Fueron el primer anuncio del profundo malestar que iba a manifestarse en la monarquía hispana en la década de los cuarenta y que alcanzará su cenit en la rebelión de Cataluña y Portugal, sin olvidar los intentos de *independencia* de Aragón con el duque de Ijar y el de Andalucía con el duque de Medinasidonia [...] Las características del levantamiento vizcaíno son semejantes a las que tuvieron lugar por la misma época en Francia. La principal causa, al menos la más aparente, fueron los nuevos impuestos."

Felipe V (1683-1746) inherited the Spanish crown (1700), most Basque industry lost favor with the monarchy; foundries and shipbuilders experienced a severe economic crisis; the industrial economy of the Basque Country was seriously compromised.

Yet, at the same time, Basque merchants began a new form of commerce in the 18th century to counteract the industrial decline: colonial trade. Several noble men and merchants, such as Francisco de Munibe e Idiáquez, Count of Peñaflorida and father of the central figure of the Basque Enlightenment, Xavier María de Munibe e Idiáquez, founded The Royal Guipuzcoan Company of Caracas in 1728 in order to counteract the *de facto* illegal monopoly held by Dutch companies over the trade of cocoa and tobacco in Venezuela and Brazil. This commercial initiative furthered the political and economic power of the Basque elite and shaped the Basque Enlightenment to its core as a colonial, Atlantic phenomenon.

By 1794, when the French invasion of Guipuzcoa triggered the dismantling of the enlightened organization founded by the count of Peñaflorida—The Royal Basque Society of Friends of the Country—the majority of members of the society were located in the Americas, not in the Basque Country.[79] If Caracas became the initial point of dissemination for enlightened and independentist culture at the end of the 18th century in Latin America, it is partly due to the enlightened ideas brought by the Basque merchants along its exploitative, monopolistic commerce, which served as target for early uprisings against Spanish colonialism (Astigarraga 67-69; Basterra). When finally The Royal Guipuzcoan Company of Caracas was dissolved in 1785, after repeated local protests and rebellions against the Company's price-gouging practices, the owners moved their monopolistic enterprise to the Philippines and founded The Royal Company of the Philippines in the 19th century.

Not only the origins but also the interests and projects of the founders of The Royal Basque Society of Friends of the Country, also known as the *Caballeritos of Azkoitia*,[80] were Atlantic and colonial. As Jesús Astigarraga demonstrates, the enlightened organization sought industrial solutions to the agricultural crisis in the Basque Country following similar trends in Europe (23-76). Their interest in the French Enlightenment as

---

[79] They were 868 in Madrid, Seville, Cadiz, Mexico, "toda America" and the Philipines in in 1810 (Ortiz de Urbina Montoya, 43).

[80] "Caballerito" stands for the diminutive of *caballero*, meaning "knight, lord, or nobleman." The diminutive here has more likely a dismissive or pejorative value.

well as in the new agricultural technology developed in northern Europe iwass Atlantic in spirit and configured the model that they transmitted to the rest of the enlightened *Royal Societies* in Spain. It is not a coincidence that Swedish and German scientists, brought to the Basque Country by the *Caballeritos*, yielded industrial and scientific discoveries such as platinum and tungsten. Although this fact remains to be studied, there is enough evidence that points to the fact that the colonial activity and discourse of the Company of Caracas not only created the economic basis for the financing of the Royal Societies of Friends, but also shaped the way in which the latter organized their knowledge and discourse, so that ultimately the Basque and Spanish enlightenment must be reconsidered a colonial effect or result (Gabilondo "The Atlantic-Iberian Enlightenment"). In short, the Basque enlightenment is, historically speaking, an Atlantic reaction to an Atlantic problem.

The enlightenment was also the period in which the centralizing crown took active part in repressing non-state languages such as Basque. Although the normative became extensive, it is worth mentioning the two that had the most far-reaching effects. In 1766, the Count of Arana enacted legislation prohibiting the publication of books in Basque. In 1768, the teaching of Basque was banned in elementary schools (Madariaga Orbeaga 121, 240-1).

Larramendi

Manuel Larramendi (1690-1766) is known as an apologist of the Basque language as well as an enlightened linguist who published the first grammar (*The Vanquished Impossible*, 1729) and comprehensive dictionary (*Trilingual Dictionary*, 1745) of the Basque language; that is, he organized the language and its elements following the classificatory, epistemological thrust of the Enlightenment (Foucault, *The Order*). Yet, there is still another line of enlightened inquiry that Larramendi pursued in his later years. In his latest work, *Corografía de Guipúzcoa* (*Chorography of Guipuzcoa*, 1754), next to a political defense of Guipuzcoa, Larramendi also elaborated a new enlightened discourse on the social and economic elements that formed and defined the province of Guipuzcoa. This enlightened, descriptive discourse registered the economic crisis of the province and moved away from the apologist discourse and its generalizing goals.

In Larramendi's discourse, the villages and the *ferrerías* (foundries) take center place, along other forms of industry (shipyards, anchor manufacturers, arm factories, etc.). Given the pastoral and nationalist turn that literature will take in the 19th century, it is important to analyze Larramendi's enlightened, descriptive discourse in order to understand the specific history that leads to nationalism in the 19th century.

Larramendi's *Chorography of Guipuzcoa* represents a defense of a very specific location, Guipuzcoa, against the changes that the absolutist monarchy of the Bourbon dynasty brought to Spain with Felipe V in 1700. Larramendi was acquainted with the royal family and court due to the fact that he had been the personal confessor of Mariana of Nuremberg, widow of Charles II, during 1730-34, in her exile in Bayonne. Felipe V had banished her from court. Larramendi's view of the Spanish monarchy must have been influenced to a certain extent by her opinions.

When Larramendi approaches Guipuzcoa, he does so in order to differentiate it from the foreign (Spanish and otherwise) perception that all Basques are "vizcainos:" "The purpose of this work is to show the widespread confusion with which people speak about these provinces of the Basque language [...] the stupidity of most Castilians when in writing and speech identify all Basques as Biscayans [...] and Aragonese and Valencians who call Basques Navarrans" (3).[81] Larramendi also cites Murillo Velarde's *Historic Geography* to explain that similar stereotyping takes place also in learnt works. In short, his is an attempt to differentiate and make concrete the historical reality of his province. Larramendi's defense relies on Guipuzcoa's history and characteristics (economic, social, etc.). There is no essence or identity that defines Guipuzcoa in Larramendi's work. There is no one idealized location, feature, or historical foundation that defines the core or identity of Guipuzcoa, which then could be expanded to the rest of the Basque Country.

Larramendi's text, which follows the descriptive protocols of the enlightened discourse, lists different features that help situate and grasp Guipuzcoa in its diversity. Because of the attention given to history and economics, realities such as the countryside and the farmstead—the object of any Basque pastoralizing, nationalist discourse—are secondary in Larramendi's work. The village and the local industries, as well as their economic decline, concern mainly Larramendi, since the agricultural farmstead was not central to Guipuzcoa's economy in the 18th century. In the geographic section entitled "Formas de las caserias y pueblos de

---

[81] "El motivo de esta obra es ver la grandisima confusion con que se habla y escribe de estas provincias del vascuence [...] la boberia del comun de los castellanos cuando en lo hablado y en lo escrito entienden a todos los vascongados con nombre de vizcainos... y de aragoneses y valencianos, que llaman navarros a los vascongados."

Guipuzcoa" ("Different Forms of Farmsteads and Villages in Gipuzcoa" 81-7), these economic and social units are described as part of the same continuum, whereby the farmstead is given a shorter treatment than the village. Furthermore, when Larramendi approaches, not the physical aspect of Guipuzcoa, but its economic units and their functions, the agricultural farmstead (*casería*) comes second to the industrial farmsteads centered on foundries (*herrerías*): "The large and small foundries are the ones that have, since time immemorial, sustained the farmsteads of Guipuzcoa and a major part of its neighbors and inhabitants [...] Another type of farmstead is the *caserías* [farmsteads properly devoted to agriculture]" (197-98).[82]

Furthermore, when approaching the farmstead, Larramendi does not note any pastoral, essentializing characteristic defining Basqueness or Guipuzcoanness, but rather a rural decline, economic and social, prompted precisely by the new habits and uses brought by modernity, which also refrain Guipuzcoans from going outside the province to seek education. As he laments,

> We know that in the past with these very same farmsteads, these individuals had enough to keep their houses with decency and give their children an outstanding education by sending them to universities and colleges, which they attended in great numbers. However, today few can be seen at either universities or colleges, who can be support themselves with help from their parents. What is the reason except that [these individuals] lived in their ancestral homes, managed their stocks and farmstead by themselves, were satisfied with little, dressed without sophistication, abhorred sartorial fashion, fancy refreshments and their increasing subtleties? And the same was true for those who lived in villages. They raised their children in a harsh way and without spoiling them [...] Nowadays, the opposite takes place: they disdain living in their ancestral homes and deride managing their foundries and other farmsteads; do not settle for little and live with all kinds of fashions and means [...] they raise their children with spoil; dress them like princes, satisfy all their demands [...] Because of these foolishness the revenue of their farmsteads is no longer sufficient: taxes here and there; debts with the merchant, in the store,

---

[82] "Las herrerías grandes y pequeñas han sido las que de tiempos antiguos principalmente han mantenido las haciendas de Guipuzcoa y mucha parte de sus vecinos y moradores [...] Otra especie de haciendas son las caserias."

with the transporters, butchers, and other stores. It is a very good way indeed to keep their children in universities and colleges. (198-99)[83]

Therefore, Larramendi notes the new influence of European modernity in the habits and uses of the Guipuzcoans. However, this is also the limit of Larramendi's analysis and criticism. He was not able to criticize politically the increasing oligarchic elitism that defined the Guipuzcoan social structure and sank most of the peasantry into poverty and destitution.

Forty eight years later, in his *Peru Abarka* (*Peter Espadrille*, 1802), Juan Antonio Mogel naturalized and essentialized the farmstead as the self-sufficient and sole possibility for a Basque imaginary that no longer was Guipuzcoan or Alavan, but Basque and rural. The new self-sustained universe portrayed by Mogel, the farmstead, was socially, economically, educationally and linguistically self-sufficient, and its subject became the rural patriarchal farmer, which then nationalism retook throughout the 20th century as the core of its imaginary. Yet, Larramendi, from within an enlightened discourse, did not, could not, essentialize such a situation. As far as he criticized the new modern habits of Guipuzcoan society, he did create a situated anti-modern discourse, which, nevertheless, remained enlightened and modern in its anti-modernity. Ultimately, Larramendi proposed a modern resistance to a modernity imposed by the institutions of the despotic, enlightened monarchy originating in France (and Spain).

---

[83] "Sabemos que antes con estas mismas haciendas tenian los particulares bastante para mantener sus casas con decencia y dar una gran educacion a sus hijos, enviandolos a las universidades y colegios mayores, donde concurrian en grande numero; y hoy se ven muy pocos, asi en los colegios como en las universidades, que puedan mantenerse a cuenta y con asistencia de sus padres. ¿En que ha de consistir sino en que, viviendo por lo comun en sus casas solares, gobernaban por si sus haciendas, se contentaban con poco, se vestian sin delicadez, aborrecian las modas de galas y vestidos, de refrescos y sus multiplicadas diferencias? Y lo mismo sucedia a los que vivian en los pueblos. Criaban a sus hijos duramente y sin melindres.... Hoy sucede todo lo contrario: se desdeñan de vivir en sus solares y de gobernar por si sus herrerias y demas haciendas: no se contentan con poco; se visten de todas modas y modos [...] crian a sus hijos con melindres, vistenlos como principitos, cumplenles todas sus mañas [...] Para estas locuras no basta la hacienda: censos aquí, censos alli: deudas en el mercader, en la tienda, en los arrieros, carnicerias y otros puestos. Buen modo por cierto para mantener los hijos en los colegios y universidades."

Munibe

Francisco Xavier María Munibe (1723-1785), 8th count of Peñaflorida, and son of the founder of The Royal Guipuzcoan Company of Caracas, lived in Azkoitia and, after studying in Bordeaux, began informal gatherings with two of his friends, Manuel Ignacio Altuna and José María de Eguía, 3rd marquis of Narros. They became known as the *Caballeritos of Azkoitia* (The Little Noblemen of Azkoitia) and were the nucleus and impetus for the organization of The Royal Basque Society of Friends of the Country in 1765, following similar models already existing in England and France. Felix María Samaniego was Munibe's nephew and a founding member of the Royal Basque Society. This Basque organization served to foster the formation of other Royal Societies throughout the Spanish empire with the main objective of disseminating scientific, industrial, agricultural, and literary knowledge during the rule of the enlightened Spanish monarch, Carlos III (1759-1788). The Basque Organization also founded the Royal Seminary of Bergara in 1770, where education and scientific research were promoted even to creole children from across the Atlantic.

Unlike previous generations of *letrados* (scribes) and men of culture on the Spanish side, the *Caballeritos* studied in France (Bordeaux and Paris). Moreover, Samaniego and Eguía were processed by the Inquisition. In turn, Altuna, although educated in Madrid, met Rousseau in Venice and became good friends, to the point that Rousseau entertained the fantasy of moving to Azkoitia: "[W]e became so intimate that we planned to spend our lives together. I was to go to Ascoytia, after some years, and live with him on his estate" (*Confessions* 308). Thus, the Caballeritos knew from their own educational experience that the Spanish university system, where science was barely taught, was anachronistically anchored in the Renaissance.

Munibe translated François-André Danican Philidor's *The Blacksmith Marshal* (1761) into Spanish and wrote two original pieces where the enlightened tensions between subaltern and oligarchic classes were explored: *Gabon sariak* (*Christmas Carol*, 1762) and *El borracho burlado* (*The Tricked Drunkard*, 1764). The first work is a musical piece and is integrally in Basque; the second and third are bilingual.

It is important to situate these theater plays in the context of the popular revolts against the tax and food-price hikes (bread, corn, etc.) provoked by the speculation of merchants, mainly situated in San Sebastian, but also property owners and rural oligarchs such as Munibe who were scattered throughout the province. These revolts, known as *matxinada*-s, took place all over the Basque Country in the 17ᵗʰ and 18ᵗʰ centuries. Yet, one of the most virulent ones broke out in Azpeitia and Azkoitia in 1766. The same year, and in Madrid, another important revolt known as the "Esquilache Mutiny" also took place. Given that the people of Azkoitia and Azpeitia were mostly Basque monolingual speakers and most of the cultural activities undertaken by the Basque elite were in Spanish or French at that point, it is important to understand the reasons why Munibe wrote theater in Basque and Spanish, for it shows the ideological shape and limits of the enlightened project in the Basque Country.

Munibe's *Christmas Carol* follows traditional rhythms and even rhetorical devices such as bringing attention to the singer's physical exhaustion as an excuse to end the song and the carol. It is presented as a work produced by a certain "Luis" of *Miserikordia Etxea* or the orphanage. It is reasonable to assume that it was written so that children and youth performed it. Thus, it falls within the category of works produced by the elite for charitable purposes, which ultimately reinforced the existing social division. In these works, the author showed full knowledge and control of popular culture and poetry. The fact that the carol was meant to be performed in church, following the popular religious performances that the church fostered as means to secure popular worship, shows that Munibe's work falls within social categories and practices that already existed. As we will see, Barrutia's Christmas carol is also similar in this respect.

Yet, the framing of the carol is important linguistically speaking. Munibe resorts to a vocabulary that is not popular or vernacular in order to explain the characteristics of his work. For example, he explains that the references to the shepherds in the carol are also a "metaphor" to speak of God as the supreme shepherd. Since the explanations must be given in Basque, the author uses a neologism for the word 'metaphor,' which, nevertheless, he has to explain due to the coinage's novelty. He writes: "artzaiaren egokikilde edo metafora" (16). The neologism "egokikilde" is borrowed from Larramendi's *Trilingual Dictionary* (1745), where it appears written as "egoquilquida" (II, 87). There are few more terms that come from the same dictionary. In short, even when the purpose of the carol is to control subaltern classes and to legitimate the social order, there is a hybrid moment of instability: the writer has to contaminate his own elite discourse (Spanish or French, with terminology such as "metaphor") and turn it into a subaltern discourse (Basque, with neologisms).

Moreover, if the author of the carol is actually Munibe and he borrowed from Larramendi, we have the beginning of a coherent enlightened discourse in Basque. If we consider that one of Larramendi's canonical references is Axular, here "Basque enlightenment" is a linguistic as well as geopolitical term. It has not been determined if Larramendi and Munibe met and had an ongoing dialogue. Given their geographic proximity, it is very likely: they lived in adjunct towns and Larramendi died in 1766 when Munibe was 43 years old. We only know that Munibe read some of Larramendi's works.

Although *A Christmas Carol* contains very few terms of social contamination, Munibe's next work, shows a more elaborate and interesting case of linguistic and social hybridity. In his *The Tricked Drunkard*, the recited parts are in Spanish and the sung parts are in Basque; the ratio is probably three quarters of the text in Spanish and one quarter in Basque. This play is not intended for the people, but for the elite circle of *Caballeritos* and other "notable" people. In short, this is an enlightened work for the legitimation of the enlightened elite, in the form of "pleasure" or "entertainment." Munibe explains the organization of languages in the introduction. He adds two notes or caveats to his work:

> The first note is directed to those who will notice the mixture of Basque and Spanish in the play, and might conclude that it is more normal for the entire work to be solely in either language. I say, thus, my first idea was to have *this entire opera in Basque*: but then the difficulty of choosing the dialect I would use to write it failed me. If I were to make use of the dialect of Azkoitia, it would have been of little enjoyment for the rest of the Country all the way to the border with France, given the concern they show against the Basque or dialed of Goiherri [region where Azkoitia is situated]; and if I wanted to use the dialect of Tolosa, Hernani, San Sebastian, etc., I had to expose the actors to ridicule, as it would be difficult for all of them to imitate the used dialect correctly. Because of this reason, thus, I had to content myself to limiting Basque to the sung parts, and making all the acted parts in Spanish. (9, my emphasis)[84]

---

[84] "La primera se dirige a aquellos que notarán la mezcla que se hace del vascuence y castellano, pareciéndoles más regular el que todo fuese en uno de los dos idiomas. Digo, pues, que *mi primera idea fue de que toda esta ópera fuese en vascuence*: pero luego me faltó la dificultad del dialecto de que me había de servir en ella. Si me valía del de Azcoytia, hubiera sido poco grato a todo el resto del País hasta la frontera de Francia, por la preocupación que tienen contra el vascuence o dialecto de Goi-erri; y, si quería usar del dialecto de Tolosa, Hernani, San Sebastián, etc., exponía a los actores a hacerse ridículos; pues sería difícil que todos pudiesen imitarle bien. Por esta razón, pues, me

The opera is about a low-class husband, Chantón Garrote, who is a drunkard. The butlers and assistants (*pajes*) of a nobleman, the Marquis of Trapisonda, decide to pull a prank on Garrote and teach him a lesson about morality: "a good husband does not drink." Therefore, it is natural that the opera, like the Christmas carol, is meant to be performed in Basque. The Marquis of Trapisonda is not present in the play and, therefore, the true oligarchic voice is not subject to language contamination. Munibe does not mention the fact that the audience, an enlightened oligarchic class, might not understand the play or cannot perform it, thus, assuming that the audience is knowledgeable about *euskara*. Although the printed version adds a translation of the passages in Basque, it is only in order permit the printed version to circulate outside the province of Guipuzcoa. Munibe clearly states that, when he wrote it, he did not intend to publish it, and therefore, the help of a translation for the Basque parts was not an issue: "I will not stop repeating what I said in the other opera in order to prove that it was never my intention to print this one or the other; for the extensive content in Basque is proof of it. It would amount to presenting the public with a piece that is not acceptable and this fact is not expected in any author" (9).[85] Here "public" and "author" are not the close circle of enlightened Basques for which the play was intended in the first place. Therefore, the original audience, the Marquis' friends, could understand the play.[86] Yet, the question remains why the entire opera or theater work was not written in Spanish, since that was the cultural language of the audience (next to French, Latin, and English).

In short, the question is why expose the audience to such a moment of social contamination by which the lower classes are given a Basque voice when they sing. The very same characters, when reciting, speak in Spanish. One can conclude that a text fully rendered in Spanish is not realistic and does not deliver a convincing effect of representing the other: the lower classes whose native language is Basque. The inclusion of Basque is necessary for the enlightened discourse to be truly realistic

---

hube de contentar con reservar el vascuence para lo cantado, haciendo que todo lo representado fuese en castellano."

[85] "No me detengo en repetir lo que dije en la otra ópera para probar de que nunca fue mi intención el imprimir ni ésta ni aquélla; pues lo mucho que lleva de vascuence ésta, es una prueba evidente de ello, porque sería presentar al público una pieza poco recomendable, y esto no es regular en ningún autor."

[86] The case of Felix María Samaniego, one of the performers from an area, Álava, in which Basque was still probably spoken in the mid 18th century, remains an issue to be solved.

and, thus, enlightened. In short, these moments of linguistic contamination point to the true historical discourse of the Basque Enlightenment where social tensions were represented in the work of art not as simple objects of contemplation but rather as languages in conflict: the cultural language, Spanish, and the subaltern language, Basque.[87]

However, there is a very interesting moment in which, from within the Basque language, Munibe guarantees that even the lowest classes understand the language of trade. He is referring in Basque to the Atlantic trade, which secured his own oligarchic position, i.e. the monopolistic commercial trade from which his father benefited with the Royal Guipuzcoan Company of Caracas. It is important to note that, although it begins in verse form, the following replies are not sung but recited, as prose or dialogue, against the original plan of the author:

La otra tendera *(a Txanton)*	**The other seller** to Txanton:
Nagusi jauna, berorrek estrenatu bear	Your lordship, you will be the first one to buy
nau. Ona tabako ederra piparako, nai	From me. Here he has good pipe tobacco;
badu Habanako hoja lejitimo-lejitimoa;	Leaves from Havana, completely legitimate
ta ala propio Holandako pikatua, ta autsa,	And even shag from Holland, and snuff,
berriz, naiz Habanakoa, ta naiz hoja Virginiakoa,	From Havana, and even Virginia leave
a escoge.	A escoge [in Spanish, to choose from]
Txanton	**Txanton:**
Brasillik ez dezu?	Do you have [tobacco from] Brazil?
...	
Don Pedro	**Don Pedro** [one of the helpers to the Marquis]:
Emakumea, ez dago emen guk bear degunerako	Woman, there is not here, for what we need,
gauza dan lienzorik: fiñagoak bear ginduzke.	Fabric that is fit; we would need more refined ones.
La primera tendera	**The first seller:**
Jauna, fiña bear badu, ez du orren mesedeak	If his lordship needs fine fabric, he will not find

---

[87] Agamben's *State of Exception* explains well the importance of the carnival/saturnalia and the charivari in the way in which the law is subverted and suspended (71-73).

| Donostia-Baionetan aurkituko, nik dudan | In San Sebastian or Bayonne, a bet-ter and more |
| baño Holanda fiñ-fiñ preziatuago-rik. (50-51) | Refined Hollandaise than I have. |

The fact that even the subaltern classes have developed, in the text, a commercial language in Basque, which recognizes the signs and commodities that signify class status, guarantees that the lower classes are part of the same enlightened, oligarchic project and subjection. At this point, Munibe even drops the pretense of differentiating between the recited parts in Spanish and the sung parts in Basque. Here, the sung part reverts to recited Basque. At this moment of clear social re-organization and re-cognition, the lower classes regain the space of the recited discourse. By turning this spoken part on trade into Basque, they also partake of the Basque enlightened discourse: a discourse in which there is a recognition of both the commercial trade that structures it socially and the language that subverts that order.

Few years after the two plays were written, in 1766, a *matxinada* or revolt erupted in Azkoitia due to the price increase of wheat. The revolt spread to Azpeitia and other parts of Guipuzcao and Biscay. It was directed to the *jauntxos* or nobles such as Munibe who were suspected of hoarding and moving the grain around in order to sell it to inflated prices. At this point, the discursive containment seen in the two plays became untenable. Munibe, the Count of Peñaflorida, and his peer the Marquis of Narros fled to San Sebastian and returned with a militia army led by the mayor of the city in order to squelch the revolt. At that time, the *jauntxos*, against the Jesuits, demanded harsh punishments. There no executions but 60 leaders were sent to prison (Larrea 238-39). The tensions between the streets of Azkoitia, its palaces, and Caracas defined the real space of the enlightenment and its ultimately failure. The discursive containment of the subaltern and colonial subjects performed in the theater plays (or operas) showed its limit and ultimate truth in the violent revolts that eventually erupted on the streets. Thus, the Enlightenment can be defined as a failed attempt to contain by discursive inclusion the local subaltern and colonial subjects.[88]

---

[88] A more extended analysis would prove that this containment structured not only the plays but also the essays Munibe and its society wrote (Gabilondo, "The Atlantic-Iberian Enlightenmen").

The tension between Jesuits and the enlightened *jauntxos* must also be incorporated in a longer analysis.

Antonio Zabala, in his history of the *bertsolaritza* or verse improvisation, makes a comment on the final fate of many compositions, such as those of Munibe, in the early 19th century. As he states: "I believe it can be ascertained that the "bertso-papera" [improvised oral poetry transcribed and printed] was initiated by the cult elite of the Country, but the people saw it, they liked the method, and ended up assimilating it to the point of creating the most interesting print literary phenomenon in Basque language" (34).[89] Yet, the introduction to Munibe's operatic work gives another interesting moment of social conflict and contamination that he ultimately dismisses. He refers to the "bait of love" that usually attracts theater audiences and captures their interest. Instead, he chooses to refrain from the issue of "love affairs" because of the status of the people who are performing the play: "[the theater work or opera] does not have the interest that captures normally the audience, as it is missing the bait of love, an overused resort in theaters to attract and capture the attention of everybody [...] if I did not mix any amorous matter, it was because of the circumstances of the people who were in charge of representing it" (8).[90] Although most *Caballeritos* were anti-clerical or had enlightened ideas about the church and the Catholic religion, the topic of sexuality and the irrational drive of Eros was not a topic they dared touch. This was another area of contamination where the socially arranged and orchestrated family unions, always on the verge of endogamy, could be challenged and contested by the drive of sexuality and desire. Here, unlike in the representation of lower classes in Basque, the enlightened discourse had not a way to isolate the elements that could threaten that very same oligarchic order and, therefore, it omitted such elements. It was also the case of Félix María Samaniego.

Samaniego

Felix Maria Samaniego (1745-1801) was the nephew of Munibe and one of the richest oligarchs in Alava. The Inquisition prosecuted him twice on account of his writings and opinions. He became the introducer of

---

[89] "Yo creo que se puede asegurar que el "bertso-papera" lo inició el sector culto del País, pero los vio el pueblo, le gusto el método y se lo asimiló hasta formar de él el fenómeno literario impreso más interesante en lengua vasca."

[90] "no tiene aquel interés que empeña comúnmente al auditorio, pues la falta el cebo del amor, agente tan socorrido en los teatros para atraer y fijar la atención de todos… si no he mezclado nada de amores, ha sido por las circunstancias de las personas que estaban destinadas para su representación"

the fable as literary genre in Spain as well as its most accomplished practitioner, next to Tomás de Iriarte. He wrote his fables for the students of the Royal Seminary of Bergara as a way to enlighten them. He was also sent as representative of the province of Alava to Madrid to negotiate and change the laws enacted by Charles III in 1778 and 1783 concerning the curtailment of some commercial rights upheld by the *fueros*. He left for Madrid in 1783 and stayed at the "court" for three years.

During his stay in the capital, Samaniego had access to different intellectual and political circles as well as to many salons and social gatherings (Martín Nogales 57-68). In this milieu, he was celebrated for his loquacious personality and the risqué verses he used to prepare for elite gatherings. Here, unlike in the case of the students of the Royal Seminary of Bergara, the goal was not to enlighten but, rather, to entertain and scandalize high society, his own peers. As a result, he wrote a series of erotic poems that eventually were published by Joaquín López Barbadillo under the title of *Jardín de Venus* (*The Garden of Venus*) in 1921.

Unlike in the case of Munibe and his reduced familial circle of persons, here, Samaniego had the numerous aristocratic elite of Madrid as his public and, thus, did not face the problem of morality or sexuality, rather the opposite. It was a well-established society that sought "entertaining" encounters with different types of others—subaltern others—from the safety of the court. This was not a new enlightened circle, such as the one in Azkoitia, which had yet to establish itself as such. As a result, Samaniego brought, for example, the discourse of the colony, not in order to enlighten the elites about (colonial) subaltern classes, as in the case of Munibe's operas, but in order to reassure the elites in their hegemonic position and safety vis-à-vis any other. Thus, Samaniego had to provide this class with a source of pleasurable, piquant entertainment derived from any form of subaltern difference, such as the colonial.

In his "El país de afloja y aprieta" ("Land of loosening up and tightening up/pushing in"), a young man's ultimate fantasy of plenty is evoked by Samaniego, whereby the protagonist equivocally equates sexual and economic plenty: he enters an exotic (i.e. colonial) country where he can live leisurely as long as he can perform sexually. Although the young man thinks at first that he is in a sexual paradise, he soon finds out that his sexual drive has a limit. He cannot perform as often as required and, thus, desire turns into the nightmare of the law. The poem chastises the young man because he confuses sex and (colonial) economy, desire and law. Ultimately, the poem enforces the idea that only economic wealth is real as it is enforced by the law, whereas sexual excess is simply a fantasy that no enlightened man could or should achieve beyond heteronormative monogamy.

In order to illustrate the difference between economy and sexuality, Samaniego resorts to the specter of the colonial subject: "three big black men of Guinea" (Equatorial Guinea is handed by Portugal to Spain in 1778). The fantasy of the young man is to go to an exotic land in which, as long as he can perform sexually on demand, he is given free lodging, food, and entertainment. The irony is that no man can perform to the sexual expectations of others ("aflojamiento"), and therefore the poor young man is chastised ("aprietar") and, ultimately, exiled from the land. The punishment is colonial sodomy or "aprietar" performed by "three large black men:"

… el gobernador entró al momento	The governor came right the way
y, al ver del joven el aflojamiento,	And seeing the young man's loosening up
dijo en tono furioso:	Said in furious tone:
- ¡Hola!, que aprieten a ese pere- zoso.	I order that this lazy man is tight- ened up
Al punto tres negrazos de Guinea	Right the way, three large black men from Guinea
vinieron, de estatura gigantea,	Came in, and with gigantic height,
y al joven sujetaron,	Held the young man
y uno en pos de otro a fuerza le apretaron	And one after the other tightened him up
por el ojo fruncido,	Through the forced eye
cuyo virgo dejaron destruido.	Whose virgo they left destroyed.
Así pues, desfondado,	In this way, without bottom,
creyéndole bastante castigado	Judging he had been chastised enough
de su presunción vana,	Of his vein presumption,
en la misma mañana,	That very same morning
sacándole al camino,	Taking him out on the road,
le dejaron llorar su desatino,	They left him crying out his er- ror,
sin poderse mover. Allí tirado	Unable to move. There lying
le encontró su criado, (72-3)	His servant found him.

In short, even when the (colonial) limits of the enlightenment are explored, they are ultimately used to enforce social boundaries. Yet, Samaniego was mindful that the limits of the Spanish enlightenment were ultimately colonial. Just as in the case of Munibe, Samaniego also was aware of the colonial anxieties underlying the Spanish and Basque enlightenments in their Atlantic history.

Barrutia

Pedro Ignacio Barrutia (1682-1759), born in Aramaio (Alava), worked as town secretary in Arrasate (Guipuzcoa) between 1710 and 1753. Around 1750, he wrote *Acto para la Nochebuena* (*A Christmas Carol*). Unlike the work of Munibe or Samaniego, Barrutia's was not published in his lifetime, although it is very likely that it was performed.

Considering the leading role town-secretaries played in the popular revolts or *matxinadas* of the 18th century, it is natural that this piece of theater was not written according to the hierarchical, enlightened model used by Munibe. Rather, Barrutia's theater play follows traditional, popular models such as baroque theater, the Christmas carol, and the "teatro de magia" or "theater of magic," which persisted through the 19th century. Next to the older baroque ideology of Christian fatality and resignation, Barrutia summons, in his play, a popular ideology of carnival and paganism in the figure of "Gracioso" (Joker), thus fusing the locations of Bethlehem and Arrasate in the same performance, so that the arrasatear audience is incorporated in the Christian play about the Nativity.

Without any space-time transitions, the play jumps from a recitative by the Virgin Mary to a conversation between three demons, Lucifer, Asmodeus, and Beelzebub. They meet Gracioso in Arrasate. Gracioso recites (and probably sings) a carnivalesque song in which a long list of foods and drinks are mentioned with the opening alliterated line of "Lian, lan bere..." which has no ready meaning in Basque and serves as musical bridge. Beelzebub recognizes Gracioso as one of their own: "He lacks no grace to blame the entire world / ... / he is our lazy, hunting lad" (17).[91] After the three demons decide to beat him, he cries out to his wife (Mari Gabon, literally "Mary Christmas"), whom accuses him of being a drunkard and proceeds to beat him too. The motive of the drunken husband despised by the wife was popular and both Munibe and Barrutia used it.

---

[91] "Mundu guztia kolpatzeko echaio [sic] falta grazia / ... / Auxe dok gure morroe alper kazadorea" (17).

Yet, unlike in the work of Munibe, here there is not an enlightened teaching of morality, following Aristotle rules of dramatic unity, but rather the magic and miraculous transformation of the physical situation of Gracioso. As he encounters the Virgin Mary and Jesus Christ, all the aches produced by the beatings go away (27). Moreover, pagan motives appear, as when Gracioso offers Baby Jesus a falcon paw to protect him from evil eye.[92]

Overall, however, Gracioso proceeds to mock and criticize some of the shepherds' conversions and rapturous trances, ultimately making room for the critique of the people of Arrasate. To Gabriel's description of his trance, induced by his meeting with Baby Jesus, Gracioso replies with mockery and doubt:

Gabriel:
Aren aoko berba dulzea aditu neban puntuan
Sentidu neban argi andibat neure biotz barruan
Arzain ignorantea ninzan biurtu naiz sabio
Ene ustez mundu guztiak eztau zuribat balio
Gracioso:
Parabolok esan franko Gabrieliko gureak
Biar goiseko beste alderuz izulikoxok aizeak
Beistegiko Gabriel kañaberan kaskabel

Lindo mozo despachazeko de vino blanco un pichel

Sekula iñok eztau ikusi onereango konturik
Ezta posible eztaodela ene lagunak ordirik
Ez aldezu dijeridu arrasaldeko salsea

Chakolin orrek turbadu deusu begietako bistea

Gabriel:
As I heard the sweet words from his mouth
I felt a bright light inside my heart.
I was an ignorant shepherd, now I am wise.
To me the whole world is not worth a cent.
Gracioso:
Our Gabriel has said enough parables.
Tomorrow morning the wind will turn him around.
Gabriel from Beistegi is a bell in the reedbed
A handsome young man capable of finishing off a pitcher of white wine.
Nobody has seen ever similar events
It is not possible that my friends are not drunk.
Have you not digested the sauce from this evening?
This wine has blurred your sight

---

[92] "Azkonarraren azamarchoa... begizkorik eztegizun bularchoaren isegi;" (28).

| Sermonadore barri orri egonaizako begira | I am staring at this new preacher |
| Orida buru moz Oñatiko Peru Jainkoen mutila. (22) | He is the son of the dim-witted Peter Jainko from Oñati. |

Unlike in the case of Munibe's theater, Barrutia does not hesitate to mix, in his play, Spanish and Basque as a way to reinforce the polyphonic power of Gracioso's subaltern voice. Here, linguistic and class contamination is sought as a powerful dramatic device of subversion.

This type of representation must have been more widespread and shows that theater, in many of its manifestations, was one of the genres in which the popular contestation of social structures took place, even when it was embedded in hegemonic spaces such as church rituals. As Antonio Zavala states, citing other similar manuscripts of the 18th century, "[T]he carols or "Gabon kantas" is one of our oldest poetic genres. There are some from the 18th century, but most of them remain as manuscript sheets" (34).[93]

If Munibe's theater was structure as an enlightened containment of subaltern classes, Barrutia's play, instead, establishes cultural continuity: his play and subaltern culture contained social and cultural forms, genres, and tropes that shared the same political and contestatory structure of performance. From Barrutia's theater to the popular revolts or *matxinadas*, which served as forms of contestation against a century marked by traditionalization and ruralization, there is only subaltern continuity.

As Urkizu has documented, the end of the 18th century was also the moment in which other three main forms of popular theater appeared in written form: the pastorals, the charivari or *astolasterrak* and the carnival (*Historia* 78-103). Although, etymologically, "pastoral" refers to the shepherds of the adoration of the Nativity, historically speaking, it evolved into the liturgical dramas celebrated mostly in Easter. Basque pastorals, still performed today, are 3- to 10-hour reenactments of Biblical episodes, epic stories, and historical characters. This shift in names from Christmas (pastoral-shepherd representation of the Nativity) to Easters (liturgical drama void of shepherds) makes clear that, similarly to the Christmas carols analyzed above, the pastorals also referred to the religious calendar.

---

[93] "Los villancicos o *Gabon kantas*" es uno de nuestros géneros poéticos más antiguos. Hay alguno del XVIII, pero todos ellos se encuentran en hojas manuscritas."

Only the *astolasterrak* or farces, in which the scandals of a town were aired, and the carnival comedies represented a space and time that escaped the Catholic calendar; they referred to older pagan practices. Furthermore, the fact that the pastorals moved out of the space of the church and were celebrated in the public sphere demonstrates that all this theater lived and evolved at the intersection of the religious and pagan worlds. Theater served as a practice of contestation and expression within a cyclical calendar of seasons. Considering that in both pastorals and Christmas carols the most interesting and subversive characters are the demons, one must conclude that there is a cultural continuation from the pastorals of the Soule to Barrutia's *Christmas Carol* written in the Biscayan dialect in Guipuzcoa—that is, there is a continuity across the Basque Country.

It seems that the liturgical drama or pastoral was present throughout the Basque Country in the Middle Ages and the Renaissance and disappeared in the 17th century from Basque culture, thus being kept only in Soule. Yet, Munibe and Barrutia's theater prove that other forms of the same theater, the Christmas carol, persisted in the southern Basque Country through the 18th century. The fact that Munibe's theater had to address this earlier, popular theater in order to establish a "new enlightened form of representation" shows that the Enlightenment in the Basque Country was a project very much contaminated and subverted by popular practices that it had to contain as the "true" object of its oligarchic culture.

Finally, and given the fact that the Basque Enlightenment's project was ultimately Atlantic in its inception and goals, one can conclude that popular theater was perhaps the space in which the effects of the Enlightenment were represented more clearly: the newly ruralized peasant masses contested and contaminated the enlightened discourse and, by doing so, also criticized its universalism. In short, they showed the Atlantic subaltern base, colonial and rural, that the enlightened project had to contain and repress in order to claim its rational universality.

It remains to study in a comparative way the ways in which the colonial revolts in Caracas, Venezuela, mirrored the *matxinadas* in Azkoitia and elsewhere against which the Enlightenment was deployed. If this were the case, then, we would have to posit an Atlantic Basque Enlightenment as the shared political space of subaltern contestation and elite containment.

Oral Lyrical Poetry

Perhaps the most important form of literary expression in the 18th century, next to theater, was oral lyrical poetry. This literature had older origins, but consolidated as an autonomous, highly stylized, and codified genre in the 18th century. However, this literary genre was collected and printed in the 19th century. Agustin Chaho prepared for the press the first collection of songs of this nature in 1844, but he never published it. Francisque Michel published *The Basque Country: Its Population, Language, Customs, Literature, and Music* in 1857 where he also collected a set of popular songs (263-324). J.D.J. Sallaberry published another important collection in 1870 with the title of *Popular Songs of the Basque Country: Original Lyrics and Music*. Finally, José Manterola published his *Basque Songbook* in 1877 - 1880. Although many collections have been published since, to this day, there is not a comprehensive, critical, historical study of this important cultural discourse and corpus.

This literature, which comprises somewhere between 100 and 300 songs, was published in many instances with its corresponding musical score. Some still survive in contemporary popular memory. Others became popular again in the 1970s and 1980s with folk singers. As a result, this tradition is very much alive in the Basque Country today. Its lyrical force and beauty can only be appreciated when the songs are heard accompanied with music in their original format.[94]

Given that this poetry follows the mythical juxtaposition of natural and human elements already present in ballads and improvisational poetry of the 15th and 16th centuries, it is safe to conclude that this genre is a continuation of different older oral traditions and, in the case of some of the songs, could go back to the 15th century.

For example, the Souletin song known as "Eijerra zira, maitia" ("You are beautiful, my love") captures the lover's invitation through mythical juxtaposition. The force of the song relies on several juxtapositions, which are not logically connected through syntactic connectors; even the verb is dropped in the first two lines in order to accentuate the image of the referent (fern, cow, you):

Mendian eder iratze,	Beautiful the fern on the mountain
Behi ederrak aretxe,	The beautiful cow a calf.
Zü bezalako pollitetarik	From one as beautiful as you
desir nüke bi seme.	I would like to have two sons

---

[94] Benito Lertxundi's records are a good example.

The other element that is present in many lyrical songs as well as in the improvisational poetry of the 15th-16th centuries is the dialogue or response-structure of the verses, whereby the lovers elaborate on their stories:

[Lover 1:] Eijerra zira, maitia	[Lover 1:] You are beautiful, my love
Erraiten deizüt egia	I pledge it is the truth.
Nork eraman ote deizü	Who might have taken away
zure lehen floria?	From you your first flower?
[Lover 2:] Eztizü egin izotzik	[Lover 2:] There was no freeze
Ez eta ere karrunik,	Nor hail that
Ene lehen floreari	My first flower
kalte egin dienik.	Might have damaged
(basquepoetry.eus)	

Other songs such as "The Embarked Damsel" or "Buketa" ("The Bouquet") also prove that the borders between epic and love songs is quite permeable and flexible. The story of the newlywed wife whose husband dies the day of the wedding but she keeps embalmed for 7 years is a good example:

Goizian goizik jeiki nündüzün,	I woke up early at dawn,
espusa nintzan goizian,	I was wed in the morning.
Bai eta zetaz ere beztitü	And I also dressed in silk
ekia jelki zenian,	When the sun rose.
Etxekandere zabal nündüzün	I was beautiful wife
egüerdi erditan,	By mid-noon
Bai eta ere alargüntsa gazte	And also a young widow
ekia sartü zenian.	When the sun set.
(basquepoetry.eus)	

Given that the topic of the last song is common to many literatures and traditions, one must conclude that this genre had the influence of different courtly literatures; this influence, however, remains to be studied in detail.

This genre shows that, by the 18th century, when the peasant classes were forced into a new ruralization and the monopolistic tendencies of the nobility created an almost unbridgeable gap between "people" and "elite," the subaltern classes had a well-developed cultural and literal code by which to conduct and regulate courtship, marriage, and love, outside the strict precepts of the Catholic Church. If the enlightened aristocracy had to develop two different discourses to address the issues of social difference, marriage, and desire, as the cases of Munibe and Samaniego show, the peasantry still retained a single discourse of love and desire that derived from an earlier mythic and improvisational tradition. In its historic continuity, this tradition challenged the ruralization to which the lower classes were forced.[95]

Etxeberri of Sara

Joanes Etxeberri (1668-1749), traditionally known as "Etxeberri of Sara," to distinguish him from another Joanes Etxeberri (c. 1580-1638), known as "Etxeberri of Ziburu," represents a marginal case in the Basque Enlightenment. Yet, in his marginality, his work must be read as the most central to a Basque Enlightenment that never fully materialized.

He was born in Sara, the town of Axular. A doctor by training, he wrote four works in the Basque dialect of Labourd, and eventually crossed the border, working as doctor in Bera (Navarre), Hondarribia (Guipuzcoa), and finally Azkoitia where he lived from 1725 to his death in 1749. Larramendi makes reference to one of Etxeberri's works, a now lost trilingual dictionary, and therefore it is safe to conclude that they met in Azkoitia or Azpeitia. It remains to be determined whether Etxeberri also met Munibe, since the latter returned from Bordeaux in 1746 and established his salon or *tertulia* with the other *Caballeritos* in 1748. Out of the four works Etxeberri wrote, only one was published in his lifetime: *Lau-Urdiri gomendiozko carta edo guthuna* (*Letter of Advise to Labourd*, 1718). His most important work *Eskuararen hatsapenak* (*Introduction to the Basque Language*) as well as his Basque method to learn Latin remained unpublished until the 20th century. Although Etxeberri's printed work had a very limited impact in the 18th century, it is safe to assume that even his unpublished book manuscripts were widely circulated and read.

---

[95] An extended analysis of this period would require discussing the religious attempts to control and abolish the culture of dance. It became the other main source of control and contestation.

It is worth mentioning that the "technology of the self" developed by Baroque culture founds its final consolidation in the numerous publications that the religious manual experienced in this century. The manual was the best-selling book of the 18th century.

There is only one precedent to Etxeberri's project: Domingo Bidegaray addressed the Navarran states in 1676 and received financial help to edit a tetralingual dictionary and a Basque school manual, which nevertheless was never finished due to the early death of the author (1679) and to other bureaucratic problems (Villasante 109). Thus, Etxeberri's proposal represents the only enlightened project designed from within the Basque language and directed to the middle- and lower-middle classes whose main language was still Basque in the 18th century. In his *Letter of Advise to Labourd,* he addressed a proposal to the parliament of Labourd to fund the publication of both his Basque method to learn Latin and his dictionary. In short, Etxeberri's enlightened project is democratic, in the historical sense of the word, and points to the only incipient nationalist project of the Basque enlightenment.

What at first seems a simple bureaucratic request—to provide the middle and lower middle classes with instruction in their own language— reveals a greater historical and political project in Etxeberri's part, which is contained in his unpublished *Introduction to the Basque Language.* What begins as yet another apology of the Basque language, following the 16th-century tradition, becomes a new enlightened discourse that no longer is apologetic, since it is written in Basque and, therefore, is not addressed to the to the subject of empire (Castilian, French, etc.) but to the Basque readership, i.e. an internal Basque reader. The goal is no longer to defend political rights, by means of the Basque language, but rather to demonstrate the internal capability of the Basque language for an enlightened project. In the book, after establishing the Babelic genealogy of Basque, Etxeberri shifts to a mechanicist discourse where human language is analyzed as a finely tuned device for communication. Although Etxeberri does not make any reference to the work of Huarte de San Juan (1575) or the Grammar of Port Royal (1660), he begins his argument by explaining the rationality and perfection of the Basque language, which is to be found in its natural state:

Therefore, it would seem that no proof could be given of the wisdom of Basque. Because no author can be found, among all the histories that correspond to this topic, who has published a single copy. However, when in lack of copies, one seeks the original, and there is no more secure copy than the original, and more truthful. That is why I wish to find the true original to devote myself to this topic, which is no other than the Basque language itself, or its speech, and I hope that, from it, I will draw necessary proof and full reasoning, for there is no more worthier witness than language, nor more truthful proof to know one, nor more common proof, which can be found more abundantly, in the natural law, in the written law, and in the divine law, than the one derived from language; (5)[96]

The counter-position between natural speech ("mintzoa"), on the one hand, and society, on the other ("in the natural law, in the written law, and in the divine law"), already points to a tension that the Enlightenment further problematized by the hand of Rousseau.

Although resorting to classical and Renaissance arguments, Etxeberri further describes language as a natural machine provided of "resorts" or devices ("erresort"), which lacks irregularity ("anomaloez eta defektiboez"):

> That is, wisdom and prudence come out shouting from the mouth of Basques; and even if Aristotle said, *Nemo est natura sapiens*; that is, nobody is born wise, just the same, had he known Basque, I believe, he would have said, *Cantabrismus est natura sapiens, (et doctus indoctus)*. Basque is, without professors and universities, wise and learned (and it is a thing to marvel and to study, how this language displays these mechanisms, since it has but two full conjugations, which are *naiz* [I am] and *dut* [I have], and although one could doubt that one of the two is defective, the rest of the conjugations of all the verbs follow them, outside [except?] the verbs that are known in Latin as anomalous or defective). (10)[97]

---

[96] "Beraz badirudi, gure Eskuararen zuhurtziaz ezin frogarik emanditekela? zeren ezpaita edireten Autor, eta istorio guztien artean egiteko huni dagokala, kopia bat bedere atheraduenik, baina nola kopia faltadenean orijinala bilhatzen ohi baita, eta ezpaita kopiarik hura baino seguragorik, eta fidelagorik; hargatik bada nik ere nahidut bilhatu egiteko huni dagokan egiazko orijinala, zeina baita Eskuara bera, edo hunen mintzoa, eta hunetarik beretik esperanza dut, atherako dudala beharden froga, eta argitasun ossoa, zeren ezbaita mintzoa baino lekhuko seguragorik, ez egiazkoagorik bat bederaren ezagutzeko, ez eta ere ezta froga komunagorik (eta) naharoago ediretendenik, hala lege Naturalean, nola iskiribatuan, eta Garaziazkoan ere, nola baita mintzotikkakoa;"

[97] "Erran nahida, zuhurtzia, eta prudenzia ojhuz daude Eskualdunen ahotik; eta Aristotelek erranbazuen ere, *Nemo est natura sapiens;* nihor eztela sortzen jakinsun, guztiarekin ere jakin izanbalu Eskuara, uste dut, erranenzuela, *Cantabrismus est natura sapiens, (et doctus indoctus)*. Eskuara da irakatslerik, eta Eskola nausirik gabe jakinsuna, eta jakina (eta ikhasia eta miresteko den gauza da, nola erresort hauk hunela jokatzen tuen, eztituelarikan, bi koniugazino baizik ossorik, zeinak baitira *Naiz*, eta *dut*, eta oraino hautarik batez dudatzeko da ea defektiboa ala ez, haukien gainean dohazi bertze gainerako berbo guztien koniugazinoak, latinez deitzen diren berbo anomaloez eta defektiboez kanpoan)."

155

Finally, Etxeberri defines language as an "instrument" that is devised to name and to refer to things, real and mental. The fact that language is an instrument that mediates between real and mental things already situates Etxeberri within a modern and enlightened understanding of language, close to the universalism of the grammarians of Port Royal and, more generally, to Cartesian philosophy:

> For Man cannot express the things he has in his mind, nor can he hear those that others hold in theirs, unless they go through the senses first. *Nihil est in intellectu quod prius non fuerit in sensu.* Because of this, language is a tool by which Man perceives and comprehends everything said by others with words, and so does he express what he has in mind. V. Advise, letter, pag. 1, 28 and 29.
> Our Basque language too is meant for this very same purpose, because through it, we communicate the thing we want to express; and in the same way, they comprehend what we say. (56)[98]

This linguistic departure has very important consequences for Etxeberri's enlightened project. First, he re-centers a linguistic Basque Country in a Basque geography, so that, the kingdom of Navarre becomes the origin of Basque history: he literally calls the Navarran kings "kings of the Basque Country" (34-35).[99] Furthermore, Etxeberri, prompted by his enlightened thinking, resituates the kingdom of Navarre at the origin of the French kingdom (through Henry IV who was first king of Navarre before becoming ruler of France) and the Spanish (through Phillip V who was of French origin). In this way, Etxeberri concludes that Pamplona is

---

[98] "Zeren Gizonak ezin adiaraz ahal baitetzake gogoan tuen gauzak, ez eta-ere adi ahal bertzek gogoan tuztenak, non lehenbizirik eztiren sentsuetarik iragaiten. *Nihil est in intellectu quod prius non fuerit in sensu.* Hargatik bada hizkuntza da lanabes bat zeinaren bidez Gizonak aditzen baititu bertzek hitzez erraiten tuzten gauzak, bai halaber adiarazten-ere berak gogoan tuenak. V. Gomendioz. carta, pag. 1, 28 y 29.
Eginbide hunetako bereko da bada gure Eskuara ere, zeren hunen bidez adiarazten baitugu, aditzera eman nahi dugun gauza; eta bide beraz aditzen baitarokute erraiten duguna. »

[99] « Eta azkenean hauk guztien khoroatzeko, erranen dut, Eskual herriak izan tuela bere Erregeak: *Ad Joannem Cantabriæ Regem aufugavit: Jonius in Elogio Valentini Ducis.* Bernardinus Gomesius. lib. 8. de gestis Regis Jacobi. Ihes egin kuen Joannes Eskual-herriko Erregerengana; ordea hemendik erran nahi dana da, Errege hek Eskualdunak zirela ezen istorioen eredura Eneko, eta Semeno Nafarroako Errege izan ziren, zeinen izenek aski klarki aditzera emaiten baitarokute Ekualdun izenak direla. »

the center and "queen" of the French and Spanish monarchies (36). Finally, and referring to Ignatius of Loyola and Francis of Xavier, he further expands the universality of the Basque Country by stressing the role of these two saints in expanding the imperialist reach of the Catholic Church across nations and continents (39-43).

Once Etxeberri establishes the rationality and universality of the "Basque Country" and its language, he even proceeds to describe his country as a geopolitical entity (49, 53). Finally, by establishing the work of Axular as the canonical reference for all enlightened Basques (59-60), Etxeberri turns Sara, the former's residence and the latter's hometown, into a Basque Athens (71-3), its classical city and reference.

Because the Basque language and its use are class-defined, Etxeberri, unlike his enlightened counterparts, also advances a social critique of diglossia, which the elite classes create when resorting to Spanish and French:

> In truth, the fate of this region has been quite different from those of other languages. For these languages become embellished and grow further among cultured classes and worsen among peasants. More so, Basque has been treated to the contrary; for it has preserved and still preserves its purity among rural, illiterate people. And if anything polluted has been attached to it, or has worsened; it has come from Universities and from the mouth of learnt people, who have spread and sown foreign names in the place of Basque words, or because they have forgotten their Basque correspondents, or they have never learnt those of the Basque Country. (93-4)[100]

In short, Etxeberri denounces the ruralization of his Basque enlightened project. As a result, he proposes to expel or exile from the Basque Country the cultured, elite classes that do not use or do not have a good command of the Basque language: "In this way, it would be convenient to expel such shameful Basques from the country; (I suspect some are willing to leave, and so would others move out of good will if they would

---

[100] « Egiaz alde guztiz hunen zorthea izan da hagitz diferenta bertze lengoaienetarik; zenbatenaz-ere hauk edertzen, eta hazten baitira gehiago jende letradunen artean, eta gaizkoatzen nekhazalenetan; Hanbatenaz Eskuara kontrarago da tratatua; zeren bere garbitasuna konserbatu, eta konserbatzen baitu jende nekhazale estudiatu gaben artean; eta baldin jeus nahastakadurarik lothu bazajo, edo lizundu bada; hori ethorri zajo Eskola-nausien eta presuna estudiatuen ahoetan, zeinek eskuarazko hitzen lekhuan hedatu, eta erain baitituzte izen arrotzak edo dela zeren ahantzi baitzitzaizkoten eskuarazkoak, edo ezbaitzituzketen behin-ere ikhasi Eskual-herrikoak. »

157

find somebody willing to give them similar positions and gifts)" (85).[101] Finally, he is the first enlightened author establishing a link between language and territory, as well as a "duty" to both. He encourages the reader to join his enlightened project and to contribute to it. According to Etxeberri, it is the reader's duty:

> The door remains open for you, if you want to redo or improve anything; and more so nowadays, for my little text is missing many things to achieve perfection: thus, you should exercise yourself in fulfilling your duty, for you are obliged to work for the benefit of your country; especially if what Cicero says is true... Although it is great the indebtedness towards parents and relatives, it is even greater towards the homeland. (96)[102]

Etxeberri's work is too short to evaluate truly all its possible implications, especially since we do not know to what extent it was read and discussed. At a time in which the nobility and its Atlantic enlightened project threatened the majority of the Basque population with ruralization and impoverishment, Etxeberri's attempt to articulate a democratic, enlightened project, stands out as a unique Basque Enlightenment that situated the Basque Country between two empires while counteracting the latter's diglossic and despotic projects with another more democratic one.

Nationalism and the Enlightenment

From the above analysis, it is now possible to analyze any consideration of the Basque Enlightenment as the origin of Basque nationalism. Mikel Azurmendi, in his most complex and comprehensive work on Basque history, *Y se limpie aquella tierra* (*Let Them Clean that Land*, 2000), finds the origins of Basque nationalism at the end of the 18th century among Jesuits and enlightened noblemen such as Manuel Larramendi and Xavier

---

[101] "Halatan egungo egunean-ere on lizateke halako Eskualdun ahalkagarrien herritik igortzea, eta khentzea; (badut uste kausi litezken zenbait joaiteko onik, bai halaber gogotik lihoazkenik, baldin kausi baledi bertze halako kargu, eta present emaille bat)."

[102] « athea bethi zabaldua gelditzen zaitzu, baldin jeusik berretu nahi baduzu: eta oraino are baino gehiago zeren nere obratto huni hainitz gauza falta baitzaizko behar den perfezinora heltzeko: halatan beraz enplega zaitea zeure eginbidearen egiten, zeren obligatua baitzara zeure herriaren progotxutan traballatzera, baldin egia bada Zizeronek erraiten darokuna... Burasoentzat, eta ahaidentzateko obligazinoa handia delarikan, handiagoa da Sort-herri arentzatekoa."

María Munibe respectively—he does not study Etxeberri. For Azurmendi, this enlightened nationalism results from an atrophy of an earlier Basque discourse, the apologist discourse of the Renaissance, which legitimized the Basques as the original inhabitants of Spain. This author denominates this atrophy "traditionalization" (13). More specifically, Azurmendi traces this "innovative traditionalization" to the enlightened work of Larramendi. He claims that the Larramendi rewrote the apologistic discourse of the Renaissance according to the new social and economic conditions that regulated agriculture in the 18th century in Guipuzcoa: the *mayorazgo* (landed property) and the leaseholds (or farmsteads) owned by oligarchic absentee landholders:

> Larramendi constitutes with his work a landmark in Basque mythologization because Tubal ends up transformed into a landholder (mayorazgo), founder from its inception of the ruling social-economic system of the 17th and 18th centuries; initiator of the *foruak* and of the customs or way of life of Basques supposedly since their origins. Thus, Guipuzcoa ends up represented as a big family, a single ancestral home or constitutional entity, compact, unique, and sovereign since the beginning, in charge of the General Assembly [Juntas generales] (312-13).[103]

Azurmendi notes that, because of "traditionalization," both Larramendi and the enlightened Basque nobility began to develop, in different forms and degrees, projects and ideas that pointed to an independent Basque Country, one endowed with its own history. Furthermore, Azurmendi finds that the "othering" of the Spanish monarchy and state by the Basque Enlightenment lies at the core of this traditionalization and nationalization of the Basque Country:

> Despite the unpremeditated nature of the device, Puztaburu's proposal [Larramendi's alter ego] could appear as an extemporaneous radicalization of the elementary narcissism of the Founding Fathers' myth. Nevertheless, it is devised from a radically new conception: the presence of the Other, dirty and dangerous, *as an identitarian and political unifying factor.*

---

[103] "Larramendi constituye con ello un hito en la mitologización vasca pues Tubal queda convertido en mayorazgo, fundador desde los inicios del sistema económico-social vasco vigente entre los siglos XVII y XVIII; instaurador de los fueros y costumbres o modo de ser y de vivir de los vascos supuestamente desde sus inicios; y Guipúzcoa queda significada como una gran familia, un único solar o entidad constitucional compacta, única y soberana desde sus inicios, al mando de las Juntas generales."

> If Tubal's tale was concocted to sanction within the Hispanic monarchy a position of privilege and honor for 16ᵗʰ-century Basques, how come that of Puztaburu, with the same elements, is forged to legitimize an *autonomous and independent* position vis-à-vis the Monarchy? (320, my emphasis)[104]

However, this autonomous and independentist trend is not nationalist. The Basque Enlightenment reacted to the decline of the Spanish empire and to the rise of an absolutist north-European hegemony, which resulted in the triumph of the French Bourbon dynasty in Spain. The decadence of Spanish imperialism and the rise of a new absolutist monarchy that no longer favored the Basque industry resulted in an agricultural refashioning of the Spanish Basque Country—hence its traditionalization. Yet, this reorganization of the Spanish Basque Country could not coincide with the project of the nation-state, since the latter was a result of the rise of industrial capitalism in countries such as England or France.

The fact that ultimately the Spanish monarchy and the church curtailed and destroyed this Basque enlightened project shows its non-nationalist nature. It was a modern and enlightened Basque response to the ancient-regime crisis in the Spanish monarchy; it is only historically logical that the result did not follow the project of the nation-state. Yet it is also clear that, throughout the 19ᵗʰ century, the Spanish monarchy did not manage to solve this Basque Atlantic problem. Spanish liberalism failed in its centralist attempts in the 19ᵗʰ century.

The Basque Enlightenment marked the beginning of a non-Hispanic, Basque modernity that did not follow the project of the nation-state and, rather, attempted to give an Atlantic solution to an economic problem. The shrinking Basque economy lost its industrial might and, thus, condemned the subaltern classes to a very new phenomenon: the re-ruralization of the Basque Country. It is this problem that then exploded with the Spanish civil conflicts of the 19ᵗʰ century, known as the Carlist Wars.

---

[104] "Pese a lo inopinado del artificio, la propuesta de Puztaburu [Larramendi's alter ego] podría parecer una radicalización intempestiva del elemental narcisismo del mito de los Padres Fundadores, no obstante se halla tensado desde una concepción radicalmente nueva: la aparición del Otro, sucio y peligroso, como factor de *unificación identitaria y política*. Si el relato de Tubal fue confeccionado para sancionar dentro de la monarquía hispana un puesto de privilegio y honor de los vizcaínos del siglo XVI, ¿Cómo es que el de Puztaburu, mediante los mismos elementos, esté forjado para legitimar un puesto *autónomo e independiente* respecto a la Monarquía?"

Only towards the end of that century, did this problem give rise to both Basque and Spanish nationalisms.

Benedict Anderson locates the origin of nationalism, against Hobsbawn's theories, in the processes of colonial independence of Latin America, when the creole elites of each commercial center mobilized against the Madridean metropolis. It was the same metropolis that condemned this creole elite, because of its American birth, to never fully form part of the metropolitan elite.[105] At that point, the creole elites embraced the racially marked subaltern masses of their respective regions in order to create a mass movement that gave rise to a nationalist sentiment. Ultimately, and following Anderson, nationalism is an eminently Atlantic phenomenon that took place in the decadent Spanish empire of the end of the 18th century and beginning of the 19th. Given that the enlightened ideas that propelled American independentist nationalism spread from Caracas to the rest of the continent and the Basque Enlightenment played a role in the Atlantic voyage of those ideas from Europe to Caracas, a new reading of the Basque Enlightenment can be effected from Latin American history. Had not the Inquisition and the Napoleonic invasion dismantled the Basque Enlightenment, then, we might have had a very Atlantic and Basque phenomenon: a parallel growth of nationalism on both sides of the Atlantic, in both Caracas and the Basque Country.

Instead, the independence of the American colonies ended the Atlantic commerce and expansion of the Basque Country and, thus, the Basque bourgeoisie turned its interests towards the Peninsula and its new liberal, nationalist project. The rural masses further suffered under this new internal arrangement, which further increased the process of ruralization and poverty. While, in the 19th century, anthropologists, tourists, and writers would further enforce this rural image by turning it into a "colonial scenario" of authenticity and antiquity (the oldest, indigenous people of Europe), the rural masses turned to the Atlantic and began the second largest wave of emigration to the Americas, triggered by increased poverty and wars.

---

[105] Anderson does not mention the North American revolution of 1776. Despite the fact that this independence movement presents significant differences with its South American counterparts, ultimately does not represent an exception to Anderson's model.

4. Colonial Difference and the Nation

1. The Tradition of Invention (Humboldt, Mogel, Chaho, Hugo, Mérimée)

If the 19th century in Europe is characterized by uninterrupted historical turmoil, simultaneous imperialist advance (Great Britain, France) and decadence (Spain, Portugal), racialization, nationalist and populist uprisings, as well as class and gender contestation and struggle, the emerging new Basque literary discourses of that time present a rather puzzling endurance and pervasiveness: they somehow address all these historical scenarios in their complexity, while interpellating very different social groups and constituencies by resorting to a complex discourse that at first appears anachronistically "romantic." In this respect, 19th-century Basque literature would seem to be a "century-long romanticism" that shapes even the 20th century. Needless to say, this "prolonged romanticism" makes no sense by any Spanish or French literary, historical standards, although Octavio Paz has hinted to a similar theory for Latin American and European modernism in his *The Children of the Mire*. In the period spanning from the French revolution (1789) and the emancipation of the Latin American colonies (1810-26) to the USA's rise to global-power status (1898) and World War I (1914-1919), Basque literature represented these events and their geo-biopolitical effects in complex ways that, to this day, remain poorly analyzed and, moreover, defy the idea of a protracted Basque romanticism.

Although labels such as "romantic," "fuerista," "costumbrista" (from literature of customs), or "historical" are helpful when approaching these texts, those denominations betray the historical continuity and complexity of 19th-century Basque discourses, for they are fraught with a very interesting and perplexing irony: they appear to be outrageous historical fabrications and, yet, they prevail and persist through the 20th century as some of the most popular and influential works—to the point that they become the imaginary foundation for the emerging Spanish, French, and Basque nationalist discourses of the turn of the century. The first influential text written by the founder of Basque nationalism, Sabino Arana, falls within this discursive tradition of "historical fabrication:" *Biscay for its Independence* (*Vizcaya por su independencia,* 1890). Similarly, the first novel written by one of the founding fathers of 20th-century Spanish nationalism, Miguel de Unamuno (1864-1936), also is a historical novel: *Peace in War* (*Paz en la Guerra,* 1897) which, as Juaristi clearly demonstrates, derives from this Basque literary tradition (*Linaje* 209-69). Similarly, Hugo,

165

Mérimée and Loti's orientalist fantasies about the Basque Country shaped the French nationalist imagination in ways that remain unexamined. In short, this Basque literature appears to represent the quintessential example or epitome of what Hobsbawn denounces as "invented tradition"—a denunciation Juaristi has expanded for the case of the Basque Country, in the following terms:

> The defenders of Basque privileges resorted to literature to invent a new tradition. The historical novel, the legend, a new brand of historical romance, and the legendary poem of Ossianic coinage provided the prenationalist writers the formal means for that invention. As any invented tradition, Basque historical-legendary literature addresses the need to reinforce the cohesion of a society whose organic ties have undergone considerable tear, to legitimate authority's institutions and relationships, and to inculcate among the masses value systems, beliefs and behavioral patterns. (*Linaje* 16-7)

Yet this literature's popularity and historical resilience defies such an obvious and self-evident accusation of fabrication.

Hobsbawn approaches the idea of "invented tradition" in the following way: "insofar as there is such reference to a historic past, the peculiarity of 'invented traditions' is that the continuity with it is largely fictitious. In short, they are responses to novel situations which take the form of reference to old situations, or which establish their own past by quasi-obligatory repetition" (2). Therefore, Hobsbawn emphasizes the fictitious temporal continuity that new traditions create in order to legitimize themselves as old and traditional. As Hobsbawn implies throughout his text, invented traditions represent a new response to new historical problems. When he further analyzes the different groups that have recourse to invented traditions, he places nationalist movements at the core of this process of invention:

> [I]t is clear that plenty of political institutions, ideological movements and groups—not least in nationalism—were so unprecedented that even historic continuity had to be invented, for example by creating an ancient past beyond effective historical continuity, either by semi-fiction (Boadicea, Vercingetorix, Arminius the Cheruscan) or forgery (Ossian, the Czech medieval manuscripts). (7)

Yet, it is important to emphasize that at the bottom of Hobsbawn's definition there is a clear dichotomy between what is genuine and invented, what is historical and fictitious, as when he concludes that "the strength and adaptability of *genuine traditions* is not to be confused with the 'invention of tradition'" (8, my emphasis). A historical analysis of 19th-century Basque literature proves that this differentiation responds to the old Marxist distinction of ideology and truth, and, thus, must be revised in relation with the distinction between "genuine" and "invented" traditions.

However, if we resort to the also Marxist-Gramscian elaboration of "subalternity, Basque literary history appears under a very different light: many subaltern groups and contending political classes developed new traditions that were very much enmeshed with older traditions to the point that the genuine/fictitious divide cannot be upheld. Furthermore, rather than helping to explain the historical origins of nationalism, such a divide obscures and reifies (others) history and turns it into ideology. The interconnection between subaltern culture and nationalist ideology is so complex and historically rooted in the Basque Country that it survives the lifespan of the social groups, Basque and foreign, old and new, from which many traditions emerge. Moreover, these traditions continue to mutate and transform into new postnationalist formations in the 21st century. Therefore, rather than "invented traditions," it is more accurate to speak of "a tradition of invention" in the Basque Country. Ultimately "inventing" is a historical tradition that goes back to the Renaissance and the Middle Age; moreover, it encompasses Basques and foreigners alike.[106]

Humboldt

Wilhelm von Humboldt (1767-35), diplomat, famous linguist, and founder of the Berlin University (1810), is the most prominent figure in the tradition of inventing a Basque tradition in the early 19th century. Although he published his seminal work on Basque language in 1818, he traveled to the Basque Country in 1799 and 1801. He collected his impressions and findings in a manuscript that was published posthumously

---

[106] Just to mention a distant case that, nevertheless, resembles the Basque: "Analogous to European concepts of renaissance, Islamic intellectuals in the nineteenth century fell back upon a 'Golden Age' of Islam. But even here, the European Orientalists provided precious assistance by explaining to them what the classical Islamic period was, and how it was to be understood and assessed historically" (Schulze 191–92). Schulze does not analyze the input of subaltern classes in this complex invention of tradition.

in his complete works in 1841-52. His linguistic work is the most important, namely his *On the Primitive Inhabitants of Hispania* (1818). However, his minor *The Basques, or Observations on a Journey through Bizkaia and the French Basque Country in the Spring of 1801* (*Die Vasken, oder Bemerkungen auf einer Reise durch Biscaya und das französische Basquenland im Frühling des Jahrs*, 1801), gathers Humboldt's thinking about the Basque Country. Furthermore, his writing inaugurated the romantic understanding of the Basque Country as the oldest and purest remnant of a newly invented "white Europe." In this respect, he was the first modern traveler to the Basque Country. If the enlightened members of the Royal Basque Society awaited for Rousseau, due to his friendship with Altuna (*Confessions* 308), at the end, they ended up being visited by Humboldt instead.

It is not a coincidence if Humboldt sums up his romantic sensibility towards people and places unscathed by civilization when he states that "I will always think of this spring at the shores of the Bay of Biscay as one of the loveliest of my life" (12). Furthermore, Humboldt's new romantic sensibility is most clearly present in his melancholic narration of a Basque Country that is losing its original language because of the impact of modernity:

> These [European] influences more and more drive out their language and so, inevitably, their national character is lost at the same time. Even now the language, being persecuted from all sides and neglected, above all, by the most enlightened parts of the nation, has decade by decade to withdraw deeper into the mountains and it is foreseeable that its decay will occur at an even faster pace from now on. (8)

After predicting the disappearance of Basque language in a century, Humboldt condenses the contradiction that marks modernity and romanticism. On the one hand, he states that "[I]t seems to be irrevocably determined in the course of human culture that the differences that separate the minor tribes from each other must necessarily fade away" (8). However, he also states,

> But the other question, and surely a not unimportant one, is whether or not this should have its limits; whether or not education can come to a point at which, in order to preserve society's warmth and strength without which it will bear no inner fruit, it becomes just as necessary to keep the imagination and sentiment within a tight circle as it is to lead reason toward a broader sphere (8-9)

In Humboldt's discourse, the Basque Country and its language stand not simply as proof of the original languages of Spain and Europe, but also as the ideal of this romantic and anti-modern search for a new sphere of humanity: "warmth, strength, imagination, sentiment." Thus, Humboldt actively seeks this romantic ideal—modern in its anti-modern utopianism—in the Basque Country.

In this respect, Humboldt reified the Basque Country as the privileged other of modernity: it is the oldest remnant of the original Europe. Yet, in its status of other, the Basque Country, once again, occupies a very modern position in the European intellectual and political imagination. With Humboldt's discourse, the Basque Country shifts its position from a Hispanic modernity, in which it was its "purest racial" subject ["the oldest inhabitants of Spain without Jewish or Moorish taint"], to a north-European, capitalist modernity, in which it becomes its oldest and most original object—the French Basque Country does not change in this respect. In his travel, Humboldt met Basque scholars such as Pablo Pedro Astarloa and Juan Antonio Mogel and his romantic discourse absorbed and reformulated the older ideology of apologism that the latter explained to him. In this way, Humboldt rearticulated the Basque apologist ideology deployed against a Hispanic modernity and turned it into a modern European one, in which the Basque Country occupies Europe's oldest and, therefore, most anti-modern position. This moment is crucial in order to understand the anti-modern thrust that prevailed in the Basque Country for the rest of the century, for it was the one sought by the modern, European subject: the romantic traveler, the scientific linguist, the anthropologist, the tourist, etc.

Unlike the ideology of apologism, this new anti-modern ideology was not simply a Basque reaction to modernization, as most Basque historiography has defended till our days, but rather the internalization of a non-Basque, European, modern reaction against modernity, so that ultimately European modernity was legitimized on its Basque reflection of originality. From Mogel and Chaho to Sabino Arana, Unamuno, and Txomin Agirre, this European and modern yearning for an anti-modern position and object constituted the geopolitical and discursive foundation of 19th-century Basque literature. Ultimately, it was a very modern yearning from an anti-modern *essence* that resisted history.

I have already discussed in the case of Larramendi and the Royal Basque Society, the Atlantic origins of an anti-modern reaction to the economic and geopolitical decadence of the Spanish empire, which already yielded formulations that seem, at first sight, to be nationalist or essentialist. Yet, with the new European discourse of romanticism, this enlightened anti-modern Basque discourse and position became essentialized: it became fully internal to a new industrial, white, colonialist Europe that sought its origins within itself in the shape of an anti-modern utopia. The Basque Country played precisely this role, along with other colonial realities, to the point of becoming an imaginary "internal colony," as I will discuss in the following. The Basques made a strategic use of such essentialist "originality," which refashioning Gayatri Spivak's proposal (*The Postcolonial Critic* 45), I will denominate "strategic essentialism."

19th-century Basque literature is defined precisely by its use of *strategic essentialism* towards a reality that remained subaltern. Instead of searching for an enlightened, rational, modern discourse, Basque writers resorted to modernity's own search for an anti-modern, utopian *essence and originality*: they invented a Basque tradition of anti-modernism that attracted linguists, anthropologists, and tourists alike by representing a space that was, on the one hand, originally European and pristine, and, on the other, as savage as any colonial space.

Yet this invention relied on a strategic use of an essentialism, which emerged from within European modernity. Thus, rather than an *invention of tradition*, Basque essentialism represents a continuation with an older *tradition of invention* that originated in an earlier Hispanic modernity: Jimenez de Rada and the apologists of the Renaissance. As such, the tradition of invention remained as modern as apologism, although now this modernity was signified as the essence of an anti-modernity that was ultimately north European and capitalist. Moreover, as I will discuss at the end of this chapter, Basque essentialism ended up becoming, via Unamuno, the "essence" of modern Spanish nationalism: *casticismo*, a racial formation that resists history and biology.

Mogel

The French revolution had clear effects on the Basque Country. On the French side of the Basque Country, many Catholic priests and young men, avoiding the military draft, crossed the border and took refuge on the Spanish side. At the same time, the romantic reaction that the revolution generated throughout Europe prompted new travelers to search for the non-modern origins of Europe, as discussed in the case of Humboldt.

170

Juan Antonio Mogel (1745-1804), a cleric from Elgoibar who worked as parish priest in Markina (Biscay), had the opportunity to encounter both types of travelers. He was a priest who worked locally but, because of his awareness of the historical changes taking place in Europe, wrote a manuscript, *Peru Abarka* (1802), which was not published until the end of the century (1881) but was circulated among Basque readers as manuscript early on.

This manuscript already registers and captures the new position that the Basque Country was bound to occupy for the rest of the century in Europe and Spain. The discursive formulations in which later nationalist literature was going to rely (Sabino Arana, Unamuno, Txomin Agirre....) were already advanced by this text—even Sabino Arana published one of Mogel's philological texts in his journal *Bizkaitarra* in 1895-96. Mogel also became the founding figure, with Pedro Antonio Añibarro (1748-1830), of the Biscayan-dialect literary tradition.

Peru Abarka consists of a long introduction in Spanish and six dialogues or chapters in Basque. The author narrates the encounter between a villager, Maisu Juan (Mister John[107]) the barber, and a farmer, Peru Abarka (Peter Espadrille; the last name is also the alias of Navarran king Santxo Garzia II, 970 – 994, which might denote a social class distinction). They meet in an inn, where Maisu Juan trumps the hotelier and causes her to break several bones so that he can offer his services as barber and, in this way, avoid the high costs of their stay. They both travel to Peru's farmstead where Maisu Juan gets a tour of rural life. While Maisu Juan is in the farm, the hotelier finds out about the former's treachery and sends the bailiff after him. Maisu Juan manages to avoid arrest by passing as a farmer in Peru's farmstead; he repents from his sins and goes back to his village. In a seventh and final dialogue or chapter, one of the secondary characters, a priest, who is Mogel's own alter ego, emerges as the main character and engages a friar, Pedro Astarloa's persona, in a dialogue about the Basque language. The text ends with several translations of classical Latin texts into Basque and with a "nomenclatura" or short dictionary.

Peru Abarka is not an isolated text. A similar genre, written as dialogues addressed to farmers, also exists in Galician culture. As Carballo Calero explains, it constituted a popular genre in the Galicia of the first third of the 19th century (*Historia* 39-40, 47-53). Pedro Boado Sánchez, for example, published *Dialogue between Two Distressed, Galician Farmers and*

---

[107] "Mister" or also "barber" or "surgeon" in the old sense of "doctor."

Compassionate, Carefree, Cultured Lawyer (1832). As Carballo Calero states "They used to print, additionally to this [books], some times more or less regularly and other times occasionally, several leaflets of political propaganda that adopted the form of dialogues, tailored to the popular style" (48).[108] In the case of Galicia, however, it was mostly the urban, liberal class who wrote this literature. If, in the Basque case, the urban class was the addressee, in the Galician case, it was the addresser; hence the more political and less essentializing character of the Galician dialogues.

For the first time in Basque literature, Mogel formulated in *Peru Abarka* the myth of the independent farmer who lives a self-contained and natural life outside modernity—the anti-modern subject that Europeans, such as Humboldt, seek. The farmer Peru Abarka becomes the epitome of anti-modernity and, thus, the ideal of Basqueness, which the rest of urban Basques, exposed to modernity, must know and admire. Mogel naturalizes and essentializes the farmstead as the self-sufficient and sole possibility for a Basque imaginary that no longer is Guipuzcoan or Biscayan, but Basque and rural—thus fully essentializing and de-historicizing the re-ruralization process that took place during the Basque Enlightenment with Larramendi and Munibe. The new autonomous universe portrayed by Mogel, the farmstead, is socially, economically, educationally, and linguistically self-sufficient; its subject becomes the rural patriarchal farmer, whom Basque nationalism retakes in the 20th century as the core of its imaginary. If Basque language was portrayed as an old matriarch in decadence by the genre of apologism, the new strategic-essentialist discourse of Basque modernity, inaugurated by Mogel, chose instead to represent superego-like patriarchal figures: Peru Abarka, and later, Zumalakarregi, Aitor, etc.[109]

Yet, if Peru Abarka is a mythic or superego-like character in its anti-modernity, the text is directed to the urban, morally dubious, speaker of a corrupt, Castilianized, Basque language: the likes of Maisu Juan, the treacherous barber. The reader is positioned in the place of Maisu Juan and, thus, as the latter experiences his discovery of and "conversion" to the essentialist, rural ideology of Peru Abarka, the reader, alongside

---

[108] "Se imprimían, además de esto, con carácter más o menos regular unas veces, otras aisladamente, diversos papeles de propaganda política que adoptaban la forma de diálogos, adecuada al estilo popular."

[109] Ultimately, this essentializing process is homosocial and therefore creates a new other within: woman, the non-political, natural, affective and domestic woman who stands for the allegorical representation of the motherland.

Maisu Juan, becomes a fully modern Basque subject. As such modern subject, the reader becomes fully aware of the importance of seeking an anti-modern utopia. However, and unlike the texts of most travelers, anthropologists, and linguists that visit the essentialized Basque Country of the 19th century, Maisu Juan (and the reader) is made to experience the anti-modernity of Peru Abarka as his own, not as that of an exotic other. As Maisu Juan identifies himself as Basque, he experiences his position as both modern and anti-modern, subject and exotic other. Therefore, the collapse of the other into the self yields an identitarian excess that makes room for the appearance of the strategic nature of *Peru Abarka*'s essentialism. Maisu Juan, and the reader with him, experience an excess of modernity, as both subject and other, which introduces the reader to the possibilities of strategic essentialism, a fully enjoyable political scenario in the sense that the reader identifies its symptom (anti-modernity) and can also enjoy it (as modern reader). Nationalist identification derives in the 20th century from the political enjoyment that Peru Abarka's strategic essentialism inaugurates. This symptomatic identification generates *jouissance* in its European excess: it represents the possibility of being modern and anti-modern at the same time.

In *Peru Abarka*, the reader[110] is faced with the perfect, patriarchal picture of rural life, Peru Abarka, and, as a result, has no choice but to identify with Maisu Juan, the villager, the outsider who comes to visit the farmstead. In the introduction, Mogel makes this identification explicit when he claims: "they [urban ideal reader] are so little knowledgeable in their home language; they cannot even imitate the Barber who becomes in the dialogue the disciple of the Chairman of the Woods!" (8). In contrast to Peru Abarka's idealized and self-contained personality and life, Maisu Juan is presented as an imperfect character who undergoes change in the text by traveling to the farmstead, by learning about rural life and, finally, by passing as farmer. Hence, it is important to emphasize that *Peru Abarka* is not a static text, like previous pastoral literature (Lazarraga), but rather the opposite: it is a travel narrative written from a non-rural point of view, that is, from the point of view of a modern European subject---from that of foreign travelers such as Humboldt.

In short, *Peru Abarka* is a modern travel narrative. At the end, Maisu Juan does not stay and, instead, returns to the village. In this sense, the author acknowledges that Maisu Juan, and thus the Basque readership, is

---

[110] The homosocial nature of strategic essentialism excludes woman as reader or forces the female reader to a position of masochism.

on the side of modernity and has its own internal anti-modern object and reference. *Peru Abarka* is the first text to narrate a modern point of view and position—a modern subject position—as internal to the Basque Country and Basque language—unlike apologism or religious manuals. This is the first radical change brought about by this narrative. Maisu Juan's travel to Peru Abarka's farmstead cannot be differentiated, in that sense, from that of Humboldt's to the Basque Country just three years earlier.

Yet, Mogel formulates another very modern subject: the subaltern classes as discursive characters that have a cultural, social, and economic history, but do not occupy an ideological or hegemonic position—do not have a political voice—in the new discourse of strategic Basque essentialism. They are the rural characters who do not join Peru Abarka's anti-modern utopia and, thus, remain "simple farmers." As I will discuss below, the subaltern classes are repressed by *Peru Abarka*'s ideology of the Basque rural essence and, as a result, remain on the fringes of both the new modern rural ideology articulated by Peru Abarka and the text itself. The subaltern classes are neither modern nor anti-modern, but non-modern. The formulation of a rural, anti-urban ideology that represses subalternity defines Mogel's text and, later on, Basque nationalism. *Peru Abarka* is the double narration of a subaltern subject that lingers on the edges of the text, on the one hand, and of a hegemonic subject that embodies the anti-modern effects of modernity, on the other—hence the paramount importance of this text.

In other words, Mogel's rural idealization, modern and anti-modern at the same time, creates its own non-modern fractures and inconsistencies. Between the essentialist purity of the rural Basque language and life so much admired by Maisu Juan, on the one hand, and the impurity of modern, urban life, from which Maisu Juan hails, on the other, a fracture emerges: the peripheral and repressed discourse of a rural, subaltern subjects who voices his/her presence through the structure of the carnival. Mogel resorts to the popular tradition of the *charivari* (local carnivalesque performance) in order to create a narrative substratum below modernity. Unlike Peru, Maisu Juan is demonized as an incompetent barber by one of the songs other peasants sing at the inn. When Peru Abarka and Maisu Juan are about to go bed at the inn, they hear a song sung by two drunk men, father and son, against Maisu Juan. One of the men satirizes the way in which Maisu Juan attempted earlier to heal his wounds:

Ecarri eusten egun sentijan   They brought to me at dusk

Maisu Juan Barberuba,	Maisu Juan the Barber
Gurago neban neure albuan	I had preferred by my side
Euqui Gaisquin Diabruba.	To have the Wicked Devil
…..	…
Cangrenatzat bat jajoco jaco	[MJ said:] The wound will turn into gangrene
Ondo ezpadogu segeetan;	If we do not saw it well.
Ezdira ez olango heridac	Wounds such as this one are not
Bedarchubaz osetan.	Cured just with plants.
Jaurtigui neutsan osticadiaz	With the kick that I gave him
Ezarri neban lurrera	I threw him on the ground,
Sartu eztedin Maisu Juane	So that Maisu Juan
Nire echian ostera. (62-64)	Never enters my house again.

In short, there is an underlying discourse that structures the narrative of *Peru Abarka*, which *is* neither modern nor anti-modern, but subaltern and non-modern; it only emerges in songs such as the one cited above. The above song is full of "impurities" in its language, open to any influence, and fully aware of its carnivalesque and subversive potential. This discourse cannot be reduced to either side of the romantic split between modernity and anti-modernity; it ultimately explains both the suture attempted by *Peru Abarka* as well as its fractures. [111]

Ultimately, *Peru Abarka* is a polyphonic (Bakhtin) text in which different forms of discourse, from the dictionary and the *charivari* to the enlightened dialogue and translation of classical texts, are introduced. In this respect, Mogel's work is also similar to one of the original texts that start the Galician renaissance: Juan Manuel Pintos's *The Galician Bagpipe* (1853), which is composed by a variety of subaltern and non-subaltern texts, discourses, and voices.

As stated earlier, the subject *and* object of *Peru Abarka* are modern and anti-modern respectively, but, ultimately Basque. At this point, modernity is recentered within the Basque Country, and the Basque villager becomes the new subject of a modernity, from which Basque culture is no longer excluded. This new modern Basque subject can contemplate his (or her) own Basque anti-modernity in *Peru Abarka* in an identitarian

---

[111] There are three women mentioned in *Peru Abarka*: the keeper of the inn, the medicine woman brought to the wounded man after Maisu Juan is thrown out of the house, and Peru Abarka's wife. All three are kept outside the strategic essentialist project, and divided on both sides of subalternity. This issue requires a more detailed study that exceeds this history; it will be developed in future editions.

and positional excess that yields modern *jouissance* and abjection. However, the non-modern and subaltern subject, present in the carnival, is pushed to the periphery of the text: outside the new modern ideology of the text.

Yet, in *Peru Abarka,* the reader can enjoy the ideological fantasy of being both a Basque modern subject and a Basque anti-modern object, while negating Basque subalternity, where the historical rural subject remains---including women. This is the ultimate effect of Mogel's strategic essentialism and its affirmation of Basque modernity. The way the rural masses of the Basque Country are mobilized by the French revolution and Napoleon, on the one hand, and by the Carlist Wars, on the other, is already articulated by Mogel in his *Peru Abarka*. These subaltern classes are forcefully mobilized to join the Napoleonic and Carlist causes by republican officials and clergymen, respectively, in the clash between modernity and anti-modernity for political discourses and hegemonic articulations that do not address the subaltern history of those rural subjects. As I will explain in the next chapter, this is the reason why the voice of the *bertsolari* (subaltern verse improviser) is so important to understand the political complexity of modernity and subalternity in the Basque Country.

Chaho

It is not a coincidence if another important author of this period, Agustin Chaho (1810-58), recreates two historical figures that embody Basque strategic essentialism; both are mythical figures and both are marked by war and resistance. One is imaginary, the other is historical: Aitor[112] and Zumalakarregi. Both represent the origin and the final development of a Basque history that, for Chaho, is a single continuous narrative. In his *Voyage en Navarre pendant l'insurrection des Basques* (*Voyage to Navarre During the Insurrection of the Basques*, 1836), Aitor represents the old Basque patriarch who is the origin of the Basque "race." Zumalakarregi is the Carlist general that embodies Aitor's spirit in the present.

Yet, this local and fantastic mixing of Basque mythology and history responds to a larger modern, European reorganization of racial, sexual, and geopolitical discourses and institutions, which Said has studied in its

---

[112] The popular Basque name « Aitor » derives from a misreading of the word « aintonenseme, » which literally means son of good parents or, in its current use, noble man, gentleman. Chaho misread it as "Aitor-en seme," i.e. son of Aitor, and wrote his novel *Aitor, a Cantabrian Legend.*

institutional and discursive structures by uniting them under the rubric of 'Orientalism.' Although Said does not dwell on the epistemological and discursive fracture that Orientalism represents vis-à-vis previous discursive structures within Europe, Leon Poliakov, in his *The History of Anti-Semitism*, explains that Orientalism also represents a reorganization of the epistemological discourses of the West (183-214). As a result, Europe's origins no longer are considered Biblical and, thus, ultimately subject to a Jewish origin, but rather Oriental and subject to archaeological, linguistic, and anthropological discourses pointing to India. Poliakov calls this reorganization "the quest for the new Adam" (183). He concludes:

> Thus, we see that a wide variety of authors and schools located the birthplace of the entire human race between the Indus and the Ganges. It only remained for linguistics to make its contribution, in a decisive though ambiguous manner, by dispelling with one certain truth a fog of adventurous suppositions, and at the same time advancing a new hypothesis as fragile as any of those which preceded it. According to this new theory it was not the whole of human race but one particular race—a white race which subsequently became Christian—which had descended from the mountains of Asia to colonize and populate the West. It seemed as if the Europeans of the scientific age, having freed themselves from the conventional Noachian genealogy and rejected Adam as a common father, were looking around for new ancestors but were unable to break with the tradition which placed their origin in the fabulous Orient. It was the science of linguistics which was to give a name to these ancestors by opposing the Aryans to the Hamites, the Mongols—and the Jews. (188)

In this space, India and Sanskrit language stand for the new white or Arian origins of the West, no longer African or Middle-Eastern. Therefore, it is important to emphasize that Orientalism was not simply a discipline to regulate and exploit the colonial other (Said) but also a new scientific and racial reorganization of the West by which "whiteness" was proclaimed as originating elsewhere than in Africa and the Middle-East (Biblical origin). In short, the divide between the Orient and the West was clearly effected by the invention of "whiteness" and, thus, racial superiority could be claimed and mobilized to colonize the Orient—which even in the case of India lost its original "whiteness" and had degenerated into racial and colonial inferiority.

German romanticism was central to the discovery of the Orient and, more specifically, of the Sanskrit language and traditional Hinduist religious discourse. Goethe, the Schlegel brothers, and Novalis proclaimed the Far East, the heart of the Orient, as the origin of the West. Subsequently, Friedrich Schlegel inaugurated the science of philology beginning with his studies on Sanskrit. In France, and next to Madame de Staël, Charles Nodier (1780-1844) was the central and most important writer, the first romantic, to embrace the new ideas of German romanticism, while also combining them with the new historical, literary discourse coming from England: McPherson, Scott, and the Gothic writers.

Augustin Chaho was a student of Nodier and thus it is not a coincidence that Chaho's refashioning of Basque history and discourse was connected with his frequenting of Nodier's salon in Paris. In short, Chaho was witness and participant to the new romantic reorganization of French literature and culture via German romanticism as well as English Gothic and historical literature. Nodier helped romantic writers such as Hugo, Musset, and Bonneville start their careers. Hugo and other writers such as Dumas and Lamartine dedicated their work to Nodier.

It is thus crucial to understand the Chaho-Nodier connection not solely at a biographical level; it must be contextualized in the geopolitical and cultural reorganization that romanticism effected in France. As Gustave Lambert, Chaho's biographer, states, "[H]e made the acquaintance of Charles Nodier, becoming his beloved student. He interested himself in linguistics" (375). Chaho moved to Paris in 1831 and stayed there intermittently through 1843. By the time Chaho arrived, Nodier had published most of his influential work, to which Chaho had access. Among others, it is important to mention Nodier's travel to Scotland, *Promenade from Dieppe to the Mountains of Scotland* (1821), which became the inspiration for Chaho's most important work: *Voyage to Navarre during the Insurrection of the Basques* (1836). Similarly, Nodier published in 1830 his influential *On the Fantastic in Literature*, which set the basis for a new conception of knowledge and literature, based on his romantic recuperation of orientalist studies, linguistics, hermeneutics, Masonic doctrines, British Gothic literature, medieval French tradition, and English and Spanish Renaissance-baroque literature (Shakespeare and Cervantes).

Nodier's combination of arcane and linguistic knowledge constituted the basis for Chaho's literary work. Chaho's first two works were precisely studies of cosmology and linguistics, so that the Basque Country and its language became foregrounded at the intersection of the new romantic and orientalist discourse outlined by Nodier. Besides a Basque grammar written with Anton Abbadie, he also published other three works where linguistics and cosmology were fused, of which *Letter to Mr. Xavier Raymond on the Analogies that Exist between the Basque Language and Sanskrit* (1836) is the most revealing. Chaho later wrote on the comparative philosophy of religions, authored two novels, edited the newspaper *Ariel,* and co-wrote a *History of the Basques since Their Settlement in the Western Pyrenees until Our Days* (1847) with his friend the Marquis of Belsunce. Chaho's extensive work represents the consolidation and expansion of an orientalist ideology that he had already outlined by 1836 in his early work.

The fact that Chaho began by opposing Spanish liberalism and embracing Carlism, but remained a republican all his life (and viewed the Basque Country as a republic) and, at the end of his life, even forsook Carlism, did not substantially alter the orientalist ideology and cosmovision he formed early on, regardless of the concrete, historical reality of the Basque Country. Chaho's changes responded to a larger picture in which different political movements such as Carlism and religions such as paganism were explained as steps or moments in a larger history: one that actually begins with Aitor (the original Basque patriarch of antiquity invented by Chaho) and ends with Zumalakarregi (the leading general of the Carlist troops in the 19th century).

In his *Voyage to Navarre*, Chaho condenses Christian and pagan religions in passages in which the name given to God by the Basque apologists of the Renaissance is rescued (Aio, Iaeo) in order to connote the new orientally-defined antiquity and originality of the Basques: "The vaulted ceiling of churches, painted in sky blue and sprinkled with stars, imitates the vault of the heavens; a superb pavilion under which the ancient Iberians celebrated the night, the happy festivals in honor of eternal AIO" (*Voyage* 162).[113] In this way, and following Humboldt's new linguistic ideas, Chaho retraces Basque language to the Iberians; in turn, the Iberians become one of the original tribes hailing from the Orient. Consequently, for Chaho, the Basques are related to such different countries as Iran or India, but not to the tribes contained in the Bible, thus, adjusting his theories to the new anti-Semitic racial ideology fostered by Orientalism in Europe (Poliakov 1965). Hence, Chaho states:

---

[113] "La voûte des églises, peintes en bleu d'azur et parsemée d'étoiles, imite la voûte du ciel; pavillon superbe sous lequel les anciens Ibères célébraient, la nuit, leur fêtes joyeuses en l'honneur du LAO éternel."

Long time before the formation of the Jewish people and the humiliating servitudes that made this handful of fugitive slaves expire, in such a harsh way, their pretenses to nationhood, the name of 'God's people' was applied originally to the only patriarchs of the South: it reminds us of the theism the ancient Euskarians professed, without symbols, without sacrifices, without prayers or cult. (*Voyage* 233)[114]

Finally, Chaho's *Voyage to Navarre* also represents the discursive form of travel narrative that most outsiders adopt throughout the 19th century when describing the Basque Country. In the text, Chaho travels from Paris to Navarre, crosses the border and meets the new patriarch of the Basque republic: Zumalakarregi, the Carlist general, who, in Chaho's eyes, becomes "the heir to Aitor."

In this sense, the very same trope of *Peru Abarka* is at work in *Voyage to Navarre*. This voyage is also set from a modern position, Paris, and ventures into the heart of the Basque republic and its leader, Zumalakarregi. In this sense, the representation of the Basque patriarch Zumalakarregi is similar to that of Peru Abarka. Here too, we have an idealized representation of the farmer who, in Chaho's historical version, is also a soldier: "if it were not for the need to plow the land from which they obtain sustenance, the mountaineers would be happily disposed to spending the entire year at war" (*Voyage* 136).

Ultimately, Chaho repositioned the Basque Country in a strategic and essentialist way, but by doing so, also invented a very modern tradition that marked the rest of the century. Retaking the way in which apologists reacted to the advances of Hispanic imperialism in a modern fashion in the Renaissance, Chaho also countered the new orientalist advance of northern European imperialism by strategically repositioning the Basque Country in a very modern, yet essentialist and anti-modern, location: Europe's white origins. In that sense, Chaho consolidated the Basque tradition of invention and recentered Basque strategic essentialism at the core of European Orientalism, imperialism, and racism. Just as with Mogel, the subaltern masses that fought in the Carlist Wars did not matter to Chaho either—and women were left outside this homosocial, patriarchal project.

---

[114] "Bien long-temps avant la formation du peuple juif et les servitudes honteuses qui devaient faire expier si durement à ce ramas d'esclaves fugitifs leurs prétentions à la nationalité, le surnom de peuple de Dieu s'appliquait originairement aux seuls patriarches du Midi : il rappelle le théisme que professaient les Euskariens antiques, sans symboles, sans sacrifices, sans prières et sans culte."

After Chaho, Aitor became the "newly found" old patriarch of the Basques. After Zumalakarregi died and the Carlist movement became a decadent political cause, the legend of Aitor continued to serve other cultural and political agendas in the Basque Country throughout the 19th and 20th centuries. Most importantly, Francisco Navarro Villoslada, the other great tradition inventor of the 19th century, retook it, and redeployed it to consolidate a foundational history that would have horrified Chaho: the Basque (Navarran) origins of imperialist Spain.

Hugo and Mérimée

As Edward Said states, Orientalism is the founding discursive structure and institution by which "the difference between the familiar (Europe, the West, 'us') and the strange (the Orient, the East, 'them')" is established as a way to proclaim Western superiority (43). Although the association of the Basque Country with the Orient led Chaho to identify the Basques with the Arians, foreign writers such as Hugo and Mérimée identifiedy the Basque Country with oriental Africa and used this identification to reformulate French nationalist identity. Opposite Chaho, Victor Hugo and Prosper Mérimée linked the Basque Country to Spain while identifying Spain as the southern European gate to the Orient that starts in North Africa.

Victor Hugo (1802-1885) stated that the Basque Country was historically Castilian but also oriental. The year before the premiere of *Hernani*, in 1829, Hugo published *Les Orientales* (*The Orientals*). In this collection of poems, Hugo connects the medieval world with the Orient, in a geopolitical and historical continuity that centers Spain and the Basque Country inside the Orient. When Hugo advances his definition of literature and oriental representations in the introduction to *Les Orientales*, he opens with a reference to Spain: "Why couldn't a literature in its entirety, and particularly the work of a poet, be like those old villages in Spain, for example, where you find everything" (8).[115] After this opening allusion to Spain, suddenly the Orient, with Spain as its European edge, is foregrounded. Spain becomes a space where the border of modernity disseminates into the Orient. Hence, Spain becomes the gate to the Orient, the passage to Africa and Asia:

---

[115] "[P]ourquoi n'en serait-il pas d'une littérature dans son ensemble, et en particulier de l'œuvre d'un poète, comme de ces belles vieilles villes d'Espagne, par exemple, où vous trouvez tout".

Today we are concerned, and this is the result of thousands of causes that have brought progress, we are more concerned with the Orient than ever before… As a result of all these developments, the Orient, as image, as thought, has become, for both the intellects and the imaginations, a sort of general preoccupation to which the author of this book has responded of his own accord… [this book's] reveries and thoughts have become in turn, and almost without wishing it, Hebraic, Turk, Greek, Persian, Arabic, and even Spanish, for Spain is still the Orient; Spain is half-African and Africa is half-Asiatic. (10-11)[116]

In this context of orientalization, the Basque Country occupies a central place in Hugo's imagination. In 1843, nine years before Hugo went in exile as the famous and celebrated genius of French culture, he stopped at the Basque Country for about a month on his way to Cauterets where he wanted to subject himself to a treatment of medicinal waters. On his journey, Hugo wrote notes for a future publication; yet, they were published posthumously along with other notes from a trip to the Alps (*Les Pyrénnées*; *The Pyrenees*). After leaving Paris, Hugo finally arrived to Bayonne, in the Basque Country, where he remembered his childhood: "I could not enter Bayonne without emotion. Bayonne is a childhood memory for me. I came to Bayonne when I was little… in the time of the great wars" (35).[117] Since his father had been part of the army that invaded Spain under Napoleon, Hugo connected his visit with his father in Spain, with happiness, and with "the great wars."

Imperialism and childhood come together in Hugo's mind and, as a result, become connected to the Basque Country. As a genealogical reminder of his future orientalization of the Basque Country, he mentions one of the first theatrical representations he ever saw, an orientalist drama entitled *Ruins of Babylon*, which was performed in Bayonne: "Oh! The good times! The sweet and bright years! I was a child, I was little,

---

[116] "On s'occupe aujourd'hui, et ce résultat est dû à mille causes qui toutes ont amené un progress, on s'occupe beaucoup plus de l'Orient qu'on ne l'a jamais fait…. Il résulte de toute cela que l'Orient, soit comme image, soit comme pensée, est devenu, pur les intelligences autant que pour les imaginations, une sorte de preoccupation générale à laquelle l'auteur de ce livre a obéi peut-être à son insu…. [this book's] reveries et ses pensées se sont trouvés tour à tour, et presque sans l'avoir voulu, hébraïques, torques, grecques, persans, arabes, espagnoles même, car l'Espagne c'est encore l'Orient; l'Espagne est à demi africaine, l'Afrique est á demi asiatique."

[117] "Je n'ai pus entrer à Bayonne sans émotion. Bayonne est pour moi un souvenir d'enfance. Je suis venu à Bayonne étant tout petit… à l'époque des grandes guerres".

and I was loved. I didn't have experience, and I had my mother" (57).[118] As soon as he crosses the border and reaches the Spanish Basque town of Irun, Hugo explains the importance of Spain in his formative years; it is his most personal experience with imperialist otherness: "It is there that Spain appeared to me for the first time and impressed me strongly... I, the French child raised in the cradle of the Empire" (60).[119] His romantizacion of the Spanish Basque Country as fully Spanish is clear. Even in his play *Hernani*, Spain, whose ultimate hero has a Basque name, is a land of smugglers and robbers as well as poets, that is, Spain is outside the law and, thus, is the ultimate land of modern transgression and anti-modern utopia.

But as soon as Hugo invokes the romantic stereotype of Spain in the Basque Country, he also slips into a more abject and disseminative logic, by which the Basque Country becomes both Spain vis-à-vis Europe but also Europe vis-à-vis Spain—due to the Basques' putative historical originality in Europe. When in San Sebastian, he claims, "I am in Spain. I feel lighter. This is a country of poets and smugglers.... But am I really in Spain? San Sebastian is connected to Spain the same way that Spain is to Europe, by an extension of land .... One is barely Spanish in San Sebastian; one is Basque" (65).[120]

However, it is important to see how the slippery oscillation between Europe and the Orient takes place in the Basque Country for the romantic imagination. For Hugo the Basque Country is both, Europe and Africa, Europe and the Orient.

The slippage and dissemination into Orientalism is a direct consequence of Hugo's identification of the Basque Country with Spain. First, the Basque Country becomes imperial Castile. When he enters a house in Pasai San Juan, he exclaims: "You enter; you are at the home of the hidalgos; you breathe the air of the Inquisition; you can see the livid specter of Phillip the Second appearing at the other end of the street" (77).[121]

---

[118] "Oh! Le beau temps! Les douces et rayonnantes années! J'étais enfant, j'étais petit, j'étais aimé. Je n'avais pas l'expérience, et j'avais ma mère".

[119] "C'est là que l'Espagne m'est apparue pour la première fois et m'a si fort étonné... moi l'enfant français élevé dans l'acajou de l'empire".

[120] "Je suis en Espagne. J'y ai un pied de moins. Ceci est un pays de poètes et de contrebandiers.... Mais suis-je bien ici en Espagne? San-Sébastian tient à l'Espagne comme l'Espagne tient à l'Europe, par une langue de terre.... On est à peine espagnol à Saint-Sébastien; on est basque."

[121] "Vous entrez, vous êtes chez les hidalgos; vous respirez l'air de l'Inquisition ; vous voyez se dresser à l'autre bout de la rue le spectre livide de Philipe II."

Then, the other side of the harbor becomes an almost full orientalist scenario: "The street of Pasaia is a true Arabic street; whitened houses, massive, beaten, barely plucked with few holes. If there were not but roofs, one would think we are in Tetuan [Morocco]. This street, where the ivy spans from one corner to another, is paved with bricks, long scales of stone that swerve like the back of a serpent" (93).[122] For Hugo's romantic imagination, the slippery and disseminative continuity of Orientalism spans from Pasaia to Tetuan, Morocco.

Hugo also resorts to the alternative form of otherness that defines the Basques: they are the oldest people of Europe, the true natives. Hugo perceives that this slippery orientalist scenario is arrested by a Basque specificity that is neither Oriental nor Spanish: "Here is Guipuzcoa, it is the ancient country of the fueros; these are the old free Vascongada provinces. A little Castilian is spoken, but mainly basceunce [sic, Basque]" (65).[123] When Hugo attempts to explain the uniqueness of the Basque Country, he resorts to its historical difference vis-a-vis the advance of modern states such as Spain. In a passage that resounds with echoes of Humboldt, Hugo concludes that the Basque Country is neither Spain nor France, but the historical resistance to the advance of both modern states:

> No doubt, this Basque unity tends to decrease and finally will disappear. The large states must absorb the small ones; that is the law of history and nature. But it is remarkable that this unity, so weak in appearance, has resisted so long. France has taken one side of the Pyrenees, Spain has taken the other; neither France nor Spain have been able to dissolve the Basque group. Underneath the new history that is overlapping in the last four centuries, it remains perfectly visible like a crater underneath a lake. (66)[124]

---

[122] "La rue du vieux Pasages est une vraie rue arabe; maisons blanchies, massives, cahotées, à peine percées de quelques trous. S'il n'y avait les toits, on se croirait à Tetuan. Cette rue, où le lierre va d'un côté à l'autre, est pavée de dalles, larges écailles de pierre que ondulent comme le dos d'un serpent."

[123] "C'est ici Guipuzcoa, c'est l'antique pays des fueros, ce sont les vieilles provinces libres vascongadas. On parle bien un peu castillan, mais on parle surtout *basceunce* [sic]."

[124] "Sans doute cette unité vascongada tend à décroitre et finira par disparaître. Les grands Etats doivent absorber les petits; c'est la loi de l'histoire et de la nature. Mais il est remarquable que cette unité, si chétive en apparence, ait résisté si longtemps. La France a pris un revers des Pyrénées, l'Espagne a pris l'autre; ni la France ni l'Espagne n'ont pu désagréger le groupe basque. Sous l'histoire nouvelle que s'y superpose depuis quatre siècles, il est encore parfaitement visible comme un cratère sous un lac."

To the European eye, the Basque difference is a form of exoticism that slips into both an Orientalism that is exterior to Europe and a form of premodern historical otherness that resists European modernity from within.

This dual othering of Basques can be traced throughout the 19th century. In 1845, Prosper Mérimée wrote his famous *Carmen*. This text, which constitutes the foundational text of the articulation of modern female sexuality as *femme fatale*, narrates precisely the seductions and perils of the Spanish Orient in the form of travel narrative. The author has recourse to two characters that exceed and thus represent, in their excess, Europe and the Orient: the Basque don José, and the Romani/gypsy (not Muslim or Jewish) Carmen. In short, there is nothing Spanish about this quintessential romantization of Spain. Don José introduces himself according to the religious-racial doctrines articulated by the Basque apologists of the Renaissance: "'I was born,' he said, 'in Elizondo, in the valley of Baztan. My name is don José Lizarrabengoa, and you are familiar enough with Spain, señor, to be able to tell at once from my name that I am a Basque and an Old Christian'" (19). Furthermore, the culminating moment in Carmen's seduction of don José takes place in Basque. As he narrates:

> "*Laguna ene bihotsarena* – companion of my heart," she said suddenly, "Are you from the Basque Provinces?" [...] "She was lying, señor, as she always lied. I wonder whether that girl ever spoke one word of truth in her life; but whenever she spoke, I believed her – I couldn't help it. She spoke Basque atrociously, yet I believed her when she said she was from Navarre. You only had to look at her eyes, her mouth, and her complexion to tell she was a Gypsy. I was mad, I overlooked the most obvious things." (24)

In this novella, the Basques, because of their European originality, represent the standby for the white romantic French traveler, Mérimée himself, the narrator and author of the text. Yet, because of their Spanishness, the Basques also present a knowledge and intimacy with the Orient, which no other European subject possesses. Don José, unlike Mérimée, is capable of becoming the epitome of the savage Spanish: the apparently civilized soldier who nevertheless abandons duty and decorum for the sake of love and, thus, becomes the quintessential romantic stereotype of the Spanish *bandolero* or highway robber. He is the Spanish subject that defies the law and is also able to kill off the oriental, sexual threat that Carmen represents. Just as with *Ivanhoe*'s Rebecca, the beautiful Jewish woman, Carmen, the oriental Spanish subject, the seductive and yet dangerous embodiment of the Orient, must be dismissed at the end. Yet this time, the voyeuristic author must rely on a more capable savage form of masculinity to do the job: the Basque don José. At the end of the story, don José kills Carmen; he turns himself to justice and awaits his death sentence in jail. In short, even the Basque subject, although truly European and white, must be killed off, so that the entire Spanish field (Basque and Oriental) is turned into an object of Orientalist research, a neutralized object that, then, can be enjoyed and studied by the orientalist from a (French) distance. The final and additional chapter of *Carmen* is a treaty on Romani/Gypsy culture.

Furthermore, when Carmen tells don José that she was born in Navarre, in Etxalar, the novel does not at any point delegitimize her claim. When don José states, "[S]he was lying, señor, as she always lied. I wonder whether that girl ever spoke one word of truth in her life; but whenever she spoke, I believed her" (24), he does not delegitimize her claims, for Carmen always lies and, therefore, always simulates identity; the truth about her birthplace is beyond simulation. In this way, Mérimée opens up the possibility for the fact that the ultimate romantic embodiment of the Orient might hail from the Basque Country, which is the ultimate form of epistemological perversion, for the Orient could be located at the heart of the most "original and true Europe:" in the Basque Country. Unlike Hugo, Mérimée emphasizes the Basques' intimate knowledge of the Orient, due to their Spanish status, but, at the same time, concedes their difference with the Orient. This differentiation increased throughout the 19th century.

The reference to Hugo and Mérimée is important in order to correct the predominance given to anthropology in the construction of Basque otherness. Before anthropologists found in the Basque Country "the origins of the oldest European race" in the 1850s and 60s, writers such as Hugo and Mérimée already articulated a discourse of otherness and essentialism towards the Basque Country during the first half of the 19th century (1830s and 40s). Yet with anthropology, Orientalism took another turn, since, following linguistics, anthropology endeavored to create a biological theory of whiteness that responded to the divide between the Orient and the West.

2. Anthropologists and *Bertsolaris* (Broca, Abbadie, Etxahun)

Following the revolution of 1848 in France, and during the European conservative turn of the 1850s and 60s, the discipline of physical anthropology inaugurated by Paul Broca in Paris and Anders Retzius in Sweden looked anew for the scientific origins of humankind and, more specifically, of Europe. This new anthropological discourse found in Basques one of its richest objects. As William Douglass states:

> By mid-century, Anders Retzius, the Swedish anatomist who systematized craneomety, and Paul Broca, the founding father of French anthropology, were debating Basque anthropometry.... There was the notion, then, that Basques, if not a "pure" proto-European race, were at the least the continent's "purest" contemporary representatives of it [...]. European scientific racism largely accepted the conclusion that there was a 'Basque race,' a creation more of the intellectual circles of Paris and Stockholm than Basque (or Spanish) ones. (102)

Following earlier linguistic and apologetic discourses on the Basques, anthropology presented the Basque Country as the remnant of an old Europe. However, once anthropology developed a new biological theory of the Aryan race and whiteness, Basques became the only race left from an older pre-Indo-European-Aryan Europe, which, to the anthropological imagination, turned out to be twice white and/or twice non-Oriental. At the same time, when anthropology organized colonial subjects as exterior racial others that, in their racial difference, reflected back on Europe's newly acquired whiteness, the Basques became the only "native savages" inside Europe, who were, at the same time, white—unlike, say, the "negroized" Irish in British imperialist imagination. In other words, Basques became "European colonial subjects:" a racial contradiction in terms, which, therefore, became the site of many anthropological anxieties and fantasies.

By the 1850s, the Basques no longer were a gate to the Orient (as in the case of Hugo and Mérimée) or the descendants of the white Aryan race (as in the case of Chaho), but rather the only colonial subjects within Europe: white, yet native. Therefore, anthropology shifted literature's orientalist stress from a Basque identity that was both interior and *exterior* (European, yet part of the Spanish gate to the Orient) to a new identity that was both interior and *anterior* (the only colonial subject interior to Europe, yet older than imperialist Europe). Because of anthropology's new racial discourse, Basques' otherness and essentialism was fully situated inside Europe—while still responding to an orientalist logic.

Abbadie

One of the most interesting and famous Basque characters of the 19th century, and friend of Chaho, Antoine d'Abbadie (1810-97), was originally involved in the colonialist discovery of the sources of the Nile—the symbolic touchstone of British imperialism. Later on, he also became the central character in the revival and promotion of modern Basque literature and culture; he organized and promoted the Basque floral games, starting in 1853. Abbadie had access to the discourse of Orientalism and physical anthropology; those two disciplines, in turn, shaped his understanding and promotion of Basque culture and literature.

The Irish-born Abbadie spent the first half of his life dedicated to exploring and mapping Ethiopia—or Abyssinia as it was known then. Later, he secluded himself in the Basque Country, built a huge beautiful castle in Labourd, and spent the other half of his life devoted to the promotion of Basque culture—although he did not abandon his colonialist studies. Among other works, he elaborated an Amarinna dictionary that even Rimbaud himself requested in his failed attempts to enrich himself in Ethiopia. This transition in Abbadie's life—from Ethiopia to the Basque Country—represents the displacement of a colonialist, orientalist endeavor *outside* the West to a new "colonialist" activity *inside* the West.

Although Abbadie collaborated on a Basque grammar with Augustin Chaho back in 1836, that is, before his departure for Africa, he only devoted his energies to the Basque Country when he returned from his twelve-year long voyage to Ethiopia (1837-49). He turned to the Basque Country precisely when the scientific and academic world concluded that his claim to the discovery of the Nile's source was ultimately untenable. That is, Abbadie devoted his attention to the Basque Country only when he discovered that his main colonialist contribution to science was lost. The Basque Country became an object of interest and desire to Abbadie after he lost his colonialist discursive aim and object: the discovery of the sources of the Nile. In short, the Basque Country, its culture and literature, became for Abbadie a compensation for and introjection of a colonialist loss.

However, Abbadie's radical life-change must also be understood in the general context of the European Restoration (1814-1830) and its consequent conservative turns through midcentury. As Juaristi elaborates, this was the moment when both Spanish and French imperialisms began to decline—that is, at a moment when both nations became marked by colonial loss:

> If furthermore the humble inhabitants of the [Basque] Country—in whom no longer could be recognized the frightening partisan armed with rifle [of the Carlist Wars]—spoke an incomprehensible language that many still considered the very same spoken in the solitude of the Edenic Paradise... even better. The [Spanish] Isabeline bourgeoisie was not eager, unlike its Victorian counterpart, to find the sources of the Nile. Their souls were not corroded by the implacable spleen that pushed the English to flee anywhere, as long as it was far from home. *Why waste time looking for Doctor Livingston when one could live without risks the experience of exoticism few miles away from home?* (*Bucle* 60-1, my emphasis)

After the European Restoration and through the 1850s and 1860s, the Basque Country became an internal other to both Spain and France, which mobilized the political imagination of the aristocracy and bourgeoisie of both states. More specifically, the Basque Country was othered when both imperialist countries experienced colonial loss and decadence abroad. Thus, the anthropological obsession with the origins of Europe and the melancholia for imperialist loss met their perfect object in the Basque Country.

Although Abbadie was more central than Chaho to the invention of the Basque Country as compensatory object of imperialist loss, it is clear that such invention served both the Basques and the Franco-Spanish bourgeoisies in order to strike a symbolic and economic deal that benefited both parties through tourism. The Basques regained certain economic vitality thanks to tourism, whereas the French and Spanish bourgeoisies found their perfect object of desire—one that symbolically compensated for their imperialist losses—in the Basque Country and, thus, proceed to turn the coastal Basque Country (San Sebastian and Biarritz) into their favorite touristic destination. In this context, the essentialization of Basque culture, which Abbadie fostered, was strategic on both parts.

Although Abbadie did not publish much about the Basque Country, most of his work dating from 1849 on points indeed to this imaginative and imperialist logic of loss and compensation. However, it is important to note that Abbadie's colonialist logic was at work even before he departed for Ethiopia. In his *Analyse du Voyage en Navarre de M. Chaho* (*Analysis of Mr. Chaho's Voyage to Navarre*, 1836), Abbadie notices the importance of using an ethnographic technology, first applied in the colonial field—craneometry—, to the Basque Country. His goal is to define the Basque Country anthropologically through the concept of race and, thus, to make it comparable to any other colonial race:

> The portrait of a standing Navarran offers a true type of this Basque [euskarienne] race. Since the work of Peron in the austral lands, there has not been enough emphasis on this method so useful to establish filiation and affinity among different peoples […] Nevertheless, instead of these cranes that can hardly be obtained, good portraits will powerfully help the linguists in the still forming science of ethnography. (83)[125]

After his return from Ethiopia in 1849, this redeployment of anthropological discourse became more emphatic. In his *Travaux récents sur la langue basque* (*Recent Works on the Basque Language*, 1859), Abbadie situated the research of Basque language precisely in the context of Orientalism. However, there is a very interesting oscillation between the way in which Basque is differentiated from the orientalist field and, yet, remains an "indigenous" language, internal to the West. If Basque serves both European philology and Orientalism in their endeavor to complete the classification of all languages, for Abbadie, Basque is the only Western language that has escaped European philology, precisely because Basque is closer to the Orient than it is to the West. In short, Basque is an "exceptional Oriental language: « The new publications in the diverse languages of Europe are not in the domain of the Asiatic Society inasmuch as they help the advancement of philology. Among our indigenous languages, Basque is the only one that remains isolated in our vast classifications" (433).[126]

---

[125] «Le portrait en pied d'un Navarraise offre un vrai type de cette race euskarienne. Depuis les travaux de Peron, dans les terres australes, on n'a pas assez insisté sur cette méthode, si utile pur établir la filiation et l'affinité des peuples.... Cependant à défaut des cranes qu'on peut rarement se procurer, de bons portraits aideraient puissamment les linguistes dans la science encore si informe de l'ethnographie».

[126] "Les publications nouvelles dans les divers idiomes de l'Europe ne sont du domaine de la Société asiatique qu'autant qu'elles tendent a l'avancement de la philologie. Parmi nos langues indigènes, le basque est la seule qui reste encore isolée dans nos grandes classifications".

Within this orientalist context, however, the imperialist logic dictates that any "savage" can eventually be equated with Basque indigenous people. Thus, Abbadie continues the introduction to his work by stating that the logic and semantic structure of Basque, which contains so many complex forms, can be equated with that of any American "savage" language:

> The usage of these [Basque] complicated forms demands even more memory than intelligence; but the Basque peasant manages this prodigious conjugation with as much ease as the savage from America knows how to employ the flexions of his language, so rich and so complicated. One is tempted to believe that the sum of intelligence is the same among savages and civilized people, but that it follows different ways. (435)[127]

As the above quote proves, the Basque peasant occupies a transitional place that oscillates between the colonial field of the American "savage" and the imperialist and civilized European man. The Basque peasant is both savage—external—and civilized—internal—to the West.

In the 19th century, Basques occupied this slippery place between the inside and the outside of the West, the colony and the empire. As a result, the Basque Country became the perfect substitutive object of imperialist loss.

Bertsolaris

Following a tradition that existed in the south of France since the Middle Ages, and inspired by similar music performances he observed in Ethiopia,[128] Abbadie began to organize "floral games" or *lorejokoak* in 1853 in Urruña. Similar celebrations sprang up in Catalonia (1859) and Galicia (1861). In the Galician case, a rich promoter and sponsor, José Pascual López Corton, also played the same role. Similarly, he also came from a colonial background: he made his fortune in Puerto Rico (Carballo Calero 71). He financed the publication of *Charity Album* (1862), the book that started the new Galician poetry.

---

[127] «l'usage de ces [Basque] formes si compliquées exige plus de mémoire encore que d'intelligence; mais le paysan basque manie cette prodigieuse conjugaison avec d'autant de facilité que le sauvage de l'Amérique sait employer les flexions de sa langue, si riches et si compliquées. On est vraiment tenté de croire que la somme d'intelligence est la même chez le sauvage et chez l'homme civilisé, mais qu'elle suit des voies différentes.»

[128] Personal communication by Patri Urkizu.

These festivals celebrated tournaments among poets, but also ball games and exhibits of rural products (cows, vegetables, etc.). Abbadie provided from his own pocket the different prizes given in the festivals and thus became known as "the patriarch of Basque culture"—an adjective that also resounds with colonial overtones. The first floral game was organized in 1853 in Urruña, but eventually moved to the Spanish Basque Country. In 1879, they were celebrated in the Navarran town of Elizondo and, then, were expanded to Guipuzcoa, Biscay, and Alava. Towards the end of the century, they were organized and sponsored by the provincial governments of each Spanish Basque province. Although the poetry competitions were based on poems written in advance, many *bertsolaris* or improvisational poets who were popular also competed in these tournaments. As a result, and for the first time in Basque history, poets and *bertsolaris* from both sides of the Pyrenees participated in the same tournaments, thus, becoming familiar with their counterparts from the other state. As Patri Urkizu states, the floral games celebrated in the Alavan town of Aramaio in 1899 brought to reality the slogan of "The Seven One," referring to the unity of the seven provinces where Basque is spoken, which served as the slogan of the floral games of Saint Jean de Lux celebrated in 1892. This slogan was created by a poet attending the floral games the year before, Felipe Casal (Urkizu, *Historia* 329).

In short, the promotion of floral games in Basque produced a literature that was also Basque in a geopolitical sense. Only since the *lorejokoak* can we speak of a modern Basque literature as (subaltern) institution: one that is also geopolitically Basque, since it addresses all the Basque territories, which, until that point, never had a political unity as such. As Urkizu concludes, "the Floral Games in the Basque Country as well as in Catalonia and Galicia represented the first specific platform geared towards organizing and promoting the language and reviving [national] identities; they fostered literary creation, from which poetry first benefited and later narrative too" (*Historia* 330). It is important to emphasize that, because of the imperialist logic of loss as well as the orientalist and anthropological ideology underlying the floral games, for the first time, the subaltern Basque voice of the mostly illiterate poet, the *bertsolari*, was celebrated as the "true" voice of the Basque people—the voice of the native. Furthermore, the fact that for the first time illiterate *bertsolaris* and literate poets participated in the floral games, made the mixing of subaltern and (lower) middle-class literatures a very permeable environment where texts, myths, tropes, and rhetoric flowed in every direction while cross-pollinating each other in a polyphonic fashion. Cultured poets such as Elissamburu or Arresebetia participated in the floral games with illiterate *bertsolaris*, such as Etxahun, an improviser known for his notorious criminal past.

In the floral games, popular improvised poetry was submitted as written poem and rewarded as high literature; illiterate *bertsolaris* would have somebody else write down their verses for them. This process of incorporating subaltern voices in Basque literature eventually became central to the future of Basque literature. Similarly, literature written in Spanish or French began to contain elements from Basque oral culture (especially *costumbrismo* o custom literature, but also legend literature as in the case of Antonio Trueba). Therefore, subaltern voices and subjects were incorporated by high Basque literature in a polyphony of voices that was not reducible to the categories of genuine tradition or sheer fabrication (to use Hobsbawn's terms). It was precisely the polyphony of voices inscribed in this literature that made its invented discourse genuine and false, historical and invented, subaltern and modern. Similarly, Chaho recreated the legend of Aitor by referring to the *bertsolaris* as the true descendants of the old "bards" of the Aitorean era.

At the core of this irreducible duality, there was a second form of discussion about the "genuine or fabricated" status of *bertsolaris* as romantic poets. As *bertsolaris* constituted the subaltern subject closest to a high-culture understanding of Basque literary authorship, they embodied the duality between subalternity and modernity. The discussion as to whether they were simply *bertsolaris* or could also be considered poets fascinated cultural promoters, observers, and critics in the 19th century. *Bertsolaris* such as Etxahun, Bilintx, or Xenpelar, because of the hardships they underwent as (illiterate) subaltern subjects, were close to the ideal of the demonic romantic or post-romantic writer à la Byron or Baudelaire. The debates as to whether these *bertsolaris* should be considered romantic poets linger in our days. The contemporary fascination with *bertsolaris* who could improvise poetry similar to romantic literature, which, nevertheless, could not be considered "true" romantic literature, further exacerbated the paradigm of the *poet maudit* or infernal poet, with which they were compared. The fact that a *bertsolari* such as Bilintx actually read Spanish romantic poetry—Zorrilla, etc.—further complicated the position of these *bertsolaris* as both subaltern and modern.

It is not a coincidence if a *bertsolari* such as Pierre Topet (1786-1862), better known as Etxahun, composed some of the most somber and melancholic poems or *bertsos* of the 19th century, as in "Mündian malerusik" ("Miserable in the World," 1827). The first three verses read as follows:

Mündin hanits malerus arauz baziraie
Bena ez ni bezaiñik ihur behinere;
Ene fons propiaren izan nahiz jabe,
Tristia ezari niz ihon lürrik gabe.

There are many of you in the world unhappy
But no one as unhappy as I am
For I wanted to own my own state,
But I've become somber without land instead.

Desertüko ihizik jenten beldürrez

Prekozionatzen (dira) ebiltera gordez;
Nik hurak imitatzen gaxoa nigarrez
Ene bizi tristiren konserbi beharrez.

The beasts of the desert, afraid of people
Take care of hiding themselves;
I, wretched soul, imitate them and cry
Trying to preserve my miserable life.

Hamar urthe hontan bizi niz esklabo,
Erdiak presuetan bestik sordeisago;
Jeloskeria baten süjetetik oro

Ni ere inpatient gerthatürik gero.
(7)

I've lived as a slave for the last ten years
Half imprisoned, half even worse;
Everything is the result of a jealousy;
I lost my patience as a result.

His abject life as outcast contributed to his fame. Similarly, Jose Maria Iparragirre (1820-1881) joined the Carlist cause in the war but, later, exiled himself to France and traveled the country earning money by singing the Marseillese on the streets. When he sang his most famous song in Madrid in 1853, "Gernikako Arbola" ("The Tree in Guernica") the non-official anthem of all the Basques, this hymn resounded with the universalism of the Marseillese. It refers to the oak tree under which the General Assembly of Biscay met and decided political and legislative matters according to the *foruak*. It became the banner under which Basque *foralistas* or *foruzaleak* rallied in opposition to the centralist doctrines of the Spanish liberal governments. The first three verses read:

Gernikako arbola / da bedeinkatua,
euskaldunen artean / guztiz maitatua.

The Tree of Gernika is sacred,
Most revered among the Basques

| Eman da zabaltzazu / munduan frutua; | Yield and spread your fruit in the world |
| adoratzen zaitugu, / arbola santua. | We worship you sacred tree. |

Mila urte inguru da / esaten dutela,	They say it's been around a thousand years
Jainkoak jarri zuela / Gernikako arbola.	Since God planted the Tree of Guernica
Zaude, bada, zutikan / orain da denbora,	Thus stand erect, now is the time,
eroritzen bazera, / arras galdu gera.	Because if you fall, we are doomed.

Ez zera eroriko, / Arbola maitea,	You will not fall, dear Tree
baldin portatzen bada, / Bizkaiko Juntia.	If the Assembly of Biscay acts in accordance.
Laurok artuko degu / zurekin partia,	The four of us [provinces] will join you
pakean bizi dediñ / euskaldun jentia. (5)	So that the Basques live in peace.

Iparragirre was neither a poet nor a *bertsolari*, but precisely another form of subaltern subject who hybridized such different genres as Italian opera, anthems (The Marseillese), popular *bertsolarism*, and romantic poetry. Until the Basque Government of the Basque Autonomous Region decided on an official anthem, "The Tree of Guernica" was sang as the national hymn of the Basques, thus exemplifying the instability and, also, durability of this production, which started as a subaltern song and ultimately became a hypercanonical anthem. As Villasante states:

Etchahun and Iparraguirre, indeed, partly so similar and partly so different from each other, ended up becoming the two most popular poets of the two Basque Countries [south and north]. One can see the similar adventurous and wandering lives in both poets, similar immortal songs and wide popularity for both. The personal unhappiness and misfortune, more felt in the flesh by Etchahun, gave a moving elegiac tone to his songs. (101)[129]

---

[129] "Etchaun e Iparraguirre, en efecto, siendo en parte muy semejantes y en parte muy distintos el uno del otro, han venido a ser los poetas populares por antonomasia de las dos Vasconias. Idéntica vida azarosa y errante en ambos, idénticos cantos inmortales y popularidad alcanzada por uno y otro. La desgracia personal y el infortunio, sentido más en carne viva por Etchahun, ha dado un tono de elegía conmovedor a sus cantos."

The fact that the other most important *bertsolari* of that period, Frantzisko Petrirena Rekondo (1835-1869), better known as Xenpelar, mocked Iparragirre in his verses for not being genuinely popular explains the polyphonic but subaltern condition that defined the origin of modern literature in Basque. Xenpelar was a factory worker. Yet he sang to Iparragirre:

Iparragirre abila dela	That Iparragirre is gifted
askori diot aditzen,	I hear from many people,
eskola ona eta musika,	He has good schooling and music
hori horiekin zerbitzen.	With which he helps himself.
Ni ez nauzu ibiltzen,	I do not wander
kantuz dirua biltzen,	Collecting money with my music
komeriante moduan,	Like comedians,
debalde festa preparatzen det	I prepare my own free parties
gogua duan orduan.	When I please so.
Eskola ona eta musika	Good schooling and music
bertsolaria gainera,	And he is also a *bertsolari*,
gu ere zerbait izango gera	We would be just as much
hola hornitzen bagera	If we were so well educated.
Hatoz gure kalera,	Come to our street
baserritar legera,	To the rural custom
musika hoiek utzita;	And leave those songs behind;
Errenterian bizi naiz eta	I live in Errenteria
egin zaidazu bisita.	Come visit me any time.
(Lekuona 231)	

Therefore, if the Basque Country becomes the compensation of a colonial loss, then, the *bertsolari* emerges as the "genuine" voice of the new, touristic, savage, Basque "native." His or her singing becomes the essence of a Basque Country that no longer poses a threat to the Spanish and French bourgeoisies.

When the entire corpus of bertsolarism in the 19th century is analyzed, it is clear that its main concerns have to do with the conditions of subaltern, rural peasants and villagers, from farm evictions and economic migration overseas to murder, alcoholism, and military draft.[130] The bertsolaris sang about economic and social problems in Spain and France in the 19th century. Yet, the cultural promotion of the *bertsolari* gave, for the first time, a voice to subaltern subjects and, at the same time, created a linguistic consciousness towards a new Basque Country that was "seven in one," that is, the seven Basque provinces on both sides of the Pyrenees. It remains to be studied the process by which Basque nationalism appropriated this subaltern production in the 20th century. Sabino Arana's earlier formulations only concerned Biscay, not the seven provinces, and they were far from the linguistic consciousness created by *bertsolaris.*

Moreover, the romantic and Ossianic dream of seeking the true bards of antiquity, fostered by Chaho in his invention of the myth of Aitor, found in the subaltern *bertsolari* its most essential representation. After Chaho, *bertsolaris* were greeted as the true bards who hailed directly from Aitor's lineage. After Zumalakarregi died and the Carlist cause faded away after the last civil war (1872-76), the *bertsolari* became the only and most central sign of the existence of an essential Basque Country founded by Aitor at the dawn of the birth of a white, colonialist Europe. The fact that the *bertsolari* did not embody any political order, given his or her subalternity, but at the same time, bore witness to the language and oral literature of a "primordial" Basque Country, made him or her the perfect representative of a nation and culture still to come. The *bertsolari* became the accidental embodiment of the nation to come: a nation whose origins were orientalist imperialism and colonial loss.

3. Foundational Fictions and Tourism (Trueba, Loti, Navarro Villoslada)

In the period that spans from the long European Restoration (1814-1848) to the Franco-Prussian war (1870-71) and the end of the Carlist Wars (1876), both Spanish and French states attempted to regulate their respective societies through different forms of centralization: national

---

[130] As Luzia Alberro states in her recent study of turn-of-century bertsolaris (Xenperlar, Bilintx, Pello Errota, Otaño, Txirrita, Lopetegi) reflected more than any other voice the contradictory thinking of Basque subaltern classes. She emphasizes that there were women *bertsolaris* but there are few records of them and further archival research is necessary.

banks, currency, railroads, schools, army, etc. Most institutions were centralized and regulated by the liberal State. This process, however, came to a standstill for both states after France's defeat in the Franco-Prussian war of 1870-71 and Spain's failure to enact a bourgeois revolution in 1868-74.

During this period, both sides of the Basque Country experienced economic decline. The old economic system of the ancien régime, based on a very precarious agricultural system and antiquated industries, did not survive the rise of British and French industrialization. Therefore, the Basque Country was turned into a pristine landscape where the new French and Spanish bourgeoisies could experience the most "original, authentic landscape and people" of their respective states. The Basque Country increasingly became a place for tourism. Although locations such as Biarritz or San Sebastian became tourist resorts, where the beach and the casino were combined to form the first modern resorts (as opposed to older forms such as "balnearios" or "health spas") by mid-century, they became popular towards the end of the century with the development of the railway. As John Walton and Jenny Smith stress, this was a phenomenon mostly centered in the Basque Country, as the Spanish and French bourgeoisies would cross the border to the other side of the Basque Country, in order to enjoy different amenities:

> Aspiring Spanish resorts also suffered from domestic and foreign competition. Despite traveling conditions, the richest Spaniards were often tempted abroad, especially to resorts in southern France such as Arcacho, Bagnéres de Luchon and (above all) Biarritz. This exodus was not balanced by an equivalent influx to the Spanish seaside, although French visitors in their thousands came to San Sebastián's August bullfights from the 1870s onwards, while Las Arenas, near Bilbao, was aiming advertisement specifically at English visitors in 1872. (24)

As a result of this touristic reorganization, very important travelers began to visit the Basque Country. They no longer looked for anthropological vestiges of an original Europe or for the colonialist compensation of orientalist losses. They sought a Basque Country that was close to nature and represented a new pastoral site for the French and Spanish bourgeoisies.

More specifically many *costumbristas* (writers of custom literature), including Basque authors such as Juan Venancio Araquistáin (1828-1906) and Antonio Trueba (1821-1889), wrote short stories that emphasized the legendary nature of the Basque Country. Half-popular legend, half-romantic cliché, their short stories added a mysterious touch to the touristic Basque Country. Their work became very popular in Spain and contributed significantly to turning the Basque Country into the land of fantastic legends that conveyed a mysterious past and a very harmless present that exorcised the specter of past Carlist Wars. Although Trueba wrote many short story collections, Araquistáin became known for his *Basque-Cantabrian Traditions* (1866).

Yet the tour de force of this touristic and legendary literature came with the encyclopedic historical novel written by Francisco Navarro Villoslada (1818-1895): *Amaya or the Basques in the Eighth Century* (1879). After the failure of the bourgeois revolution (1868-74), Spain reached a precarious political balance among its heterogeneous forces, known as the Restoration (1874-1931), and, therefore, it was in need of new myths and traditions that helped consolidate its state institutions and promote a new form of Spanish nationalism. As José Alvarez Junco states, the most important foundational myth of Spain became the "Reconquest" (424), that is, the expansionist wars, spanning from the 8th century through 1492, which were intended to expel the Muslims from Spain and "regain" the original territory for Christendom. Navarro Villoslada wrote a very compelling, narrative version of this period while also justifying the foundation of the old kingdom of Navarre as the historical starting point of the Reconquest. Furthermore, Navarro Villoslada depicted the Navarran kingdom as originally Basque and, thus, as a result, repositioned the Basque Country and Navarre at the origin of modern, conservative Spain.

Against what Jimenez de Rada wrote six hundred years earlier, Navarro Villoslada's *Amaya* portrayed the wedding between a victorious Visigoth leader, García, and the heir of the pagan Basque Country, Amaia. This union secured the lineage of the Navarran kingdom and the beginning of the Reconquest. In this way, the Basque Country became the cradle of modern Spain. With *Amaya*, the Basque tradition of invention contributed centrally to the new myths of Spanish nationalism.[131]

Navarro Villoslada's historical novel is closest to its Latin American counterpart, which Doris Sommer has named "foundational fiction" for, as she herself explains, "the inextricability of politics from fiction in the history of nation-building" defined the foundational historical novel of

---

[131] It also contributed to what, in the 20th century, became the Navarran variant of Spanish nationalism, navarrismo (Leoné).

Latin America (*Foundational* 5-6). Furthermore, and according to Sommer, in the Latin American novel of the 19th century, history and romance go hand by hand so that the mixing of genres creates the narrative foundation of the nation. At the level of the story, the mixing of genres is also mirrored by the mixing of the protagonists' different races (*mestizaje*). Usually a white *criollo* man marries a racially marked woman, thus, signifying the hierarchical inclusion of all individuals, subaltern and hegemonic, in the new project of heteronormative, racist, national construction. The participation of the racially marked subaltern masses, mainly represented as woman, is necessary to foster reproduction, biological and national, in the new, incipient republic. As Sommer states:

> After the long civil wars, progress and prosperity depended on national consolidation which needed reconciliation, not exclusion, of differences. The hegemonic project of the class that would be dominant had to win the support of other interests for a (usually) liberal national organization that would benefit them all, just as the hero of romance won the heroine and her family through love and practical concern for their well-being. A white elite, often in the large port cities, had to convince everyone, from landholders and miners to indigenous, black, and mulatto masses, that liberal leadership would bridge traditionally antagonistic races and regions in a new prosperity.
>
> Therefore, the ideal national marriages were often projected in romances between whites and Indians... or mestizas inspired no doubt by Chateaubriand's *Atala*... ("Irresistible" 81)

Similarly, in the Basque case, the literature written during the aftermath of the wars of the 1870s narrated the foundational fiction of marrying the old and the new, the subaltern and the modern, the civilized and the savage native.

Navarro Villoslada's *Amaya* tells the story of the union between the old Basque pagan race and the new Visigoth one, so that this new foundational fiction becomes the basis for the Christian Reconquest of the Iberian Peninsula. The Basque pagans are forced to convert to Christianity or perish, and the Jewish character of the novel is killed off. In this way, the new Basque-Visigoth marriage also becomes the racist foundation of a Christian Spain, clean of Basque pagans and Jewish infidels. This marriage yields the "first" new Christian king of Spain: the embodiment of the new "nation," which is bound, in the Renaissance, to become global empire and center of modernity. This is precisely the moment when, as Alvarez Junco demonstrates, Spanish nationalism stopped being a liberal project and was instead appropriated and refashioned by conservative Catholic factions, so that ultimately nationalism became a conservative project.

Unlike in historiographic narratives, the novel of Navarro Villoslada provides the "essential" native anchorage, the pagan Basque Amaya, thus, turning her marriage to a Visigoth into the true foundation for a nationalist Spain. Without this marriage, the myth of a Visigoth Reconquest remains ultimately foreign: Spain would be the result of a foreign Visigoth invasion. In short, Navarro Villoslada articulates an original, essentialist narrative for Spanish nationalism that abolishes Basque difference. However, and although it would be hard to corroborate with sociological data, it has been said that Navarro Villoslada's work had the unintended effect of converting most of its modern readers to Basque nationalism: the essentialist pull of a Basque pagan world, embodied by Amaya and her ancestors, was greater than that of the intended foundational fiction.

In the French Basque Country, both the lack of civil, violent unrest, similar to the Carlist Wars, and the decline of the economy were signified by a touristic, pastoral nature: a landscape where social change was not possible and, if pursued, always led to migrational exile. With this pastoral discourse, the French state reasserted its control over the Basque periphery and secured the latter's function as a tourist destination. In this context, Pierre Loti (1850-1923), a traveler to the French Basque Country, became the most important exponent of this new touristic, pastoral literature. His most successful novel, *Ramuntcho* (*Little Raymond,* 1897) became the epitome of the new tourist representation of the Basque Country, one that has marked the northern Basque Country until our days.

In *Ramuntcho*, Loti makes many orientalist references to describe the Basque Country. In this way, Basque churches become mosques (48), women sing Spanish songs impregnated with Arab tones (51), Basque language is compared to Mongolian or Sanskrit (58), and tolling the church bells is equated to the muezzins' singing (87). Perhaps the most striking comparison is that of Basque improvisational poets or *bertsolaris* with Muslim muezzins: "They sing with a certain forcing of the throat like the muezzins of the mosques, in a high pitch" (61).[132] Yet, Loti's orientalist rhetoric no longer constructs a compensative, imperialist dis-

---

[132] « Ils chantent avec un certain effort du gosier comme les muezzins des mosquées, en des tonalités hautes ».

course of loss. It is simply a comparative style that only emphasizes exoticism; the Basque Country is well contained within the French state even though it retains its exotic mark.

In Loti's novel, the Basque Country becomes the gate to the natural experience of French nationalism, which he pictures as ultimately a touristic experience. Thus, the novel presents the Basque Country and its hero, Ramuntcho, as fully contained in nature:

> Around the isolated house where, in the great silence of midnight, she decided alone the future of her son, the spirit of the Basque ancestors floated in the air, somber and jealous too. Disdainful of the stranger, fearful of impieties, changes, and race evolutions, the Spirit of the Basque ancestors, the old immutable Spirit which still keeps these people looking towards earlier ages. This secular mysterious Spirit by which children are driven to act like their fathers, before them, had acted on the slope of the same mountains, the same villages, around the same steeples [...] (41)[133]

The hero is introduced in similar pastoral terms: « He adored his Basque land, Ramuntcho—and that morning was one of the times when his love entered more deeply into himself" (46).[134] Yet, Loti clearly inscribes the touristic gaze of the non-Basque subject in this pastoral scene of full containment. The father of Ramuntcho is a foreigner, a projection of Loti himself, who controls the touristic gaze that overdetermines the entire description and narrative of the novel—as it is the case with Mérimée and his novella *Carmen*. When he is describing Ramuntcho, Loti creates a clear divide between maternal nature and fatherly gaze, that is, between feminized land and masculine tourist: « First the instinctive and not analyzed attachment of the maternal ancestors to their native territory, then something more refined from his father, an unconscious reflection of the artist's admiration which had detained the foreigner here for several seasons and had given him the fancy of uniting with a daughter of the mountains to

---

[133] « Autour de la maison isolée où, sous le grand silence de minuit, elle décidait seule de l'avenir de son fils, l'Esprit des ancêtres basques flottait, sombre et jaloux aussi ; dédaigneux de l'étranger, craintif des impiétés, des changements, des évolutions de races ; —l'Esprit des ancêtres basques, le vieil Esprit immuable qui maintient encore ce peuple les yeux tournés vers les âges antérieurs; les mystérieux Esprit séculaire, par qui les enfants sont conduits à agir comme avant eux leurs pères avaient agi, au flanc des mêmes montagnes, dans les mêmes villages, autour des mêmes clochers. »

[134] « Il adorait sa terre basque, Ramuntcho, — et ce matin-là était une des fois où cet amour entrait plus profondément en lui-même. »

beget a Basque descent […]" (47, my emphasis).[135] The father-son genealogy inscribes an artistic gaze in the Basque Country, thus naturalizing the landscape and the people as feminized objects of contemplation, while also legitimizing the gaze itself as masculine and exterior—the gaze of the capricious tourist.

Once the author's gaze constructs the landscape and the people as a continuum in "maternal" nature, then the Basque Country is given depth through a "natural" past. Yet, this immemorial and non-historical past justifies and fixes Basques in their location as natural inhabitants, as objects. Loti has recourse to several stereotyping tropes, such as mystery: « the remains of a mysteriously unique people, without analog among other peoples » (67);[136] and exoticism: "Is it simply the *irrintzina*, the great Basque cry that has been transmitted with fidelity from the abyss of times to the men of today, and is one of the oddities of this race of origins shrouded in mystery" (94).[137] At that point, the Basque cry no longer is equated with oriental practices but with the other important trope of nativism and origins, the North American natives: "[T]his resembles the rallying cry of certain tribes of Redskins in the woods of the Americas" (94).[138] In the mist of these tropes of originality and nativism, the author inserts a love story that is as pure and natural as the landscape. When Ramuntcho the Basque young man and his girlfriend Gracieuse meet in the dark, no sexual or passionate actions follow; rather they act out a perfect Christian, pastoral scene of chastity: "[O]n the contrary, at the intimate time of farewell, they felt even more chaste, such was the eternal love with which they loved each other" (153).[139]

Yet in order to keep the Basque Country as a touristic landscape, Loti has to vacate any form of autonomous life and reproduction, so that

---

[135] "D'abord l'attachement institinctif et non analysé des ancêtres maternels au territoire natal, puis quelque chose de *plus raffiné provenant de son père, un reflet inconscient de cette admiration d'artiste* qui avait retenu ici l'étranger pendant quelques saisons et lui avait donné *le caprice* de s'allier avec un fille de ces montagnes pour en obtenir une descendance basque […]"

[136] "les débris d'un peuple très mystérieusement unique, sans analogue parmi les peuples"

[137] "Est c'est simplement l'irrintzina, le grand cri basque, que s'est transmis avec fidélité du fond de l'abîme des âges jusqu'aux hommes de nos jours, et qui constitue l'une des étrangetés de cette race aux origines enveloppées de mystère."

[138] "Cela ressemble au cri d'appel de certaines tribus Peaux-Rouges dans les forêts des Amériques."

[139] "Au contraire, à l'instant si recueilli de leurs adieux, ils se sentaient plus chastes encore, tant ils s'aimaient d'amour éternel."

there is no economic or social life that might disrupt the natural space available to tourists—only smuggling is celebrated as an illegal yet romantic means of sustenance. Thus, the author first shows the unbearable feelings of existential angst suffered by the hero of the story: "[A]nd then he was taken by his desire to know what is beyond, and then even beyond... Oh! To go elsewhere ... To escape, at least for a time, the oppression of this country—yet so loved!—Before death, to escape the oppression of this always identical and hopeless existence. To try something else, to get out of here, to travel, to know! ... " (108).[140] Then, counterpoising poverty to love, the author makes the romance between Ramuntcho and his girlfriend, Gracieuse, impossible. She enters a convent and he has to migrate to the Americas:

> It is a plant uprooted from its dear Basque soil, which a breath of adventure takes elsewhere [...] Ahead of its road lies the Americas, exile without a likely return, the immense novelty full of surprises and now faced without courage: an entire life still too long, without a doubt, during which his soul, uprooted from here, will have to suffer and to toughen over there ; his vigor, to be spent and extinguished who knows where, in labors, in struggles unknown [...] (245)[141]

Conversely, Loti naturalizes the life in the convent and turns religion--- the medium that makes human suffering tolerable in the Basque Country---into the only hope (*spes*): "Up there, in their small convent, in their small sepulcher with walls so white, the quiet nuns recite their evening prayers... O crux, ave spes unica! ... "(245).[142]

---

[140] "[E]t alors, il est repris par son désir de connaître ce qu'il y a au delà, et au delà encore… Oh ! s'en aller ailleurs !… Échapper, au moins pour un temps, à l'oppression de ce pays, — cependant si aimé ! — Avant la mort, échapper à l'oppression de cette existence toujours pareille et sans issue. Essayer d'autre chose, sortir d'ici, voyager, savoir ! …"

[141] Il est une plante déracinée du cher sol basque, et qu'un soufflé d'aventure emporte ailleurs… En avant de sa route, il y a les Amériques, l'exil sans retour probable, l'immense nouveau plein de surprises et abordé maintenant sans courage: toute une vie encore très longue, sans doute, pendant laquelle son âme arrachée d'ici devra souffrir et se durcir là-bas; sa vigueur, se dépenser et s'épuiser qui sait où, dans des besognes, dans des lutes inconnues […]

[142] "Là-haut, dans leur petit couvent, dans leur petit sépulcre aux murailles si blanches, les nonnes tranquilles récitent leurs priers du soir… *O crux, ave, spes unica!*…"
The convent retreat will appear in Agirre's *Garoa*.

In short, Loti turns Basque people into subaltern subjects: natural objects for the contemplation and amusement of the foreign French tourist. If the Basques want to pursue any form of non-natural life, they must vacate the landscape and exile themselves outside the natural country (convents, America), so that the landscape is preserved pristine for the tourist gaze. This tourist representation and economy persists in the Basque Country until the arrival of industrialization and nationalism at the turn of the century in Biscay and Guipuzcoa. Yet, in the Northern Basque Country, it continues to shape the economy throughout the 20th century.[143]

4. Basque and Spanish Nationalisms (Arana, Unamuno, Agirre)

It is rather puzzling to observe that one of the founding ideologues of 20th-century Spanish nationalism, Miguel de Unamuno (1864-1936), and the founding politician of Basque nationalism, Sabino Arana (1865-1903), both were Basque and both became interested in Basque language to the point of applying for the same position in 1888: the first Chair of Basque Studies sponsored by the Provincial Government[144] of Biscay. Neither one won the position. The future president of the Academy of the Basque Language, Resurrección María de Azkue, was chosen instead.[145]

Few years later, Unamuno gave a lecture at the Basque floral games of 1901 in Bilbao and proposed the "balming and burial" of Basque language—a dying language, according to him, which deserved proper scientific preservation. Arana, although he changed his position several times in his lifetime, advocated for the purity of a Basque race that could only be expressed in Basque; later he valued race over language. Similarly, Unamuno upheld the superiority of the European race over the African, based on cranium volume, in his *On Regards to Casticism* (1894; *Obras completas*, III 92), and ultimately propounded a "spiritual racism" that would unite all Hispanic races under the banner of their cultural heritage: the

---

[143] A more extended analysis of this period would have to include the work of Jean Etxepare Bidegorri. His *By Car* (1931) and earlier *Thought* (1910) show the Basque counter-narrative to Loti's touristic discourse.

[144] Provincial government of Biscay.

[145] A full description of this period requires to incorporate the Basque diaspora into this continental history. The case of Jose Manuel Etxeita, one of the first Basque novelists and last mayor of Manila, the Phillipines, is also important (Gabilondo "Galdós, Etxeita, Rizal").

language of the Spanish empire. Yet, towards the end of their lives, the positions of these two authors changed once again. Unamuno defended religious, authoritarian politics, lingering on fascism, in works such as *Saint Manuel, the Good, Martyr* (1936), while Arana opted for a possibilist position within Spain, thus foregoing his previous political views on an independent Basque Country.

As Elaine Showalter explores for the case of Britain and north Europe, the fin-de-siècle was a moment of turmoil, uncertainty, and shifting social boundaries. Thus, the ever-changing and innovative nature of Unamuno and Arana's lives and works is not exceptional in this context. However, in the mist of all these shifts, these two authors prompted a radical political change in both Spain and the Basque Country: they refashioned both realities as nations. For these two authors, the Spanish and Basque nations were timeless and unchanging realities endowed with a soul or essence. Therefore, their lives and works became defined by this seeming contradiction: their ideological and intellectual shifts ultimately yielded an essentialist and unchangeable political construct, the Spanish and Basque nations. In the French case, War World I represented the beginning of a full assimilation of the northern Basque Country to the national project (Weber).

A close reading of the claims made by these two Basque authors strikes the modern reader as utterly racist, reactionary, and authoritarian; yet their legacy has shaped modern Spanish and Basque politics and culture in central and constitutive ways. There is no way to understand Spain and the Basque Country without these two authors. As we will see later, the only prominent author who escaped the nationalist turn of fin-de-siècle is Pío Baroja, although even he oscillated between fascism and libertarianism.

This ever changing fin-de-siècle is called in Spain "The Restoration;" it follows the tumultuous six-year period of revolution and civil war (1868-74), in which the Spanish bourgeoisie failed to impose its hegemony. The Restoration, thus, was an attempt to balance many unsolved historical problems that, in their precarious equilibrium, led to the Spanish Republic of 1931 and the ensuing Civil War of 1936-1939. This war was the final chapter of a long protracted fin-de-siècle that was defined by unsolved historical problems. The Franco-Prussian war of 1870-1871, which ended with a French defeat, made room for a similar phase of instability in France, which culminated in World War I.

The apparent conundrum that defines Arana and Unamuno can be best studied and analyzed precisely from within Basque literature, for ultimately their contradictions are shaped and articulated by the conditions by fin-de-siècle Basque literature. At the same time, these two authors generate the ensuing nationalist understanding of Spanish and Basque literatures, which still prevails today. After their work, Basque literature written in Spanish began to be considered Spanish and, conversely, Basque literature written in Basque was held as the sole and genuine conduit for the Basque nation. Txomin Agirre (1864-1920) and his novel *Garoa* (*Fern*, 1912), became the first and most important exponent of the new nationalist understanding of Basque literature. Therefore, any postnational understanding of Basque writing must retrace its steps back to Arana and Unamuno.

As many critics have noted separately, the above three authors, Arana, Unamuno, and Agirre began their literary careers precisely by writing historical narrative: Unamuno published in 1897 *Peace in War* (*Paz en la guerra*), Arana gave to the print *Biscay for Its Independence* (*Bizcaya por su indepenencia*) in 1892, and Agirre made his literary entrance with *The Flower of the Pyrenees* in 1898. Each book is very different from the other two, yet they all share a fundamental characteristic. All three works, although infused by history, are ultimately ahistorical; they represent a foundational fiction that situates the Basque Country outside modernity. If the previous generation of writers—Araquistáin, Trueba, Loti, and Navarro Villoslada—wrote fictions that could serve as the foundation of a new nationalist Spain-France by resorting to a pastoral and touristic Basque Country, the new generation of nationalist authors negated such possibility and relocated the Basque Country outside the French and Spanish nation-states—Unamuno did so by promoting the assimilation of the Basque Country into Spain and the abandonment of its language.

The reason for this nationalist shift was the new irruption of industrial capitalism in the Basque Country, which also brought a large influx of immigrants from other parts of Spain. This new reality broke down the foundational understanding of a pastoral and touristic Basque Country and made that ideal incompatible with the new reality of industrialization, which was fostered by a local *haute bourgeoisie* allied with the Spanish ruling classes.

As José Luis de la Granja and Santiago de Pablo state, industrialization started in Biscay in 1876 and in Guipuzcoa in 1900. By 1930, 40% of the active population in Guipuzcoa and 50% in Biscay worked in the secondary industrial sector, whereas agriculture only occupied 20 and 25

% of the population respectively (Bazán 542). In Navarre and Alava, agriculture continued to be the main economic sector that employed 60% and 50% of the working population respectively. During this period, the population in the Peninsular Basque Country grew 64% (and, at its extreme, in Biscay, the population grew 250%). The influx from other areas of Spain was immense. According to the census of 1910 and 1920, 27% of the population of Biscay was born outside the Basque Country (Bazán 543). Although the numbers were lower for Guipuzcoa, the influx was also significant.

As a result, the Basque Country went from being a re-ruralized and impoverished region to becoming a burgeoning industrial center. As de la Granja and de Pablo summarize, "the river of Bilbao became the center of the steel industry and the largest industrial concentration of early 20th-century Spain" (Bazán 548).[146] The economic and social effects of industrialization were also radical: "through these uneven processes of modernization, the Basque Country came to be, after Catalonia, the most industrialized community and the one with the highest rent per capita in Spain in the 1920s" (Bazán 556).[147] Yet, the cultural effects of and reactions to this growth were heterogeneous. The Basque bourgeoisie that controlled the industrial capital turned its economic interest towards the Peninsula, its most important market after 1898, and, thus, developed a Spanish nationalist ideology. The small bourgeoisie and middle class slowly shifted to Basque nationalist positions, which excluded the Spanish state as its sphere of economic and social expansion. Finally, the working class, split in socialist, communist, and anarchist factions, took a more internationalist stand, which, nevertheless, ended up supporting a Spanish nationalist ideology, as its political structures and institutions were organized following state lines.

In this context, the historical novel of the end of the 19th century gave sense and meaning to recent history. In his first novel, *Peace in War* (1897), Unamuno resorted to the most recent historical events that preceded the Spanish Restoration: the Carlist War of 1872-76. Furthermore, the author claimed to have historically documented every single narrative detail. Nevertheless, in the novel, he ends up narrating a mythical return to a

---

[146] "la ría de Bilbao se convirtió en el centro de la industria siderometalúrgica y en la mayor concentración industrial de la España de principios del siglo XX"

[147] "mediante estos procesos de modernización tan dispares, el País Vasco llegó a ser, después de Cataluña, la comunidad más industrializada y con mayor renta per cápita de España en los años veinte"

place that is outside history: the essentialist locus of the previous Basque literary tradition. In the final chapter, the protagonist climbs a mountain and, in a Tabor-like trance, he arrives to an anti-historical and anti-modern realization, i.e. a very modern realization of his anti-modernism. In short, he recreates the same pastoral essentialist space narrated by *Peru Abarka* almost a hundred years earlier. The protagonist of the novel undergoes a transformation similar to that of Maisu Juan, although this time, the conversation takes a more metaphysical tone:

> In him, a communion wakes up between the world around him and the world inside him: the two worlds fuse. Free from the consciousness of time and space, he contemplates them in their fusion. There in that silence beyond silence and in the aroma of the diffuse light, all desire extinguished and in tune with the song of the soul of the world, he enjoys true peace, as if in the life of death […] What time is to eternity, war is to peace: its fleeting form. In peace, death and life seem to join as one. (*Selected* 382)[148]

After returning from his journey to an anti-modern and fabricated place that escapes history in its pastoral, essentialist setting, the hero ends the novel by claiming an impossible modern progress within this anti-modern location: "Up there serene contemplation gives him eternal and transcendent resignation, mother of temporal irresignations, of not ever settling down there, of demanding higher wages, and he descends to provoke unrest among the rest, first engine of all progress and of all good… peace in the mist of war" (313).[149] Similarly, to *Peru Abarka*'s Maisu Juan, the transformed protagonist returns to the urban, modern life endowed with an anti-modern identity. But here, rather than excess of identity, modern and anti-modern, we find an attempt to reduce this contradiction

---

[148] "Despiértasele entonces la comunión entre el mundo que le rodea y el que encierra en su propio seno: llegan a la fusión ambos; el inmenso panorama y él, que libertado de la conciencia del lugar y del tiempo lo contempla, se hace uno y el mismo; y en el silencio solemne, en el aroma libre, en la luz difusa y rica, extinguido todo deseo y cantando la canción silenciosa del alma del mundo, goza de paz verdadera, de un como vida en la muerte…. Es la guerra a la paz lo que a la eternidad el tiempo; su forma pasajera. Y en la paz parecen identificarse la Muerte y la Vida" (312).

[149] "Allí arriba la contemplación serena le da resignación transcendente y eterna, madre de la irresignación temporal, del no contentarse jamás aquí abajo, del pedir siempre mayor salario, y baja decidido a provocar en los demás el descontento, primer motor de todo progreso y de todo bien… paz en la guerra misma" (313)

to a metaphysical "peace" that also encompasses "war." In order to understand this seemingly contradictory final synthesis, it is important to follow Unamuno's trajectory.

Towards the end of his life, the same Unamuno, after many changes, alterations, and reformulations of his foundational contradiction, rewrote an earlier anti-modern and ahistorical Basque Country as a contemporary Castilian town, Valverde de Lucerna, in *Saint Manuel, the Good, Martyr* (1936). This anti-modern Basque space refashioned as Castilian is a religious town, led by a priest who is both religious and political authority and, thus, preserves the town from any modern influence. This town, shielded from modernity and guided by an existential religious leader, Saint Manuel, becomes Unamuno's final and ideal refashioning of his initial Basque "peace in the mist of war." Departing from his Basque original formulation, Unamuno proceeds to articulate a metaphysical Castile, empty and ahistorical, as Spain's new national identity. It is Unamuno's Basque nationalist response to Spain's identity crisis in the aftermath of its imperialist defeat in 1898. Yet, at the root of this "metaphysical or religious nationalism" that claims an empty, postimperial Castile, we can find the strategic essentialism that derives from Basque literature since the Enlightenment. The religious Saint Manuel is the descendant of a Basque genealogy that begins with Peru Abarka—even though the nationalist and essentialist split created by Unamuno and Arana between the Spanish and the Basque "nations" makes almost impossible to retrace this genealogy. But this time, this new leader, unlike Peru Abarka, points to a more dangerous essentialism: an idealized and metaphysical authoritarianism that lingers on fascism. Although Unamuno fought political fascism, he idealized the figure of an authoritarian, intellectual leader who ultimately stood for a "higher" form of fascism.

Similarly, in his *Biscay for Its Independence* (1889-90), Arana narrates and refashions legends made popular by the previous generation of writers whom, in several instances, had also borrowed from apologist literature. However, as Arana concludes, by referring to "The Battle of Arrigorriaga," he no longer has a "legendary" goal in mind, but rather a nationalist one: to assert the immemorial essence of the Biscayan nation. As he states, "[T]he *señorío* [signori, independent territory ruled by a lord] of Biscay dates from this time, but not, as certain Spanish historians pretend, its Independence: which is as old as its blood and language" (34).[150]

---

[150] "De aquí data el *Señorío* de Vizcaya, mas no, como pretende algún historiador español, su independencia: la cual es tan antigua como su sangre y su idioma."

At the end of this essay, Arana summarizes the different battles that prove the immemorial independence of Biscay and, consequently, turns history into national destiny—a destiny marked by its opposition to Spain.

The industrialization and migration brought to the Basque Country by modernity at the turn of the 19th century altered the essentialist articulation that previous authors had strategically developed since the end of the 18th and beginning of the 19th centuries. For Arana, this essentialist past is only a starting point for a future Basque nation:

> **Yesterday.** —Biscay, a confederation of independent Republics, fights against Spain, which pretends to conquer it, but vanquishes the latter in Arrigorriaga (888), thus remaining free.—Biscay, independent lordly Republic, being subject of Castile-Leon its lord, fights against Spain, which pretends to conquer it, but vanquishes the former in Gordexola and Otxandiano (1355), remaining free.—Biscay, independent lordly Republic, being its lord, at the same time, king of Castile-Leon, fights against Spain, which pretends to conquer it, and vanquishes the latter in Mungia (1470), thus remaining free.
> **Today.** Biscay is a province of Spain.
> **Tomorrow.** —¿......................................?
> The Biscayans of the 19th century have the final word, as the future depends of their actions. (69)[151]

Yet, because this Basque nationalist essentialism no longer is strategic but utopian—although genealogically derived from the tradition that spans from Mogel to tourism—Arana has a hard time fixing and freezing it in time and space. Thus, eventually Biscay becomes the seven Basque Provinces in his discourse; race replaces language; and ultimately independence is substituted by a possibilist discourse within Spain. Yet, even

---

[151] **Ayer**. —Bizkaya, Confederación de Repúblicas independientes, lucha contra España, que pretende conquistarla, y la vence en Arrigorriaga (888), permaneciendo libre.—Bizkaya, República Señorial independiente, siendo súbdito de Castilla-León su señor lucha contra España, que pretende conquistarla y la vence en Gordexola y Otxandiano (1355), permaneciendo libre.—Bizkaya, república Señorial independiente, siendo su señor a un tiempo rey de Castilla-León, lucha contra España, que pretende conquistarla, y la vence en Mungia (1470), permaneciendo libre.
Hoy. —Bizkaya es una provincia de España.
Mañana.—¿......................................?
Tienen la palabra los vizcaínos del siglo XIX, pues que de su conducta depende el porvenir.

211

at the end of his life, Arana continues to ascertain an essentialist understanding of Basque nationalism, even though he has to resituate it within the framework of the Spanish state.

In an article he published a year before his death, which was written in prison, he states: "I have not declared myself Spanish. One can be Spanish in two ways: naturally or constitutionally [...] Well then: in the first way, that is, from the ethnic or racial point of view, I am not Spanish and I could say that I am, except if I lie, which I usually do not... . In the second way, that is, constitutionally, I'm certainly Spanish" (387).[152] By restating the difference as one between politics and ethnicity-race, he still holds on to an essentialist view, an essentialism that no longer is strategic and thus always ends up becoming racist.

Similarly, Txomin Agirre, after writing a historical novel (*The Flower of the Pyrenees* 1898) and a very vivid account of a fishing town in the Biscayan coast (*Saltpeter*, 1906), ends up writing the ultimate narrative of Basque nationalism at the turn of the century: *Garoa* (*Fern* 1912). Unlike in the case of Mogel's *Peru Abarka*, modernity is excluded from Agirre's representation of the Basque Country and is posited as a radical exterior, one defined precisely by the urban life of the cities, Spanish language, and industrialization; they are essentialist but not strategic. His portrayal of the main character of *Fern*, Joanes, the patriarchal authority of the Basque farm, defies time and space, and becomes pure ethnic essence:

> What a man he was!
>
> He was seven feet and a half tall, straight like the poplar, wide as the thicket beech tree, thick as the tough holm oak, and flexible as the green holly tree.
>
> That was Joanes when I met him.
>
> The veiny arms of the old shepherd were still muscular; his feet were very fast; his lungs were full of vigor.
>
> He had seen seventy two times the green leaf sprout in the oak forests of the Aloña mountain; but a nineteen-year-old boy would not rival him in the game of the ax, throwing the heavy javelin, or running up and down the mountains and across the valleys. (41)[153]

---

[152] "No me he declarado español. De dos modos puede ser uno español: de modo natural o de modo constitucional... Pues bueno: del primer modo, es decir, bajo el punto de vida [sic] étnico o de razas, no soy español ni he podido decir que lo soy, a no ser mintiendo, cosa que no acostumbro.... Del segundo modo o constitucional, soy ciertamente español."

[153] "Ura zan gizona, ura!

The decline of the old patriarchal figure, Joanes, and the inability of his male heirs to follow on his footsteps, as well as the cloistering of the most eligible female of the family in a convent, mark the end of Agirre's essentialist narrative that, nevertheless, cannot but acknowledge the advance of modernity. Unlike in *Peru Abarka*, modernity is exterior to Agirre's portrayal of an essentialist Basque Country and, thus, essentialism becomes the impossible basis of nationalism. Unlike Maisu Juan, here the protagonists do not undergo a transformation nor return to the urban space—they are dismissed through Manichean melodrama.

In the three authors studied above—Unamuno, Arana, and Agirre—we see the influence of a strategic essentialism displayed since Larramendi and Mogel at the end of the 18th and beginning of the 19th centuries. Here, however, this essentialism ceases to be strategic and attempts to legitimize itself as fully anti-modern and ahistorical: Unamuno's Castile, Arana's *Euzkadi* (his neologism for the Basque Country), and Agirre's ideal farmstead, are divorced from modernity and, instead, are defined by their complete opposition to it, so that they articulate an ahistorical, utopian essence for the foundation of the Basque and Spanish nations. As a result, their essentialism simply becomes ahistorical and anti-modern, which eventually finds its formulation in racist, fascistic, and authoritarian representations of the nation. Their works formulate modernity as the traumatic moment they cannot represent in their portrayals of an essentialist nation.

This nationalist essentialism was new both in the Basque Country and in Spain—and indirectly in France. Yet, it dominated the cultural landscape through the 1930s when the instauration of the Spanish Republic altered the entire political and cultural landscape. By then, the nationalist legacy of these authors had a very precise and lasting effect: each language (Spanish and Basque) became the repository of the essences of its respective nation as well as the only medium in which each nation could represent itself. As a result, the entire Basque 20th century was defined by the

---

Zazpi oin ta erdi bai luze, makal zugatzaren irudira zuzen, pagorik lodiena baizen zabal, arte gogorra bezala trinko, gorosti ezearen antzera zimel.

Orrela zan Joanes nik ezagutu nuanean.

Sendoak zeuden oraindik artzai zarraren beso zaintsuak, txit azkarrak bere oñak, zindoak bere bular-auspoak.

Irurogeita amabi aldiz ikusi zuan, Aloña mendiko ariztietan, ostro berdea berriz jaiotzen; baña etzion eramango emeretzi urteko mutil batek ez aizkora jolasean, ez burdin astuna jaurtitzen, ez mendietan gora edo ibarretan zear laisterka".

literary imperative to represent the nation, Basque and Spanish, mainly through allegory, while also registering the impossibility of such essentialist representation, due to its nationalist inability to incorporate the impurities of modernity and capitalism.

Only one Basque author, a prolific novelist, admired by writers such as Ernest Hemingway and John Dos Passos, Pío Baroja (1872-1956), emerged in this situation and was able to defy both nationalist ideologies, Spanish and Basque, even though from a marginal political position that was individualist and oscillated between libertarianism and fascism. Although he lived in Madrid in his youth, he moved back to the Basque Country (1894) and, after a return to Madrid, spent his writing career between Bera (Navarre), close to the French border, and Madrid. He wrote the most challenging literature of that period and, unlike all the writers mentioned above, he survived the Spanish Civil War.

The last novel of his tetralogy of the Basque land, *The Legend of the Lord of Alzate* (1922), best captures his understanding of the Basque Country and modernity.[154] In this somewhat avangardist text, which borders theater, Baroja retakes the legendary literature written by the previous generations and deconstructs it through the views of its protagonist, the lord of Alzate, who lives in the Middle Ages but foresees the crisis that the imperialist Christian states will eventually bring in the Renaissance. As a result, Baroja creates a protagonist, the lord of Alzate, who is also known by its Basque name, Jaun. He is utterly modern and yet he remains a pagan who converses with the mythic and essentialist characters produced by the previous generation of writers. Moreover, Jaun is always critical of any institutionalized body of beliefs, including Catholic religion. Positioned locally in his place of birth, yet on the border of two states, Jaun becomes the alter ego of Baroja and the ultimate allegory of a Basque Country that is both anti-modern and modern, in a very calculated and strategic-essentialist balance. After the Spanish Civil War, however, this lucid, pre-war representation of the Basque Country was abandoned by the author on behalf of more fascistic political ideology.

Finally, it is important to note that, by the early 1900s, there were several Basque periodicals published in the diaspora, from Buenos Aires to California. For example, the first Basque newspaper in Los Angeles was launched in 1885: *Euskal kazeta*. They were created responding to very local needs and their goal was to strengthen networks of support and

---

[154] The other three novels that consitute the tetralogy are: (*The House of Aizgorri*, 1900; *The Lord of Labraz*, 1903; *Zalacain the Adventurer*, 1908).

information in the Basque communities. They were also a result of the nationalist ideas that several emigrants took with them to the Americas (Totoricaguena 69). These periodicals are still not well known by Basque literary criticism and, thus, they require an extensive research, especially in order to determine whether they fostered some of the diasporic literature that multiplied after the 1940s. However, they are the most important written source of subaltern literature of the period. Similarly, the working-class journals published mostly in Bilbao and its vicinities remain to be studied and incorporated to a postnational history of Basque literature.

Although this requires a lengthier analysis, it is important to emphasize that nationalism, unlike previous political and cultural movements, required that bourgeois and middle classes identified with the subaltern classes and included them in the national project. This contradictory and failed demand shaped and defined the nationalist project.

5. State Difference and Nationalist Essentialism

1. Modernism (Lizardi, Lauaxeta, Orixe, *Hermes*)

In the 1920s and 1930s, Unamuno and Arana's nationalist theories had the effect of turning Basque literary production into literature written solely in Basque—and correspondingly texts written exclusively in Castilian into Spanish literature, regardless of whether they were written by Basques writers or from other nationalities. The purpose of this new reorganization of Basque literature was nationalist. Literature was to write the allegory of the Basque nation as a way for the Basques to imagine themselves as a sovereign community (Anderson 14) and, conversely, for other communities to imagine them as Basque too—i.e. to write the literary masterpiece that would give Basques local and international recognition.[155]

At that point, this nationalist, literary utopia represented a pervasive project among many minorities around the world. The Nobel prize given to the Occitan writer Frédéric Mistral in 1904 for his long narrative poem *Mirèio* (1859) was a catalyst for the Basque case (ironically enough, Mistral shared the prize with Spanish dramatist José Echegaray). Furthermore, from the Harlem Renaissance in the USA and the Irish Revival in Ireland to the Catalan Renaixença in Catalonia or the Nós Generation in Galicia, many minorities or oppressed cultures attempted to write a similar national work that would legitimize them as a nation in their own and other nations' eyes. Jameson uses the term "national allegory" to refer to this political component that, according to him, "all Third-World texts" have:

> All third-world texts are necessarily... allegorical, and in a very specific way: they are to be read as what I will call *national allegories*, even when, or perhaps I should say, particularly when their forms develop out of predominantly western machineries of representation, such as the novel…. Third-world texts, even those which are seemingly private and invested with a properly libidinal dynamic—necessarily project a political dimension in the form of national allegory: *the story of the private individual destiny is always an allegory of the embattled situation of the public third-world culture and society.* (69)

Although Jameson's description has received much deserved criticism, still his claim is valid if it is taken out of the context of "the Third

---

[155] Theater and opera experienced a very important resurgence in Basque. They must be studies in detail to rewrite a more encompassing history of this period.

World" and is applied, instead, to many political or national contexts not regulated by a hegemonic nation-state during this time, as it is the case of the Basque Country. Furthermore, it is important to realize that the allegorical nature of these works is not something that is unconscious or historically inherent as Jameson claims: it is a clear, political choice made by some minority writers.

Yet at this moment, modernism, the literary trend that defined the last decades of the 19th century, at least since the late work of Flaubert and Mallarmé, found its most canonical and representative moment in T.S. Eliot's *The Waste Land* (1920). This poetry was ultimately dystopian and brought modernism to its conclusion—a conclusion that the visual arts pushed even farther by questioning the institution of art itself. Peter Bürgher explains the logic of modernism, which leads to the avant-garde, in the following way:

> The recipient's attention no longer turns to a meaning of the work that might be grasped by a reading of its constituent elements, but to the principle of construction. This kind of reception is imposed on the recipient because the element necessary within the organic work when it plays a role in constituting the meaning of the whole merely serves to flesh out structure and pattern in the avant-gardist work. (81)

In short, the poem takes the reader away from its meaning and turns the the principle of poetic construction into its true meaning. *The Waste Land*, accordingly, became an allegory of the impossibility of writing and conveying poetic meaning. Nevertheless, by doing so, the poem reinforced the institution of literature through the allegory of its impossibility. In short, in hegemonic cultures such as English, the dystopian and allegorical self-cancellation of the poem led to the reinforcement of a highly stylized type of writing that only the most knowledgeable people in the institution of literature could read. This phenomenon is known as "high art."

Literatures such as the Basque had recourse to modernism in a contradictory way. On the one hand, the poetic allegory had to be meaningful since it had to represent the nation. On the other, the allegory had to be written in such a way that resisted meaning and signified the cancellation of poetry so that it was acknowledged by other literary traditions and, consequently, accepted in the high-art institution of modernism. In short, it had to be modern and anti-modern at the same time. These two goals are contradictory and explain the development of Basque modernist poetry in the first half of the 20th century. Ultimately, such development was a continuation of the older negotiation between modernity and anti-modernity that defined modern Basque literature as (strategically) essentialist since the 18th century.

In the Basque case, the debates between Aitzol (José Ariztimuño, 1896-1936) and Orixe (Nicolás Ormaetxea, 1888-1961), the leading cultural intellectuals of the moment, focused on the populist or elitist style in which the national allegory had to be written, thus, performing the new modernist refashioning of the anti/modernity debate in a nationalist space. Given the Basque genealogy of the project, there was a consensus about the genre to use: poetry was the only legitimate discourse in which to write a national allegory. It had to be epic poetry. Yet, the populist tendency defended by Aitzol gave priority to the subaltern tradition (*bertsolaritza, kopla zaharrak*, etc.), whereas the classicist alternative defended by Orixe opted for a more elitist, purist poetic option, which was supposed to be based on both classical poetry (Greek and Latin) and Catholic religion. Ultimately, Orixe's proposal gained wider acceptance than Aitzol's (Otegi) but led to a modernist poetry that did not overcome the former's classicist tenets and, ultimately, showed the contradictions in which a project of writing a modernist, national, Basque allegory was trapped. Orixe's was twice anti-modernist, as it opposed the subaltern tradition that a nationalist literature was supposed to incorporate and did not meet the high-art standards set by modernism.

The two most influential modernist poets of the time, Lizardi (Jose Maria Agirre, 1896-1933) and Lauaxeta (Esteban Urkiaga, 1905-1937) were consecrated and marginalized respectively because of their positioning vis-à-vis Orixe's program. Lizardi's poem "Asaba zaarren baratza" ("Garden of Our Ancestors") published in his *Biotz-Begietan* (*On the Eyes and Heart*[156] 1932) represents the canonical rendition of nationalist literature. Yet this poem, modernist in nature, encapsulates the contradictions of the nationalist project without overcoming them, as I will discuss below. The two poets died by the time the Spanish Civil War ended—Lauaxeta was executed by the fascist faction—and thus their chance to write a complete and definitive allegory was eclipsed. Although Orixe finally wrote a long, classic epic poem, *Euskaldunak* (*The Basques*, written in 1935, published in 1950), which can also be sung in its entirety, as

---

[156] It can also be translated as *On the Eyes of the Heart*

Virgil's *Aeneid*. His classicist, purist, and ahistorical use of language, completely divorced from the high-art modernist tenets of the time, rendered his poetic attempt anachronistic by the time it was published. It reads like a pastoral poem in the midst of an industrialized country: neither subaltern nor modernist, it became twice anti-modern.

As Iñaki Aldekoa notes, Arana's legacy also had another consequence: "In reality, the influence exerted by Sabino Arana on later poets is not due to his poetic work but rather to his theoretical work. The norms dictated by Sabino Arana on the poetic meter, on the necessity of rhyme, etc. were scrupulously respected in the decade of the thirties" ("La poesía" 482). The other important effect Arana's nationalism had over the poets of that generation was the purist language they adopted. Theirs was a literary language meant to reflect an essence void of any Latin or Castilian corruption. In Lizardi's case, the purist mandate helped him create a very modernist poetry, which was as sophisticated and refined as difficult to understand, thus bringing the reader's attention to the linguistic construction of the poem. His *On the Eyes and Heart* was originally published in Basque with a translation in Spanish on the side; it was hard to read even for the cultured Basque reader of the time. Nationalist purism, ironically enough, helped to create the modernist effect that both Aitzol and Orixe rejected: it brought the reader's attention to the construction of the poem. This strange marriage between nationalist essentialism—as poetic and linguistic purism—and modernism defined Lizardi's poetry. Yet, Lizardi's poetry void of any reference to subaltern poetry, lacked readers. It was addressed to an empty nation.

Poems such as Lizardi's "Garden of Our Ancestors," are both highly nationalist in their allegorical thrust and modernist in their purist language. The poem tells the story of three generations of a Basque family who meet on the home garden; their encounter allegorizes the Basque Country. Yet, the poem cannot solve the problem between an essentialist understanding of the Basque Country and the modernist credo that it propounds—except in a negative way. The poem tells the story of the half-blind grandmother who does not recognize her grandson, the poet, and, instead takes the latter's son for her grandson. In that way, the poet, the subject who allegorizes the present, excludes himself from the nationalist recognition that takes place between past (grandmother) and future (great-grandson). The self-exclusion of the grandson and, thus, of a non-nationalist present, for which he stands, becomes a way to represent modernity as a negative, yet utopian, scenario that will be achieved with the great-grandson's maturation in a near future. The lack of any reference to the poet's parents is meant to underline the exceptional, modernist moment of creation, which has no direct precedents (the parents); it is a creation *ex nihilo*. The end of the poem, where the recognition between disconnected generations takes place, resounds with older references; the tree, for example, is a reference to Iparragirre's "Tree of Guernica."

Ordun eguzkiz yantzi zan	Then, was covered with sun
Asaba zaarren baratza;	my ancestors' garden;
Ordun, zuaitzak igaliz;	Then, the trees were covered with fruits
Ordun baratza leeneratu zan	Then, the garden went back to its past
Mugak berriro zabaliz	Widening its narrow limits
Ta leen ikusi-gabeko	And, not seen before,
Zuaitz berri bat zegoan	A new tree stood there
Erdian, guzien buru…	In the middle, presiding over the rest
Aren gerizak erri-baratzak	Its shade has made nations
Ezin-ilkor egin ditu.	and gardens immortal
Nire Tabor-mendi: nire	My Tabor Mountain: transfiguration
Baratz zaarraren antzalda!,	Of my old garden!
Egi, mami, biur adi:	Become truth and matter!
Leenaren muñak aldatu beza	May the core of the past change
Baratz zaarra baratz berri! (61)	The old garden into a new one!

Yet, the allegorical exclusion of both the poet and the present time from the poem has also another allegorical meaning: the exclusion of the reader. This exclusion would have had a positive effect in the case of a hegemonic literature such as English: it would have been admired by the complexity of its exclusionary structure, thus, forcing the reader to embrace its elitist meaning as a sign of class distinction and identification. In the Basque case, the exclusion had the opposite effect: it triggered the failure to create a Basque readership able to complete and give meaning to the national allegory. The poems were published with a Spanish translation on the side. This is where the reader was situated in the poem book: between the original and the translation, going back and forth, alienated and fascinated by the essentialist, purist language of Lizardi, yet realizing the impossibility of becoming a nationalist reader in Basque, a reader without the impure help of Spanish. At that point, the reading (listening) subject of Basque poetry was still the subaltern and working classes. There was not a middle-class or bourgeois readership.

Similarly, in poems such as "Langille eraildu bati" ("To a Slaughtered Worker"), from the poem book *Arrats beran* (*At Dusk*, 1935), Lauaxeta combined a nationalist treatment of the landscape with the representation of a modern reality such as a strike by Biscayan miners. Purist words created by Aranist linguistics such as "urrutizkin" (telephone, far-word-device) only highlight the modernist thrust of the poem:

¡Ene Bizkai'ko miatze gorri	Oh my red mines of Biscay
zauri zarae mendi ezian!	You are wounds in the humid mountain.
Aurpegi balzdun miatzarijoi	You, miner of black face
ator pikotxa lepo-ganian.	Come with your pickax on your shoulder.
Lepo-ganian pikotx zorrotza	With the sharp pickax on your shoulder.
eguzki-diz-diz ta mendiz bera.	With the shiny sun, down the hill.
Ator bideskaz, -goxa sorbaldan-,	Come down the trail, the sun on your
kezko zeruba yaukon olera.	shoulder, to the factory of the smoky sky.
Opor-otsa dok txaide zabalan,	There is talk of strike in the pavilion,
-ukabil sendo, soñanzki urdin-.	—Strong fists, blue uniforms—.
Jaubiak, barriz, nasai etzunda,	The bosses, instead, sitting comfortably
laguntzat auke, i, urrutizkin.	Have you as help, oh phone.
Aurpegi balzdun miatzarijoi	Miner of black face,
ari bittartez deyak yabiltzak.	Calls go through the line.
¡Bideskan zelan dirdir-yagijek	How they shine on the road
txapel-okerren kapela baltzak!	The ranger police's hard hats.
¡Orreik yaukoen gaizkin-itxura	They truly have a criminal aspect
sispa luziak lepo-ganian!	With their rifles on their shoulders.
¡Ene Bizkai'ko miatze gorri,	Oh my red mines of Biscay
zauri zarae mendi ezian! (65)	You are wounds in the humid mountain.

The ultimate contradiction of this modernist poetry relied on the fact that it had no readership. Most of the Basque speakers still preferred *bertsolaris* (a national tournament was held precisely in 1934 in San Sebastian) or popular theater (mainly comedy written by authors such as Toribio Alzaga, Ignazio K. Nuñez Arizmendi, and Marcelino Soroa) while the educated masses favored reading in Spanish or French. Gregorio Mujika's humorous tales about a popular character, compiled in a book with the homonym title of *Fernando of Amezketa* (1925), were probably the most read and celebrated narrative of the time. In short, subaltern culture began to have modern media in which to represent itself. Furthermore, subaltern culture became internal to the nationalist project, but it remained separated and dismissed by the modernist agenda of high-literature writers.

Against what Lizardi allegorized in his poem, there was no nationalist recognition between old language (grandmother) and new readers (the literary offspring of Lizardi's poetry). Modernism was only an option in hegemonic literatures in which already an existing readership had a literary habit against which modernist poetry could become meaningful—and even revolutionary as counter-literature. In the Basque case, the lack of a historically constituted Basque readership further accentuated the divorce between modernism and nation—thus moving the social split between elite and subaltern classes inside the nationalist project. Ultimately, Basque modernist poetry was designed to be published and purchased, but not to be read. This means that such literature, instead of promoting the language, actually accentuated its subalternization, thus creating the opposite effect of what essentialist nationalism, such as Arana's, required from poetry.

In Bilbao, the journal *Hermes* (1917-1922) represented an attempt to create a more avant-gardist nationalism in Spanish. Many artists and some of the writers mentioned earlier (Unamuno, Baroja) collaborated. However, it is important to note that many Basques, such as Pedro Mourlane Michelena or Rafael Sanchez Mazas---born in Madrid but raised in Bilbao by his Basque mother---participated actively in that journal and eventually became founders of Spanish fascism. The Spanish fascist hymn *Cara al sol* (*Facing the Sun*) was composed by a group of Basque writers in Madrid.

The many periodicals published by the working class around Bilbao have been studied as sociological or political objects, but have not yet been incorporated to a postnational literary history.

2. National Allegories (Txillardegi, Laxalt, Martín Santos)

After the Spanish Civil War and the German occupation of France in World War II, Basque literature ceased to be published, especially on the Spanish side where it grew strongest in the 1930s. Franco's dictatorship played a very active and violent role repressing Basque culture, as the nationalist Basque government of the Republic sided with the legitimate government against the fascist coup of 1936. Only towards the late

1950sand early 1960s, did Basque literature become once again a significant cultural field, written in several languages and countries, which nevertheless was devoted to a critical and allegorical representation of the nation. Yet, it was mainly diasporic and exilic (internal and external), because of the historical and political situation of the southern Basque Country under the dictatorship.

In the 1940s and early 1950s, Basque cultural production almost stopped in the southern Basque Country with the exception of Salbatore Michelena (1919-1965), a Franciscan priest who took advantage of the cultural shelter offered by the monastery of Arantzazu and wrote *Arantzazu, Poem of the Basque Faith* (1949). Another priest writing on the French side, in the convent of Belloc, Iratzeder (Jean Diharce), was the other isolated voice who wrote against the general cultural despair that prevailed in the Basque Country. Catalan and Galician writers wrote similar poems in that existential moment such as Salvador Espriu, *The Skin of the Bull* (1960), and Celso Emilio Ferreiro, *Long Night of Stone* (1962).

Most of the literary work was carried out in exile or was shaped by a diasporic-exilic sentiment even when it was written in the European Basque Country. Jokin Zaitegi, a Basque who migrated before the Spanish Civil War to Guatemala, created a literary periodical entitled *Euzko Gogoa* in 1950, which gave voice to all the diasporic and continental writers in Basque. The periodical was shipped to twenty-six countries and, till the late 1950s became the center of literature written in Basque. By the end of that decade, however, a new periodical, *Egan*, published in San Sebastian with the financial help of the provincial government gathered the youngest writers.

Parts of the first novel of the post-bellum, written in Basque with a conflictive hero, were originally published in *Euzko Gogoa* in 1956: Txillardegi's (José Luis Alvarez Enparantza) *The Secret Diary of Leturia*, published in book form in 1957 (*Leturia*). This author was one of the founders of the terrorist group ETA and the one who proposed its name. After joining ETA's ranks in 1958, he was arrested and, eventually, went on exile to Belgium where he stayed until his return to the Spanish Basque Country in 1975 after the death of Franco; he wrote two more novels in exile: *Peru of Leartza* (1960) and *Elsa Schelen* (1969).

These later novels have always been considered existential and close to Sartre's *The Nausea* (1938) and Camus's *The Stranger* (1942). However, Basque critics have not underlined the colonial setting and connotations of these existentialist works. Similarly, *Leturia* takes place between Paris and certain places that have Basque names but are not real. The love story between Leturia and Miren, which ends with the former's suicide and the latter's death from sickness, can only be understood within the specific situation of the Spanish Basque Country and the sense of alienation that prevailed. The fact that an existentialist style is deployed in a colonial setting (Sartre/Camus) and in a dictatorship (Txillardegi), gives a very specific meaning to *Leturia*, which to this day has not been studied as such. In this sense, *Leturia* is an existential, exilic allegory of the Basque Country, which nevertheless remains utterly modern in its articulation, references, and style.

Similarly, the son of a French Basque émigré to Nevada and brother to the most influential governor of that state, Robert Laxalt, wrote another critical and diasporic allegory of the Basque Country by resorting to the foundational link between diaspora and "motherland:" family ties. His novel, *Sweet Promised Land*, published in English the same year of *Leturia*, 1957, centers on father-son relations and echoes the most popular poem of that era, written seven years later by Gabriel Aresti: "The House of My Father" (1964). Yet, the novel conveys the idea that the wandering life of a Basque shepherd in Nevada, the novelist's father, is the experience of any Nevadan. In this novel, we have a reversal of the European Basque nationalist allegory that shapes literature from Agirre to Txillardegi and Aresti: Basque history stands for the experience of all immigrants to the United States. The novel counters with the subaltern, exilic notion that the "garden of our ancestors" (Lizardi) or "the house of my father" (Aresti) is built on whichever land gives the subaltern emigrant an opportunity to do so. In short, "the house of my father" can be built in any "sweet promised land," as long as it is precisely that: welcoming and sweet.

Moreover, the "true" "house of my father" is revisited in the novel on a trip: a touristic visit that the narrator and his father take together to the latter's hometown in the northern Basque Country. When the father visits the last house of his relatives, he makes a short appearance and leaves. His relatives ask him to return, but the father does not respond and continues to walk away. The son and also author-narrator of the novel notices this misunderstanding and writes:

> I looked at my father, but he did not seem even to have heard. His face was white and grim and violently disturbed, and he was breathing in quick gasps. I reached out and touched him on the arm and said uncertainly, "They want us to come back."

Without turning, he shook his head and cried shakenly, "I can't go back. It ain't my country any more. I've lived too much in America ever to go back." And then, angrily, "Don't you know that?" (176)

Two paragraphs later, after the narrator describes their return to Nevada, the novel ends. This is perhaps the most powerful allegorical rendition of the Basque Country written after World War II. The author does not condemn or glorify the Basque Country as a nationalist space, but rather, inserts it in an Atlantic space of passage and migration, in which the "garden of our ancestors" or "house of my father" becomes a traumatic space that cannot be inhabited by a migrant subaltern Basque, although it must be revisited. Thus, the house/garden is ultimately reinvented on the other side of the Atlantic. In this novel, "true" Basque essence disappears and a more historical discourse, involving class, poverty, and migration emerges, as the ultimate Basque experience—a subaltern experience— any immigrant group can embrace. This experience also announces what a global Basque Country is meant to become years later. This is the novel that most clearly takes apart the nationalist character of all the essentialist literature written up to that point. In the 1950s, the difference between strategy and nationalist essence was best seen from the diaspora.[157]

During this time, several Basque novelists wrote in Spanish; Ramiro Pinilla and Ignacio Aldecoa are only two of a longer list. Yet, Luis Martín Santos (1924-1964) stands out not only as the greatest Basque writer in Spanish of that era, but also as the most celebrated novelist of Spanish literature in the 20th century with Juan Goytisolo. Born in Larache, Morocco, he grew up in San Sebastian and finished his studies in Madrid. At a time when any novelist writing in Spanish had to move to Madrid to triumph, and the Spanish Basque Country remained oppressed by the Franco regime, Martín Santos moved back to San Sebastian and lived in the city as the Director of the Psychiatric Institute. Although his *Tiempo de Silencio* (*Time of Silence*, 1962) is considered the most canonical novel of 20th-century Spanish literature, due to its technical complexity, narrative power, and ability to represent critically Franco's Spain, it has never been linked to the Basque position of the author.

---

[157] There are two books in Basque, which have not received enough attention and must be incorporated in a wider analysis of this period: Sebastian Salaberria's *I Would Have Shot Them Myself* (1964) and Martin Ugalde's *The Killers* (1961). These two works constitute unique reflections of the violence of the Spanish Civil War and its aftermath.

Besides the title of the novel, the narrative is also structured allegorically. A young scientist who comes from the provinces and arrives to Madrid to conduct some scientific research with rats, in order to find a cure for cancer, ultimately finds his efforts frustrated by the lack of resources and the backwardness of science in Spain. After he becomes accidentally involved in an abortion, he is exiled to the provinces again. His dreams of becoming an internationally known scientist have been shattered.

The novel is an allegory of Martín Santos's own situation as a writer who is also a scientist and writes a national Spanish allegory of the 20th century, but is fully aware that such a fiction can only be written from the exile of "the provinces;" only such peripheral location permits the novel to retain its meaning. In short, the chronotope of silence/province, written by a Basque writer living in the Basque Country, gives a critical and modern account of Spain, so that his literature and position, as provincial and silent, exceeds the allegorical Spanish nation and finds a critical space from which to criticize and articulate that nation. This critical and narrative excess is ultimately Basque.

Towards the end of the novel, in stream-of-consciousness form, the protagonist narrates his exile back to the provinces through the tropes of castration and colonialism:

> If I could enter the ecstasy, if I could fall to the ground and kick in front of the missionary I would be converted, I would submit to the necessary brainwashing and become converted to a hunter of fat partridges and submissive village girls. But we're not Negroes, we're not Negroes. The Negroes jump, laugh, shout, and vote to elect their representatives to the United Nations. We are neither Negroes, nor Indians, nor people of underdeveloped countries. We are dried mummies stretched out in the pure air of the meseta, hanging by a rusty wire waiting for our small silent ecstasy. (245)

Martín Santos very strategically begins by making a sarcastic reference to a colonial setting, but his protagonist ends up asserting that Spain is not a colony; thus Spanish literature has not the existentialist alternative of French writers such as Sartre or Camus. The only space for existential agony results from the ironic excess created by criticizing Unamuno's articulation of Spain as the empty, metaphysical Castile of Don Quixote ("dried mummies stretched out in the pure air of the meseta") from a Basque position of excess. Martín Santos, from his Basque location as province and excess, represents the critical closing of a Spanish nationalist ideology that is originally articulated by Basque intellectuals such as Unamuno. This time, Martín Santos's strategy is precisely to de-essentialize Spanish nationalism and bring back the ambivalence between "inner colony" and "interior savage space" that defines the Basque Country vis-à-vis Spain (and France) since the 19th century.

Finally, it is important to emphasize that the existentialist angst that define the novels of Txillardegi and Martín Santos leads to dystopia, to an internal exile, whereas only Laxalt finds an alternative space for Basques precisely in a place that is subaltern, migrant, and diasporic: the deserts of Nevada. In short, all the spaces defined by these authors are exilic and diasporic in their Atlantic spread; the difference lies in their final utopian or dystopian result. It is not a coincidence if the American West is connected with North America's internal imperialist expansion towards the West, whereas the existentialism and critique of Txillardegi and Martín Santos are connected to the European experiences of colonialism and dictatorship. They all share the colonial and imperialist anxieties that are triggered by the increasing decolonization of the world after 1948.

3. Neolithic and Industrial Basques (Krutwig, Oteiza, Aresti)

If literature was marked by critical allegories of the nation in the late 50s and early 60s, so that both Spanish and French nationalisms were criticized, the same period also presents the most nationalist and essentialist allegories of the Basque Country, mainly exemplified by the work of Oteiza and Aresti; their allegories marked the 60s and early 70s. Although other writers such as Jon Mirande or Frederico Krutwig also participated in this discourse, the dialogue between Oteiza and Aresti is the one that determined culture in the Basque Country at that time.

Basque sculptor Jorge Oteiza (1908-2003), published in 1963 his influential *Quosque Tandem! Interpretación estética del alma vasca (Till When! Aesthetic Interpretation of the Basque Soul)*, which revolutionized Basque culture and gave rise to many cultural movements—even ETA found inspiration in this book.[158] Oteiza's book represents the ultimate exponent of a nationalist discourse of "true" Basque essence. Oteiza claims in his *Quosque Tandem* that the Basque "man" found "his" full realization as man already

---

[158] The other main book that inspired and gave theoretical grounding to ETA was Krutwig's *Vasconia*, published the same year as *Quosque Tandem*.

in the Neolithic by resorting to the aesthetics and politics of emptiness,[159] as it was made evident, according to Oteiza, by Basque cromlechs:

> Now, in the abstract, in this Neolithic cromlech, the artist invents the habitation for his metaphysical root in the precise external space of reality. Unamuno would call it his intrastue—his soul cupboard—his intrahistory. Man has stepped outside of himself, outside of time. An aesthetic solution—religious reason—for his supreme existential anguish….Everything, we might say…. must be reduced to cromlech, to zero as formal expression. (*Selected* 327).

As the reference to Unamuno makes clear, Oteiza's approach is genealogically linked to the Basque formation of Basque and Spanish nationalisms; it represents a reformulation of the same essentialist discourse.[160] Obviously, part of the importance of this book lies in the fact that its theories justify a Basque identity fully realized in the Neolithic. Oteiza presents the Basques as the perfect reference and solution to modernity's contradictions, except that the Basques have achieved such solution in the Neolithic, that is, in prehistoric times. This radical prehistoricism renders the Basques the perfect other of the West. If one were to follow Oteiza, contemporary Basques do not have much to do but to revert, rather than to evolve, to that state of full realization already established in the Neolithic. There could not be a richer response to a very subaltern and oppressed culture that was not allowed to evolve during Francoism.

At the same time, Oteiza's take on Basque (pre)history and identity is most modern, for Oteiza found in the Basque Neolithic the response that the European avant-garde—from impressionism and modernism to

---

[159] Chaho already elaborated this idea of religious emptiness in the 19th century: "the theism that the ancient Euskarians professed, without symbols, without sacrifices, without prayers or cult" (*Voyage* 233).

[160] Oteiza's proposal was not unique in Spain. As William Washabaugh argues in his *Flamenco: Passion, Politics and Popular Culture*, a similar elaboration took place in Andalusia with flamenco: "Anselmo González Climent promoted such a view in his *Flamencología* (1953) which is considered a genre-defining opus. He described flamenco as a mysterious song, an "intuitive metaphysics" (González Climent 1964: 166), an embodiment of the fundamentals of human experience (1964: 168), a musical realization of what Unamuno described as 'the tragic sense of life' (González Climent 1964: 170; Ríos Ruiz 1988: 242; 1993: 33)" (32). Octavio Paz's essentialist definition of Mexican identity in his *The Labyrinth of Solitude* also nears Oteiza's proposals for the Basques. In short, these essentialist attempts at defining national identity were widespread among non-hegemonic areas.

constructivism and Dadaism—sought for the problem of modern art in an international context. The Kantian definition of the sublime required that art be contemplated without any interest, thus turning it into an autonomous discourse and institution (next to the other two institutions of modernity: science and politics). Nevertheless, the commodifying logic of capitalism undermined the autonomy of art to the point of turning it into a practice and institution whose ultimate meaning lied on its resistance to the capitalist market, hence the avant-garde's final self-realization in the modernist tropes of void and silence (also present in Unamuno, Lizardi, and Agirre).

Oteiza was very aware of the development of the European avant-garde and, thus, proceeded, very strategically, to empty Basque culture of meaning, in an anti-anthropological fashion, to the point that he equated Basque culture with void, silence, and ahistoricity. In *Quosque Tandem*, Oteiza turns (Neolithic) Basque culture into an essentialist culture that, at the same time, becomes "the essence" of the European avant-garde and, more generally, of modern art. In short, thanks to Oteiza, the Basque Neolithic becomes the teleology of modern art.[161]

This idea also influenced poet Gabriel Aresti, hence the title of his most important work, *Rock and Country* (*Harri eta Herri*, 1964). In the 1960s, Aresti marked the beginning of modern Basque poetry, of the reunification of the Basque language, and, most importantly, of the first successful representation of a Basque nationalist identity centered on the metaphor of the rock. His poem collection *Rock and Country* makes many references to the Basque sculptor Jorge Oteiza and represents the first popular rendition of a national allegory of the Basque Country, thus, solving the modernist dilemma that Lizardi and Lauaxeta posed; Aresti's poetry was popularly sung as Orixe and Aitzol had wanted yet it responded to the highest standards of the international literary style of the moment. His most famous poem, "Nire aitaren etxea" ("The House of My Father") stands as the central representation of that nationalist ideology of Basque essence: the rock. In the poem, Aresti claims that, even when his entire family and succession will die, the house of his father will

---

[161] In this respect, Oteiza extended from language to culture the Basque ideology of Renaissance apologists who defended that Basque language already contained a perfect Christian philosophy and logic. From a more metaphysical position, Unamuno also fashioned Spanish nationalism in the same way: its essence was the empty landscape of Castile, where Spanish imperialism and Catholic religion emerged not as a positive content but rather as the metaphysical, empty essence of modernity—a very anti-modern essence at that.

survive in a way that defies history. This poem echoes Lizardi's 1932 poem, "Garden of our ancestors."

As in the case of Oteiza and his aesthetics, Aresti's poem also works by the essentialist strategy of emptying the Basque Country of any meaning. Here, "the house of my father" becomes another cromlech, another stone monument, which also signifies emptiness and thus the ultimate essence of the Basque Country: silence and void. If Oteiza's cromlechs defied history because of their prehistoric chronotope, Aresti's house also steps out of history at the end of the poem, as the poet loses his soul and descendants but, nevertheless, the house stands still as an eternal stone monument, void of (Basque) humanity:

Nire aitaren etxea	I shall defend
defendituko dut.	The house of my father.
…	…
Galduko ditut	I shall lose
aziendak,	Cattle,
soloak,	Orchards,
pinudiak;	Pine groves,
galduko ditut	I shall lose
korrituak,	Interest
errentak,	Income
interesak,	Dividends
baina nire aitaren etxea	But I shall defend
defendituko dut.	The house of my father.
Harmak kenduko dizkidate,	They will take my weapons,
eta eskuarekin defendituko dut	And with my hands I shall defend
nire aitaren etxea;	The house of my father,
eskuak ebakiko dizkidate,	They will cut off my hands,
eta besoarekin defendituko dut	And with my arms I will defend
nire aitaren etxea;	The house of my father;
besorik gabe,	They will leave me armless,
sorbaldik gabe,	Without shoulders,
bularrik gabe	Without chest,
utziko naute,	And with my soul I shall defend
eta arimarekin defendituko dut	The house of my father.
nire aitaren etxea.	I shall die,
Ni hilen naiz,	My soul be lost,
nire arima galduko da,	My descendants will be lost;
nire askazia galduko da,	But the house of my father
baina nire aitaren etxeak	Will endure
iraunen du	On its feet.

233

In short, the discourse of the 1960s, from Oteiza to Aresti, followed Benedict Anderson's definition of a community imagining itself as sovereign and limited (even if this imagination could only be deployed towards the past or the future, when Basques were or would be independent again by reaching emptiness). There was political enjoyment here too, but it was of the masochist type as the Basque reader could enjoy his/her most modern non-modernity (its modern Neolithic position) by vacating himself/herself from the nationalist, essentialist Basque Country. This Basque Country had to be empty in order to be politically enjoyed. This essentialist and nationalist representation of the Basque Country further shows its non-strategic nature, once the migrational dimension of these authors is reconsidered—a dimension that is not evident and thus requires further analysis.

Oteiza left the Basque Country for Latin America in 1935. He spent fourteen years overseas and returned to Bilbao only in 1948. As a consequence of his American journey, Oteiza published in 1952 *Aesthetic Interpretation of the American Megalithic Statuary* where he refers to pre-Columbian cultures as "matrix cultures" and celebrates their sculpture and architecture as "fantastic statuary left by an unknown people" (12). Actually, Oteiza discovered the model for the fully realized Basque man of the Neolithic in Latin America, among pre-Columbian ruins. In the Columbian city of San Agustín, where he contemplated pre-Columbian statues, he found the program that then he carried on in the Basque Country in the 1960s.

When referring to "the pre-Columbian sculptor," Oteiza concludes: "He is the first sculptor of the first stone, the sculptor of the first signs, the first engineer of the Augustinian soul;" then, Oteiza claims the necessity to repeat the same aesthetic feat in the present, "the necessity of recreating in ourselves a similar spiritual resolve... with equal faith and parallel ambition" (135). In Latin America, Oteiza understood the function of modern art by observing pre-Columbian statues that defied the history and modernity brought by Spanish imperialism: to empty contemporary culture of all its meaning until one arrives to prehistory. As Oteiza concludes: "by limitation alone we will be unlimited and eternal... a sculptor is neither more nor less than the initial and dramatic form of a universal type of man—he is just that. A statue is a political solution" (145). Therefore, the central work that defined recent Basque culture as essence, as truly other, *Quosque Tandem*, was also a result of a Basque Atlantic voyage. To put it in ironic terms, the "the house of my father" of Aresti's *Rock and Country* was Latin American in origin and became only Basque as a result of Oteiza's Atlantic journey and return to the house of his father, the Basque Country—the reverse journey of Laxalt.

Furthermore, the recurring metaphor in Aresti's *Rock and Country* is not the rock, ironically enough, but the Atlantic Ocean. More specifically, Aresti refers to the passage from land to the sea where he finds the true modernity of the Basques: the docks at the port of Bilbao. As Aresti writes, referring to Oteiza, his true sculpture is not carved out stone but sea water:

Nik	I
Poetatzatik	From the profession of poet
Dimisioa	Presented
Presentatu nuen	My resignation
Kantsazioaren aitzaikiarekin	With the excuse of exhaustion.
Baina nola aitzakia hura gezu-rrezkoa zen,	But as that excuse was made out of lies,
berriz ere hartu nuen eskuan mailua,	I took once again the hammer on my hand
Eta Kantabriako itsasoa jo dut kolpeka.	*And I hit the Cantabric* Sea blow by blow.*
Jurgi Oteizak ere	Jorge Oteiza too,
Kromlekaren aitzakiarekin	With the excuse of the Cromlech
Dimisioa presentatu zuen	Presented his resignation
Eskultoretzatik,	From the profession of sculptor.
Baina hala ere	But even so,
Inork eztio Euskalerriari Penamenik eman	Nobody has given their condolescences To the Basque Country
(131, my emphasis)	
	*Bay of Biscay

In both cases, Oteiza and Aresti effected a very modern recuperation and self-fashioning of an essentialism that ultimately was nationalist and Atlantic. In the case of Aresti, furthermore, the reference to the Atlantic was connected with the immigrant workers who came from other parts of Spain to work in Bilbao at the seaport. Thus, Aresti, unlike Oteiza, was capable of fully inscribing modernity within his nationalist, poetic project. He understood that the migrant experience was central to any future articulation of Basque nationalism. In this respect, Aresti stands as the work that came closest to including subalternity within the nationalist project.

Yet, precisely because of the ultimate modern and inclusive nature of Aresti's work, towards the end of his life, he was denounced by Basque nationalists as being "españolista" (pro-Spain, Hispanophile) and was ostracized and exiled from the Basque Country. Oteiza's constant status as outsider and madman followed the opposite direction. After the Spanish transition was finalized in the 1980s, Oteiza achieved a canonical position and was celebrated by Basque institutions in dire need of cultural legitimation and capital. Had Aresti lived longer, he would not have been canonized the same way. Although he wrote a poem about not wanting to have a street named after him. His death eventually erased his "españolista" trace and the city of Bilbao went against the wishes of the poet: there is a street in the city named after him.

Blas de Otero and Gabriel Celaya are the other two important poets of this moment. In an extended, postnational exposition of this period, their work must be incorporated as central.

4. Modernity's Failure (Saizarbitoria, Lertxundi, Guerra Garrido)

Only when a newer generation of authors born during Francoism or in the aftermath of World War II began to write, did Basque literature finally shift genres and topics, so that the new nationalist goal became to write the first modern, Basque *novel*, rather than poem, which could allegorize the urban and contemporary Basque Country, rather than the pastoral countryside or a Neolithic, metaphysical space beyond modernity. The challenge then was to represent a modern Basque Country that was also nationalist, without falling into any essentialist or self-canceling, masochist situation, as the previous generations had. Yet, this challenge implied ideologically that linguistic and social subalternity had been overcome in the Basque Country. In short, it was a political fantasy, which nevertheless was necessary in order to overcome that very same subalternity.

The first attempts were made in the 70s in the continental Basque Country. It is not a coincidence if this new generation attended the university and had a more complete, middle-class education. The most important author and novel of that decade were Ramon Saizarbitoria (1944-

) and his *100 Meters* (*100 metro*; 1976).[162] Raúl Guerra Garrido, an immigrant to the Basque Country, and his most famous novel, *Unexpected Reading of the Capital* (1976), were also an attempt to formulate the same problem in Spanish, with a similar multi-perspectivist narrative and a more historical point of view. Saizarbitoria's novel centered on an ETA member, whereas Guerra Garrido's focused on an industrialist kidnapped by ETA.

Saizarbitoria's *100 Meters* was the result of a very serious reflection on Basque literature carried in San Sebastian among several writers who wrote in an avant-garde journal, *Ustela* (*Rotten*) in the 1970s, and constituted themselves as a group. Bernardo Atxaga, the other important writer of that period, was also part of this group but, due to several disagreements, later joined another one in Bilbao, which also published a journal: *Pott* (*Kiss/Failure*) and had a different literary program. The disagreements between Saizarbitoria and Atxaga, that is, between *Rotten* and *Kiss/Failure*, points to a more important phenomenon: the field of literature in Basque language was for the first time organized as a field (Bourdieu). Until this point, Basque literature was rather an intermittent activity that experienced some successes but only in an isolated form. Now, Basque literature was a cultural field and institution with an inner coherence and a political mandate: to write the modern Basque novel par excellence as a way to overcome allegorically its historical subalternity.

A similar consolidation was taking place in the newly inaugurated democratic Spain and, thus, Basque writers writing in Spanish found more access to the publishing houses of Madrid and Barcelona and to the literary debates originating in those cities, which became their literary field of reference. Thus, the split inaugurated by Arana and Unamuno between languages was further accentuated by its economic and institutional consolidation after 1975. Unlike literature written in Basque, the one written by Basques in Spanish became absorbed by the Spanish markets and institutions and never found a political location in the Basque Country until the late 1990s, as I will explain below. Basque writers on the northern or French side of the Basque Country, due to the lack of local political and cultural support, became subject to the institutionalization and economics of the South.

---

[162] As Juaristi rightly points out, this is the Basque version of the *compte rendue* between the existentialist novel and the *nouveau roman*, the former exemplified in the Basque case by Txillardegi (*Literatura* 124).

237

Basque literature written in Basque defined the literary field in the Basque Country. Consequently and once every writer became positioned within the new Basque literary field, each of them had to take a position in order to create the national allegory. Thus, Atxaga published *On the City* (1976), Mario Onaindia brought out *The Tree Trunks Lying on the Snow* (1977), Joxe Agustin Arrieta wrote *The "After Lunch" of the 15th of August* (1979), Koldo Izagirre contributed with his *Because* (1976), and Itxaro Borda, the only woman and writer of the French side positioned within the field as such, published her polemical *Basilica* (1984) few years later.

Yet all these attempts to write the national allegory relied on the modernist European tradition spanning from Kafka to the *nouveau roman*. All these texts were highly innovative in the form; as the French terminology of the period tended to proclaim, novels such as Saizarbitoria's *100 Meters* were "scientific novels"—a formal experiment conducted with the precision and method of a lab test. In short, these novels were written for the writers themselves, were highly polemical, and in general had no mass appeal. The most important effect of these novels was to create a new and modern literary field whereby every author knew that he or she had to have a literary and symbolic capital in order to take a position. At the same time, this field consecrated Saizarbitoria as the canonical writer of modern Basque literature, which, then, had the negative effect of paralyzing his writing. After publishing *Oh Jesus* (1976), a Beckettian novel, he stopped publishing for nineteen years.

100 Meters requires a summary analysis to explain why it does accomplish a new modern and nationalist allegory of the Basque Country. In the novel, Saizarbitoria tells the story of an ETA member who is cornered in the central square of the Old Town (*alde zaharra / parte vieja*) of San Sebastian. He runs a hundred meters before the police shoot him down. The novel represents, in a fragmentary and non-continuous way, the activist's life by resorting to different discourses (dialogue, police interrogation, inner monologue, media releases, touristic guides, etc.). At the same time, the novel captures the voices and reactions of all the people surrounding the death of the terrorist.

At most levels of the novel, one can isolate a three-dimensional structure that is ultimately topological and allegorical. Every level is divided in three spaces: the personal space of the main character, the public and political space against which he defines himself, and the outside space that surrounds the struggle between the personal and the public. A chart of the different levels and spaces can be summarized as follows:

Levels	Personal space	Public space	Exterior space
Political	Basque Country	Spain	Europe
Linguistic	Basque	Spanish	Foreign Languages
Social	Family	Country	Abroad
Family	Mother	Lover	Father
Temporal	Past	Present	Future
Narrative Person	I	You	It/he/she / they
Narrative Space	Open part of Square	Arches	Street

The fact that the novel combines successfully all these levels and spaces gives its discourse a complexity and depth that had not been achieved in Basque literature before. The Basque Country and the main character emerge with a conflictedness that makes them fully Basque and modern: there are no traces of essentialism at the level of what is represented. The only formal shortcoming is the shortness of the novel (less than 100 pages). Moreover, the linguistic subalternity of Basque is included in the novel, although social subaltern classes are not.

Yet, the novel is essentialist at another unsuspected level: representation. The fragmentariness and juxtaposition of different discourses turns the novel into a modernist novel that is completely disconnected from previous Basque narratives and, thus, ultimately, alienates the reader. The Basque reader of the 1970s was not prepared for this novel and he or she only accepted it as a literary fetish of quality because the critics had decided so. In this sense, the essentialism of Saizarbitoria is not Basque but modern—hence its label of "scientific novel." This is not an isolated phenomenon. The *nouveau roman* in France or the modernist novel of Martín Santos and Benet in Spain had a similar effect.

However, at that moment, and for the first time in Basque literary history, the market of Basque literature was being organized as a field with a readership. The reading public, who was looking for that new representation of a Basque modernity, rejected the novel but also purchased it. Although *100 Meters* had many editions, these were due mainly to the educational institution where the novel was taught; the readers were told to purchase the novel. Thus, Saizarbitoria's next novel, *Oh Jesus!* (*Ene Jesus, Maria ta Jose*, 1976) further alienated his readership, had smaller sales, and led the author to a silence of nineteen years, in which the more readable literature of Bernardo Atxaga became the new canon and reference.

After Atxaga had replaced him as the most canonical writer of Basque literature in the 1980s, Saizarbitoria broke his literary silence and began to publish novels with regularity in the 1990s: *Countless Steps* (1995), *Two Hearts: War Chronicles* (1996) and *Bury Me in the Ground* (2000, a compilation of previous novels and novellas published separately). These new novels represented a radical departure from Saizarbitoria's previous production, for, this time around, his literature addressed the issue of violence (the Civil War and ETA) and contemporary Basque society, head-on, in its historical and narrative richness without falling into modernist, fragmentary narratives (*100 Meters*). *Countless Steps*, for example, tells the story of a protagonist who wants to write a novel about an ETA member killed by the police and, at the end, is haunted and destroyed by an accidental encounter with current ETA members. In this process, Saizarbitoria tells the sentimental education of a generation of young Basques who came of age between the mid-1970s and early 1980s, that is, in the transition from the dictatorship to the democratic regime. In order to capture the radical departure this novel represented, it is worth quoting Jesús María Lasagabaster's remarks made in 1990 about contemporary Basque literature: "It seems as if Basque writers are afraid to face historical and social reality, be it past or present" ("Introduction" 19). Without a doubt, Saizarbitoria's novel is the most important Basque novel of the 1990s.

In the 1970s and 1980s, ETA was being approached by Basque, French, and Spanish literatures as either the leading political movement of Basque nationalism or the exotic political other of the Spanish state. In either case, ETA's terrorism merely served as political justification or background for the development of narratives that were little concerned with the Basque problem in itself. As Darío Villanueva already pointed out in 1987, this treatment was connected with a literary tendency, journalistic and otherwise, to feed on the immediacy of contemporary events: "The novel in general, not only those written by journalists, takes advantage of events deriving from the most immediate, and frequently painful, reality. Terrorism has been, in this order of things, one of the most exploited topics" ("La novela" 45). Even *100 Meters* did not fully escape this exploitative effect.[163]

In the context of Basque literature, the new novels by Saizarbitoria

---

[163] Perhaps the most popular and exploitative novel, worldwide, about Basque terrorism is mostly unknown to Basque readers: Robert Ludlum's *The Scorpio Illusion* (1993). He became a global best-seller with his *Bourne* series.

(and, as we will see later, Atxaga's) represented the first attempt to break away from this opportunism as well as from the literary reluctance, prevalent in previous years, to address the issue of terrorism in its social and historical complexity. They constituted the first attempts to write historically about ETA without either endorsing or marginalizing it in a Manichean way. Yet it is important to understand the other reason that pushed Saizarbitoria to write about ETA and (state) violence.

As a result of the rise of a Basque literary market in the 1980s, which was brought about as an unintended effect by the nationalist literature of these authors (see next chapter), Saizarbitoria's new literature was confronted with the fact that its main recognition came from the official spheres (government, prizes, critics) rather than from a readership who was not willing to read complex and challenging literature, beyond a certain point. Consequently, canonical literature such as Saizarbitoria's resorted to *the politicization of narrative* as a way to hold on to its dwindling nationalist, canonical status.

Clearly since the 1990s, the new consumerist Basque market required narratives based on individual characters with a rich interior and intimate life or narratives that paralleled other consumerist experiences. The contradiction between this demand for a narrative of individual, affective experiences and the political need to represent political violence as a way to remain institutionally recognized defined the latest work of Saizarbitoria. Although since the 1990s, Saizarbitoria continued to write in a complex, modernist style, he also moved from representing national allegories (*100 Meters*) to more reduced narratives of the domestic space where the presence of historical, political violence, nevertheless, does not go away (*Two Hearts*). To this day, Saizarbitoria continues to be the most accomplished realist chronicler of everyday life in the Basque Country. However, the impossibility of containing violence within a personal space, such as the domestic, forced the novel to narrate the protagonist's neurotic enjoyment and suffering, thus, masterfully representing the inner life and troubling ghosts of a very specific Basque generation who has grown up with ETA but has also abandoned violence as a means of politics.

As I will explain below, Saizarbitoria's most important novel, *Martutene* (2012), closes what I call "the long Basque 20th century" (1898-2011) and becomes its most important and canonical novel.

6. Global Difference and Postnationalism

1. Globalizing Basque Otherness (Atxaga, Irigoien, Pinilla)

In the 70s, there was a third group of writers who were not directly involved in the power struggle that defined the literary field between the San Sebastian group heralded by Saizarbitoria, on the one hand, and the Bilbao group led by Bernardo Atxaga, on the other. This group resorted to a very different literary capital: "Third-World" magic realism, which proved to be so successful in Latin American literature with García Márquez and, later on, in Indian literature written in English with Salman Rushdie as well as in African American literature with Toni Morrison.

Among these writers, Anjel Lertxundi published the first national allegory based on the tenets of magic realism: *The Town of Urturi Is Hangover* (1971). Juan Mari Irigoien, who lived in Latin America for several years, followed with *The Cock's Promise* (1976). Txillardegi also wrote a similar novel, although more mystical than realist-magic, entitled *From Beyond the Wind* (1979), which also pointed to a departure from the modern, urban setting of earlier productions.

Bernardo Atxaga, after ending his earlier modernist phase with the Bilbao group *Kiss/Failure*, also published some of first short stories of what later would constitute his canonical *Obabakoak* (1988). His short story *An Exposition of Canon Lizardi's Letter* (1982), won the prestigious Irun prize and made the author famous as magic-realist short-story writer. This new literature, unlike that of Saizarbitoria, had enormous success among readers, partly because it was more accessible, due to its realist and mythic style, and partly because it resorted to the literary register of magic realism, which represented the Basque community as endowed with a new magic essence—the Basque Country was presented as exotic "other." This new magic-realist literature worked as a reactive to the earlier urban, modern narrative: the new rural and magic realities represented by this literary style were more in line with the traditional imaginary of Basque nationalism. The idea of a Basque modernity expressed by the urban novels of authors such as Saizarbitoria did not have an ideological echo among its readers. Ultimately, magic realism became a way to re-represent the subalternity that had historically defined the Basque language and its classes---and earlier proposals such as Oteiza's or Saizarbitoria's had left out. The political contradiction and fantasy of this new approach rested on the fact that subalternity was exoticized as other, as magic, and became highly enjoyable in its anti-modernity.

Given the large success of these magic-realist novels, some authors repeated the formula by representing the rural-subaltern world in different ways, as in the case of Lertxundi's *At the Sixteenth Time, Apparently!* (1983) and *Otto Pette: In Death as in Life* (1994) or Irigoien's *The Polyhedron's Leaves* (1983) and *Babylon* (1989).

Yet, the most canonical novel among these works was Atxaga's *Obabakoak* (1988), which received the most prestigious awards in both the Basque Country and Spain. This work was translated to over twenty-three languages and landed a full page in the *New York Times Book Review* (Suárez Galbán). In short, this work represented the full political, economic, and cultural materialization of Basque literature as the allegory of a nationalist community which was both anti-modern (magically essential) and modern (new style), subaltern and elite-sanctioned, and, thus, could be represented as magic and realist. Atxaga's novel was a full answer to the main pursuit of 20th-century, nationalist, Basque literature since its inception in the 1910s and 20s: the essentialist, national allegory.

Ironically enough, if Saizarbitoria's *100 Meters* is considered the first modern and urban allegory, opposite Atxaga's rural and magic one, it is important to emphasize that both are dystopian in last instance and, thus, they are closer than their respective standpoints might suggest at first sight. In *Obabakoak*, the Basque Country presents itself to the Basques and to the rest of the world as a realist "other," endowed with a magic essence (subalternity) and, so, the exoticism of Basque terrorism in *100 meters* parallels that of *Obabakoak*. The fact that the latter is not a "true" novel but a very elaborate topological intertwining of short stories that refer to the town of Obaba, does not disqualify the work as a novel but rather complicates the novel's form.

However, the essentialism of *Obabakoak* had a global dimension that previous Basque literature did not. It constituted the first successful representation of the Basque Country as a perfect, minority, subaltern culture endowed with all the characteristics—magic essence—that the West sought in minority, subaltern cultures and literatures—opposite *100 meters*, which emphasized the modernity and European-ness of the Basque Country, even when it exoticized terrorism. This is the reason for the local and global success of Atxaga's novel. *The New York Times* had already hailed García Márquez and Salman Rushdie as "a continent [Asia/Latin America] finding its voice" (Johnson 133). It was also the case of Atxaga: the Basque Country had found its voice. *Obabakoak* represented the Basque Country as a perfect, minority, subaltern community—and its literature as the perfect epitome of a subaltern literature.

W.E.B. Dubois discusses the meaning of having a "double consciousness" for the African American experience of the USA in these terms: "this double-consciousness, this sense of always looking at one's self through the eyes of others, of measuring one's soul by the tape of a world that looks on in amused contempt and pity" (5). This sense of "double consciousness" has also defined Basque culture and literature in the 20th century; this double consciousness defined it as a minority, subaltern culture. Early Basque nationalism represented the most powerful attempt to overcome this double consciousness and to pose a "true essence," rather than a strategic essence, thus joining the racist discourse that prevailed at the time in Europe. Yet, at the end of the 20th century, when the continental Basque Country gained autonomy again, *Obabakoak* emerged as the full assumption of this double consciousness by which the Basque Country became simultaneously essentialist—as other, subaltern, minority, exotic, archaic, magic, etc.—and a modern, quality, first-world literature celebrated by the media all over the world. In short, the Basques could look at themselves through the eyes of global, first-world readers in *Obabakoak*. Yet, and if Dubois's words are paraphrased, the measuring tape of the "Basque soul" remained nationalist essentialism: the otherness of a minority, subaltern culture. The world looked at the Basques as "magic others" and forced the latter to look at themselves as such "others." This is the normative definition of what a minority, subaltern literature means in globalization.

The reason for global culture to accept *Obabakoak* as a "true work of art" endowed with the essence of a minority culture—with its otherness—begins in Spain. The fact that Spain had no colonies since the early 20th century[164] and, even with the boom of Latin American literature, Spanish remained a subaltern language in the first world (unlike French, English, or even German), neutralized the difference between Basque and Spanish. Both were equally subaltern languages incapable of developing their own internal "minority" literatures.

Yet, the linguistic difference between Spanish and Basque helped emphasize a difference that otherwise would have gone unnoticed to the European readers and, more generally, to the global readers and critics. If English had a presence in the postcolonial world of Asia and Africa, or France celebrated its own "minority" literatures as Francophone literature in Africa and Canada, Spanish did not have a parallel in its own

---

[164] With Equatorial Guinea and the Western Sahara as separate semi-colonial developments.

247

geopolitical area: the Latin American boom of the 60s was never perceived or celebrated as a Spanish postcolonial phenomenon, i.e. as "Hispanophone literature:" that would be an anachronism. Moreover, the literary production of ex-colonies such as Equatorial Guinea or Western Sahara was not yet considerable: in 1987 writers Donato Ndongo and Ana Lourdes Sohora published what are considered two of the first modern Equatorial Guinean novels, *Shadows of Your Black Memory* and *The Loyal Friend* respectively.[165] Therefore, the only conditions by which a minority literature could take place in Spain were precisely given by linguistic difference, such as Spanish/Basque. That became the Spanish brand of "Third-Worldism."

The review of *Obabakoak* in *Le Monde* is illustrative of this Third-World-like character attributed to Basque literature: "He [Atxaga] names things like Adam in paradise, like Bernal Díaz del Castillo [Hernán Cortés's chronicler] in front of an unknown world" (Chao).[166] In short *Obabakoak* represents the transition from nature to culture in a "savage, uncivilized, and almost Third-World like culture;" hence its essentialism. The reference to Bernal Díaz del Castillo further emphasizes the postcolonial overtones of an unconscious Spanish imaginary long gone in Latin America. Finally, the fact that *Obabakoak's* all twenty-three translations were based on the Spanish translation rather than on the original Basque, which nevertheless was directed and supervised by Atxaga himself, further emphasized its minority status. The fact that it was originally written in Basque is simply a symbolic sign of its "genuine minority status," its essence, for ultimately the text that served as the basis for translation was not the original but its Spanish translation.

However, *Obabakoak* also represented the full materialization of a Basque literary field and market in the aftermath of Francoism. In this respect, the novel was the most modern Basque literary production until that point. That is, with *Obabakoak,* literature became a Basque cultural reality, both as field and institution (publishers, reviewers, critics, academic courses, translators, agents, etc.), so that finally also had a well-defined canon. As Bourdieu explains, Atxaga's "position taking" as magic-realist writer, which ensured him a canonical and teleologically central place in the nationalist pursuit of 20th-century Basque literature, also had an economic and social effect that the author did not anticipate.

---

[165] His earlier *Antholog of Guinean Literature* (1984) represented the first compilation of literature of Ecuatorial Guinean writers.

[166] Original quote in French no longer available.

Moreover, this unintended effect changed radically the Basque literary field altogether: it brought the commodification and commercialization of Basque literature. *Obabakoak*'s success became central to the formation of a market whose readership no longer responded to the nationalist ideal of literature but rather to that of consumerist, individual tastes. *Obabakoak* was the first modern best-seller of Basque literature with sales over 40.000 copies. Few works had sold 40.000 copies before and never as a "mass literary phenomenon;" *Obabakoak* was consumed by the public as an event, as a cultural phenomenon to the point of becoming an overnight bestseller—hence its modernity. At the same time, the canonization of *Obabakoak* had a secondary and important effect: it forced the rest of Basque authors to take positions as canonical, counter-canonical, or para-canonical, thus consolidating the *Rotten/Failure* conflict. That is, after *Obabakoak* every author had either to duplicate its success or to neutralize it with an alternative counter- or para-canonical work.

Since the global recognition of *Obabakoak* at the end of the 80s and early 90s, Atxaga followed an interesting path, including his 1999 announcement about considering quitting literature (Efe). The main reason he gave was the commercial and commodified turn taken by literature—precisely a turn triggered by him and fostered by the spread of globalization in Basque culture, which could be symbolically dated to 1992.

From a political perspective, Atxaga's work represented the crowning moment of a whole period of literary production—the modern, nationalist one—in which Basque literature had been engaged in representing the Basque community as an essential "nation" and "subject." Perhaps the most concise way to define the history of modern Basque literature in the 20th century is precisely this: *a series of allegorical attempts to represent strategically the Basques as a modern nation and subject endowed with an anti-modern essence.* Although one could rewrite this history in many ways, a look at most literary histories (Villasante, Sarasola, Kortazar, Juaristi, Aldekoa, etc.) demonstrates that most of them have been written and chronicled following the writers' involvement and success in representing the nation.

In this context, Atxaga's *Obabakoak* represented the powerful moment when a writer finally found both the "form and content" to produce a successful essentialist, national allegory, one that was widely acknowledged as such by the Spanish state as well as by most first-world languages and countries. Thus Atxaga's subsequent difficulty in writing, his consideration of abandoning literature, derived from his success in naming and representing the allegory of the Basque nation. As I have discussed elsewhere, this is a one-time economy that precludes the writer and the readers from repeating it; ontologically speaking, "naming," giving the true name to a being, naming its essence, can only take place once ("Bernardo Atxaga's Seduction").

Yet, the global acceptance of the national Basque allegory had a very pernicious effect that ultimately delegitimized the history of nationalist, Basque allegories and, more specifically, Atxaga's *Obabakoak*: the national allegory was globally celebrated because of its self-exotization and self-othering. Thus, rather than a full political recognition that would help turn the Basque Country into a global, political subject, this work had the opposite effect of reifying or reinforcing the subaltern position of Basque literature and culture at a global level. In short, Obabakoak marked *the new global subaltern status* of Basque literature and culture. The violence present in the novel and its final self-cancelation took place at a time in which the violence of ETA reached its most deadly levels, thus, contributing to the perception of an essentialist Basque nation as violent.

Atxaga's ulterior work has encountered serious difficulties in overcoming *Obabakoak* and making sense of this new global subalternization of Basque literature. As a result, just like Saizarbitoria, Atxaga has tended to politicize his narrative by resorting to stories involving ETA and the Civil War. This trend has continued to our days. So far, Saizarbitoria has been more successful in surviving his own canonical status than Atxaga, as the scandal with the latter's *The Son of the Accordion Player* (2003) proves: it was criticized for being a pastoral novel close to custom literature (Echevarria). Basque institutions such as Etxepare have reinforced the global subalternization of Basque literature by presenting Atxaga as the face of Basque literature: for example, this institution named an endowed chair at New York University after this writer. As the years pass, Atxaga is more widely criticized for its effects in Basque literature (Apalategi; Galfarsoro *Subordinazioaren*; Atutxa).

Furthermore, as the new literature of the 1980s and 1990s made clear, the project of the essentialist national allegory showed some insurmountable limits: it was a masculinist project centered on the ABC, so that women and other Basque regions were marginalized.

Although Basque authors writing in Spanish or French had success in publishing in multinational companies centered in Barcelona, Paris, and Madrid, the rise of a local independent Basque publishing industry with companies such as Elkar, Erein, Pamiela, or Susa had the political effect of consolidating literature written in Basque as the central literary activity of the Basque Country. As stated above, the centrality of the project of the essentialist national allegory, focused on the novel as a genre, and legitimatized a southern, masculine literature in Basque as hegemonic. Yet, the centrality of literature written in Basque helped consolidate a second Basque literature in the shadow of the more hegemonic one: literature written in Basque in the North. Partially as a result of the rise of literary journals such as *Rotten* and *Failure/Kiss* in the South, northern writers launched their own journal on the French side in 1981: *Maiatz* (May). Authors Piarres Xarriton, Itxaro Borda, Lucien Etxezaharreta and Aurelia Arkotxa launched this journal, which has been published since continuously till our days and has launched most of the writers from the North. The political divide between states, the ever increasing subalternity of Basque language in the north, and their linguistic difference from the standard Basque adopted in the South, gave them an identity but also relegated them to a more marginal position, as the main industry and readership of literature in Basque was located in the South. The journal *Maiatz* also became a publishing company in 1984 and eventually received the help of the Council of Basque Culture, the sole institution that fosters Basque culture on the French side. Itxaro Borda was perhaps the only northern writer who managed to cross over to the south and gain a readership on both sides of the Basque Country. At the time of the publication, her *Basilica* (1984) became scandalous, due to its very ironic and critical take on the project of the national allegory.

Outside literature written in Basque, two names have to be mentioned in Basque literature in Spanish: Ramiro Pinilla and Miguel Sánchez Ostiz. Ramiro Pinilla is perhaps a singularity in Basque literature. He wrote several interesting novels which he self-published; he was finalist to the prestigious Planeta prize in 1972 and, in 2004-2005, he published his best-known work: the trilogy *Green Valleys, Red Hills*. Ironically, after having written many social novels, it was his three-volume national allegory who won him acclaim and praise; yet, his work did not manage to overcome the essentialist and exoticizing pull also seen in Atxaga. Only, the Navarran Sánchez Ostiz has managed to write a truly realist novel that portrays the complexities of the Basque Country. Yet, he has undergone the opposite evolution: the more critical and locally situated he has become, the less accepted and celebrated his work has ended up being. Novels, such as *Pirannas* (1992) need to be studied and reconsidered.

2. Women's Literature and Exile (Urretabizkaia, Mintegi, Borda, Jaio)

Although there were few writings by Basque women early in history (Maite Nuñez-Betelu lists several women writers from the 18th century onwards; vii), women became recognized writers at the end of the Franco dictatorship: Amaia Lasa, Lourdes Iriondo, Arantxa Urretabizkaia, Laura Mintegi, and Itxaro Borda. In the 1970s and 1980s, they introduced and elaborated individual desire rather than a national or communal identity, as literary subject, due to fact that women were always exiled from the nationalist allegorical project. Masculine literature did not elaborate individual desire because it always stood for the essentialist nation and its allegorical subject, thus becoming *the* subject of national identity. Women were only accepted as part of the nationalist project in so far as they agreed to occupy a non-subjective position: the reproductive mother *qua* nature, which did not have social agency. Women writers did not accept such a position and thus needed to elaborate a non-nationalist, non-communal position and desire, i.e. an individual one. As a result, women had to exile themselves from Basque culture and nationalism; they had to become exilic subjects. Therefore, they organized sex and gender—and thus desire and identity—according to a different structure from the normative one imposed by nationalism and its essentialist allegory. This fact shaped and determined not only women's writing, but also the future of the entire field of Basque literature when the nationalist project faced a crisis triggered by globalization and consumerism. Therefore, women's literature began to shape all Basque literature starting in the late 1980s.

In order to understand the masculinist structure of the national allegory, it is important to understand the context in which women's writing emerged in the 1970s. In 1976, the most important writer of that generation, Ramon Saizarbitoria, published his third novel. The title of his novel, *Oh Jesus*, refers to the sentence that the phallic mother of the story endlessly repeats as the opening line of her monologues. The character of the mother is as important as peripheral in the novel. Nevertheless, this novel consecrated Saizarbitoria as the central and outmost important Basque writer of the nationalist and realist tradition in vogue in the 1970s. At the same time, Saizarbitoria's third novel also anticipated the crisis of such a realist-nationalist model of writing.

Six years later, in 1982, Bernardo Atxaga published his first important short story, *Camilo Lizardi*, which later on became one of the keystone stories of his novel *Obabakoak*—precisely the novel that in 1988 conse-crated his author as the canonical writer of Basque literature of the 1980s. In this work, a new literary paradigm—the magic-realist, national alle-gory—was developed as a response to Saizarbitoria's previous realist writing style. In the story, women's absence is associated with magic na-ture. In the middle of the magic wilderness, a child who can turn into an animal and becomes a sacrificial victim of the town of Obaba, shouts "mother, mother" before he dies metamorphosed into a white boar (*Oba-bakoak* 47). Here too, the mother symbolizes a reproductive and phallic subject that, moreover, does not only regulate biological reproduction in nature but also the magic realist-style of the story.

Halfway in the canonical relay between Saizarbitoria and Atxaga, pre-cisely in 1979, Arantxa Urretabizkaia became the first "official" woman writer with a short novel entitled *Why Darling?* In the novel, a narrative voice in style of stream of consciousness introduces another type of mother. Here the mother-woman is abandoned by her lover, a narcissistic man with childish tendencies. The mother feels insecure; she is searching for company while the thought of her son becoming another narcissistic man like his father haunts her. This novel, which underscores the cen-trality of the mother position and gives her a voice, did not consecrate her author as canonical, although it became a best seller (Kortazar and Olaziregi 4). Furthermore, this work did not manage to interrupt the na-tionalist perpetuation of the phallic mother, both natural and peripheral, in contemporary Basque literature, as the continuity between Saizarbito-ria and Atxaga testify.

The comparison of the motherly representations effected by the three authors mentioned above with their respective institutional positions makes clear that the image of the mother was central to Basque literature up to the 1990s. The more peripheral to the story this image was, the more phallic and semi-natural it became—it controlled and threatened the narrative center occupied by the masculine protagonist. This moth-erly voice, in its peripheral and yet phallic power, was literally represented by a single sentence: "Oh Jesus!" "Mother, mother!" etc. In last instance, the single sentences representing the mother legitimized the stories and their respective authors as canonical. In turn, the more central and real the mother became to the story, the more defenseless and abandoned she appeared—although her voice acquired a more personal and individual tone. In short, the positioning of the maternal voice was always carried out at the expense of both the author's and the novel's centrality. As long as women writers resisted and dreamt other identities that were not motherly-nationalist, they were actively marginalized. These women were exiled, or exiled themselves, from the literary system and canon imposed by the nationalist culture of the Basque Country. At the same time, it should be clear that women writers did not approach motherhood as an identity problem but as an option: they chose to be or not to be a mother. Nevertheless, these women did reformulate and represent attempts to overcome the social and political limitations imposed by nationalism on motherhood.

Still in the mid-1990s, some fifteen years later, the maternal figure was central to women's literature. The novel by Laura Mintegi *Nerea and I* (1994) is centered on the figure of another mother also abandoned by an irresponsible and immature lover. Arantxa Iturbe published a narrative essay and biography on her experience on motherhood: *Oh Mother!* (1999). However, in both cases, the mother was not defined by her motherhood, but rather by her own individual subjectivity as mother. Actually, both authors explored the social limits imposed on women through the institution of motherhood. That is, in the twenty years elapsing from Franco's death in 1975 to the publication of Mintegi and Iturbe's work in the mid and late 90s, the figure of the mother remained central to Basque literature. Only in 2006 did Karmele Jaio published *Mother's Hands* where the relationship between daughter and mother became the center of the novel.

The centrality and continuity of the maternal figure ran parallel to women writer's marginalization. Women writers continued to be marginal until the late 1990s. In sight of which, it could be stated that, as a result of the hegemony of the Basque nationalist imaginary, the figure of "woman," be it heterosexual or lesbian, native or immigrant, did not exist as such social construction till the 2000s. For the Basque nationalist imaginary, the only existing "woman" was "the mother." Maternity continued to be the only space from which hegemonic, nationalist, Basque culture constructed and allowed the existence of people who were not of masculine gender. In other words, the gender opposite nationalist Basque masculinity *qua* Basque historical and political subject was not "woman" but "mother:" a mother who was ahistorical, natural, and phallic.

The category of "Basque women writers" did not exist as such until the year 2000—beyond a critical or political-misogynistic construction— because what they had in common was a negative identity. It was precisely the identity they all wanted to overcome: nationalist motherhood. Curiously enough, the alternative to nationalist motherhood was always exile: if they accepted the mother position, they imposed exile from and on themselves, whereas if they did not accept it, they were exiled from the cultural system of Basque nationalism. Nevertheless, it is important to emphasize that such an exile and identity were basically negative and did not give place to what Blau DuPlessis, and other feminists in favor of the thesis of a different writing by women, call "feminine aesthetics" or "feminine writing."

The work of most Basque women writers until the 2000s was defined by their personal voice, which manifested in forms that were different and sometimes even irreconcilable among themselves. Each narrative voice constructed a literary space that became a utopia against the nationalist, motherly position. Here, "space" and "utopia" are used in order to convey the fact that these enclaves did not exist in hegemonic nationalist culture and, thus, literature became, in the most literal and material sense, the only site where a utopian space could materialize and exist. In Benedict Anderson's terms, these literatures were not attempting to "imagine a community" but rather the opposite; they imagined "a personal space outside the community." It is precisely from this utopian space outside the nationalist imaginary that women articulated their lack as desire: a desire for another type of gender and sex articulation where motherhood and nation were not equated. Thus, the nationalist motherly position against which women wrote explained why they wrote as individual subjects, as individual voices, rather than as the voice of the nation or the subject of the nation (masculinist literature). As a result, they ciphered their efforts in formulating a discourse of desire, rather than one of political violence, death, etc.

Despite all the differences among all the above writers in their representations of desire and identity (exile and alienation), all shared two negative qualities, two characteristics that defined them negatively. Firstly, as I have already discussed, Basque women writers did not represent a motherly or national voice. These writers' narratives organized an individual and personal voice that did not attempt to represent, or legitimize, the political body of the Basque national *socium*. As a result, women writers opted to explore, from their personal and individual spaces of (inner) exile, new forms of articulating their lack through desire. In their writing, desire was a way to reach *jouissance*, that is, irrepresentable spaces where women writers transcended the nationalist order through its cracks. Perhaps Laura Mintegi is the writer who explains *jouissance* more clearly among Basque women writers. Her knowledge of Lacanian and feminist psychoanalysis makes her point radically pertinent as she explains in an article entitled "Emakumearen orgasmoa" ("The Orgasm of Women"):

The case of woman is the same: man could never fulfill the love request posed by woman. Because it is an infinite request, unsatisfiable. Psychoanalysts could not explain why women's expectation was infinite and, therefore, they concluded that women's orgasm was infinite, insatiable for men's capacity.

They did not realize that, the infinitude did not emanate from an unsatisfiable orgasm, but from the position that woman has been given in the structure, because her expectations cannot be fulfilled as long as she continues to be placed in that space. Woman will be insatiable until she becomes a subject, until she completes her structure. Only then, will we able to see if it has anything to do with orgasm.[167]

The second negative, discursive characteristic shared by all women writers, results from their position in the Basque structure of identity and desire. It is their reliance on voices other than the first-person narrative as well as their tendency to locate spaces that are not situated in any precise geography, Basque or otherwise. Several strands of European and North American feminism posit the idea of a writing style that is feminine by nature (Irigaray, Wittig, Duplessis. etc.). Following this trend, but from a more historical perspective, critics such as Birute Ciplijauskaité affirm that the contemporary female novel in Europe is defined by the first-person narrative—the most subjective and individual of narrative persons. As she states: "[C]ommenting on fiction written in German and French, several critics observe a clear tendency towards the narration in first person and emphasize the high percentage of women writers. A similar assessment could be extended to the literary production in England, the United States, Spain and, to a certain extent, Italy and Portugal" (13). She concludes that "[I]n order to affirm themselves, women turn inwards and find their most persuasive voice through the use of the first person" (30). In the case of Basque women writing in the 1970s through the 2000s, the "I" was not the prevalent narrative person, although personal

---

[167] "Emakumearen kasua bera da: gizonak inoiz ezin izango lioke erantzun emakumearen maitasun eskaerari. Eskaera infinitoa delako, bete ezina. Psikoanalistek ez zuten jakin azaltzen zergatik zen infinitoa emakumeen espektatiba maitasunarekiko, eta ondorioztatu zuten emakumeen orgasmoa dela infinitoa, asegaitza gizonen ahalmenerako.

Ez zuten ikusi, infinitotasuna ez datorkiola orgasmo aseezinetik, baizik eta egituran egokitu zaion espaziotik, beraren espektatibak ezin dituelako bete espazio horretan kokaturik dagoen artean. Emakumea asegaitza izango da subjektu bihurtu arte, bere egitura osatu arte. Ondoren ikusiko dugu orgasmoak zerikusirik duen ala ez."

and individual voices were. These voices were constructed through the combination of different narrative strategies, persons, and locations. Perhaps, the reason for the lack of predominance of first-person narratives was due to the fact that women were situated in positions of exile and estrangement vis-à-vis nationalism and, thus, were not located in subjective spaces that allowed them to speak from one single place: the first person.

However, at the turn of the new millennium, the above situation changed with the arrival of a new group of women writers. These women were part of a younger nationalist generation that achieved local hegemony in the Basque Country. It also coincided with the crisis undergone by the project of the nationalist allegory and its masculinist subject, on the one hand, and the emergence of desire as the ultimate form of capitalist activity, consumerism, on the other. Therefore, the work of these women writers moved inside a nationalist, Basque, hegemonic discourse, which was in crisis and helped produce a new Basque consumerist subject. Among these younger women, motherhood no longer was the issue that centrally defined their articulation of desire and identity. Moreover, these writers began to use the 1st person more often.

As in the case of Jasone Osoro, Lourdes Oñederra and Ana Urkiza, women writers received wide social recognition and had success in sales. They were also promoted as the forerunners of a new wave of Basque literature, which defined the literary field: "women's literature."[168] However, these women wrote about women—younger women—who felt stranded or alienated. Unlike the previous group of women writers, these younger writers were not able to represent the origins and causes of their alienation. Their writing chronicled the identity and desire of women who were estranged from themselves. Authors such as Osoro or Oñederra wrote about personal anguish or ennui. In short, they did not write from a position of exile vis-à-vis nationalism and motherhood, but one of exile or estrangement from themselves, and from within a hegemonic, nationalist class that was undergoing a crisis.

This turn, from motherhood and exile to desire and self-estrangement points to a historical change that helps us understand desire and

---

[168] Several of these writers held meetings, organized themselves as a group (*Working Group of Basque Women Writers*), and published an ensemble work (*Whims/Desires* 2000). Lourdes Oñederra, received all the prestigious Basque awards in 2000 for her first novel published the year before and Itxaro Borda received the most prestigious national prize, the Euskadi prize, in the year 2001 for her *100% Basque*.

identity across the gender and national divide in Basque culture after the arrival of globalization (neoliberalism). In so far as women writers have written in exile outside the project of the national allegory, or inside a consumerist hegemonic nationalism that nevertheless is experiencing a crisis, women writers have been the first *postnational subject* of Basque culture and politics, and in that respect, they have shaped the entire field of literature and politics in the new millennium, as the Basque Country has become postnationalist and global.[169]

As of 2001, this was the sociological picture of women writers: the official number of writers affiliated to the Association of Basque Writers totaled 242. The total of women writers was 28 (11.5%), of which 16 (6.6%) were engaged in creative writing. Furthermore, more than half of these women had joined the association in the previous last three years (15 or 53% of all women writers joined between 1998 and 2001). At the risk of simplifying, one could name the eight most active women writers of Basque literature until the year 2001: Arantxa Urretabizkaia, Mariasun Landa, Laura Mintegi, Tere Irastorza, Arantxa Iturbe, Amaia Iturbide, Aurelia Arkotxa, and Itxaro Borda. The last two are French and the rest are Spanish.

As of 2016, the number of writers in Basque is 512, of which 387 are active and 96 are women (EIE email communication). Therefore, the number of women writers has increased from 11.5% in 2001 to 24% in 2016.

3. Postnational Hybridity (Borda, Sagastizabal, Epaltza, Montoia, Osoro, Martínez de Lezea)

The exilic situation experienced by women writers in the 1970s and 1980s became generalized in the 1990s in Basque culture. The market, the only space of culture sanctioned by neoliberalism and globalization, forced most writers into a situation that women writers had lived before vis-à-vis nationalism. Most writers, like women authors before, found themselves at the end of the nationalist project, facing a new postnational scenario that women had experienced before as exile. Now the exile from nationalism was forced, not by nationalism itself, but by the market: the

---

[169] Here postnationalism means the new political situation in which the project of a nation-state no longer is feaseable; the state and nation become out of sink. Yet, postnationalism (after the nation, following the nation) also means that nationalism does not disappear but rather experiences a new politicial strength, from fundamentalism to anti-neoliberalism, which is caused by its unhingedness with the state, hence its crisis.

essentialist, allegorical project of the nation was in crisis. The desires and tastes of the individual consumerist reader and its private self became the new postnational space in which most writers had to write. Ironically enough, this coincided with the rise of a local, Basque, nationalist, intellectual and political class that still held to a nationalist ideology. Therefore, nationalism was politically hegemonic but culturally and economically was experiencing a crisis.

This was the decade when most Basque literary and cultural institutions, from academia to the press, from the Association of Basque Writers (EIE) to publishing houses, gained some stability. Most notably the first newspaper in Basque language, *Egunkaria*, started in 1990, and an older initiative, the yearly Durango Market (*Durangoko Azoka*), became the Basque book fair that marked the publishing calendar of Basque literature. As stated above, this moment coincided with the generalization of mass culture and globalization, which prompted the neoliberalist ideology that equated individual desire with consumerism and thus relegated any other form of citizen participation to the margins. The encounter between the recently nationalist stabilization of culture and the irruption of globalization created forms of hybridity that, sometimes, served to celebrate a new postnational culture of consumerism, and other times, helped contest neoliberal globalization. ETA's failed attempts to negotiate a cease-fire in Algeria with Spanish state representatives in 1994 and the new cease-fire announced in 1999, also pointed to a postnational situation of crisis and change, which could not be solved. Basque and Spanish nationalisms were in crisis in the globalized aftermath of the fall of the Berlin Wall but, at the same time, remained the main political horizon in which politics were conducted.

Nothing can capture better the hybridity of that moment than the clash between an alternative culture centered on what was known as Basque Radical Rock, which in the 1990s gained mainstream acceptance with groups such as Negu Gorriak, on the one hand, and the official culture that embraced neoliberalism and celebrated it with the inauguration of the Guggenheim Museum in Bilbao, on the other. The hybrid mixing of *bertsolaritza* and hip-hop by Negu Gorriak had its echo in the mixing of works of Basque sculptor Eduardo Chillida and North American architecture by the Guggenheim at its newly inaugurated museum at Bilbao.

Authors publishing in the 1990s for the first time confronted globalization and its effects in Basque culture with very interesting and even contradictory results. Over all, none of these authors tried to address and legitimize the hegemonic subject of nationalism and, thus, no longer posited the idea of strategic essentialism as a literary task or goal. Yet, the new political hegemony of a nationalist class haunted these writers with the ideology of the nation. The tentative term that helps to understand this new literary production is "hybridity" and the genre that captured this complex situation and became central to Basque literature was the novel.

Unlike the long tradition that, since the Renaissance, presented Basque culture and literature as different, as endowed with an essence that was either strategic or nationalist, this new literature emphasized the impurity of that essence, its hybrid nature; it was half-global and half-local. In short, this literature proposed a new Basque location and community based on a hybrid difference; they tried to imagine "the nation after the crisis of the nation" and in this respect, they were postnational.

Homi Bhabha theorizes this hybridity as neither local nor global but as a third space. In a rather condensed passage, he declares:

> The non-synchronous temporality of global and national cultures opens up a cultural space—a third space—where the negotiation of incommensurable differences creates a tension peculiar to borderline existences…. The problem is not of an ontological cast, where differences are effects of some more totalizing, transcendent identity to be found in the past or the future. *Hybrid hyphenations* emphasize the incommensurable elements… as the basis of cultural identifications. What is at issue is the performative nature of differential identities: the regulation and negotiation of those spaces that are continually, *contingently*, 'opening out', remarking the boundaries, exposing the limits of any claim to a singular or autonomous sign of difference—be it class, gender or race. (219 my emphasis)

The other proponent of hybridization, Nestor García Canclini, elaborates a different theory of hybridity, which, nevertheless, complements Bhabha's (206-63).

Although the concept of hybridity is fraught with historical and political problems and ultimately is untenable, it is historically operative as a starting point to analyze the interaction between local and global cultures. Although there are many names that represent this new globalized, hybrid, Basque literature, here I will concentrate on six: Itxaro Borda, Aingeru Epaltza, Joxean Sagastizabal, Xabier Montoia, Jasone Osoro, and Toti Martínez de Lezea.[170] Their work represents six large tendencies in Basque literature and therefore these authors help us understand not only a specific body of texts but also the literature of the 1990s and early 2000s at large.

Borda

The work of Itxaro Borda stands out as unique and separate from the rest of her peers, both women and northern writers. Her lesbian standpoint allows her to articulate motherhood as desire for the mother-land; in this respect her writing, and especially her novels, are centered on articulating a lesbian, nationalist desire. As her trilogy of detective novels centered on the sleuth Amaia Ezpeldoi exemplifies, her desire is about a subject who cannot go home but wishes to find a home where her motherly and lesbian desire can find its object/subject of desire. Her trilogy is formed by *Until They Leave Us Alone* (1994), *Just a Love Disappointment* (1996), and *While I Live in the World* (1996).

Her writing does not aim at the historical and real Basque Country, nowadays centered on the Basque Autonomous Community and its hegemonic social class: the new consumerist, heteronormative Basque middle class. Rather, Borda's writing points to a Basque Country that has never existed, historically speaking, and, nevertheless, is not imaginary but utopian: a Basque Country that encompasses all the regions and social classes that historically have been part of Basque culture or politics, beginning with her homeland in the French Basque Country. In order to do so, Borda resorts to hybridization.

Because Borda's writing is not hegemonic, but at the same time remains nationalist, the process of hybridization in her work starts within the borders of the Basque Country and expands outwards into global culture. Hers is probably one of the most inclusive bodies of literature as far as the heterogeneous objects and subjects it incorporates. Her novels include endless references to global culture, detective stories, road films, reggae, rock, etc. In addition, archaic, rural, and camp forms of Basque culture are also incorporated in her work in innovative ways. The almost obliged visit paid by the detective to the shepherds of the area in each novel is part of

---

[170] A longer list should also include at least the following names: Paco Aristi, Rikardo Arregi, Hasier Etxeberria, Joxemari Iturralde, Mikel Hernandez Abaitua, Koldo Izagirre, Edorta Jimenez, Pello Lizarralde, Xabier Mendiguren, Joxan Muñoz, Ixiar Rozas, Joseba Sarrionaindia, and Iban Zaldua.

261

this hybridization of non-modern elements of Basque culture. Such moments pay tribute, a hybridized tribute, to the foundational narrative of the Basque novel: the nationalist, essentialist custom literature of Agirre (*ohiturazko literatura, costumbrismo*). Furthermore, Spanish and French are also spoken in her work. In *Till They Leave Us Alone*, one can read several "Basquized" French and Spanish dialogues.

Moreover, the literary convention of the lonely private eye allows her protagonists to travel throughout the Basque Country and map it, while remaining in a permanent state of migrancy. Her detective's migrancy allows the author to "re-produce" literarily the Basque Country. Unlike most Basque literature written on either side of the French-Spanish border, Borda's narratives always cross this border and move on both sides, so that they create a single space: one that constitutes precisely the geography of the nationalist Basque Country. This crossing is a permanent feature in all her novels. Furthermore, crossing also affects the innermost part of the detective's own self: her desire. Usually the lover who appears at both the beginning and end of the novel comes from the opposite state side of the border, in which the case takes place. As a result, her writing is not defined by a position of exile, unlike most of her heterosexual counterparts from the southern Basque Country, but rather by one of migrancy. She articulates a sense of home, nation, and motherhood that does not exist yet, and thus, is desired from a position that is lesbian, melancholic, and migrant towards the mother-land.

Her non-heteronormative, migrant, yet nationalist approach to the Basque Country, led her to win the Basque national prize of literature in 2002 with her *100% Basque*. Yet, this very same position has also taken her in recent years to speak up against both nationalism and terrorism, in works such as *Triad* (2003).

Epaltza

The Biscayan writer relocated in Navarre Aingeru Epaltza published a novel in the early 1990s *Ur uherrak* (*Troubled Waters*, 1991). Perhaps *Troubled Waters* is the most interesting and undervalued Basque novel of the 1990s. A narrative work that resounds with the same dense style of Faulkner or many other modernist novelists, successfully achieves the dislodgment of the Basque nationalist subject and its essentialist effect. *Troubled Waters* creates a literary language that is highly hybrid in its combination of linguistic and cultural registers, and yet is able to represent the Basque spoken in Navarre, the region where Epaltza lives, with a strength that is unparalleled. However, the literary and topological location of the novel already displaces the essentializing effect of a nationalism that is centered on the ABC. Furthermore, this novel, rather than representing the hegemonic subject of Basque nationalism, presents a regional, particular subject and position. The novel tells the story of several individuals in a Navarran town named "The Town." There are no direct references to Navarre, as a way to universalize the story, but at the same time, the literary language itself, full of Navarran dialectisms, manages to hybridize standard Basque language as Navarran. This hybridization has the effect of locating the story linguistically in the Navarran area of the Basque Country while representing it as universal: the Navarran Town could be any town.

There is no single protagonist in the novel; rather a set of four characters creates a double narrative structure. Juanito is a villager who leaves home and migrates to the USA, fights in Vietnam, marries an African American woman, and eventually returns to his hometown with his wife and daughter Billie. Jazinto is a dysfunctional, old man from the village who is saved by Billie from his attempt to commit suicide and gradually develops a complex and loving relation with her. Finally, Medina is the fanatic police officer (*guardia civil*) who is obsessed with discipline and eventually loses his job in The Town, although he returns to try to hunt down Juanito, who is suspected of having killed a villager. The novel is structured along two axes: the violent confrontation between Juanito and Medina, on the one hand, and the loving and yet troubled relation between Billie and Jazinto, on the other.

Billie becomes the lead singer of a rock band who sings in Basque, achieves international recognition, and, at the end of the novel, returns to The Town for a concert held during the summer festivities. A brawl ensues across the Town. At the very end, Juanito kills Medina and turns himself in. As Billie is about to leave The Town in a bus, her embrace of Jazinto marks the end of the novel.

In the narrative, the violent instances connected with both American and Spanish state violence (Vietnam, Francoism) cancel each other out and, consequently, are vacated from the novel. In turn, the embrace between a dysfunctional, old man from the village, Jazinto, and an "African-American-Spanish-Basque-Navarran" woman, Billie, who is becoming an international music star, represents the new hybrid reality of the Basque Country. The novel implies that old nationalist masculinities must be first vacated before new hybrid realities occupy their place. However, the embrace between the old man and the new woman is void of sexual desire, as if sexual desire is still impossible in a space from where the masculinist, national subject has recently been vacated but still lingers as a ghost. In this sense, this novel does not represent a "radically new Basque reality," but rather one where past and present are also hybridized. The absent yet over-present violence of ETA and the Spanish state thus are criticized by vacating them from the novel while representing violence otherwise.

Epaltza celebrates and relocates the hybridity of globalization by way of recentering it at the core of a Basque location, which nevertheless is peripheral to Basque nationalism. *Troubled Waters* has the effect of finally finding a Basque location and identity in globalization. The final embrace between Billie and Jazinto points to a reality that, in its absence of sexual desire, transcends nationalist masculinity; it hints at a new space and time that cannot be represented. In other words, the embrace delineates a hole, a lack, in the middle, precisely one that results from the vacation of the nationalist subject and its violence (ETA/Spanish state). This absence transcends the nationalist order and hints at a reality that cannot be represented yet. At the end of the novel, the reader enters this absence, in a way, or is possessed by this absence, and, thus, can experience postnational *jouissance*, a reality impossible to represent within the contemporary nationalist, hegemonic discourse, and yet one that can be enjoyed in its impossibility.

Epaltza's later work has become highly original and hybrid in its combination of genres and topics, from the detective novel to the historical novel. Yet, in his more recent work, the original hybridation has blocked the writer from representing newer and older realities in their complex historicity, and thus, ultimately have become formal, stylistic, and without necessary depth. Many gifted writers, not only Epaltza, continue trapped in this "postmodern trap," and represent one of the main tendencies of Basque literature.

Sagastizabal

In 1994, Joxean Sagastizabal published *Kutsidazu bidea, Ixabel* (*Show me the Way, Isabel*) a novella that became an automatic best seller and whose sales equaled those of *Obabakoak* (around 40.000 copies). The novella's story is about a Spanish-speaking Basque man who decides to learn Basque by moving to a "boarding school" or *euskaltegi* in the mist of the rural Basque Country. The book is a romantic comedy where the colonial discourse and tropes of Conrad's *Heart of Darkness* are deployed in order to parody the "Heart of Basque Nationalist Darkness:" this heart is precisely essentialist nationalism and its allegorical project. The rural "natives" living in a farmstead are portrayed as more (post)modern and daring than the protagonist is and, at the same time, the latter finds his own urban, imperialist condition "naïve" and "native." The novel manages to vacate all its protagonists from the "pure" and "pristine" location of the heart of Basque nationalist darkness. This empty location is then used as the cultural norm to parody, tease, and subvert. But interestingly enough, the parody is made in Basque language so that both spaces—interior and exterior to the space of Basque nationalism—are rendered in Basque, thus radically de-essentializing Basque identity while affirming it. In short, here we have a very hybrid anti-essentialism. Sagastizabal's novella is therefore a critique of the essentialist tradition strategically inaugurated by Mogel and his *Peru Abarka* (1802), which found its final and failed nationalist formulation in Atxaga's *Obabakoak*.

The novel is hybrid in very enjoyable and productive ways. At a linguistic level, the novel plays with the entire spectrum of language "impurities" that the standardization and normalization of Basque has created by default over the last few years. Hybridization ranges from the non-normative dialectal forms of the "natives" (reflected in the title), to the new "dialect" of *euskaldunberris* (new Basque speakers) and the Spanish and English registers of mass culture and commercials. *Euskaldunberris* are "new Basque speakers" who have learnt Basque later in life and, in the learning process, have created a new "dialect" (closer to the standard version than to the historical dialects), which also has some idioms of its own based on grammatical and lexicographical errors that sometimes border genuine enjoyable surrealism.

The novel does not only satirize the essentialist, nationalist construction of the Basque Country, but also creates a form of Basque literary hybridity that is at the core of the reason of its success. Sagastizabal's novel manages to connect the reader's real situation (as either dialectal speaker or *euskaldunberri*; influenced by either Spanish or French) with the Basque standard norm that is only spoken in the media and official milieus. The playfulness of this novella exceeds simple pleasure and reaches real political and historical *jouissance*. The novella suggests a Babelic Basque: an impossible hybrid form that comprises the norm and its infraction, the underlying essentialist, nationalist ideology and its subversion, the colonizer and the imperialist, the local and the global, etc. In a sense, this novel is close to a comedy-version of Juan Goytisolo's *Count*

Julian. It also represents a full reversal of *Peru Abarka* and the most important critique of Basque essentialism and anti-modernity of the last 200 years. Like *Peru Abarka*, this is also a travel narrative.

As a result of this linguistic enjoyment, Sagastizabal created a new space that was Basque but exterior to the Basque nationalist discourse and formation. *Show me* moved the reader outside Basque nationalism and within Basque language. The reader could look at the nationalist construction of the Basque Country looking back at him or her in the same way that any global subject can: from the exterior. In more Lacanian terms, it could be said that, in *Show me*, the Basque readers were looking at themselves from a global position (the Other) that allowed them to contemplate themselves as subjects of global and local hybridity---this would be "the mirror stage" of a new global Basque subject. However, this look could only be placed within Basque language, since the enjoyment of the novel relies in its linguistic register. Thus, this position, global and Basque at the same time, opened up Basque literature to a local hybrid enjoyment of globalization. The result was sheer enjoyment or *jouissance* of a Basque hybridized essence *qua* national identity: the reversal of *Peru Abarka*.

In this respect, Sagastizabal's novel was also the opposite of Atxaga's *Obabakoak*. With *Show me*, Basque literature no longer presented its national essence for the world to see, as in *Obabakoak*, thus submitting it to further subalternization, but rather performed it in order to take narrative control over the gaze that global culture imposes over minority, subaltern cultures. As a result, *Show me* turned globalization into a Basque phenomenon that Basque readers could enjoy as Basques rather than as "minorities" or "others"---i.e. as subalterns. I would conclude that, with his novel, Sagastizabal closed the nationalist phase of Basque literature and its project of (strategically) representing the Basque Country as nation and essence. He has continued this line of criticism with even new installments of the *Show me* novella.

Sagastizabal also opened up a new genre, which can be called mass-literature. With the precedent of Iñaki Zabaleta's *The Subway Station of 100the Street* (1988) and with later works such as Jon Arretxe's *Thursdays* (1997), a new more massive readership, constituted often by *euskaldunberris* learning the language and seeking pleasurable and fun narratives of love, sex, and partying, has consolidated the genre. As of 2016, Zabaleta's novel is on its 41st edition and Arretxe's on its 45th.

The Victorian Xabier Montoia comes from the alternative music world where he decided to learn Basque to sing in that language. After playing in several bands (Hertzainak, M-ak), he began to write in the early 1990s. He has published four poetry books, five short story collections and seven novels. His short stories have had the biggest impact, especially *Gazteizko hondartzak* (*The Beaches of Vitoria*, 1997) and *Euskal hiria sutan* (*The Basque City in Flames* 2006); he won the Basque national prize for literature, or *Euskadi Saria*, for the latter. His alternative and critical view of the Basque Country and its hegemonic classes has given his literature a very specific hybrid form, which has opened the way for many forms of alternative literature close to the progressive left.

The poem "For Some" from his early *Anfetamiñak* (an untranslatable word play between "amphetamine" and the Basque word *miña* which means "pain or hurt") defines his alternative hybridity:

Batzuentzat	For some,
Jesukristo gurutzera	When Jesus Christ rose
(lapurren artean)	to the cross
igo zenean,	(among thieves)
hasten da historia.	Begins history.
Beste batzuentzat, aldiz,	For others, instead,
Leninek —txapela kenduz—	When Lenin —taking off his hat—
«Botere osoa sovieterako»	Shouted
deiadar egin zuenean,	"All power to the Soviets,"
Finlandiako geltokian.	At a Finnish train station.
Niretzat	For me
David Bowiek ilea moztu zuen	The day David Bowie cut
egunean.	His hair.

Most of the short stories in the mentioned two books have become increasingly long, between 15 and 25 pages. They also tend to end abruptly with a rather shocking, traumatic, or violent resolution. This is not a coincidence or an idiosyncratic anecdote; it points to the core of Montoia's writing.

The length of his short stories allows him to introduce an immense heterogeneity of geographies, classes, races, and sexualities inhabited by subjects whose heterogeneous language reflects and represents this social diversity. Bakhtin has named this variety of subjects and languages heteroglossia, and Montoia's short stories are inhabited by the richest and most complex heteroglossia in Basque literature. Furthermore, it is not a stretch to claim that Montoia's heteroglossia captures the Balzacian diversity of the Basque social landscape better than most novels, and thus his short stories remains the best novels of Basque literature. Furthermore, he seeks elements that cannot be easily reconciled in order to create a sense of hybridity. In the initial short story of *The Beaches of Vitoria*, entitled "Black as Coal," Montoia tells a flashback story, in the first-person, of a Basque nationalist young man who, during the Civil War, came of age and found an outlet for his gay sexuality with a Nazi pilot at the hotel in which he worked as bellboy. The room of the German pilot in a Victoria hotel seized by the Nazis becomes the only space in which the Basque young man can explore his bourgeoning gay sexuality and eventually finds love. This short story allows the author to introduce the bombing of Guernica, in which the German pilot takes places, and a gay love story in which opposed political views can be filtered and altered by sexual desire. The story ends abruptly when the plane piloted by the young Nazi lover is shot down and lands in front of the young Basque man. The fact that an old Basque man recalls his youth in a flashback style and, fully aware of the Nazi pilot's participation in the bombing of Gernika, still propels to claim, or at least to nostalgically remember, his love story with the pilot as the great love of his life, explains the hybridity and heteroglossia of Montoia's novels. In the short story collection, the main character of one story appears marginally in another, so that ultimately the collection gives a Balzacian view of the Vitorian life in the last 60 years. This Balzacian, heteroglossic waving of interconnected stories explains the main characteristic of Montoia's short stories.

Similarly, in the short story entitled "Film," from *The Basque City in Flames*, Montoia takes the international San Sebastian Film Festival as excuse in order to explore the new neoliberal, (post)nationalist, elite class of the Basque Country. The protagonist, Lola Pagola, focalizes the story in Spanish---a Spanish that is rendered, nevertheless in Basque. Although the act of narrating in Basque language the thoughts of a character speaking and thinking in Spanish is not unprecedented, Montoia manages to create a more hybrid and complex reality. The reader finds out that Lola is a native Basque speaker, cultured, who, nevertheless, hates the Basque language and its speakers to the point that, after watching a film with lush, green Basque landscapes, she ends up imagining the beauty of a green, natural Basque Country without Basque speakers. She even calls the civil servants of the Guipuzcoan Provincial Government, who are intent on speaking Basque, "talibans." In short, Montoia masterfully portrays a character who has internalized self-hatred for the sake of a consumerist society associated with English and Spanish and in which plastic surgery or fashion are more relevant than minority languages. The story also ends up abruptly when she is attacked in the bathroom of a bar and she does not find out who is the perpetrator.

The other interesting aspect of Montoia's short stories, which apparently contradicts the tendency to narrate detailed, complex, hybrid and heteroglossic realities, is their abrupt and often violent end. Reminiscent of some of best Chekhov's stories, the end interrupts unexpectedly the complexity of stories where Basque police officers, farmers, jet society women, immigrants, and punk youth come together. I have elsewhere suggested that there is an inherent sadism in this authorial tendency to end violently his stories ("Euskal literatur genero"). "Long" short stories that otherwise risk becoming longer novellas or even novels, end unexpectedly and traumatically at the hands of Montoia.

In order to understand the meaning of these ends, and, more generally the place of Montoia in Basque literature, it is important to remember that the title of the second short story collection makes a reference to Bernardo Atxaga's proposal to envision the Basque Country as a single city, the Basque city, where people can live harmoniously and democratically in different neighborhoods, and so Basque speakers can find their own location/neighborhood. Montoia allegorizes burning a model of the Basque city, which two characters are building on scale at home in the last short story entitled precisely "The Basque City in Flames" (405-14). This end has an earlier precedent: the character mentioned above, Lola Pagola, is unwilling to read the novel *Obabakoak* and settles for its filmic version, directed by Montxo Armendariz; however, she also becomes bored with the film before it ends.

Thus, the final reference to the destruction of the Atxagan Basque city in the last short story represents an utter repudiation of the essentialist, nationalist ideology that Atxaga and the project of the national allegory embody. Moreover, Montoia's narrative is also intent in violently destroying and criticizing the new consumerist, hegemonic culture that a Basque nationalist elite has embraced although it also represents its crisis. Thus Montoia is bound to criticize and symbolically destroy this reality he portrays so masterfully. In this respect, Montoia represents an entire tendency in Basque literature, which is critical of the contemporary (post)nationalist, consumerist, globalized Basque Country.

Osoro

The other writer who emerged over the last few years as a new celebrity is Jasone Osoro. She has published two short stories and three novels. Yet she is known for her first short story collection entitled *Tentazioak* (1998, *Temptations*). With it, Osoro became an overnight bestseller and celebrity, and, as a result, she was offered a position in the Basque television as presenter. The unifying topic of most short stories is gender and sex, understood in its broadest sense. The stories are short, and as Patxi Ezkiaga already announces in the introduction to the collection, when referring to Raymond Carver, they could be categorized under the rubric of "dirty realism" so characteristic of the latter's narrative—most tellingly *Cathedral*.

The way in which her work was received somehow resonates with the reception given to Helen Fielding's *Bridget Jones's Diary,* Banana Yoshimoto's *Kitchen* or Almudena Grandes's *Las edades de Lulú*, although the dominant sadomasochistic tone of the latter does not prevail in Osoro's collection. In other words, this short story collection was also received with a sophisticated level of voyeurism that did not exist before in the Basque Country. Rather than pure eroticism, *Temptations* is a combination of a minimalist anguish—an almost non-expressed existential malaise—and sexuality, which makes the collection very compelling and attractive. A barely intimated and yet very real anguish over a minimal problem, such as getting dressed ("On a Friday"), combined with a high degree of narcissism and exhibitionism, gives Osoro's story collection its specific character and popularity.

Ironically, enough, this story collection also captures the problem of locating the global hybridity that defines Basque young culture. These stories present a desire that is global: consumerist in nature and not related to any Basque nationalist discourse or ideology. However, the stories displace desire onto the (mostly female) body, as the latter engages in different sexual activities. The contradiction of this displacement lies on the fact that it is violent. As the stories rescue the (female) body as a new site of desire, the latter also becomes a domestic site violently voided of any positioning vis-à-vis Basque culture, history, social classes, and politics. This lack of positioning, beyond that of the body itself, turns the body, not the subject, into the new object of hegemonic, Basque nationalist desire embodied by the voyeuristic readers. In other words, the sexualized treatment of the body with no references to Basque culture and society, automatically converts this body, by default, into a site of Basque nationalist desire and voyeurism—which does not have to be necessarily masculine. The body becomes a fetish of desire, whereby other types of desires and hybrid realities are suppressed.

Yet, the repressed eventually returns with affective force: light anguish, ennui, boredom, etc. This is the characteristic affect celebrated by hegemonic middle- and upper-middle-class global literatures, such as Generation X's. Osoro's story collection presents desire and anguish as irreconcilable and yet unavoidable. This contradiction is not given up by the stories, but is not solved either. This is the new hybridity that Osoro's work brings into Basque culture: global, consumerist desire is unconsciously hybridized with Basque nationalist culture in the fetish of the mostly female body.

Osoro's literature might be one of the first representations of a desire that is class-marked and internal to Basque nationalism. Her works points to a new hybrid reality that emerged within Basque nationalist culture in the 1990s, which no longer coincided with the masculine subject of Basque nationalism, as represented in the work of Atxaga or Saizarbitoria, but was contained within Basque nationalism.

Yet, this hybridization of desire and nationalism yields anguish and existential ennui. In short, Osoro's work is one of the first chronicles of the birth of a new nationalist self, no longer hegemonically signified by a political and masculinist subject, but rather by a non-political, individual, feminized self, marked by its bodily fetishization. In this sense, Osoro's work is a witness of the "birth of a new Basque, individual, nationalist, desiring self." Yet, the affective conflictivity of this new self also points to the crisis of nationalism triggered by consumerist, global culture.

Also in 1998, the publishing house Elkar, in collaboration with some private patrons, organized the Igartza Prize for young writers. From 1998 to 2004, all the winners were men (Osoro was a finalist in 1999). However, since 2004, only three men have won the prize. Some of the most famous young female writers have emerged from this prize and have gained the aura that Osoro brought with *Temptations*. This prize is the main reason why these days there is a widespread believe that "Basque literature is ruled by women." Although factually this is not correct by any stretch of the imagination, it points to the shifting, postnational, historical situation that emerged since the 1990s.

271

It is important to highlight that, although Toti Martínez de Lezea writes in Spanish, her primary reading community is in the Basque Country and, therefore, she must be approached primarily as a Basque writer, not as a regional Spanish writer dependent of the Spanish literary system (publishing companies, critics, agents, etc.). Today, the center of the literary market in the Basque Country is constituted by literature written in Basque and, thus, Basque literature in Spanish is at best another extension of this Basque market and reading community. Even though any Basque writer who uses Spanish as his or her literary language contributes to the diglossia that the Spanish state still enforces, a counter-diglossic reading might address this issue: Basque writers in Spanish are situated as secondary to a local Basque literary community in Basque, which makes those writers Basque, rather than regional and Spanish. The fact that Martínez de Lezea's books in Basque translation are more popular than those of many writers originally writing in Basque explains the complexity of her position.

The majority of her novels take place in the Basque Middle Ages or the Renaissance; they narrate fictional or historical minority-subaltern characters such as Jews, women, witches, etc. By resorting to history, Martínez de Lezea creates a space and time that is outside or beyond the reach of contemporary violence and nationalism (globalization, the Spanish state, ETA…). The Middle Ages and the Renaissance are the historical periods in which the French and Spanish states have not yet fully consolidated: they are still being formed and thus modernity and capitalism have not taken center place. In this new chronotope, Martínez de Lezea can explore other Basque biopolitical differences outside the indifference generated by globalization and (post)nationalism. This is precisely the reason for her incredible success and importance. Her literature asserts the fact that even the Basque readership seeks a literature of subalternity and differences that escape globalization and nationalism (Spanish and Basque). It must be emphasized that, unlike in the case of the essentialist allegorical-national literature studied earlier, Martínez de Lezea's position against globalization, modernity, and nationalism allows her to explore not just Basque difference, as the only difference that negates other differences, but a varied array of Basque geopolitical and biopolitical differences.

Martínez de Lezea follows a genre that is well rooted in the 19th century Basque literature: the historical legend, which later also becomes the historical novel. In this respect, rather than a break or sudden novelty, Martínez de Lezea's novels are a continuation of Navarro Villoslada's

Amaya and its Jewish, Basque-pagan, Gothic, and Muslim characters. Given that the historical legend was developed as a genre precisely at a time in which the Spanish state unsuccessfully attempted to consolidate itself as a nation, in the mist of the Carlist civil wars and colonial loss, one could also conclude that the legend was also written from without the state and modernity. Martínez de Lezea, and Joan Mari Irigoien, explore this tendency, which is very popular in the Basque Country.

4. Neoliberalism, Autobiograph, and Affect (Juaristi, Savater, Onaindia, Uribe)

So far, I have defined from within the Basque literary field the shift towards a postnational, hybrid, literature, which is a result of essentialist Basque literature's own failure and exhaustion in representing the national allegory (*Obabakoak*). Yet this shift must also be analyzed from the political field in order to understand the other important development in recent Basque postnational literature: confession-memoirs, self-fiction, and autobiography written in both Spanish and Basque.

In the early 2000s, several Basque intellectuals wrote memoirs or biographies: Jon Juaristi's *The Troubled Tribe* (2002), Mario Onaindia's *Freedom's Wages, a Memoir (1948-1977)* (2001), Juan Aranzadi's *Arquiloque's Shield: On Messiahs, Martyrs, and Terrorists* (2001), Mikel Azurmendi's *Pictures from El Ejido: A Report on the Immigrant's Integration* (2001), and Savater's *Pardon for the Inconveniences: A Chronicle of a Battle Without Guns Against Guns* (2001), among others. It is important to note that at least two of these writers had written novels in Basque (Onaindia and Azurmendi) and another had published an essay in Basque too (Jon Juaristi, *Ideologies of the Basque Language*, 1976).

In the late 2000s, and especially after the publishing success of Kirmen Uribe's novel *Bilbao-New York Bilbao*, sanctioned by the institutions with several prizes, a genre known as *autofikzioa* or self-fiction became popular in Basque literature. Although finer differences can be established between fictional memoirs, biographies, self-fiction, chronicles, etc., the simultaneous appearance of all these books points to the fact that those precise boundaries were blurred. All these works pointed to a new obsession with writing the self. Miren Agur Meabe published *A Glass Eye* (2013), Bernardo Atxaga *Nevada Days* (2013), Ixiar Rozas *Black and White* (2014), Mikel Hernandez Abaitua, *Refined Sugar, Coarse Salt* (2010), Arantxa Urretabizkaia *Photos in Black and White* (2014), Itxaso Martin *I, Vera* (2014) and writers writing in Basque such as Mariasun Landa, Maite

Gonzalez Esnal, and Marisol Bastida wrote autobiographies in Spanish. The list can be further expanded but the above titles give a sense of the trend.

Finally, even if it did not coincide fully with the above trends, writers and poets alike began to perform their work in public in sophisticated performances that blended reading, music, and acting. In short, as some writers began to write about the self, others began to use their selves to perform their literature, that is, to re-locate their physical self at the center of their literatures, by performing themselves, their bodily selves, while performing their literature. Kirmen Uribe combined the performative act of reading his work with the performative writing of his self, which extended to articles he wrote for newspapers and afterwards incorporated in his novel.

In order to understand this shift towards writing the self, in its many forms, it is important to understand the historical shifts that took place in the Basque Country in the late 1990s and early 2000s, which culminated with ETA's permanent cease-fire in 2011.

In the 1990s and early 2000s, Basque terrorism lost its infrastructural support in France, especially after the raids in Bidart in 1992 (Elorza). At the same time, the Basque population of the Autonomous Basque Community took massively to the streets to protest against terrorism, especially after the assassination of the PP council member, Miguel Angel Blanco in 1996. Simultaneously, the semi-federal arrangements of the southern Basque Country settled down and, a new form of nationalism emerged in the northern Basque Country (Ahedo). As a result of all these developments, the nationalist project that, in its radical and democratic forms, inspired the nationalist majority of the Basque Country over the last three decades (1970-1990) began to lose its hegemonic hold. In 1996, the right wing Spanish party, PP took power and began a redoubled effort to repress Basque terrorism and nationalist, leftist politics by resorting to military, police and judicial means. Although ETA called a cease-fire in 1998, the Aznar government continued with its policy of judicial and police interventions. The attack extended to Basque culture: in 2003, a Spanish judge closed the only newspaper published in Basque under the pretense that some of its editors were associated with ETA. The case was closed in 2015 with no charges filed. In 2004, the PP attempted to blame ETA for the Madrid bombings perpetrated by a group allied with Al Qaeda. As a result, and starting in the mid-2000s, the two main Spanish parties, PP and PSOE, began to lose steadily support in the Basque Country.

In the late 1990s, many non-political organizations such as *Elkarri* or *Movimiento por la paz* took to the streets to demonstrate peacefully. At the same time, the radical left counteracted with the "kale borroka" or street fight, led by masked youth who terrorized the streets of many towns and vandalized institutions, public buildings, and private property. These two movements, non-political citizen organizations and violent youth, responded to the dissolution of a Spanish/Basque nationalist hegemony in which no political party could embody and channel hegemonically a nationalist project any longer. The nationalist project lost its definition, its clear political embodiment, in the late 1990s. Begoña Aretxaga has explored some of the repercussions of this dispersal of nationalist politics; she concludes that its result is a phantasmatic politics where the nationalist political body disappears and gives rise to a hall of mirrors. In this transitional space, political paranoia and hallucination were the order of the day.

This dissolution of nationalist politics had direct repercussions on the political discourse itself. Until the late 1990s, the responsible subjects for the production of political writing about the Basque Country were intellectuals who had actively participated in the nationalist struggle of the 1960s and 1970s as well as academics who, until recently, denounced Basque nationalism and terrorism from the objectivizing perspective that a state-regulated academia granted. Yet, these intellectuals and academics continued to write in Manichean terms on the Basque political body through the 1990s, thus, ignoring the historical crisis of the nationalist project (both Basque and Spanish). At the same time, ETA threatened many of them. Thus, they experienced the effects of violence in their own bodies and selves at a point when the dissolution of the nationalist political body left their discourses without a clear critical aim. The new non-party politics led by citizen movements and the masked violent youth co-opted their position as intellectuals who could objectively know and write about the Basque political body.

As a result, Basque political, intellectual writing also underwent a similar dissolution, which turned the intellectuals' very same bodies into the only "political body" left. Consequently, their discourse shifted from politics to confession, from the discourse on "the body of the nation" to the discourse on "the body of the self." At the same time, this shift in body politics also created an unintended geopolitical effect. In the past, the academic and intellectual discourse on the national body was written from a universalist point of view in Spanish (and French), which usually was co-opted by and resituated within the general state discourse of Spain and France— the state always embodies the universal position of power/knowledge (Foucault). The new stripping of the intellectuals' political discourse to their bare bones, to the intellectuals' body itself, had the effect of relocating their discourses, not in a Spanish/French/universalist location, but rather on a local level, that is, on a postnational Basque Country whose body no longer was hegemonically nationalist.

The other important discursive effect of this bodily shift—from the nation to the self—was the phantasmization of the political nationalist body, which became an uncanny leftover, a traumatic kernel, embodied within the self of the intellectual. Ultimately, political, intellectual discourse turned into fiction: the confession/memoirs of the intellectual's body and self. This hybrid of confession and memoir became the representational location where the kernel or traumatic leftover of the nation continued to live on, in a spectral or phantasmatic way.

The combined result of the new geopolitical relocation and fictionalization of the Basque intellectuals' political discourse made room for a new type of writing: the confession-memoir-autobiography in Spanish language, a very new and important form of postnational Basque literature. In short, the dissolution of the nationalist body also had the effect of forming a new Basque literature in Spanish written locally for and by the Basques. This possibility had disappeared since the end of *fuerista* literature in the 19th century, after which the nationalist discourses of Unamuno and Sabino Arana polarized languages into two separate nationalist bodies.

The literary, political confession-memoir written in Spanish in the early 2000s by intellectuals is another new development of postnational Basque literature, which also forces the critics to re-read Basque literature written in Spanish at least since the beginning of the 20th century. Basque literature in Spanish must now be considered not as national and Spanish, but rather as postnational and Basque; not as a literature regionally or accidentally Basque, but rather as a literature defined by the presence or lack of the Basque, nationalist, political and linguistic body.

It is important to remember that the most well known writers in Basque (Atxaga, Saizarbitoria, Urretabizkaia, Lertxundi) underwent a similar experience of losing a canonical position due to the failure of the national allegory and, thus, in the 1990s resorted to the opposite option: to politicize literature by writing novels about ETA and the Civil War.

From this newly regained perspective one can also see the symmetry between hegemonic Basque (post)national literatures written in Basque and Spanish: *whereas Basque writers in Basque politicized literature as a means to resort to the political Real (violence) in order to gain nationalist legitimacy, Basque writers in Spanish fictionalized politics as a means to contain the spectral state of the nationalist body.*

This situation has a very interesting parallel in Latin America where a similar form of political discourse of the self was also produced in the postnational aftermath of the dissolution of the socialist utopias of Cuba, Chile, and Nicaragua: *testimonio* literature. In his seminal essay on the issue, John Beverley reflects on the literary shift from magic realism to *testimonio*, as he recaps the aftermath of the Chilean coup of 1973:

> Testimonio began as an adjunct to armed liberation struggle in Latin America and elsewhere in the Third World in the sixties. But its canonization was tied even more, perhaps, to the military, political, and economic force of counterrevolution in the years after 1973. It was the Real, the voice of the body in pain, of the disappeared, of the losers in the rush to marketize, that demystified the false utopian discourse of neoliberalism, its claims to have finally reconciled history and society. At the same time, testimonio relativized the more liberal or even progressive claim of the high-culture writers and artists of the book to speak for the majority of Latin Americans. It marked a new site of discursive authority, which challenged the authority of the "great writer" to establish the reality principle of Latin American culture and development. (281)

Similarly, the new Basque memoir of the intellectual self is also a *testimonio* to the (neo)liberal failure to solve political violence in the Basque Country. Yet, here the "great intellectual," rather than the subaltern masses that endure the violence of ETA, wrote the Spanish-Basque *testimonio*. In this sense, Basque *testimonio* is the political opposite of its Latin American counterpart. Yet, in both cases, we have a postnational literature that emerges in the aftermath of the crisis of the "great writers," who narrate the Basque and Latin American national allegories respectively (García Márquez, Saizarbitoria, Atxaga). Furthermore, because of the dissymmetrical location of the Latin American and Spanish-Basque *testimonios*—Third and first worlds respectively—we see that the *testimonio* form can be mobilized to give voice to the subaltern masses—Latin America—or to actually uphold the national project in its neoliberal version—Basque Country.

Intellectuals in privileged positions of power write most of Spanish-Basque *testimonios*. Yet, at the same time, it is important to emphasize that most of these intellectuals were threatened by ETA and, as the nationalist political body was in crisis, this intersection of violence—personal violent threats, the irresolution of the Basque problem —brought about this new literary genre. The Basque postnational confession-memoir served as bodily host to the trauma (the Real) of Basque violence and history, which still marks the Basque Country even after the permanent cease-fire of ETA in 2011.

The fiction of the self written in Basque emerged later, in the late 2000s, as a result of the political climate outlined above, which, nevertheless was further aggravated by the relentless attack of the conservative party in power PP and ETA's unwillingness to cease its activities. This situation was aggravated by the economic crisis that began in 2008. As a result, the fictionalization and writing of the self gained ground in the Basque Country around the phenomenon known as *autofikzioa* or self-fiction.

Initially, this literature claimed to problematizes the boundaries between self, literature, and reality by resorting to complex mechanisms of referentiality in which the narrator or protagonist could claim to be the author, or pretend to appear to be the author, or, conversely, the author narrated biographical elements while claiming their ultimate fictionality. The side effect of all these new frictions between self, discourse, and reality was the emergence of affectivity as the ultimate form of political activity. The self resorted to nostalgia, melancholia, anger, boredom, etc. in order to claim a new fictional mastery of reality. *Politics became reduced to affect.*

The fact that in the case of writers such as Kirmen Uribe, the author further problematized those boundaries by writing some of the pieces of the novel earlier in a column in the newspaper *Egunkaria* and performed them in recitals with music and video. He is the author that most problematized the boundaries between self, fiction, and reality. Here, unlike in the *testimonio*-confession written in Spanish by Basque intellectuals, the author articulated the discursive fantasy that the self could organize the surrounding reality and give meaning to it, by problematizing its boundaries. At the end, the fantasy was to uphold authorial mastery over reality: the author problematized a more complex organization of self/reality only to create at the end a more fantastic effect of mastery, by which literature retook its lost control over reality.

Yet in order to understand the new fictional refashioning of the self in Basque, we must go further back in history, to its foundational moment. In his seminal *Confessions* (1782), Rousseau's compulsion to tell it all represented a new development in which the self became the romantic site that could uphold the advances of industrial capitalism while also becoming the harbor of the historical trauma of industrialization. The ancien-regime history that resisted commodification and change remained within the self as its ghost, as its traumatic trace. Ultimately, Rousseau's inaugural *Confessions* legitimized the ancien régime as the new modern stronghold, the romantic self, from which to embrace and resist simultaneously capitalism. In the Basque case also, we have a very Rousseauean compulsion to tell it all through the self—most of these Basque writers grew up in Catholic Spain—so that the self and its trace of history, its traumatic violence (the Real), become a new fantastic and affective stronghold against the advances of globalization and political violence. From this newly gained position, these writers fantasize about fashioning a new self that simultaneously embraces and resists the violent dissolution of the national body and the arrival of globalization. In this sense, modern bourgeois literature finally arrived to the Basque Country in the 2000s, in a new postnational fashion, to narrate a neoliberal and globalized Basque self.

Both hegemonic forms of Basque literature, the politicized fiction told in Basque, and the fictionalized politics written in Spanish and Basque, are a double but complementary formation that aims to remain central to a new global, consumerist, postnational Basque culture. Yet, the fantastic reduction of Basque history and reality to an affective self as only means of literary activity must be challenged, as it excludes most forms of subalternity.[171]

5. The End of the Long 20th Century: Saizarbitoria, Rodriguez, Lujanbio, Galfarsoro

The Basque 20th century, unlike the one posited by Hobsbawn (*The Age of Extremes*), seems to be a long one. It began with the new postimperial reformulation of Basque and Spanish nationalisms in 1898 and the rise of industrialization, which slowly turned the French Basque Country into the South's periphery, and ended with the economic crisis of 2008 and ETA's permanent cease-fire in 2011.

As for literature, the monumental novel published in 2012 by Saizarbitoria, *Martutene*, a behemoth of 758 pages, became a summary and culmination of the entire century. This novel represents the acknowledged

---

[171] Basque writers in French who have gained state-wide variety have begun to rethink their position in the Basque Country, notably Jean Echenoz and Maria Darriussecq.

failure of the project of the national allegory. It is also a combined history of the entire 20th century. From the early 1910s, through the Civil War and ETA, all the way to contemporary globalization, which is allegorically signified by the irruption of a young north-American character whose arrival turns the protagonists' Basque world asunder, Saizarbitoria's novel narrates the entire long Basque 20th century. More specifically, *Martutene* narrates the long Basque 20th century and its end by resorting to the political idea of failure: the failure of a nationalist project. Yet this idea becomes the basis of a transmitted historical memory that announces the new 21st century and announces the continuity of a postnational Basque Country. In a way, after *Martutene*, a new century and a new moment open up for Basque literature and culture. Although it is hard to historicize such a recent history, it is the ethical imperative of the historian to do so.

The first element that defines this new historical moment is the ineffective institutionalization of Basque culture at the hands of a nationalist, hegemonic class. There is a major institutionalization of Basque literature and culture, most notably signified by the inauguration in 2010 of the Etxepare institute (following the model of other postimperial state languages: the Cervantes Institute, the Alliance Française, Goethe Institute, etc.). Its functioning so far has been conservative and lacking the postnational imagination required by the times; its accountability has also been questioned (Olasagarre). The other example is Basque television (ETB1) whose low ratings could provide a window of opportunity for experimentation but, instead, point to a systematic lack of willingness to change course and become innovative and socially relevant (Landabidea). Moreover, and as Imanol Galfarsoro has stated, this ineffective institutionalization is upheld by the nationalist, liberal, equidistant elite that dominates Basque culture (*Subordinazioaren*), which acts as if Basque language and culture were out danger of disappearing. The sociological reality shows the opposite.

Besides the ever-increasing presence of women in literature, and specially the raw short stories of Eider Rodriguez, another new important development is the resurgence of the essay: the genre whose authors have gained the social "aura" that novelists have had till recently. After two decades in which Joxe Azurmendi single-handedly kept the intellectual and philosophical essay alive, a new generation has taken the baton. The proliferation of essays from feminism (Ziga) to the issue of independence (Galfarsoro *Subordinazioaren*; Olariaga et al.) points to the fact that Basque literature is ready to reimagine the postnational reality of the Basque community beyond institutional conservatism and neoliberal fictions of the self.

Finally, it is worth mentioning that the core of Basque literature, its oral tradition, has made a smooth transition to globalization. The *bertsolaris* or verse improviser has reemerged as the other auratic "writer" who is followed not only on stage but also across different platforms such as twitter, radio, television, youtube, or facebook. The *bertsolaris* hold a national championship every four years, which usually is sold out and gathers a public of over 10.000 spectators. From Xabier Amuriza and Andoni Egaña to Maddalen Lujambio, the first woman bertsolari to win the championship, they represent one of the liveliest aspects of Basque literature.

Yet, after more than 40 years of liberal, centralist democracy in the entire continental Basque Country, the Spanish and French states have proven to be adverse to multicultural diversity. The survival of Basque language and culture points more than ever before to a single solution, which nevertheless is no full guarantee of success: self-determination and state independence.

Cited Works

Abbadie, Anton. *Antoine d'Abbadie*. Vol. 2. *Recueil des texts, ethnographiques, géodésiques, linguistiques, littéraires*, Patri Urkizu (ed.), Bilbo: Euskaltzaindia / San Sebastian: Eusko Ikaskuntza, 1997.

Abrams, M. H. et al., eds. *The Norton Anthology of English Literature*. 6th ed. 2 vols. New York: W. W. Norton, 1993.

Adams, John. "A defense of the Constitution of the United State." *The Works of John Adams, Second President of the United States: with a Life of the Author, Notes and Illustrations*. Vol. 4. Boston: Little, Brown, 1850-1856. 267-573.

Agamben, Giorgio. *State of Exception*. Chicago: University of Chicago Press, 2005.

Agirre, Txomin. *Kresala*. klasikoak.armiarma.eus/pdf/AgirreDKresala.pdf. 1-10-2016.

—. *Aunamendiko lorea*. klasikoak.armiarma.eus/pdf/AgirreDLorea.pdf. 1-10-2016.

—. *Garoa*. klasikoak.armiarma.eus/pdf/AgirreDGaroa.pdf. 1-20-2016.

Ahedo, Igor. *Entre la frustración y la esperanza: política de desarrollo e institucionalización en Iparralde*. N.l.: IVAP, 2003.

Aizpeolea, Luis. R. "Pugna por el patriotismo constitucional", *El País*. 4 Nov. 2001. Lexis-Nexis. University of Nevada, Reno Getchell Library. 7 Jul. 2003. www.library.unr.edu/subjects/databases.html.

Alberro, Luzia. "Bertsolariek lagundu zuten gertatzen ari zenari hitzak jartzen." Berria 1-22-2016. www.berria.eus. 1-22-2016.

Aldekoa, Inaki. "La poesía del siglo XX." Urkizu, Patricio, ed. *Historia de la literatura vasca*. Madrid: UNED, 2000. 480-504.

—. *Historia de la literatura vasca*. San Sebastian: Erein, 2004.

—. "Bernard Etxepare: «Doctrina Christiana» y poesía amatoria." ASJU, XLIV.2 (2010): 1-40.

Alfonsi, Petrus. *Dialogue Against the Jews*. Washington, DC: The Catholic University of America Press, 2013.

Al-Makkari, Abu-l-'Abbas Ahmad ibn Mohammed. *Analectes sur l'histoire et la literature des arabes d'Espagne*. I-II. Amsterdam: Oriental Press, 1967.

Althusser, Louis. "Ideology and Ideological State Apparatuses." *Lenin and Philosophy and other Essays by Louis Althusser*. Trans. Ben Brewster. New York: Monthly Review Press, n.d. 127-186.

Alvarez Junco, José. *Mater Dolorosa. La idea de España en el siglo XIX*. Madrid: Taurus, 2001.

Anderson, Benedict. *Imagined Communities. Reflections on the Origin and Spread of Nationalism.* London: Verso, 1983.

Anzaldúa, Gloria. *Borderlands: The New Mestiza. La Frontera.* San Francisco: Aunt Lute, 1987.

Apalategi, Ur. "Rossetti's Obsession by Ramon Saizarbitoria: on the seduction of minority literary fields". *Nationalities Papers: The Journal of Nationalism and Ethnicity* 40:3 (2012): 321-340.

Appadurai, Arjun. *Modernity at Large.* Minneapolis: University of Minnesota Press, 1996.

Arana Goiri, Sabino. *La Patria de los Vascos. Antología de escritos políticos.* San Sebastian: R&B ,D.L, 1995.

Aranzadi, Juan. *El milenarismo vasco: Edad de Oro, etnia y nativismo.* Madrid: Taurus, 2000.

—. *El escudo de Arquíloco: sobre mesías, mártires y terroristas.* Madrid : Machado Libros, 2001.

Araquistáin, Juan Venancio. *Tradiciones Vasco-Cantabras.* San Sebastian: Roger, 2000.

Aramburu, Enrique and Mikel Eskerro. "Historia del euskera en la Argentina." Juan de Garay. Fundación vasco-argentina. http://www.juandegaray.org/2012/08/el-euskera-en-la-argentina.html. 1-10-2016.

Aresti, Gabriel. *Harri eta herri. Gabriel Arestiren literatur lanak.* 2. N.l.: Susa, 1986.

Arnaiz Villena, Antonio and Jorge Alonso García. *El origen de los vascos y otros pueblos mediterráneos.* Madrid: Editorial Complutense S.A. 1998.

Arretxe, Jon. *Ostegunak.* San Sebastian: Elkar, 1997.

Arrieta, Joxe Agustin. *Abuztuaren 15eko bazkalondoa.* San Sebastian: Caja de Ahorros Provincial de Guipuzcoa, 1979.

Astarloa, Pablo. *Apologia de la lengua bascongada.* Echevarri, Spain: Amigos del libro vasco, 1983.

Astigarraga, Jesús. *Los ilustrados vascos: ideas, instituciones y reformas económicas en España.* Barcelona: Crítica, 2003.

Atxaga, Bernardo. *Ziutateaz.* I-II. San Sebastian: Kriselu, 1976.

—. *Etiopia.* San Sebastian: Erein, 1983.

—. *Camilo Lizardi erretore jaunaren etxean aurkitutako gutunaren azalpena.* San Sebastian: Gipuzkoako Aurreki Kutxa Probintziala, 1982.

—. *Obabakoak: A Novel.* New York: Pantheon Books, 1992.

—. *The Lone Man.* Trans. Margaret Jull Costa. London: Harvill Press, 1996.

—. *The Lone Woman.* London: Harvill Press, 1999.

——. *The Accordionist's Son*. Minneapolis: Graywolf Press, 2009.

——. *Nevadako egunak*. Pamplona: Pamiela, 2013.

Atutxa, Ibai. *Kanonaren gaineko nazioaz: euskal nortasunaren errepresentazioei buruzko azterketa* Ziutateaz *eta* Bilbao-New York-Bilbao-*n*. Donostia: Utriusque Vasconiae, 2011.

Axular (Pedro Agerre). *Gero*. klasikoak.armiarma.eus/idazlanak/A/AxularGero.htm. 1-10-2016

Ausubel, Nathan and Marynn. *A Treasury of Jewish Poetry: From Biblical Times to the Present*. New York: Crown Publishers, 1957.

Ayerbe Echebarria, Enrique et al. *Literatura vasca*. Lasarte-Oria: Ostoa, 2002.

Azurmendi, Joxe. *Volksgeist. Herri gogoa*. San Sebastian: Elkar, 2007.

Azurmendi, Mikel. *Y se limpie aquella tierra. Limpieza étnica y de sangre en el País Vasco (siglos XVI-XVIII)*. Madrid: Taurus, 2000.

——. *Estampas de El Ejido: Un reportaje sobre la integración del inmigrante*. Madrid: Taurus, 2001.

Bakhtin, Mikhail. *The Dialogic Imagination*. Austin, TX: University of Texas Press, 1981.

Bakker, Peter. "'The Language of the Coast Tribes Is Half Basque': A Basque-American Indian Pidgin in Use between Europeans and Native Americans in North America, ca. 1540-ca. 1640," *Anthropological Linguistics* 31 (1989): 117–143.

Ballesteros, Isolina. "Counted Days for the Lone Man: Decentered Masculinity and Ideology Fatigue in *El hombre solo* (1994), by Bernardo Atxaga, and *Días contados* (1994), by Imanol Uribe." *Anales de la Literatura Española Contemporánea* 27:2 (2002): 5-30.

Baroja, Pío. *Trilogías* I. Tierra vasca: La casa de Aizgorri, El mayorazgo de Labraz, Zalacain el aventurero, La leyenda de Jaun de Alzate... Madrid: Fundación José de Castro, 2009.

Barthes, Roland. *Sade, Foucault, Loyola*. Baltimore: John Hopkings University Press, 1997.

Bailyn, Bernard. *Atlantic History: Concept and Contours*. Cambridge, MA: Harvard University Press, 2005.

Barrutia, Pedro Ignacio. *Acto para la Nochebuena*. klasikoak.armiarma.eus/pdf/BarrutiaIkuskizuna.pdf. 1-10-2016.

Basquepoetry.eus. "Eijerra zira maitia" basquepoetry.eus/?i=poemak&b=859. 1-10-2016.

——. "Buketa." basquepoetry.eus/?i=poemak&b=855. 1-10-2016.

Basterra, Ramón de. *Una empresa del siglo XVIII. Los Navíos de la Ilustración*. Madrid: Cultura Hispánica, 1970.

Baudrillard, Jean. *Simulations*. New York: Semiotext(e), 1993.

Bazán, Iñaki, coord. *De Túbal a Aitor: Historia de Vasconia*. Madrid: La Esfera de los Libros, 2002.

Beauvoir, Simone. *The Second Sex*. New York: Vintage Books 1989.

Benjamin, Walter. "Theses on the Philosophy of History." *Illuminations*. New York: Shocken, 1969. 253-64.

Benjamin of Tudela. *The Itinerary of Benjamin of Tudela*. Cold Spring, NY: NightinGale Resources, 2005.

Bertranpetit, J. and Cavalli-Sforza L. Luca. "A Genetic Reconsctruction of the History of the Population of the Iberian Peninsula. *Annals of Human Genetics* 55.1 (1991): 51-67.

Beverley, John. "The Real Thing." Gugelberg, George M., ed. *The Real Thing. Testimonial Discourse and Latin America*. Durham: London, 1996. 266-86.

Bhabha, Homi. *The Location of Culture*. London: Routledge, 1994.

Bijuesca, Josu K. "Aránzazu y Sor Juana. Hacia una interpretación global del final de los Villancicos de la Asunción de 1685." *Litterae Vasconicae. Euskeraren Iker Atalak*. 7 (1999): 153-75.

—. "Fragmentos de poesía vasca en la literatura española de los Siglos de Oro, reescritura y manipulación." *Oihenart: cuadernos de lengua y literatura* 21 (2006): 61-72.

—. "Praktika literarioaren esparru sozialak eta XVIII. mendeko euskal literatura penintsularra: *Naissance de l'écrivain?*" *Euskera* 55.2 (2010): 877-914.

—. "Literatura eta mezenasgoa XVI eta XVII. mendeetako Euskal Herri Penintsularrean: Mikoletaren "Vuestra Merced"-en aitzakiaz." *Oihenart: cuadernos de lengua y literatura* 25 (2010): 7-40.

—. "Euskara eta vascuence hitzen adiera metriko-poetikoaz: katebegi ostenduak, aroen mitoa eta periodizazio irizpideak euskal literaturaren historian." *Euskera* 58.2 (2013): 577-608.

Blanco Pérez, Domingo. *Historia da literatura popular galega*. Santiago de Compostela: Universidade de Santiago de Compostela, 1994.

Bohigas, Pere. *Aportacio a l'estudi de la literatura catalana*. Badalona: L'Abadia de Montserrat, 1982.

Borda, Itxaro. *Basilika*. Zarautz, Sp.: Susa, 1984.

—. *Bakean utzi arte*. Zarautz, Sp.: Susa, 1994.

—. *Amorezko pena baño*. Zarautz: Susa, 1996.

—. *Bizi nizano munduan*. Zarautz, Sp.: Susa, 1988.

—. *100% Basque*. Zarautz, Sp.: Susa, 2000.

—. *Hiruko*. Irun: Alberdania, 2003.

Bourdieu, Pierre. *The Field of Cultural Production: Essays on Art and Literature*. Cambridge: Polity Press in association with Blackwell Pub., 1995.

Brotherston, Gordon. *Book of the Fourth World: Reading the Native Americas through Their Literature*. New York: Cambridge University Press, 1992.

Bürgher, Peter. *Theory of the Avant-Garde*. Minneapolis: University of Minnesota Press, 1984.

Burns, William E. *Which Hunts in Europe and America: An Encyclopedia*. London: Greenwood Press, 2003.

Butler, Judith. *Gender Trouble: Feminism and the Subversion of Identity*. New York: Routledge, 1990.

Cabo Aseguinolaza, Fernando, Anxo Abuín González, and César Domínguez, eds. *A Comparative History of Literatures in the Iberian Peninsula*. Philadelphia: John Benajamins Publishing Co. 2010.

Calin, William. *Minority Literatures and Modernism: Scots, Breton, and Occitan, 1920-1990*. Toronto: University of Toronto Press, 2000.

Camus, Albert. *The Outsider*. London: Penguin, 2013.

Carballo Calero, Ricardo. *Historia da literatura galega contemporánea: 1808-1936*. Vigo: Galaxia, 1981.

Caro Baroja, Julio. *The Basques*. Reno: Center for Basque Studies, 2009.

—. *Los vascos y la historia a través de Garibay*. Madrid: Caro Raggio, 2002.

—. *Las brujas y su mundo*. Madrid: Alianza, 1966.

Castro, Américo. *España en su historia. Cristianos, moros y judíos*. Barcelona: Crítica, 1983.

Cavalli-Sforza, L. Luca. *Genes, Peoples, and Languages*. New York: North Point Press, 2000.

Chaho, Augustin. *Voyage en Navarre pendant l'insurrection des Basques*, Bayonne: L. P. Lespés, 1865.

—. *Lettre à M. Xavier Raymond, sur les analogies qui existent entre la langue basque et le sanscrit*. ParisL Arthus Bertrand, 1836.

—. *Aïtor, légende cantabre = Aitor, leyenda cántabra = Aitor, kantabriar kondaira*. Bilbao : Academia Lingüística Internacional , 2008.

—. and Marquis of Belsunce. *Histoire des basques: depuis leur établissement dans les Pyrénées Occidentales jusqu'à nous jours*. Bayonne: P. Lespés, 1847.

Chao, Ramon. "Espagnols en quête de littérature." *Le Monde* 1-17-1992. Online, Lexis-Nexis, 5-2-1994.

Chibber, Vivek. *Postcolonial theory and the specter of capital*. London: Verso, 2013.

Ciplijauskaité, Biruté. *La novela femenina contemporánea (1970-1985): hacia una tipología de la narración en primera persona*. Barcelona: Anthropos, 1988.

Colebrook, Claire. *New Literary Histories: New Historicism and Contemporary Criticism.* New York: St. Martin's Press, 1997.

Corcuera Atienza, Javier. *Orígenes, ideología y organización del nacionalismo vasco, 1876-1904.* Madrid: Siglo XXI, 1979.

Coromines, Joan. *Estudis de toponímia catalana.* Vol 1. Barcelona: Biblioteca filológica Barcino, 1965.

Cruz, Juan. "Yo intento fracasar major." *El Pais.* 8-24-2008. www.el-pais.com. 1-14-2015.

D'Abartiague, William Lewy. *L'Atlantide et les Basques. Essai de bibliographie.* Bayonne: Courrier, 1937.

Damrosch, David, ed. *The Longman Anthology of British Literature.* New York: Longman, 2002.

Deleuze, Gilles and Félix Guattari. *Kafka: Toward a Minor Literature.* Minneapolis: University of Minnesota Press, 1986.

De Certeau, Michel. *Heterologies: Discourse on the Other.* Minneapolis: University of Minnesota Press, 1986.

Del Valle, Yvonne. "Jesuit Baroque." *Journal of Spanish Cultural Studies* 3.2. (2000): 141-63.

De Quincey, Thomas. Joan of Arc: *The English Mail-Coach, and the Spanish Military Nun.* New York: Mcamillan, 1912.

Derrida, Jacques. *Specters of Marx: The State of the Debt, the Work of Mourning & the New International.* New York: Routledge, 1994.

Diputación de Álava. www.alava.net/publicar/Veleia. 6-10-2009.

Douglass, William. "Sabino's Sin: Racism and the Founding of Basque Nationalism." *Ethnonationalism in the Contemporary World: Walker Connor and the Study of Nationalism.* Ed. Daniele Conversi. New York: Routledge, 2002. 97-112.

Dubois, W.E.B. *The Souls of Black Folk.* New York: Dover, 1994.

DuPlessis, Rachel Blau. *The Pink Guitar: Writing as Feminist Practice.* New York: Routledge, 1990.

Echave, Baltasar de. *Discursos de la antigüedad de la lengua cantabra Bascongada.* Mexico, DF: Henrrico Martinez, 1607.

Echevarria, Ignacio. "Una elegía pastoral." El país. 9-4-2004. www.el-pais.com. 1-10-2010.

Efe. "Literaturarekin krisi bat pasatzen ari dela esan du Bernardo Atxagak." *Egunkaria*, 30 March 1999, 30.

Elorza, Antonio. *Un pueblo escogido: génesis, definición y desarrollo del nacionalismo vasco.* Barcelona: Crítica, 2001.

Emakume Idazleen Lantaldea. *Gutiziak.* Tafalla: Txalaparta, 2000.

Epaltza, Aingeru. *Ur uherrak.* Pamplona: Pamiela, 1991.

Epps, Brad and Luis Fernández Cifuentes, eds. *Spain beyond Spain: Modernity, Literary History, and National Identity*. Lewisburg, PA: Bucknell University Press, 2005.

Erauso, Catalina de. *La Historia de la Monja Alférez*. Barcelona: Linkgua Ediciones, S.L., 2007. (*Lieutenant Nun: Memoir of a Basque Transvesti in the New World, Catalina de Erauso*. Boston: Beacon Press, 2011).

Espadaler, Antón María. *Literatura Catalana*. Madrid: Taurus, 1989.

Etxahun, Pierre Topet. *Bertsoak eta kantak*. www.klasikoak.armiarma.com. 2009-10-30.

Etxeberri, Joanes. *Lau-Urdiri gomendiozko karta, edo guthuna*. klasikoak.armiarma.eus/pdf/EtxebSaraLauUrduri.pdf. 1-10-2016.

—. *Eskuararen hatsapenak*. klasikoak.armiarma.eus/pdf/EtxebSaraHatsapenak.pdf. 1-20-2016.

Etxenike, Luisa. *Ejercicios de duelo*. Vitoria-Gasteiz: Bassarai, 2001.

Etxepare, Bernard. *Linguae Vasconum Primitiae*. klasikoak.armiarma.eus/pdf/EtxepareBPrimitiae.pdf. 1-10-2016.

Etxepare, Jean. *Beribilez*. http://klasikoak.armiarma.eus/pdf/EtxepareJBideBeribilez.pdf. 1-10-2016.

---. *Buruxkak*. http://klasikoak.armiarma.eus/pdf/EtxepareJBideBuruxkak.pdf. 1-10-2016.

Even-Zohar, Itamar. "Polysystem studies." *Poetics today* 11.1 (1990): 9-78.

—. "The Role of Literature in the Making of the Nations of Europe: A Socio-Semiotic Examination." *Canadian Review of Comparative Literature/Revue Canadienne de Litérature Comparé* 24.1 (1997): 15-34.

Fedorchek, Robert M. trans. and ed. *Stories of Enchantment from Nineteenth-Century Spain*. London: Bucknell University Press, 2002.

—. *Death and the Doctor: Three Nineteenth-Century Spanish Tales*. London: Bucknell University Press, 1997.

Fernández del Riego, Francisco. *Manual de historia da literatura galega*. Virgo, Galaxia. 1971.

Fielding, Helen. *Bridget Jones's Diary: A Novel*. New York: Viking, 1998.

Foucault, Michel. *The History of Sexuality. I. An Introduction*. New York: Pantheon Books, 1978.

—. *The Order of Things: An Archaeology of the Human Sciences*. New York Pantheon, 1970.

Freud, Sigmund. "The Uncanny." *The Standard Edition of the Complete Psychological Works of Sigmund Freud*. Ed. James Strachey. London: The Hogarth Press, 1953-74. XVII. 219-259.

Frey, Nancy Louise. *Pilgrim Stories: On and Off the Road to Santiago*. California: University of California Press, 1998.

Fuchs, Eckhardt and Benedikt Stuchtey. *Across cultural borders: historiography in global perspective*. Lanham, Md.: Rowman & Littlefield, 2002.

Fuster, Joan. *Literatura catalana contemporània*, Barcelona, Curial, 1976.

Gabilondo, Joseba. "Terrorism as Memory: The Historical Novel and Masculine Masochism in Contemporary Basque Literature." *Arizona Journal of Hispanic Cultural Studies* 2 (1998): 113-46.

—. "Del exilio materno a la utopía personal: política cultural en la narrativa vasca de mujeres." *Ínsula* 623 (1998): 32-36.

—. "Before Babel: Global Media, Ethnic Hybridity, and Enjoyment in Basque Culture." *Revista Internacional de Estudios Vascos* 44.1 (1999): 7-49.

—. "Bernardo Atxaga's Seduction: On the Symbolic Economy of Postcolonial and Postnational Literatures in the Global Market." *Basque Cultural Studies*. William Douglas et al., eds. Reno: Nevada University Press, 2000. 106-33.

—. "Itxaro Borda: Melancholic Migrancy and the Writing of a National, Lesbian Self." *Anuario del Seminario Julio de Urquijo* XXXIV-2 (2000-2): 1-25.

—. "Posnacionalismo y biopolítica: Para una crítica multiculturalista del estado y su soberanía en Europa y el País Vasco (notas sobre Habermas y Agamben)." *Inguruak: Revista de la federación vasca de sociología* 37 (2003): 1-23.

—. "Galdós, Etxeita, Rizal – Madrid, Mundaka, Manila: On Colonial Disavowal and (Post)Imperial Articulations of the Hispanic Pacific-Atlantic." *452F: Revista de Teoría de la Literatura y Literatura Comparada* 9 (2013): 13-43.

—. "Spanish Nationalist Excess: A Decolonial and Postnational Critique of Iberian Studies." *Prosopopeya: revista de crítica contemporánea* 8 (2014): 23-60.

—. "The Atlantic-Iberian Enlightenment: On the Imperial-Colonial and Morisco-Basque Mediations of the Spanish Enlightenment." *A Comparative History of Literatures in the Iberian Peninsula*. César Domínguez, ed. Philadelphia: John Benjamins North America. (forthcoming).

—. "Euskal literatur genero "txiki" eta hibridoen zentraltasunaz. (oharrak euskal eleberriaren ofizialismo politiko eta ezintasun zinematikoaz)." *EGAN* 61.3/4 (2008): 21-59.

Galfarsoro, Imanol. *Multicultural Controversies: Political Struggles, Cultural Consumerism and State Management*. N.p.: The Davies Group, 2014.

— *Subordinazioaren kontra*. Pamplona: Iruñea, 2008.

García Canclini, Néstor. *Hybrid Cultures: Strategies for Entering and Leaving Modernity*. Minneapolis: University of Minnesota Press, 1995.

Garibay, Esteban. Los Quarenta Libros del compendio historial *de las chronicas y universal historia de todos los reynos de España*. Barcelona: Sebastian de Cormellas, 1628.

Gartzia, Pruden. *Lazarraga: Errenazimentua euskaraz*. Pamplona: Pamiela, 2005.

George, Olakunle. *Relocating Agency: Modernity and African Letters*. Albany: State University of New York Press, 2003.

Gerson, Paula, Annie Sahver-Crandell, Alison Stones, eds. and trans. *The Pilgirm's Guide: A Critical Edition. II. The Text*. London: Harvey Miller Publishers, 1998.

Gilroy, Paul. *The Black Atlantic: Modernity and Double Consciousness*. Cambridge: Harvard University Press, 1993.

Glissant, Édouard. *Caribeean Discourse. Selected Essays*. Charlottesville, VA: University Press of Virginia, 1989.

—. *Poetics of Relation*. Ann Arbor, MI: University of Michigan Press, 1997.

Goldberg, David T., ed. *Multiculturalism: A Critical Reader*. Cambridge, MA: Blackwell Publishers, 1994.

Gómez López, Ricardo and Blanca Urgel. "Descripción y defensa de la lengua vasca durante los siglos XVI y XVII." *Post Tenebras Spero Lucem. Los estudios gramaticales en la España medieval y renacentista*. Granada: Editorial de la Universidad de Granada, 2010. 257-320.

González Echevarría, Roberto and Enrique Pupo-Walker, eds. *The Cambridge History of Latin American Literature*. New York, NY: Cambridge University Press, 1996.

González Millán, Xoán. *A narrativa galega actual (1975-1984): unha historia social*. Vigo: Xerais, 1996.

—. *Literatura e sociedade en Galicia (1975-1990)*. Vigo: Xerais, 1994.

—. *Silencio, parodia e subversión: cinco ensaios sobre narrativa galega contemporánea*. Vigo: Xerais, 1991.

Gorrochategui, Joaquín. "Vasco antiguo: algunas cuestiones de geografía e historia lingüísticas." *Paleohispanica* 9 (2009): 539-55.

Goytisolo, Juan. *Count Julian*. Trans. Helen R. Lane. New York: Viking, 1974.

Gracia, Jordi. "Prólogo al primer suplemento." *Los nuevos nombres: 1975-2000. Primer Suplemento*. Barcelona: Crítica, 2000.

Gramsci, Antonio. *Prison Notebooks*. New York: Columbia University Press, 1991.

Grandes, Almudena. *Las edades de Lulú*. Barcelona: Tusquets, 1989.

Greenblatt, Stephen. *Shakespearean Negotiations: The Circulation of Social Energy in Renaissance England.* Berkeley: University of California Press, 1988.

—. "Racial Memory and Literary History." Hutcheon & Valdés 50-62.

Guerra Garrido, Raul. *Lectura insólita de El Capital.* Barcelona: Destino, 1976.

Guha, Ranajit. *Dominance without Hegemony: History and Power in Colonial India,* New York: Harvard University Press, 1998.

—. "On Some Aspects of the Historiography of Colonial India." *Subaltern Studies: Writings on South Asian History and Society,* Vol. 1. 1-8. Oxford University Press, 1982.

—. "Preface." Subaltern Studies. vii-viii.

— and Gayatri Spivak, eds. *Selected Subaltern Studies.* Oxford: Oxford University Press, 1988.

Habermas, Jürgen. *The Postnational Constellation: Political Essays.* Cambridge, UK: Polity, 2001.

Halevi, Judah. *The Kuzari: An Argument for the Faith of Israel.* New York: shocken Books, 1964.

—. *Ninety-Two Poems and Hyms of Yehuda Halevi.* Albany, NY: State University of New York Press, 2000.

Haritxelhar, Jean. *L'oeuvre poètique de Pierre Topet-Etchahun.* Bilbao: Gráficas Ellacuría, 1970.

Henao, Gabriel de. *Averiguaciones de las Antiguedades de Cantabria ... principalmente a descubrir las de Guipuzcoa, Vizcaya y Alaba.* Salamanca: Eugenio Antonio García, 1691.

Herder, Johann Gottfried. *Herder: Philosophical Writings.* Cambridge: Cambridge University Press, 2002.

Hernandez Abaitua, Mikel. *Azukre xehea, gatz larria.* Irun: Alberdania, 2010.

Hobsbawn, Eric. *The Invention of Tradition.* Cambridge, UK: Cambridge University Press, 1992.

—. *The Age of Extremes: The Short Twentieth Century, 1914-1991.* London: Michael Joseph, 1993.

Hollier, Dennis, ed. "On Writing Literary History." *A New History of French Literature.* Cambridge, MA: Harvard University Press, 1989. xxi-xxv.

Hugo, Victor. *Les Orientales,* Paris: Didier, 1952-54.

—. *Les Pyrénnées,* Paris: La Découverte, 1984.

Humboldt, Welhelm Freiherr von. *The Basques, or Observations on a Journey through Bizkaia and the French Basque Country in the Spring of 1801* in

Selected Basque Writings: The Basques and Announcement of a Publication.
Reno, NV: Center for Basque Studies, 2013. 5-163.

—. *Los primitivos habitantes de España: investigaciones sobre los primitivos habitantes de España con ayuda de la lengua vasca.* Madrid: Polifemo, 1990.

Hutcheon, Linda and Mario J. Valdés, eds. *Rethinking Literary History: A Dialogue on Theory.* Oxford: Oxford University Press, 2002.

Ibn Hayyan of Cordoba. *Almuqtabis II-1 (Crónica de los emires Alhakén I y Abderramán II entre los años 796 y 847).* Zaragoza: Instituto de Estudios Islámicos y del Próximo Oriente, 2001.

Igartua, Iván and Xabier Zabaltza. *Euskararen historia laburra, Breve Historia de la Lengua Vasca, A Brief History of the Basque Language.* San Sebastian: Etxepare Euskal Institutua, 2012.

Ilarregui, Pablo and Segundo Lapuerta, eds. *Fuero General de Navarra.* Pamplona: Aranzadi, 1964.

Iparragirre, Jose Mari. *Olerkiak eta eresiak.* www.klasikoak.armiarma.com. 2009-10-30.

Irigaray, Luce. *Speculum of the Other Woman.* Trans. Gillian G. Gill. Ithaca, NY: Cornell UP, 1985.

Irigoien, Joan Mari. *Oilarraren promesa.* Bilbao: Mensajero, 1976.

—. *Poliedroaren hostoak.* San Sebastian: Erein, 1995.

—. *Babilonia.* San Sebastian: Elkar, 1989.

Iturbe, Arantxa. *Ai, ama!* Irun: Alberdania, 1999.

Izagirre, Koldo. *Zergatik bai.* San Sebastian: Kriselu, 1976.

Jaio, Karmele. *Amaren eskuak.* San Sebastian: Elkar, 2006.

Jameson, Fredric. "Third-World Literature in the Era of Multinational Capitalism." *Social Text* 15 (Fall 1986): 65-88.

JanMohamed, Abdul and David Lloyd. "Introduction: Toward a Theory of Minority Discourse: What Is t Be Done?" *Cultural Critique* 6 (1987): 5-12.

Jaurgain, Jean. *Quelques légendes poétiques du pays de Soule.* Nîmes, France: Lacour, 1992.

Jiménez de Rada, Rodrigo. *Opera omnia. Pars I.* Turnhout: Brepols, 1987.

Jockers, Matthew L. *Macroanalysis: Digital Methods and Literary History.* N.l.: University of Illinois Press, 2013.

Johnson, Dane. "The Rise of Gabriel García Márquez and Toni Morrison." *Cultural Institutions of the Novel.* Deidre Lynch and William B. Warner eds. Durham, NC: Duke University Press, 1996. 146-58.

Jordan, Barry. "The Emergence of a Dissident Intelligentsia." *Spanish Cultural Studies: An Introduction.* Helen Graham and Jo Labanyi, eds. Oxford: Oxford University Press, 1995.

Jordan, David M. *New World Regionalism: Literature in the Americas.* Toronto: University of Toronto Press, 1994.

Juaristi, Jon. *Euskararen ideologiak.* Donostia: Kriselu, 1976.

—. *Literatura vasca.* Madrid: Taurus, 1987.

—. *El linaje de Aitor.* Madrid: Taurus, 1987.

—. *Vestigios de Babel. Para una arqueología de los nacionalismos españoles.* Madrid: Siglo XXI, 1992.

—. *El bucle melancólico. Historias de nacionalistas vascos.* Madrid: Espasa Calpe, 1997.

—. "La invención de la tradición vasca." in *La memoria histórica de Cantabria.* Jose Angel Garcia de Cortazar, ed. Santander: Universidad de Cantabria, 1996. 205-18.

—. *La tribu atribulada. El nacionalismo vasco explicado a mi padre.* Madrid: Espasa Calpe, 2002.

Junco, José Alvarez and Adrian Shubert. *Spanish History since 1808.* London: Arnold, 2000.

Kaplan, Caren, Norma Alarcón, and Minoo Moallem, eds. *Between Woman and Nation: Nationalisms, Transnational Feminims, and the State.* Durham, NC.: Duke University Press, 1999.

King, Stewart. *Escribir la catalanidad. Lengua e identidades culturales en la narrativa contemporánea de Cataluña.* London: Tamesis, 2005.

Kristeva, Julia. *Strangers to Ourselves.* New York: Columbia University Press, 1991.

Kortazar, Jon. *Teoría y práctica poética de Esteban Urkiaga, Lauaxeta.* 1986.

—. *Literatura vasca: siglo XX.* San Sebastian: Etor, 1990.

—. and Marijose Olaziregi, eds. "Letras vascas, hoy." *Insula* 623 (Nov. 1998).

Krutwig, Federico. (Fernando Sarrailh de Ihartza). *Vasconia.* N.l.: Astero, Herritar Berri, 2006.

Kurlansky, Mark. *The Basque History of the World.* New York: Penguin, 1999.

Kymlicka, Will. "The New Debate on Minority Rights (and postscript)." Laden and Owen, 25-59.

Lacan, Jacques. *The Seminar. Book III. The Psychoses, 1955-56.* London: Routledge, 1993.

Laden, Anthony Simon and David Owen. *Multiculturalism and Political Theory.* Cambridge: Cambridge Univesity Press, 2007.

Lakarra, Joseba A. "Gogoetak euskal dialektologia diakronikoaz: Euskara Batu Zaharra berreraiki beharraz eta haren banaketaren ikerketaz", in

I. Epelde, ed., *Euskal dialektologia: lehena eta oraina*. Bilbo: UPV/EHU, 2011. 155-241.

Lalinde Abadía, Jesús. "El pactismo en los reinos de Aragón y de Valencia." Luis Legaz y Lacambra et al., ed. *El pactismo en la historia de España: simposio celebrado los días 24, 25 y 26 de abril de 1978 en el Instituto de España, Cátedra Francisco de Vitoria*. Madrid: Instituto de España, 1980. 121-139.

—. "El sistema normativo navarro." *Anuario de Historia del Derecho Español* 40 (1976): 111-139.

Lambert, Gustave et al. *Augustin Chaho*. Hélette: Editions Harriet, 1996.

Landa, Mariasun. *The Dancing Flea*. Reno: University of Nevada Press, 1996.

Landabidea, Xabier. *Euskaldunok eta telebista XXI. mende hasieran*. Vitoria: EAE Administrazioa. Lendakaritza: 2015.

Laqueur, Thomas. *Making Sex: Body and Gender from the Greeks to Freud*. Cambridge, Mass.: Harvard University Press, 1990.

Laroussi, Farid and Christopher L. Miller. *French and Francophone: The Challenge of Expanding Horizons*. New Haven, Conn.: Yale University Press, 2003.

Larramendi, Manuel. *El imposible vencido: arte de la lengua vascongada*. San Sebastián: Hijos de I. Ramón Baroja, 1886.

—. *Diccionario trilingüe del castellano, bascuence y latín*. San Sebastian: Bartholome Riesgo y Montero, 1745.

—. *Corografía o Descripción general de la muy noble y muy leal Provincia de Guipúzcoa*. San Sebastián: Sociedad Guipuzcoana de Ediciones y Publicaciones, 1969.

—. *De la antiguedad y universalidad del bascuenze en España*. Salamanca: Antonio Joseph Villargordo, 1728.

—. *Sobre los fueros de Guipúzcoa: conferencias curiosas, políticas, legales y morales sobre los fueros de la M.N. y M.L. provincia de Guipúzcoa*. San Sebastian: Argitalpen eta Publikapenen Gipuzkoar Erakundea, 1983.

Larrañaga Odriozola, Carmen. "Del bertsolarismo silenciado." *Jentilbaratz: cuadernos de folklore* 6 (1997): 57-73.

—. "Ubiquitous but Invisible: The Presence of Women Singers within a Basque Male Tradition." *Gender and Memory*. Ed. Selma Leydesdorff, Luisa Passerini and Paul Thompson. New Brunswick, NJ: Transaction Publishers, 2005. 59-72.

Larrea Sagarminaga, María Angeles. *Historia del Pais Vasco: Siglo XVIII*. Bilbao: Universidad de Deusto, 1985.

Lasagabaster, Jesus Maria. *Contemporary Basque Fiction: An Anthology*. Reno: University of Nevada Press, 1990.

—. "Introduction." *Contemporary Basque Fiction: An Anthology*. Reno: University of Nevada Press, 1990. 1-23.

—. "The Promotion of Cultural Production in Basque." Helen Graham and Jo Labanyi, eds. *Spanish Cultural Studies: An Introduction*. Oxford: Oxford UP, 1995. 351-55.

Lauxeta (Estepan Urkiaga). *Arrats beran*. klasikoak.armiarma.eus/pdf/LauaxetaArrats.pdf. 1-10-2016.

Laxalt, Robert. *Sweet Promised Land*. Reno: Nevada University Press, 1997.

Lazarraga. See Perez de Lazarraga.

Lazarus, Neil, ed. *The Cambridge Companion to Postcolonial Literary Studies*. Cambridge, Cambridge University Press, 2004.

Lekuona, Manuel. *Idaz-lan guztiak. Vol.1. Aozko literatura*. N.p.: Librería Técnica de Difusión, 1978.

Lennon, Brian. *In Babel's Shadow: Multilingual Literatures, Monolingual States*. Minneapolis: University of Minnesota Press, 2010.

Leoné, Santi. *Euskal Herri imajinario baten alde*. San Sebastian: Elkar, 2008.

Lertxundi, Andu. *Ajea du Urturik*. Bilbo: Ediciones Mensajero, 1982.

—. *Hamaseigarrenean aidanez*. San Sebastian: Erein, 1983.

—. *Otto Pette*. Irun: Alberdania, 1994.

Lévi-Strauss, Claude. *The Raw and the Cooked*. Chicago: Chicago University Press, 1983.

Lizardi, Xabier. *Biotz-begietan*. klasikoak.armiarma.eus/pdf/LizardiBiotz.pdf. 1-10-2016.

López, Casto Fulgencio. *Lope de Aguirre*. Caracas: Ediciones Nueva Cádiz. 1953.

Loti, Pierre. *Ramuntcho*. Paris: Gallimard, 1990.

Loyola, Saint Ignatius Of. *Personal Writings*. New York: Penguin, 1996.

Robert Ludlum's *The Scorpio Illusion*. New York: Harper Collins, 1993.

Madariaga, Pedro. *Arte de escribir, ortografía de la pluma, y honra de los profesores de este magisterio. Obra dividida en XII diálogos eruditos*. Madrid: Imprenta de Antonio de Sancha, 1711.

MacClancy, Jeremy. "Biological Basques, Sociologially Speaking." *Social and Biological Aspects of Ethnicity*. Ed. Malcolm K. Chaptman. Oxford: Oxford University Press, 1993. 92-129.

Madariaga Orbea, Juan. *Sociedad y lengua vasca en los siglos XVII y XVIII*. Bilbao: Euskaltzaindia, 2014.

Mainer, José Carlos, ed. *Historia de la literatura española*. Barcelona: Criítica, 2010.

Mañaricua A.E. *Historiografía de Vizcaya*. Bilbao: GEV, 1971.

Marcus, Greil and Werner Sollors, eds. *A New Literary History of America*. Cambridge, MA: Belknap Press of Harvard University Press, 2009.

Maravall, José Antonio. *Culture of the Baroque: Analysis of a Historical Structure*. Minneapolis: University of Minnesota Press, 1986.

Martin, Itxaso. *Ni, Vera*. San Sebastian: Elkar, 2014.

Martín Nogales, José Luis. *Samaniego ante la Inquisición*. Alava: Arabako Aldundia, 1995.

Martín Santos, Luis. *Time of Silence*. New York: Columbia University Press, 1989.

Martinez de Zaldivia, Juan. *Suma de las cosas cantabricas y gulpuzcoanas del bachiller Juan Martinez de Zaldivia*. San Sebastian: Diputacion de Guipuzcoa, 1945.

Meabe, Miren Agur. *Kristalezko begi bat*. Zarautz, Sp.: Susa, 2013.

Menocal, María Rosa. *The Ornament of the World: How Muslims, Jews, and Christians Created a Culture of Tolerance in Medieval Spain*. Boston: Little, Brown, 2002.

Mérimée, Prosper. *Carmen and Other Stories*, Oxford: Oxford University Press, 1998.

Micoleta, Rafael. "Rafael Micoleta Camudio Modo breve de aprender la lengua vizcaína." *Cuadernos de Sección de Eusko Ikaskuntza. Hizkuntza eta Literatura* 7 (1988): 133-214.

Michel, Francisque. *Le Pays Basque : sa population, sa langue, ses mœurs, as littérature eta sa musique*. Paris : Librarie de Firmin Didot Frères, Fils et Cie. 1857.

Michelena, Luis. *Historia de la literatura vasca*. Donosita: Erein, 1988.

—. *Lenguas y protolenguas*. Salamanca: Acta Salmanticensis XVII, 2.1963.

—. *Sobre el pasado de la lengua vasca*. San Sebastian: Auñamendi, 1964.

—. *Textos arcaicos vascos*. Madrid: Minotauro, 1964.

—. "Contra Lekobide." ASJU 2021 (1986): 291-313.

Mignolo, Walter. *The Darker Side of the Renaissance: Literacy, Territoriality, and Colonization*. Ann Arbor: University of Michigan Press, 1995.

—. *Local Histories / Global Designs: Coloniality, Subaltern Knowledges, and Border Thinking*. Princeton, NJ: Princeton University Press, 2000.

Mintegi, Laura. *Nerea and I*. New York: Peter Lang, 2005.

—. "Emakumeen orgasmoa." GARA. 2000-4-2. www.gara.org. 10-2-2015.

Mitxelena, Salbatore. *Arantzazu. Euskal-sinismenaren poema*. klasikoak.armiarma.eus/pdf/MitxelenaSArantzazu.pdf. 1-10-2016

Mogel, Juan Antonio. *Peru Abarka*. Durango: Asociación Gerediaga, 1981.

Montoia, Xabier. "Batzuentzat." http://susa-literatura.eus/liburuak/susa0101 . 1-20-2016.

— *Gasteizko hondartzak*. Zarautz, Sp.: Susa, 1997.

— *Euskal hiria sutan*. San Sebastian: Elkar, 2006.

Montreal Zia, Gregorio. *The Old Law of Bizkaia (1452)*. Reno: Center for Basque Studies, 2005.

Moretti, Franco. *Graphs, Maps, Trees: Abstract Models for a Literary History*. London: Verso, 2005.

Mujika, Gregorio. *Pernando Amezketarra*. klasikoak.armiarma.eus/pdf/MujikaPernando.pdf. 1-10-2016.

Munibe, Francisco Xavier María. *Gabon sariak*. klasikoak.armiarma.eus/pdf/MunibeSariak.pdf. 1-10-2016.

—. *El borracho burlado*. klasikoak.armiarma.eus/pdf/MunibeBurlado.pdf. 1-10-2016.

Nature. "Editorial: Comédie-Francaise. Regional and Minority Languages Should Be Protected, in France, and Elsewhere." *Nature* 452 (2008): 1144.

Navarro Villoslada, Francisco. *Amaya o Los vascos en el siglo VIII*. San Sebastian: Ttarttalo, 1991.

Ndongo, Donato. *Las tinieblas de tu memoria negra*. Madrid: Fundamentos, 1987.

Nebrija, Antonio de. *Gramática castellana*. Madrid: Fundación Antonio de Nebrija, 1992.

Nietzsche, Fredric. *The Use and Abuse of History*. New York: Liberal Arts Press, 1957.

Nodier, Charles. *Promenade from Dieppe to the Mountains of Scotland*. Londo: T. Cadell, 1822.

—. *Du fantastique en littérature*. Paris: Chiméres, 1989.

Núñez-Betelu, Maite. *Una bibliografía anotada de obras escritas por mujeres en euskera*. Lewinston, NY: The Edwin Mellon Press, 2003.

Oihenart, Arnauld de. *Notitia utriusque Vasconiae, tum Ibericae, tum Aquitanicae, qua praeter situm regions et alia scitu digna*. Paris: Sebastian Cramoisy, 1638.

—. *L'art poetique basque*. www.euskomedia.org/PDFAnlt/literatura/15/15177208.pdf. 1-10-2016.

—. *Euskal atsotitzak eta neurtitzak. Proverbes et poésies basques. Proverbios y poesías vascas*. www.euskaltzaindia.net/dok/ikerbilduma/55225.pdf. 1-10-2016.

Olaniyan, Tejumola and Ato Quayson. *African Literature: An Anthology of Criticism and Theory*. Malden, MA: Blackwell Pub., 2007.

Olariaga, Andoni et al. *Independentzia helburu*. Tafalla: Txalaparta, 2016.

Olasagarre, Juanjo. "Etxepare." *Deia*. 2-13-2016. www.deia.com. 1-10-2016.

Olaziregi, Mari Jose. *Intimismoaz haraindi: emakimezkoek idatzitako euskal literatura*. San Sebastián: Eusko Ikaskuntza, 1999.

—. "Un siglo de novela en euskera." Urkizu, Patricio. ed. *Historia de la literature vasca*. Madrid: Uned, 2000. 504-88.

—. ed. *Basque Literary History*. Reno, NV: Center for Basque Studies, 2013.

Onaindía, Mario. *Elurtzan datzaten zuhaitz emborrak*. Bilbo: Mensajero, 1977.

—. *El precio de la libertad, memorias (1984-1977)*. Madrid: Espasa, 2001.

Oppenheimer, Stephen. *The Origins of the British: A Genetic Detectiv Story*. London: Carroll and Graf, 2006.

Ortiz, Fernando. *Contrapunteo cubano del tabaco y el azúcar*. Caracas: Biblioteca Ayacucho, 1987.

Ortiz de Ubina Montoya, Carlos. "La Patria común Bascongada: una quimera soñada por los Amigos del País." *Sancho el sabio: Revista de cultura e investigación vasca* 25 (2006) 25-50.

Osoro, Jasone. *Tentazioak*. San Sebastian: Elkar, 1998.

Otegi, Lurdes. *Lizardiren poetika Pizkundearen ingurumariaren argitan*. San Sebastian: Erein, 1994.

Oteiza, Jorge. *Oteiza's Selected Writings*. Reno: Center for Basque Studies, 2003.

Parekh, Bhikhu. *Rethinking Multiculturalism: Cultural Diversity and Political Theory*. New York: Palgrave, 2006.

Paz, Octavio. *Children of the Mire*. Cambridge, MA: Harvard University Press, 1991.

—. *The Labyrinth of Solitude. Life and Thought in Mexico*. London: Penguin, 1996.

Perez de Lazarraga, Joan. *Eskuizkribua*. *klasikoak.armiarma.eus/pdf/Lazarraga.pdf*. 1-10-2016.

Pérez de Pablos, Susana. "España retrocede en lectura." *El País*. 12-1-2007. www.elpais.com/articulo/sociedad/Espana/retrocede/lectura/elpepusoc/20071201elpepisoc_2/Tes. 12-1-2007.

Pérez Firmat, Gustavo, ed. *Do the Americas Have a Common Literature?* Durham: Duke University Press, 1990.

Perkins, David. *Is Literary History Possible?* Baltimore: The Johns Hopkins University Press, 1992.

Pinilla, Ramiro. *Verdes valles, colinas rojas*. Barcelona: Tusquets, 2004-2005.

Poliakov, Leon. *The History of Anti-Semitism*. New York: Vanguard Press, 1965.

Poza, Andrés. *De la antigua lengua, poblaciones y comarcas de las Españas: en que de paso se tocan algunas cosas de la Cantabria*. S.l.: s.n., 1987

Pozuelo Yvancos, Jose Maria and Rosa Maria Aradra Sanchez. *Teoría del canon y literatura española*. Madrid, Cátedra, 2000.

Rama, Ángel. *Transculturación narrativa en América Latina*. Mexico: Siglo XXI, 1982.

—. *The Lettered City*. Durham: Duke University Press, 1996

Rawls, John. *A Theory of Justice*. Cambridge, MA: Harvard University Press, 1971.

Real Sociedad Bascongada de los Amigos del Pais. *Ensayo de Real Sociedad Bascongada de los Amigos del Pais. Año de 1766. Dedicado al Rey N. Señor*. Vitoria: Thomás Robles, 1768.

Ribera, Julián. *Music in Ancient Arabia and Spain*. N.l.: Stanford University Press, 1929.

Río, David. "Robert Laxalt: A Basque Pioneer in the American Literary West." *American Studies International*, 41:3, 2003. 60–81.

Riquer, Martín de. *Història de la literatura catalana*. Barcelona: Ariel, 1964.

Roca-Pons, Josep. *Introduction to Catalan Literature*. Bloomington, Ind.: Dept. of Spanish and Portuguese, Indiana University, 1977.

Rodriguez, Ileana and María Milagros López, eds. *The Latin American Subaltern Studies Reader*. Durham: Duke University Press, 2001.

Rousseau, Jean-Jacques. *Instrucción de un padre a su hijo sobre el modo de conducirse en este mundo: = Instruction d'un père a son fils sur la manière de se conduire dans le monde*. Vitoria-Gasteiz: Instituto de Estudios sobre Nacionalismos Comparados = Nazionalismo Konparatuen Ikasketarako Institutua, 1996.

—. *The Confessions*. New York: Penguin, 1953.

Ixiar Rozas. *Beltzuri*. Pamplona: Pamiela, 2014

Rushdie, Salman. "Damme, This is the Oriental Scene for You!". *The New Yorker*. 73:17 (1997): 50-61.

Sagastizabal, Joxean. *Kutsidazu bidea, Ixabel*. Irun: Alberdania, 1994.

Said, Edward. *Orientalism*. New York: Pantheon Books, 1978.

Saizarbitoria, Ramon. *100 Meter*. N.l. Basque American Foundation, 1985.

—. "My Jesus" *Contemporary Basque Fiction: An Anthology*. Lasagabaster, 77-81.

—. *Hamaika pauso*. San Sebastian: Erein, 1995.

—. *Bihotz bi: gerrako kronikak*. San Sebastian: Erein, 1996.

—. *Gorde nazazu lurpean*. San Sebastian: Erein, 2000.

—. *Martutene*. San Sebastian: Erein, 2012.

Salaberri Muñoa, Patxi. *Axularren prosa erretorikaren argitan*. Bilbao: Euskal Herriko Unibertsitatearen Argitalpen Zerbitzua, 1997.

Salaberria, Sebastian. *Neronek tirako nizkin*. Tolosa: Auspoa, 1964.

Sale, Roger, George Drake, Karen Saupe, and David Damrosch. "Roundtable" *Pedagogy* 1.1 (2001): 195-214.

Sallaberry, J.D.J. *Chants populaires du Pays Basque : paroles et musique originales*. Bayonne: Lamaignère, 1870.

Samaniego, Felix María. *El jardín de Venus y otros jardines de verde hierba*. Madrid: Siro, 1976.

Sánchez Ostiz, Miguel. *Las pirañas*. Barcelona: Seix Barral, 1992.

Sarasola, Ibon. *Historia social de la literatura vasca*. Madrid: Akal, 1976.

Sarkar, Sumit. "The Decline of the Subaltern in Subaltern Studies." Vinayak Chaturvedi, ed. *Mapping Subaltern Studies and the Postcolonial*. London: Verso, 2012. 300-23.

Sartre, Jean Paul. *Nausea*. London: Penguin, 2000.

Savater, Fernando. *Perdonen las molestias: crónica de una batalla sin armas contra las armas*. Madrid: Ediciones El País, 2001.

Scanlon, Geraldine M. *La polémica feminista en la España contemporánea: (1868-1974)*. Madrid: Siglo XXI, 1976.

Schmidt, Carl. *Political Theology: Four Chapters on the Concept of Sovereignty*. Chicago: University of Chicago Press, 2005.

Schlegel, Frederick. *Lectures on the History of Literature Ancient and Modern*. London: George Bell and Sons, 1876.

Schlegel, Wilhelm. *Lectures on Dramatic Art and Literature*. N.l.: Dodo Press, n.d.

Schulze, Reinhard. "Mass Culture and Islamic Cultural Production in 19th Century Middle East." George Stauth and Sami Zubaida, eds. *Mass Culture, Popular Culture, and Social Life in the Middle East*. Frankfurt: Campus Verlag, 1987. 189-222.

Scott, James C. *Domination and the Arts of Resistance: Hidden Transcripts*. New Haven: Yale University Press, 1990.

Shohat, Ella and Robert Stam, eds. *Multiculturalism, Postocoloniality, and Transnational Media*. New Brunswick: Rutgers University Press, 2003.

— "Whence and Whither Postcolonial Theory?" *New Literary History* 43 (2012): 371–390.

Showalter, Elaine. *Sexual Anarchy: Gender and Culture at the Fin de Siecle*. New York: Viking, 1990.

Sommer, Doris. *Foundational Fictions: The National Romances of Latin America*. Berkeley: University of California Press, 1991.

—. "Irresistible Romance: The Foundational Fictions of Latin America." Homi K. Bhabha, ed. *Nation and Narration*. New York: Routledge, 1990. 71-98.

Spivak, Gayatri Chakravorty. *Death of a Discipline*. New York: Columbia University Press, 2003.

—. *The Postcolonial Critic: Interviews, Strategies, Dialogues*. New York: Routledge, 1990.

—. "Can the Subaltern Speak?" Cary Nelson and Lawrence Grossberg, eds. *Marxism and the Interpretation of Culture*. Chicago: University of Illinois Press, 1988. 271-313.

—. "Subaltern Studies. Deconstructing Historiography." in Guha and Spivak. 3-33.

Steiner, George. *After Babel: Aspects of Language and Translation*. Oxford: Oxford University Press, 1998.

Suárez Galbán, Eugenio. "A Village in the Palm of One's Hand". *The New York Times*. 6-20-1993. Secc. 7: 20.

Tarrío Varela, Anxo. *Literatura gallega*. Madrid: Taurus, 1988.

Taylor, Charles and Amy Gutman. *Multiculturalism and the Politics of Recognition: An Essay*. Princeton: Princeton University Press, 1992.

Terry, Arthur. *A Companion to Catalan Literature*. Woodbridge, Suffolk, UK: Tamesis. 2003.

Thomassen, Lasse. "The Inclusion of the Other? Habermas and the Paradox of Tolerance." *Political Theory* 34.4 (2006): 439-462.

Totoricaguena, Gloria. "The Formation of the Basque Diaspora." *Identity, Culture, and Politics in the Basque Diaspora*. Reno: University of Nevada Reno, 2004. 55-80.

Tovar, Antonio. *Mitología e ideología sobre la lengua vasca: historia de los estudios sobre ella*. Madrid: Alianza, 1980.

Trask, R. L. *The History of Basque*. New York: Routledge, 1997.

—. *Etymological Dictionary of Basque*. Brighton, UK: University of Sussex, 2008.

Txillardegi. *Leturia*. N.l.: Basque American Foundation, 1986.

—. *Peru Leartzako*. San Sebastian: Elkar, 1979.

—. *Elsa Scheelen*. San Sebastian: Elkar, 1985.

—. *Haizeaz bestaldetik*. Zarautz: Itxaropena, 1979.

Ugalde, Martin. *Hiltzaileak*. San Sebastian: Erein, 1985.

Unamuno, Manuel. *Obras completas*. Madrid: A. Aguado, 1950-1958.

--.   Saint   Manuel,   the   Good,   Martyr.   1-10-2016. www4.gvsu.edu/wrightd/spa%20307%20death/saintmanuel-bueno.htm.

—. *Selected Works of Miguel de Unamuno, Volume 1: Peace in War: A Novel.* Princeton University Press, 1983. (*Paz en la guerra.* Tafalla: Txalaparta, 2008)

Unzueta Echebarria, Antonio. "Nuevos datos sobre el reformado de ermitaños y poeta vasco Juan de Undiano." *Fontes linguae vasconum: Studia et documenta* 14.39 (1982): 329-38.

Uribe, Kirmen. *Bilbao-New York Bilbao.* San Sebastian: Elkar, 2008.

Urkiza, Ana. *Desira izoztuak.* San Sebastian: Elkarlanean, 2000.

Urkizu, Patricio, ed. *Historia de la literatura vasca.* Madrid: UNED, 2000.

—. "Roland gesta kantetan, eleberrietan, teatroan eta zinean." *Jean Haritschelhar-i omenaldia.* Bilbao: Euskaltzaindia: 2008. 645-64

Urquijo, Julio de. *El Refranero vasco. Los refranes de Garibay.* San Sebastián: n.e., 1934.

Urretabizkaia, Arantxa. "Why Darling?" Lasagabaster. 91-5.

—. *Zuri-beltzeko argazkiak.* Pamplona: Pamiela, 2014.

Urza, Monique. *The Deep Blue Memory.* Reno: University of Nevada Press, 1993.

Valdés, Mario J. and Djelal Kadir, eds. *Literary Cultures of Latin America: A Comparative History.* New York: Oxford University Press, 2004.

Vallverdu, Josep. *Història de la liteatura catalana.* Barcelona: Editorial M. Arimany, 1978.

Vennemann, Theo. *Europa Vasconica –Europa Semitica.* Berlin: Mouton de Gruyter, 2003.

Vilavedra, Dolores. *Historia da literatura galega.* Vigo: Galaxia, 1999.

Villanueva, Darío. "La novela." Andrés Amorós et al. *Letras españolas: 1976-1986.* N.p.: Castalia and Ministerio de Cultura, 1987. 19-64.

—. "Los marcos de la literatura española (1975-1990): esbozo de un sistema." Francisco Rico, ed. *Historia y crítica de la literatura española.* Vol 9. *Los nuevos nombres: 1975-1990.* Eds. Darío Villanueva et al. Barcelona: Crítica, 1992. 3-40.

Villasante, Luis. *Historia de la literatura vasca.* Bilbao: Sendoa, 1961.

Wallerstein, Immanuel. "The Inequalities that Blazed in France will Soon Scorch the World." *The Guardian.* Dec. 3, 2005. www.guardian.co.uk. 12-20-2007.

Walton, John and Jenny Smith. "The First Spanish Seaside Resorts." *History Today* (1994): 23-29.

Washabaugh, William. *Flamenco: Passion, Politics and Popular Culture*. Oxford, GBR: Berg Publishers, 1996.

Wa Thiong'o, Ngugi. *Decolonising the Mind: The Politics of Language in African Literature*. Portsmouth, NY: Heinemann Educational, 1986.

Watson, Cameron. *Modern Basque History: Eighteenth Century to the Present*. Reno: Center of Basque Studies, 2003.

Weaver, Matthew. "Angela Merkel: German multiculturalism has 'utterly failed'" The Guardian. 17-10-2010. www.theguardian.com. 21-1-2016.

Weber, Eugene. *Peasants into Frenchmen: The Modernization of Rural France 1870–1914*. Stanford, California: Stanford University Press, 1976.

Wittig, Monique. *Les guérillères*. Boston: Beacon Press, 1985.

Woodworth, Paddy. *The Basque Country: A Cultural History*. Oxford: Oxford University Press, 2007.

Xenpelar. *Bertso jarriak*. www.klasikoak.armiarma.com. 2009-10-30.

Young, Iris Marion. *Inclusion and Democracy*. New York: Oxford University Press, 2000.

Yoshimoto, Banana. *Kitchen*. New York: Grove Press, 1993.

Zabaleta, Iñaki. *110. Street-eko geltokia*. San Sebastian: Elkar, 1988.

Zaldua, Iban. *Ese idioma raro y poderoso: once decisiones cruciales que un escritor vasco está obligado a tomar*. Madrid: Lengua de Trapo, 2012.

Zallo, Ramon. *Basques Today: Culture, History and Society in the Age of Diversity and Knowledge*. Irun: Alberdania, 2006.

Zavala, Iris. *Breve historia feminista de la literatura española (en lengua catalana, gallega y vasca)*. Barcelona: Anthropos, 2000.

Zavala, Antonio. *Bosquejo de historia del bertsolarismo*. San Sebastian: Auñamendi, 1964.

Ziga, Itziar. *Sexual Herria*. Tafalla: Txalaparta, 2011.

Zizek, Slavoj. *The Plague of Fantasies*. London: Verso, 2009.